Power, Pleasure, and Profit

ER,
PLEASURE,
and
PROFIT

Insatiable Appetites from
Machiavelli to Madison

✥◦✥◦✥◦✥◦

DAVID WOOTTON

The Belknap Press of Harvard University Press
CAMBRIDGE, MASSACHUSETTS
LONDON, ENGLAND
2018

First printing

Book design by Dean Bornstein

Library of Congress Cataloging-in-Publication Data
Names: Wootton, David, 1952– author.
Title: Power, pleasure, and profit : insatiable appetites from Machiavelli
to Madison / David Wootton.
Description: Cambridge, Massachusetts : The Belknap Press of Harvard
University Press, 2018. | Includes bibliographical references and index.
Identifiers: LCCN 2018023374 | ISBN 9780674976672 (alk. paper)
Subjects: LCSH: Conduct of life—History. | Power (Social sciences)—History. |
Values—History. | Enlightenment. | Ambition—History. | Pleasure. | Profit.
Classification: LCC BJ1595 .W793 2018 | DDC 170.9/03—dc23
LC record available at https://lccn.loc.gov/2018023374

For Alison, with whom I have found happiness
&

Leone, à piedi del quale ſia vn libro poſpoſto da parte, con l'inſcrittione
IVS.

RAGIONE DI STATO.

Si dipinge armata, per dimoſtrare l'huomo che ſi ſerue di tal ragione,
vuole quando foſſero le forze il tutto dominare cō l'arme, ò altro mezzo.

Si rappreſenta con la veſte di colore torchino conteſta d'occhi, e d'orecchie, per ſignificare la geloſia, che tiene del ſuo dominio, che per tutto
vuol hauer occhi, & orecchie di ſpie, per poter meglio guidare i ſuoi diſe-
gni, & gl'altrui troncare.

Se gli dà la bacchetta per moſtrare queſta Ragione di ſtato eſſere propria di chi hà dominio, & ſignoria, dalla quale l'huomo diuiene imperio-
ſo, ancorche ogn'vno, per ben che Prencipe non ſia, poſſi hauere vna cer-
ta ragione di ſtato in propria, con la quale vogli gouernare il dominio

Dd 4   delle

"Ragione di Stato," from Cesare Ripa, *Iconologia* (4°) (1603).

Contents

It is an opinion of the ancient writers, that men are wont to vex themselves in their crosses, and glut and cloy themselves in their prosperity, and that from the one and the other of these two passions proceede the same effects: for at what time soever men are freed from fighting for necessity, they are presently together by the eares through ambition; which is so powerfull in mens hearts, that to what degree soever they arise, it never abandons them. The reason is, because nature hath created men, in such a sort, that they can desire every thing, but not attaine to it. So that the desire of getting being greater then the power to get, thence growes the dislike of what a man injoyes, and the small satisfaction a man hath thereof. Hereupon arises the change of their states, for some men desiring to have more, and others fearing to lose what they have already, they proceede to enmities and warre.

—Niccolò Machiavelli,
Discorsi sopra la prima Deca di Tito Livio
(trans. Edward Dacres, 1636)

Besides this, the desire of man being insatiable [*sendo ... gli appetiti umani insaziabili*] (because of nature hee hath it, that hee can and will desire every thing, though of fortune hee be so limited, that he can attain but a few) there arises thence a dislike in mens minds, and a loathing of the things they injoy, which causes them to blame the times present and commend those pass'd, as also those that are to come, although they have no motives grounded upon reason to incite them thereto.

—Niccolò Machiavelli,
Discorsi sopra la prima Deca di Tito Livio
(trans. Edward Dacres, 1636)

O human mind, insatiable and vain,
Fraudulent, fickle, and, above all things,
Impious, malignant, full of quick disdain!

—Niccolò Machiavelli,
"Tercets on Ambition"

From whence, then, arises that emulation which runs through all the different ranks of men, and what are the advantages which we propose by that great purpose of human life which we call bettering our condition? To be observed, to be attended to, to be taken notice of with sympathy, complacency and approbation, are all the advantages which we can propose to derive from it. It is the vanity, not the ease or the pleasure, which interests us.

—Adam Smith,
The Theory of Moral Sentiments (1759)

The principle which prompts to save, is the desire of bettering our condition, a desire which, though generally calm and dispassionate, comes with us from the womb, and never leaves us until we go into the grave. In the whole interval which separates those two moments, there is scarce perhaps a single instant in which any man is so perfectly and compleatly satisfied with his situation, as to be without any wish of alteration or improvement of any kind. An augmentation of fortune is the means by which the greater part of men propose and wish to better their condition.

—Adam Smith,
*An Inquiry into the Nature and Causes
of the Wealth of Nations* (1776)

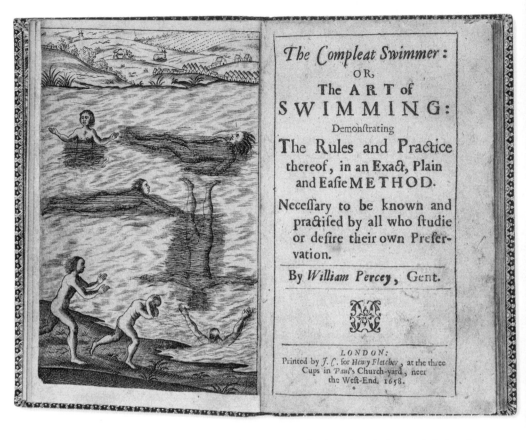

The Compleat Swimmer:
OR,
The ART of
SWIMMING:
Demonstrating
The Rules and Practice
thereof, in an Exact, Plain
and Easie METHOD.

Necessary to be known and
practised by all who studie
or desire their own Preservation.

By *William Percey*, Gent.

LONDON:
Printed by *J. C.* for *Henry Fletcher*, at the three
Cups in *Paul's* Church-yard, neer
the West-End. 1658.

Title page and frontispiece from William Percey, *The Compleat Swimmer* (8°) (1658).

To the Reader

William Percey's *The Compleat Swimmer* (1658) begins, as I do, by addressing "the ingenious, prudent, and self-preserving reader." For Percey, "There are two onely chief *ends,* which are the only *inducements* to all *Actions* in the whole *world;* and these are *pleasure* and *profit;* yea these are the mayn and only *objects* whereon all Creatures *animal* or *rational* fix their eyes; the *wheeles* upon with [*sic:* which] all our Actions turn, as the *Universe* doth upon the *Axletree,* these are the *Magnets* or *Loadstones* that attract all our *thoughts* and *actions* to themselves as their *Centre.*"[1] *The Compleat Swimmer* is only the second book in English which aims to teach the reader how to swim; the only people who would normally read it now are scholars interested in the early history of swimming as a sport, which is to say hardly anyone at all. We know nothing about its author, but it is safe to assume that he was not intending to make a particularly contentious claim when he insisted that all human activities are motivated by either pleasure or profit. Pleasure and profit were often coupled together (scholars, for example, read for pleasure and profit), but never before Percey, as far as I can tell, were they claimed to be the *only* motivations, to the exclusion of all others, such as honor, virtue, and piety.[2] Whether he intended to or not, Percey was presenting a new account of what it is to be a human being. He even went so far as to suggest that human beings are little different from the animals:

> Doth not the *indefatigable Emmet* [Ant] keep still *exercising* his restless motion all the *summer,* that he may enjoy the pleasure and profit thereof in his *low-roof,* but to himself, and his un-aspiring thoughts, a delightful *Palace.* What *incessant* pains takes the *Laborious Bee,* that she may enjoy the sweetness of the *Hony* in the *Artificial Chambers* of her well-wrought *Castle?* Herein consists pleasure and profit both. *Sed quid moror istis?* [But why do I linger over such examples?] The *prudent* and *industrious Merchant* Roames far and neer, spares neither *costs* nor *pains, danger,*

care nor *trouble;* and all for the *sacred* hunger of *Gold:* Therein consists both his pleasure and profit too. Nay, the *Toyl-embracing* husband-man [farmer] merrily *whistles* along the tediousness of his painful *furrows,* in hopes to rejoyce in a fruitful *Harvest.*

He may well have had classical philosophers such as Epicurus and Lucretius in mind, but no classical philosopher (and indeed no medieval theologian) had praised hard labor in this way, or taken economic activity as the paradigmatic example of rational activity. Something new is happening here, yet Percey seems quite unaware of it, and assumes that his readers will think as he does.

Percey is an early example of the conviction that human beings (and animals too) are always engaged in the pursuit either of immediate pleasure or of the means to future pleasure.[3] His view of human nature is reminiscent of Thomas Hobbes, who had published *Leviathan* in 1651, though Hobbes called the means to future pleasure not "profit" but "power," or of David Hume, who would publish *An Enquiry Concerning the Principles of Morals* a century later, in 1751, though Hume would call the means to future pleasure not "profit" but "utility." Pleasure and profit, according to Percey, pleasure and power, according to Hobbes, pleasure and utility, according to Hume: these are, these authors believed, the only motives to action, "the *wheeles* upon which all our Actions turn." In other words, all our behavior is self-interested. And if this is the case, morality has to be seen as a strategy for achieving our interests: thus Paul Henri Thiry d'Holbach wrote (in a shockingly atheistical work, published under a false identity in 1770), "In order that man may become virtuous, it is absolutely necessary that he should have an interest, or that he should find advantages in practising virtue."[4]

Hume thought it was "excusable" to conclude that, since all human behavior is self-gratifying, it follows that it is always motivated by selfishness. Nevertheless he rejected this view, and sought to draw a distinction between self-gratifying behavior and selfish behavior, and to argue that although moral behavior is the best strategy for attaining our personal happiness and welfare, benevolence, friendship, and justice are not motivated solely or even primarily by self-interest or self-love.[5] Others were not so subtle, and bluntly asserted what we may call the selfishness principle: that nobody can reasonably be required to act contrary to their own interests. As Thomas Nettleton expressed it in 1729, "We have frequent Opportunities every Day of our Lives, to do Good to others, without any Detriment to ourselves; or if in the Exercise of *Kindness,* we should suffer some Loss or Inconvenience, yet that will be abundantly recompensed by the Pleasure and Satisfaction which it affords: But to do Good to others, by bringing a greater Evil upon ourselves, is what no *rational Benevolence* will require; neither is it consistent with the general Good, to which a just degree of *Self-love* in every Particular, and a due regard to *Self-interest* is absolutely necessary."[6] And here is a statement of it by the Genevan professor of law Jean-Jacques Burlamaqui in a textbook (first published in French in 1747) which went through more than sixty editions in seven languages because it was a learned summary of received views: "Now let man reflect but ever so little on himself, he will soon perceive that every thing he does is with a view of happiness, and that this is the ultimate end he proposes in all his actions, or the last term to which he reduces them. This is a first truth of which we have a continual conviction from our own internal sense. Such, in effect, is the nature of man, that he necessarily loves himself, that he seeks in every thing and every where his own advantage, and can never be diverted from this pursuit."[7] The word "advantage" here is used to refer to both pleasure and the means to future pleasure. As we shall see, Burlamaqui and his contemporaries devoted a great deal of intellectual effort to showing that this overriding principle of self-interest could explain apparently altruistic behavior.[8]

Burlamaqui was, notionally, a Calvinist, but he deliberately abstained from describing human self-love as a consequence of the Fall, as a manifestation of original sin. On the contrary, he insisted that this is how God intended us to be, and to suggest there is some defect in his workmanship would be to question divine benevolence. Burlamaqui thus argued from natural reason, not from revelation—from deism, not theism. Some early writers in the tradition we will be exploring here (such as Pierre Bayle and Bernard Mandeville) deliberately masqueraded as Calvinists, and others (such as Hobbes) wanted to exploit the overlap between the selfishness principle and Augustinian theology, whether Catholic or Protestant.[9] But Augustinian theologians never hesitated to denounce such arguments as heretical, as indeed they were, whether they were presented by authors (such as d'Holbach and Hume) who were directly critical not just of Christianity but of belief in a divine providence, or by authors (such as Burlamaqui, Adam Smith, and, much of the time, Voltaire) who insisted on some form of providential design.

Underlying the selfishness principle was the conviction that it must be possible to give a scientific account of human nature—modeled on the new sciences of William Gilbert (who had published *De magnete* in 1600), Galileo Galilei (whose new physics appeared in 1638), and, by the time we get to Hume and Burlamaqui, Isaac Newton (whose theory of gravity was published in 1687). Human beings pursuing pleasure and profit will act, it was believed, in rational, predictable ways, and their behavior will thus be calculating and calculable: this is still the assumption on which the discipline of economics is founded.

This book is about the origins and implications of this new psychology and of the moral and political philosophies and economic theories that came to be associated with it.[10] There is a key feature which power, pleasure, profit, and utility have in common and which marks the difference between this new world and all that had gone before: they can be pursued without limit.[11] They can, to use a word invented in 1817 by Jeremy Bentham, the founder of utilitarian moral philosophy, be "maximized." Traditional conceptions of honor and virtue all require restraint, moderation, self-abnegation, self-sacrifice; but the new philosophy of pleasure and profit set no limit to self-interested or selfish conduct other than the need to avoid the self-defeating behavior of the drinker who wakes with a painful hangover or the gambler who fails to allow for the possibility of losing. What power, pleasure, profit, and utility have in common is that the pursuit of them is endless. As these insatiable appetites became respectable, curiosity and ambition—equally unlimited, and so once viewed as vices—were reinterpreted as virtues.

My title is *Power, Pleasure, and Profit,* in that order, because power was conceptualized first, in the sixteenth century, by Niccolò Machiavelli and his followers; in the seventeenth century Hobbes radically revised the concepts of pleasure and happiness; and the way in which profit works in the economy was first adequately theorized in the eighteenth century by Adam Smith. "Utility," my fourth key term, received its classic formulation with Bentham, also in the eighteenth century. Machiavelli, Hobbes, Smith, and Bentham did not bring about singlehanded the large intellectual and cultural shifts that we and their contemporaries see as being epitomized in their works; they were part of wider and deeper movements of intellectual change over which they had no control but for which their works now serve as useful markers. Indeed, all four embody and responded to a great transformation which has been variously described as the shift from *Gemeinschaft* (community) to *Gesellschaft* (society) or from *Homo hierarchicus* to *Homo economicus*.

This book provides a series of sketches illustrating this intellectual and cultural revolution which still shapes our own understanding of the world: the replacement of Aristotelian ethics and Christian morality by a new type of decision making which may be termed instrumental reasoning or cost-benefit analysis. Burlamaqui, again, provides a useful textbook summary: "Reason, as the very etymology of the word implies [from Latin *ratio,* reckoning], is nothing more than a calculation and account. To reason is to calculate, and to draw up an account, after balancing every thing, in order to see on which side the advantage lies."[12]

This is an astonishing claim; were it correct, proofs in Euclidean geometry and Aristotelian syllogisms would not be examples of reasoning; the experimental method, insofar as it tests hypotheses, might just pass muster. Yet Burlamaqui's mode of reasoning, which took as its model double-entry bookkeeping, remains paradigmatic today and continues to be identified with rationality itself; "rational choice theory" assumes that there are no rational choices except those which result from cost-benefit analysis.[13] Such reasoning presumes that the advantage to be calculated is itself unproblematic and is in principle measurable. The merchant knows why he balances his accounts: to see if he is in profit. Instrumental reasoning more generally is always at the service of what Burlamaqui called "advantage" or "interest." But our interest, according to the selfishness principle, is simply pleasure or the means to future pleasure. Reason, which had always been presented as the mistress of the passions, is now to be regarded as their servant. Objective "reason" had been replaced by subjective "reasons."[14] Hume stated the new doctrine, which he acknowledged must seem "somewhat extraordinary," in uncompromising terms: "Reason is, and ought only to be the slave of the passions, and can never pretend to any other office but to serve and obey them."[15] Three passions in particular—ambition, emulation, and avarice—were identified by Hume as the "chief governing principles" shaping our lives in society.[16]

Before the rise of instrumental reasoning (or rather, its extension from mundane tasks like carpentry to decisions about how best to live) the general view (at least among the ruling and writing elites) was that what mattered most was not whether you succeeded or failed, but what sort of person you were; honor, self-respect, dignity, reputation, and a clear conscience were held to be more important than success in acquiring power, pleasure, or wealth. Here, to take a single example, is Xenophon expressing views which would have been recognized by any ancient Greek or Roman citizen: "All creatures seem in a similar fashion to take pleasure in food, drink, sleep, and sex. But the love of honor does not grow up in animals lacking speech. Nor, for that matter, can it be found in all human beings. The lust for honor and praise grows up only in those who are most fully distinguished from the beasts of the fields: which is to say that it grows up only in those judged to be real men and no longer mere human beings."[17] In Xenophon's understanding, women, slaves, and those who worked for a living were "mere human beings," incapable of honor, and thus insufficiently distinguished from the beasts of the fields. Plenty of Greek and Roman citizens did not live up to their own ideals and principles, but they had no doubt that to give priority to power, pleasure, profit, or utility—to, in a word, advantage—over honor, praise, or virtue was debasing and degrading.

As for Christianity, at the heart of the Gospel message is a rejection of instrumental reasoning: "Consider the lilies of the field, how they grow; they toil not, neither do they spin. . . . Take therefore no thought for the morrow: for the morrow shall take thought for the things of itself. Sufficient unto the day is the evil thereof" (Matt. 6:28, 34). Inevitably, ordinary Christians took thought for the morrow; but they were always conscious of another, higher standard by which they would eventually be judged.

The transmutation of values with which this book is concerned can be summarized by comparing Aristotle and Smith on prudence. For Aristotle, prudence (*phronesis,* or practical wisdom) is subordinated to virtue: "for virtue makes us aim at the right mark, and practical wisdom makes us take the right means."[18] But for Smith, prudence has become a virtue in its own right, a virtue solely concerned with maximizing advantage and pleasure:

> The qualities most useful to ourselves are, first of all, superior reason and understanding, by which we are capable of discerning the remote

consequences of all our actions, and of foreseeing the advantage or detriment which is likely to result from them: and secondly, self-command, by which we are enabled to abstain from present pleasure or to endure present pain, in order to obtain a greater pleasure or to avoid a greater pain in some future time. In the union of those two qualities consists the virtue of prudence, of all the virtues that which is most useful to the individual.[19]

Prudence, which was once associated with all the virtues, is now associated only with the two virtues of industry and frugality. Aristotle surely knew what industry and frugality were, but he did not bother to include them among the virtues: they were instrumental qualities you would look for in a slave, a craftsman, or a wife, and thus not, properly speaking, virtues at all.[20] Prudence, for Aristotle, was not an instrumental quality of this sort because it enabled the individual to realize their capacity for virtue (in which lies true happiness); it had nothing to do with the successful pursuit of pleasure and avoidance of pain. For Aristotle, prudence enables one to become virtuous; for Smith, it enables one to become successful.

This transmutation of values is in part a democratization and degendering of values: as far as Enlightenment thinkers were concerned, human beings could not be separated into two distinct classes, whether they be those of "real men" on the one hand, and women, workers, and slaves on the other, or those (harder to tell apart, until the great day of judgment) of saints and sinners. Rather, we all, whether rich or poor, male or female, take pleasure in food, drink, sleep, and sex. We all aspire to prosperity and security. We are all capable of reason.* We are all, fundamentally, alike.[21]

---

* "That the capacities of the human mind have been in all ages the same; and that the diversity of phenomena exhibited by our species, is the result merely of the different circumstances in which men are placed, has been long received as an incontrovertible logical maxim; or rather, such is the influence of early instruction, that we are apt to regard it as one of the most obvious suggestions of common sense. And yet, till about the time of Montesquieu, it was by no means so generally recognized by the learned, as to have a sensible influence on the fashionable tone of thinking over Europe. The application of this fundamental and leading idea to the natural or *theoretical history* of society in all its various aspects:—to the history of languages, of the arts, of the sciences, of laws, of government, of manners, and of religion,—is the peculiar glory of the latter half of the eighteenth century, and forms a characteristical feature in its philosophy." Dugald

Instrumental reasoning is, I would acknowledge, potentially a double-edged weapon. On the one hand it cuts through traditional assumptions about status, rank, and honor; but on the other it might be thought to encourage the invention of new and ever more pernicious ways for one human being to exploit another. For the period this book covers, 1500–1800, the record seems to me clear: those who were most prominent in attacking the old moral codes were also, almost without exception, egalitarians. Machiavelli praised popular government; Hobbes founded his political theory on the claim that all human beings are fundamentally equal; John Locke fought a long campaign against slavery; Cesare Beccaria insisted that the justice system should treat everyone alike; Bentham became a democrat; Smith provided a sophisticated critique of the economics of slavery; none of the American Founding Fathers defended slavery in principle, and most acknowledged that it was a dreadful evil.[22] The Declaration of Independence states, "We hold these truths to be self-evident, that all men are created equal, that they are endowed by their Creator with certain unalienable Rights, that among these are Life, Liberty, and the pursuit of Happiness." In the nineteenth century new arguments, from history and biology, were devised to justify and foster inequality, and in response new arguments were constructed in defense of equality; but they lie outside the scope of this book.

This double revolution, of instrumental reasoning and egalitarianism, met (and still meets) everywhere with sustained resistance. It is a secular view, and so opposed by all religions. It has not had a uniform impact across the globe, and in some places, at some times, it has been to some considerable degree reversed. Nevertheless, it is one of the two fundamental transformations—the other being the development of science and technology, with which it went hand in hand—which have made our world distinctly different from all its predecessors.[23] For better or worse, willingly or unwillingly, whether believers or atheists, modernists or postmodernists, we are all caught up in the triumph of instrumental reasoning, of egalitarianism, and of technology. Wherever we turn, we find ourselves surrounded by what Max Weber called "a shell as hard as steel." This book is about how that shell came to be constructed, and about how it came to seem natural, inevi-

---

Stewart, *The Works of Dugald Stewart in Seven Volumes* (Cambridge, Mass.: Hilliard and Brown, 1829), 7:65.

table, and inescapable; how it came to seem not something exterior and imposed upon us, not (in the phrase used in the original translation of Weber into English) an "iron cage," but a structure which gives shape and purpose to our lives, a shell or exoskeleton.[24]

This double revolution took place first in a few minds and a few texts, and only slowly came to characterize whole societies; yet, in a complicated interaction, the new ideas only seemed plausible because they reflected changes already taking place within those societies. Thus the texts we will be concerned with both reflected and helped transform ordinary life. This book is primarily about texts, but power, pleasure, and profit exist outside texts—indeed, power and pleasure can be observed to exist among many animals lacking speech. Profit, on the other hand (at least as it is pursued by prudent and industrious merchants and toil-embracing farmers), is, along with money, a social construct and could not exist without language and without mathematics. There is thus something peculiar about the economy: it only exists insofar as we believe it exists, just as the English language only exists because we write and speak it. Percey hoped that the readers of his book would be saved from drowning; he was teaching them how to make it to dry land. But when it comes to our understanding of ourselves, there is no dry land to be reached, for we are immersed in the ocean of language; we cannot touch bottom, and so we must keep swimming as best we can.[25]

Frontispiece from Thomas Hobbes, *Leviathan* (2°) (1651).

1

Insatiable Appetites

This book follows in the footsteps of Alasdair MacIntyre's *After Virtue* (1981). MacIntyre made two related claims in that book which seem to me fundamentally correct. The first was that after Niccolò Machiavelli and Thomas Hobbes, moral philosophy—as that enterprise had always been understood—became impossible. In the post-Hobbesian world, what passed for virtue was merely a set of strategies for pursuing pleasure and advantage.[1] Utilitarianism was the logical outcome of this mode of thinking, and in MacIntyre's view utilitarianism made good and evil fundamentally subjective. It led inescapably to the view that moral right or wrong is simply whatever we want it to be, which he called "emotivism."[2] MacIntyre's own solution to what he saw as the bankruptcy of modern moral philosophy was to turn back to Aristotle and Thomas Aquinas and to join the Catholic Church. MacIntyre's solution is not one I advocate; but his diagnosis of the problem seems to me sound. One purpose of this book is to explore the question of what it means to live "after virtue."

Second, MacIntyre identified something he called "the Enlightenment project," whose goal was to replace traditional moral philosophy by the maximization of pleasure and advantage. Postmodernists have mounted a sustained attack on the universalist claims of the Enlightenment, while historians have responded by arguing that there is no such thing as "the Enlightenment" and have instead identified a variety of different Enlightenments.[3] What I propose to do in the chapters that follow is to build up a much more complex picture of "the Enlightenment project" than is to be found in MacIntyre and in the postmodern critics of the Enlightenment.

These chapters contain a series of arguments that rub against the grain of contemporary scholarship. Machiavelli appears here as a theorist of power, not republican liberty. Hobbes is presented as speaking the language of possessive individualism. Adam Smith is arraigned for not understanding the eighteenth-century economy. Each of these individual arguments must stand or fall on its own. But they form part of a larger picture, my attempt to identify what I call "the Enlightenment paradigm," which may be quickly summarized as the attempt to understand how selfish individuals can construct functioning societies and to propose ways in which individuals can be trained and societies can be reconstructed so that they function more successfully to satisfy our selfish appetites. The Enlightenment paradigm is thus an elaboration of what I earlier called "the selfishness principle," its extension from psychology to moral philosophy, politics, and economics.

I opt for the term "the Enlightenment paradigm" rather than "Enlightenment project" because a project implies conscious intent, while one can work within a paradigm without having identified it, without being aware of it—one may simply take it for granted, assuming there is no alternative. To argue that there was an Enlightenment paradigm is, of course, to adopt a principle of selection: there were plenty of eighteenth-century thinkers who did not work within the paradigm I identify (I discuss François-Vincent Toussaint and Adam Ferguson, for example, and a whole book could be written on Jean-Jacques Rousseau's efforts to break with the Enlightenment).

It might be helpful here to go back to the origins of the popular use of the term "paradigm" in Thomas Kuhn's *The Structure of Scientific Revolutions* (1962). No one would imagine that a history of Copernicanism which studied Nicolaus Copernicus, Galileo Galilei, Johannes Kepler, and Isaac Newton was committed to denying the existence of other world systems—the Ptolemaic, the Tychonic, the Cartesian. Nor would anyone imagine that the author's intent was to claim that Galileo and Kepler were always on the same side of every important debate, or that Copernicus in some way foreshadowed the arguments of Kepler, let alone Newton. And so I trust that no one will misinterpret this book as implying that all eighteenth-century thinkers worked within the Enlightenment paradigm, or that those who did agreed on every important question.

What the word "paradigm," as used by Kuhn—or, for example, to come closer to my subject, by John Pocock—does commit one to is a grand narrative. It commits one to a story of the construction, reconstruction, and reproduction of a paradigm, and thus to a story which is something more than a genealogy, and indeed one which might seem to some a teleological account. Such a commitment is at odds with much contemporary historical writing. A paradigm, once identified, provides a principle of selection which enables one to distinguish information from noise, crucial developments from minor variations and local disagreements, radical change from continuity.[4]

I hope, in short, to convince skeptical readers that there was such a thing as the Enlightenment paradigm; I do so neither in order to reject that paradigm (as Catholics and postmodernists must) nor in order to defend it, but in order to show that, whether we like it or not, aspects of it remain so intertwined with the key institutions and goals of our culture that there is, if we are honest, no escaping from it. A paradigm can survive simply by becoming uncontentious: we are all still Copernicans, and we all still operate (I would argue) within the Enlightenment paradigm. Readers of this book will discover, I hope, that the Enlightenment lives on in them, rather as M. Jourdain in Molière's *Le Bourgeois gentilhomme* (1670) discovered that he had been speaking prose all his life without knowing it.

But the Enlightenment has for us a strange form of continuing life: everything about it seems alien, and yet everything about it seems familiar; it is simultaneously dead, undead, and full of life. The reason for this, I will suggest, is that we still live within institutions and practices created in the eighteenth century, the institutions and practices of the free market, of free speech and freedom of religion, and of the written constitution. These institutions and practices embody ideas, and the ideas they embody are those of the Enlightenment paradigm. The institutions, the practices, and the ideas are intertwined and inseparable. The Enlightenment lives on in us, even as we attack it or deny that it ever really existed, because Enlightenment forms of life (to adopt a phrase from Ludwig Wittgenstein) continue to be our forms of life. Those forms of life are certainly under strain, and it would be wrong to assume they will survive indefinitely. Indeed their life may be coming to an end. In a postindustrial, digital world, a world of artificial intelligence and of boundless supplies of energy, new categories of thought and new institutions may supplant them; and perhaps we can see more clearly now what the Enlightenment paradigm was precisely because we are beginning to emerge from it. As G. W. F. Hegel said, "the owl of Minerva spreads its wings only with the falling of the dusk."[5]

This book is about the triumph of the passions and the enslavement of reason. For two millennia philosophers claimed to teach the mastery of the passions and, as a result, the attainment of happiness.[6] There was, it was agreed, only one true form of happiness, but different philosophical schools disagreed about how to define it and how to attain it. Happiness and excellence went together, and all the moral qualities we admire would be found united in the happy person, for virtue was, they were sure, ultimately not many things but one thing.

The first person to mount a direct and sustained attack on this way of thinking was Machiavelli.[7] He maintained that to achieve success in politics you had to do things which would normally be regarded as wicked. The point of political life was to win glory; and this was incompatible with being a "good man" as that term was understood by philosophers and theologians. Machiavelli saw human beings as being driven onward by insatiable appetites, which is to say that he saw them as being incapable of virtue as traditionally understood. At one point (in chapter 25 of *The Prince*) he even states that *all men* have the same goals, wealth and glory, although they pursue them by different strategies.[8] But it does not seem that he actually means this, for all his examples are of rulers, and the whole of *The Prince* is based on a distinction between ordinary people and their rulers. Thus, in the preface Machiavelli states that you need to be a member of the populace to understand princes and a prince to understand the populace, and in chapter 9 he says that cities are made up of two different types of people: the populace, who want to be neither bossed about nor oppressed, and the *grandi,* who want to boss people about and oppress them. Machiavelli certainly does not think that the populace pursue glory; glory is the goal of rulers, political leaders, generals, and, in well-ordered republics, of the people acting collectively as citizens and as soldiers in a citizen army. Thus although Machiavelli sometimes writes as if all human beings are alike, he actually thinks (to paraphrase F. Scott Fitzgerald) that the powerful are different from you and me, for they pursue glory and we don't. The rest of us also have insatiable appetites, but we pursue wealth, the pleasures of sex, and the respect of our neighbors, not glory.[9]

We enter a fundamentally different world if we turn to Hobbes, for as far as Hobbes is concerned all human beings really are alike. To reach this conclusion he has to radically redefine honor and glory, traditionally the preserve of a privileged few, making them subjective and universal.[10] He defines honor in chapter 10 of *Leviathan:* "The manifestation of the Value we set on one another, is that which is commonly called Honouring and Dishonouring. To Value a man at a high rate is to *Honour* him; at a low rate is to *Dishonour* him."[11] And he has just previously defined value as:

> The *Value,* or WORTH of a man, is as of all other things, his Price; that is to say, so much as would be given for the use of his Power: and therefore is not absolute; but a thing dependent on the need and judgement of another. An able conductor of Souldiers, is of great Price in time of War present, or imminent; but in Peace not so. A learned and uncorrupt Judge, is much Worth in time of Peace; but not so much in War. And as in other things, so in men, not the seller, but the buyer determines the Price. For let a man (as most men do,) rate themselves at the highest Value they can; yet their true Value is no more than it is esteemed by others.

Thus value and honor are not absolute, but relative; indeed, honor can be reduced to the price one's labor or skills will command in the market. This means that is it not just generals and judges who are men of honor, but a carpenter or a cook can be honored or dishonored. So too the carpenter or the cook can glory in their value: "*Joy,* arising from imagination of a mans own power and ability, is that exultation of the mind which is called GLORYING: which if grounded upon the experience of his own former actions, is the same with *Confidence:* but if grounded on the flattery of others; or only supposed by himself, for delight in the consequences of it, is called VAINE-GLORY."[12]

This radical insistence that we are all motivated by exactly the same psychological and social drives and that political communities consist not of different types of people (men and women; workers and gentlemen; subjects and rulers) but of people who are all fundamentally alike may usefully be said to mark the beginning of the Enlightenment. As far as Hobbes is concerned, everybody, from king to scullery maid, pursues exactly the same sorts of goods, which ultimately can be reduced to two: pleasure and power. But, if we are fundamentally all alike, we are also all different. One person plans for the future while another lives for the present. Some like to dance, others to play cards. We have insatiable appetites, but we want different things, and pursue them through different strategies. These differences do not constitute a natural hierarchy (men being superior to women, citizens to slaves, rulers to ruled) as they do in classical authors and still do in Machiavelli, but can be found distributed throughout the population.

Like Machiavelli, Hobbes grounds his account of politics in his analysis of human nature. But Hobbes's state must be constructed out of individuals who are fundamentally alike: we see this visually represented in the famous frontispiece to *Leviathan,* where the artificial person of the state is made up of a vast number of anonymous individuals. This methodological individualism is characteristic of the thinkers with whom we will be concerned. Indeed, we will be identifying a set of theories that are layered one over another or (perhaps better) nested one within another: psychology, moral philosophy, politics, and economics all, in the post-Hobbesian world, rely on the shared assumption that human beings have, in Machiavelli's phrase, "insatiable appetites."[13]

But, as we shall see, later thinkers have at their disposal intellectual tools that Hobbes lacks, and they solve the problems he raises in ways that would have been unimaginable to him. So the intellectual enterprise with which we are concerned developed over time; we find only an initial sketch of the issues in Hobbes. The full set of Enlightenment arguments is assembled in the third quarter of the eighteenth century, and appears in three great texts of 1776: the American Declaration of Independence, Adam Smith's *Wealth of Nations,* and Jeremy Bentham's *Fragment on Government.*

According to Hobbes, human beings seek pleasure and flee pain. This pleasure/pain response results in the two fundamental passions, which Hobbes calls appetite and aversion. Humans seek power because power assures them of future pleasure. But you can take pleasure in the thought of some future triumph: pleasures can be imaginary. The merchant can take pleasure in accumulating gold and silver, imagining what he could spend it on should he ever choose to do so. There is thus a constant interchange between physical sensations and the imagination, between present pleasures and future pleasures, between ends and means. Power itself can be a source of pleasure; and the prince may take pleasure in his jewels, his furs, his silks, and his other luxuries, but they are also signifiers of power. Although Hobbes is very aware of this interchange, he rarely explores the ways in which power and pleasure engage with each other. He does, however, acknowledge that they can meld in his discussions of lust and revenge. Of lust Hobbes says, "The appetite which men call *Lust,* and the fruition that appertaineth thereunto, is a *Sensual* pleasure, but *not onely* that; there is in it also a delight of the minde: for it consisteth of two appetites together, to *please,* and to *be pleased;* and the delight men take in delighting, is not Sensual, but a pleasure or joy of the minde, consisting in the imagination of the power they have so much to please."[14]

The "delight men take in delighting" is evidently a good thing, though Hobbes thinks male lovers take delight in the evidence of their own power, not in giving pleasure—we will see later that this solipsism is, in Hobbes's view, inescapable. Just as one can delight in delighting, so too one can take delight in inflicting psychological pain:

> *Revengefulness* is that passion which ariseth from an expectation or *imagination* of *making* him that hath *hurt* us, *finde* his *own actions hurtful* to himself, and to *acknowledge* the same; and this is the height of Revenge: for though it be not hard, by returning evil for evil, to make one's adversary displeased with his own fact [i.e., deed]; yet to make him acknowledge the same, is so difficult, that many a man had rather die than do it. Revenge aimeth not at the death, but at the captivity and subjection of an enemy; which was well expressed in the exclamation of *Tiberius Caesar,* concerning one, that, to frustrate his revenge, had killed himself in prison; *Hath he escaped me?* To *kill* is the aim of their *hate,* to *rid* themselves out of fear; *Revenge* aimeth at *Triumph,* which over the dead is not.[15]

Hobbes surely understood that there are endless opportunities, in ordinary conversation, to take delight in delighting or to triumph over others by humiliating them, but he was particularly aware of the second possibility; he believed, for example, that when we laugh it is always at someone else's expense, and never out of sheer delight.[16] Laughter is a display of power.

The classic text which explored the interface between power and pleasure came much later with the publication of Montesquieu's first book, *The Persian Letters*—a work which was an immediate success, with nine printings appearing (or at least claiming to have appeared) in 1721. It is a study in two sorts of despotism. On the one hand, there is the despotism that Montesquieu can name, the despotism of the Persian seraglio, which we see through the correspondence between Usbek and his wives and eunuchs. On the other hand, there is the despotism that is never explicitly named, the despotism of the French monarchy, seen through the letters of Usbek and Rica, Persian exiles in France. Montesquieu thus moves back and forth between the tyranny of the family, which he can expose directly, and the tyranny of the state, which he dares approach only indirectly. In his later reflections on the novel he tells us that a secret chain runs through it; that chain, in my view, is the love of liberty, which is a fundamental part of what it is to be human.[17]

Montesquieu, whose own views can, I would argue, be deciphered between the lines written by his correspondents, believed that all human beings love liberty, and that where it is denied there can be no authentic human relationships. But he also believed that tyranny is remarkably stable. Once a tyrannical system is established nobody, least of all those in charge, knows what is really going on; the truth is hidden under a carapace of lies; and the tyrant himself is manipulated and maneuvered by those over whom he pretends to rule; even he becomes a prisoner of a system he can neither understand nor change; Montesquieu discovered the master / slave dialectic long before Hegel.

This double vision, of our aspiration to freedom and our inability to escape despotism, resulted in a novel which is both profoundly idealistic and deeply pessimistic. In digressions Montesquieu portrayed alternative worlds in which each individual is dedicated to the public good (the society of the Troglodytes) or in which true love triumphs over every adversity (the love of Apheridon and Astarte, who are siblings; Montesquieu thought the taboo on incest was artificial, not natural). He approved of the sexual freedom exercised by French women, and argued strongly for divorce. We thus get fleeting glimpses of what a good society might look like, but the novel ends with the suicide of Usbek's wife Roxanne, whose lover has been killed, and who announces with pride that she has never loved her husband, no matter what lies she has been forced to tell.

Montesquieu may have taken his inspiration from Abraham Nicolas Amelot de la Houssaye's attack on Venice (published in 1676), which had been similarly successful and had coupled together an account of the despotism that lay hidden behind Venice's republican facade with a vivid description of the dissolute and empty private life of a nobility trapped within a system which claimed to serve them but simply imprisoned them.[18] Amelot, in writing about Venice, was striking at the French monarchy, as was Montesquieu in writing about Persia.[19] Amelot's is the earliest text I know which emphasizes the interface between power and erotic pleasure—and, if Montesquieu did not read him before writing *The Persian Letters,* then at least he must have recognized a kindred spirit in Amelot when he eventually came to read him, as we know he did.[20] Amelot translated Tacitus, Machiavelli, and Paolo Sarpi, the three key authors on the corrupting effects of power, and Machiavelli had also coupled his studies of politics with plays, such as *Mandragola,* which explored the difficulties of pursuing pleasure within the required forms of Christian family life.[21]

This intermingling of the personal and the political was not new: the rape of the Sabine women was, after all, a key event in Livy's account of the founding of Rome, just as the rape of Lucretia was a key event in the founding of the republic, and the state was often presented as the family writ large. John Milton had already treated divorce and tyrannicide as parallel problems, although he had hesitated to say as much. What was new in Amelot and in Montesquieu was a willingness to think through this traditional trope, to trace the corrupting influence of despotism through both the family and the state, and to conclude that sexuality and politics could not be separated. From Montesquieu it is only a small step to Mary Wollstonecraft, who made explicit everything that Montesquieu dared not state openly.[22]

According to Augustine, there are three fundamental passions in fallen man—the insatiable appetites for sex, money, and power.[23] (I use "appetite" here in the broad sense in which it is used by Machiavelli and Hobbes, and indeed Cicero—not in the narrow sense which would confine the appetites to hunger, thirst, and sex.) In a justly famous book entitled *The Passions and the Interests: Political Arguments for Capitalism before Its Triumph* (1977) Albert Hirschman explored what happened when the view of Machiavelli and Hobbes that human beings are governed by their passions was adopted. First, passions had to be set against each other, to check and control each other. And second, people had to be persuaded to look at the longer-term consequences of their behavior: short-term passions such as anger or lust had to be regulated by longer-term interests for wealth and security.

As Hirschman saw clearly, the idea of "interests" represented a new paradigm.[24] The word "interest" was known to Machiavelli—it was used to him and by him in his diplomatic correspondence.[25] But he never uses it in *The Prince* or the *Discourses on Livy*, where the concept is conveyed by the words *utile* and *utilità*.[26] "Interest" became a crucial term for Italian and French political theorizing with Giovanni Botero's *Reason of State* in 1589, but became widely used in English only in the 1640s.[27] In *Leviathan* Hobbes takes it for granted as a fundamental category, although one that, for all his care in such matters, he never bothers to define. The reason is simple. In Hobbesian terms we have only one true interest: pleasure. And there is only one reliable means of ensuring pleasure, and that is power. Our interest thus lies in the maximization of power in the broad sense in which Hobbes defines that term.[28] One of our most obvious interests is our interest in acquiring wealth, which is a particular type of power—in the post-Hobbesian world, pleasure, power, and profit are the three things we pursue without limit and (until death) without end. These three are our interests.

Hobbes thought we had another crucial interest: we need friends to act as allies and supporters. In this day and age, when we friend each other on Facebook, it may not seem obvious to say so, but there is a limit to how many friends you can have. Machiavelli thought there was never more than forty or fifty people who participated in power, and I doubt he would have thought he had more than forty or fifty friends, for he lived in a world where both power and friendship depended on regular face-to-face encounters, and there are only so many people you can meet and greet on a regular basis.[29] But as far as Hobbes was concerned (Machiavelli would not have agreed), friendship like wealth is simply a resource we can draw on, a form of stored-up power.* So we have no interests other than power and pleasure, and both of these must be pursued without limit.

---

* Compare François de La Rochefoucauld's *Maxims* (first published in French, 1665): "Gratitude among *Friends*, is like *Credit* among *Tradesmen*, it keeps Business up, and maintains the *Correspondence*. And we frequently pay not so much out of a Principle that we ought to discharge our *Debts*, as to secure our selves a place to be trusted in another time." And "What Men call *Friendship*, is no more than *Society*; 'tis only a mutual care of

There is a peculiar feature of the language of interests which should already be apparent from my use of the phrase "true interest." The language of power and pleasure is, at least in Hobbes's usage, value-free: we pursue them both of necessity. They are neither good nor bad; they are simply inevitable. There are, however, many different types of power and many different pleasures; pleasures, including the pleasure of having power over others, can be addictive and destructive. Hobbes is very conscious of the destructive possibilities of the pursuit of power and pleasure: what he calls the law of nature is a set of prudential recommendations on how to minimize these adverse consequences, but the recommendations only become obligations—and indeed it only becomes possible to act in the light of them—once a sovereign has been established and we have exited from the state of nature.[30] There is a paradox here: in the state of nature there is no law of nature; the law of nature only becomes binding once we leave the state of nature.

Interests are different from the laws of nature because the laws are universal while interests are situation-specific. Identifying interests involves interpretation and calculation. The laws of nature are either in force or in abeyance, and when they are in force they are either obeyed or disobeyed. In the state of nature, where the laws of nature are not in force, every individual has an interest in seeking to abide by them and implement them as far as is practically possible—which, outside a narrow circle of family and friends, is not very far at all. Claims about interests are rational or irrational, true or false. You cannot separate an interest from the thinking that identifies it. The identification of interests is inseparable from normative judgments about rationality and prudence, but it is entirely distinct from moral judgments about right and wrong. For Hobbes, interest is a critical concept, one designed to expose other people's irrational or hypocritical behavior.*

Interests, an exchange of good Offices. In a word, it is only a sort of Traffick, in which Self-love ever proposes to be the Gainer." François de La Rochefoucauld, Moral Maxims and Reflections (London: Gillyflower, Sare and Everingham, 1694), 58–59, 115; also Jonathan Swift, Verses on the Death of Dr. Swift (Dublin: Faulkner, 1739).

* Two examples, from Thomas Hobbes, Leviathan, Or, the Matter, Forme, and Power of a Common Wealth, Ecclesiasticall and Civil (London: Crooke, 1651): "And therefore in reasoning, a man must take heed of words; which, besides the signification of what we imagine of their nature, have a signification also of the nature, disposition, and interest of the speaker; such as are the names of Vertues, and Vices; For one man calleth Wisdome,

Thus the category of interest slides between the descriptive and the normative.

The word itself, in the sense of the pursuit of advantage, marks out a peculiarly modern set of preoccupations. The *Oxford English Dictionary* dates "interest" meaning "that which is to or for the advantage of anyone" to 1579, and meaning "regard to one's own profit and advantage" to 1622.[31] With the concept of interest goes the notion that just as one can calculate profit and advantage, so one can predict the behavior of political actors, who will inevitably pursue their own advantage. David Hume's claim that "politics may be reduced to a science" is a claim about the power of interest as a tool for the analysis of political behavior, and its essential role in thinking about the best form of government.[32]

It is clear that we all have a number of interests. We all want, in some measure, wealth and power (or at least those softer forms of power that are called status and influence). And we want these because we believe they will enable us successfully to flee pain and chase pleasure, because we make use of them in our pursuit of happiness. What is puzzling is the idea that the concept of "interest" is new, when there seems to be nothing obviously new about the things that we have an interest in. Did not the ancient Greeks pursue wealth, status, power, pleasure, and happiness pretty much as we do?[33] Did they not then have interests, just as we do?

The historian's answer to this question has to be no. There was general agreement that *eudaimonia,* happiness, is the ultimate end of all human activity. In Aristotle's account, philosophical contemplation is the best route to happiness, but along with the practice of philosophy (or alternative to it—Aristotle's meaning is much disputed) one may find happiness in a life lived according to virtue, providing one also has a reasonable amount of

---

what another calleth *feare;* and one *cruelty,* what another *justice;* one *prodigality,* what another *magnanimity;* and one *gravity,* what another *stupidity,* etc." (17). And, "in any businesse, whereof a man has not infallible Science to proceed by; to forsake his own naturall judgement, and be guided by generall sentences read in Authors, and subject to many exceptions, is a signe of folly, and generally scorned by the name of Pedantry. And even of those men themselves, that in Councells of the Common-wealth, love to shew their reading of Politiques and History, very few do it in their domestique affaires, where their particular interest is concerned; having Prudence enough for their private affaires: but in publique they study more the reputation of their owne wit, than the successe of anothers businesse" (22).

good luck—is not born ugly, or penniless, does not suffer a painful and lingering death, and so forth. The key to virtue, according to Aristotle, is moderation. Even knowledge is not something Aristotle imagines that one can acquire more and more of, in the way that one can collect more and more stamps or (in the manner of Henry Clay Folger) copies of Shakespeare's first folio. Just as Aristotle's cosmos was limited, so too his moral and political philosophy depended on recognizing and respecting limits. It is not at all clear, for example, that Aristotle's pupil Alexander the Great, who burst the bounds of the polis in his attempt to conquer the whole world, could possibly be described as a virtuous man.[34] Plutarch, in his essay "On the Fortune of Alexander," insisted he could—but only by claiming that he was putting into action the cosmopolitan ideas of Zeno the Stoic, conveniently forgetting that Zeno came after Alexander, not before, so that one might rather say that Zeno was transforming into ideas the actions of Alexander.[35]

The point about interests, as the term comes to be used in Italian from the fifteenth century onward, is that they have no natural limit; their fundamental principle is immoderation, not moderation.[36] How could one have too much power, or too much money, or too much pleasure? To suggest that one can (and surely one can, but that's another story) is to step outside the language of interests. That language takes as its model the example of double-entry bookkeeping, according to which the purpose of a business is to produce as much profit as possible as quickly as possible.* Double-entry bookkeeping, which goes back to the late thirteenth century, knows nothing about moderation (unlike the merchants who practiced it, who understood that one must balance profit against risk), nor anything about deferred gratification (unlike the merchants, who knew that it may be worth forgoing quick profits in order to make bigger gains in the future).

The logic of interests is a logic of maximization; Bentham invented the verb "maximize," but in Shakespeare's *As You Like It* Rosalind asks, "Why then, can one desire too much of a good thing?"[37] The answer, surprisingly, would seem to be no. In 1690 Nicholas Barbon maintained that the wants of the mind are infinite; remarkably, he argued that our capacity to

---

* See Appendix B for the way in which double-entry bookkeeping became part and parcel of Protestant theology.

supply those wants through commerce has no natural or necessary limit. What we think of as nonrenewable resources—such as coal and gold—were for Barbon renewable, growing within the ground as crops grow in the fields. If there is no limit to our desires, there is also, Barbon argued, no limit to economic growth.[38] Power, too, has no limits. Montesquieu, when he was in England in 1730, copied into a notebook a phrase from Henry St. John Bolingbroke's periodical *The Craftsman:* "The love of power is natural; it is insatiable; almost constantly whetted, and never cloyed by possession."[39]

So the key thing power, pleasure, and profit have in common, in their modern usages, is that they share the logic of maximization, and the term "interest" is used to capture this logic. Power and wealth are obviously, from a certain point of view, relative, but they are primarily accumulative. We see this clearly in Machiavelli's preference for Rome over Sparta and Venice; Sparta and Venice sought to keep their quest for power within limits, while Rome did not.[40] The only limit to power, as Alexander and the Romans understood, is the edge of the known world; and as to wealth, to that there is no limit at all.

Status, on the other hand, is purely relative. When Alexander the Great said, as he overcame yet another peril, "O Athens, can you possibly believe what dangers I undergo to win good repute among you?," he was over-looking the clash between the established culture of moderation and his own limitless aspirations: you don't have to conquer the whole world to win good repute in Athens; indeed, conquering the whole world may only en-gender hostility in a previously free city-state. Power, pleasure, and profit are the interests that are not self-limiting. But since there is a limit to status, since there is no status higher than king of the castle or cock of the walk, the quest for status is a zero-sum game—you can only move up if others move down. The quest for status is thus one of the factors making, in Hobbes's understanding of the world, for a war of all against all, for status is, of necessity, in limited supply.

It would be wrong to suggest that the idea of an unlimited aspiration was new in the early modern period. As we have seen, Alexander had burst the bounds of the polis. Theologians had long insisted that in heaven the blessed contemplate God's infinity, but they had also maintained that earthly beatitude must necessarily be imperfect. Where Aristotle had regarded happiness as something that could undoubtedly be attained in this life, medieval theologians had their doubts; only in heaven could the good life be realized. Thus, three things were necessary before power, pleasure, and profit could be raised to the status of ends in themselves: first, the limits of the city-state had to be burst asunder, moderation had to give way to excess; second, wealth had to be turned into an abstraction, an entry in a ledger book; and third, happiness in this world had to be given priority over happiness in the next.

But, unfortunately, there is no security in this world; success today can be followed by failure tomorrow. By their very nature as unlimited goods, power, pleasure, and profit could only be pursued, never securely attained. The Christian never escapes sin; maximizers, whether it is power, pleasure, or profit that they pursue, can never escape a sense that they could have done better. Even Warren Buffett must occasionally lie awake at night thinking not of the successful deals he has made but the deals that he failed to make and the deals that went wrong.

The otherworldly goals of the Christian and this-worldly goals of the interest maximizer are, as we have seen, fundamentally at odds. Until the fourteenth century, Christian ethics were largely taught in terms of the seven virtues and the seven vices. Virtue had a double role: it was both the best strategy for achieving happiness here and now, and it was the best strategy for ensuring salvation (though sinners who repented and did penance might also be saved). The traditional virtues, however, were no guide to how best to maximize power, pleasure, and profit, for they were the virtues of moderation. From the fourteenth century onward, Christian teaching increasingly focused on the Ten Commandments: what was required was not virtue, but, insofar as that was possible, obedience (and, insofar as it was not possible, grace).[41] As Max Weber recognized, obedience could, suitably interpreted, open up a good deal of scope for unlimited accumulation.[42] Obviously one had to avoid breaking the First Commandment (against idolatry) and the Tenth (against covetousness), but there was no commandment which forbade wealth or the pursuit of wealth. In any case, strict Augustinians, whether Catholic or Protestant, agreed that we are incapable of obedience. It is striking that among Catholics the only ones who could handle with ease the new language of interests when applied to the individual were the Jansenists, who took it for granted that human beings were incapable of virtue or even obedience; the pursuit of their interests was all of which they were capable.[43] Orthodox Catholics, by contrast, sought to confine the language of interests rigorously to the logic of state power, of reason of state, and to retain the traditional virtues as a guide for private individuals (although, as Blaise Pascal took delight in pointing out in the *Provincial Letters,* their casuistry often undermined the traditional virtues while pretending to respect them).

So what links power, pleasure, and profit together is that they are unlimited aspirations. Between Machiavelli and James Madison these unlimited aspirations came into their own, and with them came the new language of interests. The result was the destruction of classical ethics and politics, on the one hand, and of Christian ethics and politics on the other. Hobbes's *Leviathan* is, from this point of view, the first modern text.

The classical language of virtue was not concerned with self-sacrifice; altruism is a nineteenth-century concept. Until the invention of altruism, virtue was always supposed to bring with it its own rewards; Aristotle's virtuous man aspired to happiness and not just to a reputation for justice or bravery; and being just and courageous made him happy. But if virtue was its own reward, it was still fundamentally different, even in the thinking of the Epicureans, from the successful pursuit of pleasure. For the early modern moral philosophers with whom we are concerned here—Hobbes, Locke, Hume, Claude Adrien Hélvetius, Bentham, and their like—the good and the pleasurable are simply one and the same thing. "Things then are good or evil, only in reference to pleasure or pain," writes Locke.[44] "Good and evil, or in other words, pain and pleasure," writes Hume.[45]

This was certainly not Aristotle's view. He not only rejected the view that we should live for pleasure—the view later adopted, with reservations, by the Epicureans—but also insisted that virtue is a good in itself, even for those (those about to die on the field of battle, for example) who have no prospect of happiness. MacIntyre is right to insist that the remnants of the old language of virtue that appear in the writings of eighteenth-century authors are mere flotsam, the wreckage left behind after a terrible storm. The opening words of Voltaire's essay on virtue in the *Philosophical Dictionary* are these: "It is said of Marcus Brutus that, before killing himself, he uttered these words: 'O virtue! I thought you were something; but you are only an empty phantom!'"[46] For Voltaire, virtue, as understood by the Greeks, the Romans, and the medieval theologians, was indeed an empty phantom. Pleasure, on the other hand, was something real.

The difference between Voltaire and the ancients or the scholastics is not just that pleasure came to take the place of virtue. After all, the Epicureans had managed to construct a pleasure-based ethics which also laid emphasis on strength of character and was largely compatible with the republican virtues (strangely, there is no mention of Epicurus in MacIntyre's book). What was new was that in the past there was always understood to be a fundamental compatibility between the virtues. Courage and magnificence, for example, were both virtues, but there was nothing to prevent someone excelling in both. Courage might best express itself in battle, and magnificence in the town square; but a true leader needed both. The virtues were not mutually contradictory but rather mutually supporting. Indeed, Aristotle went so far as to argue that you could not have one virtue without having them all—the virtues were, in his view, inseparable. All this changed, as Isaiah Berlin correctly insisted in his 1972 essay "The Originality of Machiavelli," with the new power politics. As far as Machiavelli was concerned, there was no point in even attempting to be both a good Christian and a good politician—you must choose between two incommensurable systems of value.[47]

Machiavelli's thinking was born in part out of the medieval distinction between those who fight, those who pray, and those who work—knights and monks belonged to different worlds, had different ways of life, and upheld different values. But those worlds were bound tightly together by the institutions of both church and state, by shared sacraments and rituals, by mutual deference and respect. Plenty of knights retired to monasteries when their fighting days were over. Machiavelli cut through those ties. He announced that the values of politics, properly conducted, were fundamentally at odds with those of Christianity; one had to choose between them. And he was clear about which choice he had made: "I love my homeland," he said, "more than I love my own soul."[48] Machiavelli, it's true, continued to write about virtue; but by "virtue" he no longer meant the qualities that enable human beings to fulfill their true purpose; he meant those qualities that enable you to acquire glory. Only politicians and generals were capable of this sort of virtue, for virtue and glory go hand in hand. *The Prince* was the first major assault on the Aristotelian and Christian conceptions of virtue.

The question of Machiavelli's religious beliefs (or lack of them) is a vexed one in modern scholarship, though his closest friends seem to have been in no doubt that he was no Christian. When he was appointed by the Wool Guild in 1521 to select a Lenten preacher, Francesco Guicciardini wrote to him:

> It was certainly good judgment on the part of our reverend consuls of the Wool Guild to have entrusted you with the duty of selecting a preacher, not otherwise than if the task had been given to Pachierotto, while he was alive, or to Ser Sano [two well-known homosexuals] to find a beautiful and graceful wife for a friend. I believe you will serve them according to the expectations they have of you and as is required by your honor, which would be stained if at this age you started to think about your soul, because, since you have always lived in a contrary belief [*con contraria professione*], it would be attributed rather to senility than to goodness.[49]

What was Machiavelli's contrary belief? It has been known since 1960 that in 1497 Machiavelli copied out the whole, lengthy text of Lucretius's *De rerum natura,* and that his version of the text incorporated a series of deliberate and informed choices about how best to amend the numerous problematic passages over which any reader must stumble.[50] Machiavelli's engagement with Lucretius was thus sustained and intense. Some scholarship has begun to take the question of Machiavelli's Lucretianism seriously, but at least one example of Machiavelli's intimate familiarity with Lucretius has been missed: a striking echo of *De rerum natura* is to be found in the opening words of the prologue to Machiavelli's play *Clizia,* which reworks a Roman play which reworked a Greek play, thus inviting its author to play with the idea of repetition: "Se nel mondo tornassino i medesimi uomini, come tornano i medesimi casi, non passerebbono mai cento anni, che noi non ci trovassimo un'altra volta insieme a fare le medesime cose che ora." (If the same people reappeared in the world, as the same events do, a hundred years would never go by without us finding ourselves once again together doing the very same things we are doing now.)

Lucretius held that, given enough time, the same configurations of atoms will recur, so that over and over again Brutus and Cassius (or atomic configurations identical to those of Brutus and Cassius) will stab Caesar. But, Lucretius argued (bk. 3, lines 843–861), though the same events will be repeated, the same people will not reappear, for Brutus II will have no memory of having once been Brutus I. If Brutus II could remember being Brutus I they would be the same person but the two of them would not be identical, for Brutus II would have memories Brutus I did not have; if they are identical they cannot be the same person. Thus Brutus and Cassius will never find themselves once again together doing the very same thing yet again. They will have no sense of déjà vu. Machiavelli, in these seemingly throwaway lines, captures this technical distinction between the recurrence of the same events and the nonrecurrence of the same people—a distinction that was not made in Pythagorean and Stoic discussions of recurrence, which mistakenly presumed that if Brutus I and Brutus II are identical, then they are the same person.[51] In the opening words of his play, then, Machiavelli not only declares his attachment to an anti-Christian doctrine of recurrence but also commits himself to a specifically Lucretian form of that doctrine.

Lucretius was an Epicurean, rejecting the possibility of any form of life after death (which is why he was so concerned to squash the idea that we might be reincarnated in the future) and insisting that pleasure and pain are all that matter in life. Classical Epicureanism maintained that although there are numerous pleasures and pains, happiness is always the same. For Machiavelli and his Renaissance and Enlightenment successors this seemed contradictory. The notion that there are competing conceptions of the good life, and that this competition can never be resolved, followed, it seemed to them, inevitably from the conviction that we are creatures of appetite, for no one doubts that the appetites are plural. Of course, this pluralism was not acceptable to theologians. Its slow dissemination was inseparable from a process of intellectual secularization, a process which sometimes took place within a carapace of religious observance, and sometimes was avowedly irreligious and antireligious. But the theologians were not the only ones opposed to it. Great claims have been made for Baruch Spinoza as the founder of modern, secular, democratic thought; but in ethics Spinoza, despite the fact that he started from Hobbesian premises, was directly opposed to Hobbes, who had insisted that "there is no such

Finis ultimus, (utmost ayme,) nor *Summum Bonum,* (greatest Good,) as is spoken of in the Books of the old Morall Philosophers."[52] By contrast, Spinoza sought to demonstrate that there was only one true conception of the good, one that all wise men would adopt and share. Immanuel Kant, too, sought to reimpose unity upon the world of value, replacing the Ten Commandments by his own categorical imperative. Spinoza and Kant stand in opposition to Machiavelli, Hobbes, and Hume. You have to choose one side or the other. Modern moral philosophy, you might say, is an attempt to either justify or escape from pluralism—either to explain how pluralists can still claim to know what virtue is, or alternatively to explain how one can rebuild a unitary conception of virtue in a world that has lost its sense of the unity of the virtues, and the underlying sense of community in which that unity was grounded (for, as MacIntyre correctly says, a moral philosophy characteristically presupposes a sociology).[53]

This choice between the pluralists and their opponents has been memorably presented by Jonathan Israel as a choice between Voltaire and Spinoza.[54] He praises Spinoza as the founder of modern radicalism, and excoriates Voltaire as a proponent of enlightened despotism. But Voltaire was much more than that. He wrote brilliantly against slavery, and risked much in the defense of religious freedom.[55] Nevertheless, if Voltaire had a core commitment, it was to value pluralism. Take, for example, *Candide.*[56] Candide, in the course of Voltaire's short novel, is buffeted by one catastrophe after another. In the end, stranded on the banks of the Bosporus, he decides to cultivate his garden. Voltaire is not claiming for a moment that the good life Candide builds for himself at the end of the novel is the only form of the good life. He is not suggesting that we should all seek out an interstice, a privileged space on the margins of political, religious, and economic conflict, an Epicurean garden. He certainly *is* saying that this is one form of the good life, and that not everyone should be expected to perform the civic virtues. Candide discovers the pleasures of Turkish delight studded with roasted pine nuts and chunks of pineapple, and with the candied peel of oranges, lemons, and citrons. These pleasures, produced by the hard work that keeps at bay boredom, vice (a little bit of flotsam there, floating on the surface of Voltaire's text), and poverty, are all that a reasonable person could desire. There's a great deal about power and pleasure in *Candide,* but none of it counts, it seems, as political theory. Fair enough; but it is hard to see how Voltaire's rejection of every established authority is compatible with a view of him as a reactionary spokesperson for despotism.[57]

Nor should we simply assume that there is nothing to be said about the politics of Turkish delight. In eighteenth-century England it was roast beef that symbolized English liberty and the prosperity that resulted from it; before the French called the English *les rosbifs,* the English were singing of "The Roast Beef of Old England," and William Hogarth's *The Gate of Calais* celebrated the English diet of roast beef while the French made do with onion soup. "Beef and Liberty" was (and is) the motto of the Sublime Society of Beefsteaks (founded 1735), and there is, I am glad to say, a book entitled *Beef and Liberty.*[58] Voltaire would have been well aware that the peasants of France did not have luxuries like Turkish delight any more than they had roast beef: which is why *mon petit choux* (my little cabbage) is an endearment in French which has no equivalent in English.

In *Candide* Voltaire speaks for what we may call (in imitation of Judith Shklar) the ordinary pleasures, knowing full well that many people are denied even the most ordinary of pleasures. One of these is sex. Michel de Montaigne devoted a chapter of his essays, coyly titled "On Some Lines of Vergil," to the pleasures of sex: "The genital activities are so natural, so necessary and so right: what have they done to make us never dare to mention them without embarrassment and to exclude them from serious orderly conversation? We are not afraid to utter the words *kill, thieve or betray;* but those others we only dare to mutter through our teeth." They are quoted (inaccurately) by Voltaire in the chapter of his *Questions on the Encyclopedia* ambiguously entitled "On Kisses." In *Jacques the Fatalist,* Denis Diderot, who had begun his career as a best-selling author with *The Indiscreet Jewels,* a book almost entirely about genital activities, recycles and adapts Montaigne's phrases without quotation marks. The pluralist tradition I am discussing takes it for granted that we have to talk about sex: even the usually solemn Pierre Bayle had a good deal to say about kissing in the margins and footnotes of his *Philosophical Dictionary.* There are no genital activities in Spinoza; in their place we find the far from precise *corpora commiscere,* the intermixing of bodies, which presumably covers the chaste pleasures of walking arm in arm, holding hands, and hugging—and the far-from-chaste pleasures of French kissing, fellatio, cunnilingus, and genital intercourse.[59]

Montaigne's *Essays* were, inevitably, condemned by the Jansenists for his moral laxity and ended up on the Index of Prohibited Books, where Montesquieu's *Persian Letters* joined them; the books Diderot published were all banned, and *Jacques the Fatalist* was first published long after Diderot's death, in 1796.* It's worth remembering here Robert Darnton's demonstration that as far as eighteenth-century booksellers were concerned, philosophy and pornography were more or less the same thing (which explains why they stocked very few copies of Spinoza); but I have to admit I'm a little surprised to find Machiavelli's *Mandragola* being described, by a distinguished political theorist, as a "louche little play" even in this day and age.[60] Political theorists, we are to gather, can safely steer clear of these ordinary pleasures, which have nothing to do with politics. And yet, what is the point of a liberal politics if it is not to end stoning for adultery, to legalize homosexuality, to make it possible to talk freely about ordinary pleasures? Machiavelli's "louche little play" is not only an exercise in applying Machiavellian principles to private life; it also has the equally serious purpose of asking Montaigne's question, "What have the genital activities done to make us never dare to mention them without embarrassment and to exclude them from serious orderly conversation?"

But, you may want to protest, where's the theory here? Turkish delight may symbolize prosperity, but it doesn't constitute a *theory* of prosperity. Publishing *Candide* in the middle of the Seven Years' War may have been a political act, but *Candide* is not a work of political philosophy. Machiavelli's *Mandragola* may end happily with a contented ménage à trois, but it is not, you may think, to be taken seriously as an argument for sexual freedom. Pleasure, and the various pleasures that matter to us all, you might claim, lie outside the proper realm of political theory. And this is where I would disagree with you, both on my own behalf and on behalf of the long Enlightenment that runs from Machiavelli to Bentham, an Enlightenment that insisted that we must take push-pin (a game no one plays any more—think of

---

* Montesquieu's *Persian Letters* was never legally published in France under the ancien régime, but it circulated freely; Montesquieu, *Lettres persanes,* ed. Catherine Volpilhac-Auger and Jean Ehrard (Oxford: Voltaire Foundation, 2004), 23n44, 27. By 1750 this had come to seem anomalous, but the book was so widely available that it was too late for the authorities to take action.

marbles, or pick-up sticks) as seriously as we do poetry. But push-pin and poetry are not the difficult cases when it comes to thinking about pleasure; the difficult cases, then as now, have usually to do with sex. And here it is worth remarking that Machiavelli and Bentham were both advocates of sexual liberty. As Machiavelli wrote to his friend Francesco Vettori, Florence's ambassador to Rome, encouraging him to seek sexual pleasure wherever he pleased, "He who is deemed wise during the day will never be considered crazy at night, and he who is esteemed a respectable man [*uomo da bene*], and is worthy, whatever he does to lighten his heart and live happily renders him honor not blame. Rather than being called a bugger or a whoremonger, one says he is a man of broad interests, easy going, and a good fellow."[61] Throughout his correspondence with Vettori, Machiavelli treats the choice of a male or female sexual partner as purely a matter of personal preference. As for Bentham, he has the extraordinary merit of being the first to argue systematically that there should be no law against pederasty, for private pleasures between consenting individuals should be subject to no penalties and cannot be regarded as immoral; Bentham even wonders if they can properly be described as unnatural.[62] I should stress that Machiavelli and Bentham had no conception of homosexuality as we understand the term.[63] Thus Bentham (relying on examples from Greek and Roman history and on contemporary reports from Tahiti) argued that it is perfectly commonplace for men to be attracted to youths, but this attraction usually goes along with an attraction to adult women. He believed that it is very unusual for a man to be attracted to another man or a youth to a man; thus, where youths consent to have sex with men, this is generally not because of mutual attraction but is rather to be considered as a form of prostitution. But Bentham thought prostitution should be legal, and he assumed that postpubescent children are capable of consent. The views Machiavelli and Bentham held on the vexed issue of sexual pleasure are not distinct from their views on morality and politics; they are inseparably connected to them.

Let me give just one further example to show that we actually ought to think a little more carefully about pleasure than we usually do. According to David Hume, religious believers do not, in the main, really believe in an afterlife, even though they say they do. They are "really infidels in their hearts" for the simple reason that they cannot imagine what the afterlife will be like. Nevertheless, they enjoy nothing more than listening to fire and brimstone sermons:

> In matters of religion men take a pleasure in being terrify'd, and . . . no preachers are so popular, as those who excite the most dismal and gloomy passions. In the common affairs of life, where we feel and are penetrated with the solidity of the subject, nothing can be more disagreeable than fear and terror; and 'tis only in dramatic performances and in religious discourses, that they ever give pleasure. In these latter cases the imagination reposes itself indolently on the idea; and the passion, being soften'd by the want of belief in the subject, has no more than the agreeable effect of enlivening the mind, and fixing the attention.[64]

If Hume was right—and Hume had a good deal of experience of hellfire sermonizing—moderate religion will always be at a disadvantage to fundamentalist religion. The fundamentalist preacher evokes a pleasurable terror in his audience; the audience grows; and by a straightforward feedback mechanism the preacher is encouraged to reinforce his message of damnation for all but the few. As a consequence of this process he acquires first influence and eventually power. Strangely, the source of this power is not his audience's belief in what he says but their lack of belief. Fundamentalism flourishes even when—indeed because—men and women are really infidels in their hearts. Hume's theory moves from a claim about the psychology of pleasure to an analysis of the place of religion in society and politics. If this movement surprises us, it is because we are not used to taking pleasure seriously, and if we persist in the belief that all that is needed for the triumph of good sense where religious disputes are concerned is dialogue and mutual respect, that is because we fail to understand the mechanisms working against dialogue and mutual respect.

Pluralism, in its new guise of multiculturalism, is a fact of life in modern societies. It is a deep paradox that many of the people who benefit most from multiculturalism are not themselves in favor of it: Hume's analysis helps us see why this is so. It has always been the case that most of the people who benefit from toleration are, it turns out, not themselves in favor of it when they have the power to persecute others. If we turn to the principled advocates of toleration, those who genuinely believe that there is no one form of the good life, what we find over and over again is pleasure being praised in the place of virtue, prosperity in the place of godliness, limited power in the place of absolute power. I have taken a brief example from Hume in order to show that it is possible to think seriously about pleasure, that one can theorize pleasure; my argument in this chapter has simply been that if we want to understand the Enlightenment paradigm we have to learn to think, to echo MacIntyre, "after virtue"; and that means we have to put power, pleasure, and profit, and with them the appetites, the passions, and the interests at the center of our enquiry.

I DISCORSI DI NICO-
LO MACHIAVELLI, SO-
PRA LA PRIMA DECA DI
TITO LIVIO.

Con due Tauole, l'vna de capitoli, & l'altra delle cose prin-
cipali : & con le stesse parole di Tito Liuio a luo-
ghi loro, ridotte nella volgar
Lingua.

Nouellamente emmendati, & con somma
cura ristampati.

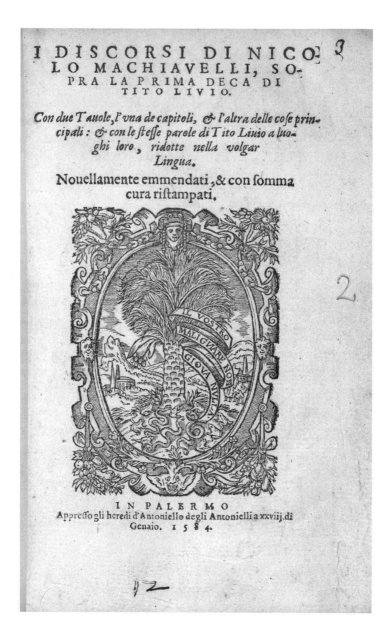

IN PALERMO
Appresso gli heredi d'Antoniello degli Antonielli a xxviij.di
Genaio. 1 5 8 4.

Title page from Niccolò Machiavelli, *Discorsi* (8°) (1584), printed by John Wolfe.

2

Power: (Mis)Reading Machiavelli

It is just over five hundred years since Niccolò Machiavelli wrote *The Prince,* although rather less since the book became famous—written in 1513, revised in 1515, first published in 1532, it became notorious in the Protestant world only after the Massacre of St. Bartholomew in 1572.[1] In the context of religious warfare, Machiavelli was read (or perhaps misread) as advocating a totally unprincipled approach to politics, as approaching power in purely instrumental terms. Already in 1573 we find Gabriel Harvey in Cambridge trying to obtain a copy of "Machiavell, the greate founder and master of pollicies," and boasting to his friend Edmund Spenser that he was familiar with people who were "pretely well acquainted," as he put it, not just with *The Prince,* but with the whole of Machiavelli's work.[2] John Wolfe (who would later collaborate with Harvey) published editions of *The Prince,* the *Discourses on Livy, The Art of War, The History of Florence,* and Machiavelli's minor works—all in Italian, and with fake Italian places of publication—in England in the 1580s; *The Art of War* was already available in English, and *The Florentine Historie* soon followed.[3] And, of course, Machiavelli was available in Latin, the language of the learned.

This chapter addresses one particular aspect of Machiavelli's legacy, his role in Elizabethan discussions of how best to maintain control of Ireland. Lisa Jardine and Anthony Grafton's essay "How Gabriel Harvey Read His Livy" is well known, and from it we learn that Harvey read Livy in order to give advice on how best to subdue Ireland, and that he read him through Machiavelli's eyes; indeed, in 1584 Harvey and Thomas Preston read the first decade of Livy and Machiavelli's *Discourses* side by side, the second serving as a commentary on the first.[4] In 1580 Sir Philip Sidney included Machiavelli on a reading list for Edward Denny, who was going soldiering in Ireland.[5] Not surprisingly, among the English settlers in Ireland we find Machiavelli cited or quoted by Sir James Croft in 1583, by Sir William

Herbert in 1591, by Richard Beacon (or Becon) in 1594, and by Edmund Spenser in 1596.[6] Their business was state policy, and so naturally they turned to Machiavelli. But what did they find? Did they read Machiavelli as he was meant to be read, or did they misread him? The question is inescapable, so let me start by questioning the readings of Machiavelli's *The Prince,* the *Discourses,* and *The Art of War,* which are currently generally accepted in the English-speaking world.

Everyone agrees that Machiavelli's primary purpose in writing *The Prince* was to make a bid for employment by the Medici, who had taken control of Florence in August 1512. Machiavelli had lost his government job in November and, suspected of opposition to the new regime, had been confined to the territories of the Florentine state for a year. In February 1513 he had been imprisoned and tortured on suspicion of participation in a plot against the Medici. He was released from prison in March under an amnesty to celebrate the election of the new Medici pope, Giovanni di Lorenzo de' Medici, who had taken the title of Leo X, and in November 1513 his period of confinement expired and he was once more free to travel, but he dared not go to Rome for fear that he would be suspected of conspiring with the Soderini family, who were in exile there, and be rearrested (and subjected to further torture).[7] But he was desperate to obtain employment, and Rome was where the jobs were being handed out.

What is not generally understood is what this means for the interpretation of *The Prince.*[8] Machiavelli, at the time he was writing *The Prince,* had no prospect of obtaining employment in the government of Florence, and any advice he had to offer on how to govern Florence would have been greeted with suspicion.[9] In chapter 5 of *The Prince* he stressed that governing cities that are used to ruling themselves is an almost impossible task. Unless one is prepared to destroy them completely one can never be confident of succeeding. This was a pretty clear warning to the Medici against regarding Florence as a secure power base. In 1513 or 1515 such advice, written for a Medici audience, could hardly be welcome; indeed, it came close to being a threat, and could only serve to remind readers that Machiavelli himself was one of those suspected of being unable to forget the word "liberty."

In writing *The Prince,* Machiavelli's mind was not (despite what commentators generally say) on Florence.[10] It was widely and correctly believed that the Medici were interested in repeating Alexander VI's project of establishing a papal nephew in a territory of his own. What Machiavelli had to offer was his intimate knowledge of the strategy and tactics of Cesare Borgia—this is why Cesare plays such a central role in the argument of *The Prince* and why Machiavelli wrote in 1515—when once again it seemed that the pope would try to establish a princedom in central Italy for Giuliano de' Medici—that he thought that a new prince should always imitate the policies of Borgia.[11] So *The Prince* is a book about how to establish yourself as the ruler of a territory which has previously lacked any well-defined state power, and which, because of the prevalence of feudal inequality and private fortresses, is incapable of political liberty. It is a handbook for someone who wants to establish a despotism, but a despotism in a region where there had previously been no consolidated state power.

Let us turn from *The Prince* to the *Discourses* (written 1515–1519).[12] There Machiavelli's prime purpose was not (as one might think from reading the standard commentaries) to provide an analysis or a defense of republican liberty. His goal was to draw from a study of politics, and particularly of Livy's history of Rome, reliable principles of action which could be employed by any state, whether princedom or republic. Thus the preface to book 1 states clearly that the work is about both "kingdoms and republics" and its purpose is to show how either a "prince or republic" can learn from the example of the ancients. In the course of doing this he undoubtedly does provide an account of the particular characteristics of republics. His admiration for ancient Rome was founded in the claim that the Roman republic was the state which had been the best in the whole of recorded history at doing what states are supposed to do. Machiavelli sums up his entire political teaching with regard to the domestic affairs of states in *Discourses*, 2.22, in a passage which is, again, carefully presented as being applicable to both republics and princes: "For government is nothing other than holding your subjects in such a way that they cannot harm you or that they do not wish to. This is done either by making yourself entirely secure against them, taking from them every means for injuring you, or by benefiting them to such an extent that they cannot reasonably wish to change their fortunes."[13]

What preoccupied Machiavelli was how to construct a political order which was secure against both internal sedition and foreign conquest. The two fundamental strategies for preventing internal sedition which he identifies in the *Discourses* are coercion and co-option, and the granting of legal security and even political liberty is the best method of co-option. From the point of view of subjects or citizens, the case for political liberty is that it is the best guarantor of their security and prosperity (*Discourses,* 1.58, 2.2). Thus, from the point of view of both rulers and subjects, liberty can be regarded as not an end in itself but a means. As Machiavelli puts it, "It is easy to learn why this love for free government springs up in people, for experience shows that cities never have increased in dominion or in riches except while they have been at liberty."[14] Turning subjects into citizens is thus not only good for the citizens themselves; it is also the most effective way of co-opting them into the service of the state.

But it is not the only way, "For when men are well governed, they do not seek for nor wish any other liberty [than to be ruled by law]."[15] One may contrast this with, for example, Francesco Guicciardini's simple statement that "those who love liberty cannot be won by good treatment, for one cannot by any kindness uproot from their breasts that desire not to hold any man superior, and to govern themselves," and indeed with many statements by Machiavelli himself, including his claim in *The Prince* that free states will always resist a government imposed upon them; by the time he wrote the *Discourses* it had become clear that the claim made in chapter 5 of *The Prince* was false at least as far as Florence was concerned.[16] For Florence, it was now clear to him, had never been a proper republic, and there was no realistic prospect of introducing a well-founded liberty there unless (by same strange reversal) the Medici should decide to become the agents of republican reform, and even then the resulting republic would look nothing like that of classical Rome.*

The measures Machiavelli thought necessary to ensure against foreign conquest are detailed in *The Art of War* (1521), the only one of his works which Machiavelli saw through the press. In this dialogue, Machiavelli's spokesperson (for most purposes) Fabrizio Colonna announces that it would not be difficult to remodel "any state in which there is still left something

---

* "The reason why Florence throughout her history has frequently varied her methods of government is that she has never been either a republic or a princedom having the qualities each requires." Machiavelli, "A Discourse on Remodeling the Government of Florence" (1520), in *The Chief Works and Others,* trans. and ed. Allan H. Gilbert, 3 vols. (Durham, N.C.: Duke University Press, 1989), 1:101.

good" after the example provided by "my Romans." What is needed is "To honor and reward excellence, not to despise poverty, to esteem the methods and regulations of military discipline, to oblige the citizens to love one another, to live without factions, to esteem private less than public good, and other like things that could easily fit in with our times." His interlocutor, Cosimo Rucellai, is struck dumb by such utopian nonsense. (Machiavelli was surely familiar with the 1519 Florentine edition of Thomas More's *Utopia,* which appeared from the same press as *The Art of War.*)[17] Cosimo responds, "I do not intend to reply to what you have said in any way, but I wish to let the decision about it be turned over to those who easily can judge it."[18] And thereafter Cosimo and Fabrizio conspire together to ensure that the discussion is confined to military matters, and that the proposals discussed are equally applicable to republics and kingdoms.[19] The key proposal is not, as is often claimed, for a citizen army (as in the early Roman republic), but rather (as in *The Prince*) for every ruler to have their own army *(armi proprie)*—that is to say an army consisting not of foreign mercenaries but of one's own people, whether conscripts or volunteers, subjects or citizens. The militia Machiavelli had himself raised in 1506 consisted of conscripted peasants, none of whom were, or had any prospect of becoming, citizens, and it is this specific military force which Colonna sets out to defend in *The Art of War.*[20]

Knowledgeable readers (who would have been a minority, since the book was intended for a wide audience) would have noticed Machiavelli's self-mocking reference to "my Romans" and grasped that his decision to use a mercenary soldier who had served indifferently in the service of Spain, the papacy, and Florence as his spokesperson was intended to point both to the difficulty of putting good theory into practice (for Fabrizio acknowledges that he has never had a chance to practice what he preaches), and to the need to abandon republican illusions if Italy were to free itself from foreign invaders.[21] How could someone like Cosimo Rucellai forget, how indeed could Machiavelli himself forget that when the cry of liberty had been raised during the Pazzi conspiracy (1478) not a single person had responded to the call to arms?[22]

Machiavelli's considered opinion was, then, that his fellow citizens had been happy to trade liberty for security.[23] And as far as security was concerned, it was security of property that mattered most to them: "men will more quickly forget the killing of their father than the loss of their patrimony" (*The Prince,* chapter 17). As a consequence, the preoccupation with the reformation of manners, institutions, and laws which runs through the *Discourses* arose not out of a desire to see liberty restored for its own sake but rather out of a desire to see effective government restored in an Italy which had fallen prey to foreign invaders; there were, in Machiavelli's view, a range of possible political structures that might serve this end. Republicanism was not the only solution, nor necessarily, in practical terms, the best one.

By the time Machiavelli wrote the *Discourses* he had reached the conclusion that there was no prospect in contemporary Italy of liberty being adopted as the true goal of political life. There were, he believed, plenty of examples in history of societies dedicated to liberty, and indeed the free cities of contemporary Germany embodied the highest ideals of republican freedom, but they did so only because they, like the Romans when the republic flourished, were poor.[24] A republican love of liberty flourished, he held, only when citizens were impoverished and had no aspiration to become rich, indeed were prepared to give freely of what little they had to ensure that the state flourished. Why were the German free cities different in loving liberty, not instrumentally, as a means to wealth, but for its own sake? Machiavelli's explanation was that "they have not had many dealings with their neighbors; the latter have not come to their cities nor have they visited neighboring places, because they have been content to enjoy the goods, to live on the food, and to be clothed with the wool provided by their country; thus the reason for all intercourse has been removed, and the beginning of all corruption; because they have had no chance to take up the customs of either France or Spain or Italy; nations which altogether are the corruption of the world."[25]

Communication with France, Italy, or Spain would in itself be corrupting, but so would the development of a commercial society, one in which people were no longer content with the produce of their own little neighborhood but traded abroad for luxuries: silks and satins, books and musical instruments, paintings and tapestries, playing cards and mirrors.[26] Thus Machiavelli implied that there were three distinct types of republican liberty: that of ancient Rome and contemporary Germany, grounded in a subsistence economy, in which citizens were prepared to fight and die for freedom; that of the commercial cities of contemporary Tuscany, where the attachment to liberty was much weaker, where mercenary armies were the norm, and where freedom was willingly traded away providing there were plausible promises of security and prosperity (prosperity being something Florence had never sought to offer its subject cities); and, between the two, the *vivere civile* that a statesman might hope to establish in a city like Florence, which would be defended by a conscript militia, and which would be a considerable improvement on the present state of affairs, but would fall far short of the unattainable ideal, *il vivere politico ed incorrotto.*[*]

On Machiavelli's analysis the social structure of Florence, a bustling commercial city without local nobles who could retreat to private castles, meant that it was unsuited to despotism but equally unsuited to the strenuous liberty of early Rome. It must, of necessity, make do with some sort of awkward compromise, as exemplified by Venice, and as embodied in the constitution proposed by Machiavelli in "A Discourse on Remodeling the Government of Florence," written immediately after *The Art of War.* Just as there was no foreseeable future in which Florence would cease to be Christian (despite the pernicious defects of that religion), so there was no foreseeable future in which it would have a proper citizen army, and none in which it would cease to be a commercial city. Girolamo Savonarola, with his bonfire of vanities, had grasped the scale of change necessary, but had also demonstrated the impossibility of carrying it into lasting effect, for even his supporters had balked when their commercial way of life was under threat; indeed, even Savonarola had approved of prosperity while inveighing against luxury.[27]

Thus one can certainly say that Machiavelli "presents a wholehearted defense of traditional republican values," but such a statement needs to be accompanied by an acknowledgment that he saw the world of true republican liberty as being lost and gone—if not forever, then at least until history went through one of its great cycles which saw all memory of previous civilizations wiped out and a new beginning almost from scratch.[28] It would take a Noachic flood, or a change of religion, or an invasion of Scythians before traditional republican values could once more be realized in an Italian city. In the meantime, the primary task of the politician was the relatively modest

---

[*] See Appendix C in the present volume.

one of constructing a political order secure against internal sedition and foreign conquest.

Of interpretations of Machiavelli there has been and will be no end. The account I have just given helps explain why both *The Prince* and the *Discourses* are open to radically contrasting interpretations, depending on whether one thinks *The Prince* is about Florence or the Romagna, whether one thinks the republican ideals expressed in the *Discourses* are thought to be realizable or unrealizable, and whether one thinks *The Art of War* to be about the need for a citizen army or a conscript army. This makes the question of Machiavelli's reception by his readers particularly difficult and problematic. Where readers of Thomas Hobbes, for example, have generally agreed on what Hobbes was saying, even if they have disagreed about how to respond to it, there has been no consensus among readers of Machiavelli on how to interpret him, and his texts have been put to work to serve radically different purposes. Since beliefs and actions are inseparably intertwined, different readings of Machiavelli have served to legitimate different political behaviors, and it would seem certain that Machiavelli has influenced his readers in ways that he would never have intended.[29]

In 1969 Quentin Skinner put the word "influence" as used by intellectual historians under a ban—though we might think that the claim he was making then, that texts can't be shown to influence their readers, was self-refuting, since his own text had an obvious influence.[30] Although he has significantly shifted his position since, no one now writes articles with titles such as "The Influence of Machiavelli on Spenser"—the title of an article which appeared in a more innocent time, in 1909. Since 1969 historians of ideas have suffered from their own "anxiety of influence," to borrow a phrase from Harold Bloom. Writing about Spenser in 1986, Ciaran Brady felt he could safely dismiss "such adventures in intellectual genealogy"—he was thinking not of Michel Foucault, but of Skinner's description of much history of ideas as being like the opening chapters of the first book of Chronicles.[31] And, of course, discussions of influence do often have the matter back to front: it is not, one might think, Machiavelli who influenced Spenser, but Spenser who took something from Machiavelli. The literary critics have a word that almost covers this: "reception." But reception, strictly speaking, implies a concern only with how Machiavelli was read, while what matters is also how he was put to work in new texts. We don't have a good word for this process of taking and using; let's make do with the word "repurposing."

So let me start my own discussion of Spenser with a word or two about influence and its alternative, repurposing, even though I know I run the risk of sounding like poor Charles Tansley in Virginia Woolf's *To The Lighthouse,* who is endlessly writing a dissertation on the influence of somebody on something (nobody in the novel, except presumably Charles himself, can be bothered to remember just who is the somebody and what is the something). *To the Lighthouse* appeared in 1927, when T. S. Eliot was happily rambling on about the influence of Seneca on Shakespeare, and it is hard to read Eliot's confident use of the word "influence" now without an inward shudder.[32] Indeed, the whole enterprise is guyed by David Lodge in his 1984 campus novel *Small World,* in which Persse McGarrigle is writing a postmodern thesis on the influence not of Shakespeare on Eliot but of Eliot on Shakespeare.

Still, I think it is straightforwardly the case that some texts are influenced by other texts, or repurpose other texts, and this is often manifested by what literary critics call intertextuality.[33] In some cases a vocabulary, an argument, or a manner of thinking is so distinctive that one can have no doubt where it comes from, just as one can trace a rare genetic mutation to its source.[34] In such cases we can be confident that a later text engages directly with its predecessor. In other cases a mutation may be quite common, so that it is impossible to say whether an author is copying a predecessor or independently making a similar conceptual or linguistic move. And in still other cases a language or a paradigm may become so common that it may be impossible to narrow down the range of possible texts in which an author might have encountered it to one particular text. Edwin Greenlaw, the author of "The Influence of Machiavelli on Spenser," thought Spenser echoed Machiavelli's phrase *medicine forti,* strong medicines, in his *A View of the Present State of Ireland.*[35] "Machiavelli's phrase often appears in *the View*" Greenlaw tells us, when, actually, it never appears, for Spenser writes of "violent medicine"; and anyway, "strong medicine" is a commonplace phrase, were Spenser to have used it.[36]

In the case of Machiavelli what we have is a text that was very widely read throughout Europe, and often quoted or paraphrased—frequently without naming the author, and often by attributing a statement of Machiavelli's to some slightly more respectable author, such as Tacitus. One could, in the spirit of Eliot, find a lot of Tacitus in Machiavelli, or, in the spirit of McGarrigle, a lot of Machiavelli in Tacitus. Echoes of Machiavelli can be found all over the place, often in writers who are not echoing Machiavelli himself but have come by his ideas second- or thirdhand, sometimes indeed by reading Machiavelli's critics, such as Giovanni Botero and Innocent Gentillet. And, of course, Machiavelli was never an isolated thinker. Guicciardini held very similar views, so that one could learn a sort of Machiavellism from his *History of Italy,* which first appeared in English in 1579, or from T. Purfoote's *A Briefe Collection or Epitomie of All the Notable and Material Things Contained in the Hystorie of Gucchiardine* (1591), or Robert Dallington's *Aphorismes Ciuill and Militarie* (1613, 1629), both of which sought to extract practical lessons from Guicciardini's *History of Italy* just as Machiavelli had sought to extract them from Livy's *History.*[37]

Moreover, concepts became attached to the name of Machiavelli which are not in fact to be found in Machiavelli. Machiavelli never writes about interests in his major political works. The language of interests seems so obviously Machiavellian that it comes as a shock to realize it isn't. Machiavelli never refers to "politics," although he uses the adjective *politico;* and yet we think of him as the founder of modern political analysis. And Machiavelli never writes of reason of state, although all the later theorists of reason of state were engaging with him and his disciples.[38]

Just as we read concepts like "interests" and "politics" and "reason of state" back into Machiavelli, so we can pick up phrases from Machiavelli and assume too easily that we know what they mean; we can think we are borrowing when we are in fact adapting and transforming. When Machiavelli said, on 10 December 1513, that for fifteen years he had been studying *l'arte dello stato,* did he mean what Jacob Burckhardt called *Der Staat als Kunstwerk,* the state as a work of art (or artifice)? Or did he mean that he had been learning the trade or business of "the state" (by which he meant not the modern state, but rather "the regime"), as one might learn the wool trade or the silk trade? In an earlier letter of 9 April 1513 Machiavelli said that he did not know how to reason about the silk trade or the wool trade *(l'arte della seta; l'arte della lana),* he couldn't reason about profits and losses, and so he reasoned about the state. Clearly, then, Machiavelli does not have Burckhardt's *Kunstwerk* in mind; he is writing about the business of politics, not the art of politics, just as in *L'arte della guerra* he is writing about military techniques, not about war as an art form. Machiavelli had made a career in the business of politics until he lost his position on the restoration of the Medici, and found himself in prison, and tortured, suspected of republican plotting.

⟨✥⟩

Realizing that for someone like Machiavelli there is a business of politics is key to understanding the term *ragion di stato*. The origins of this phrase are far from straightforward. It became widespread after the publication of Botero's *Reason of State* (1589), but Botero was only echoing a phrase he had heard frequently repeated, and indeed he had no insight into its origins. The phrase had already appeared here and there in print before 1589; it had even appeared in English. If one hunts through the early usages three things become clear: first, the phrase *ragion di stato* derives from an earlier phrase, *ragion di guerra,* which itself derives from Latin: Caesar, for example, had written of *ratio atque usus belli.* It had long been accepted that normal standards of justice and morality did not apply in warfare, when deception and dishonesty were often admirable; reason of state regarded peace as warfare conducted by other means—as the peacetime equivalent of *ragion di guerra.*

In usages such as these the word *ratio* or *ragione* is ambiguous; sometimes it means law, as in "the law of war," and sometimes it means "enterprise" or "business." So *ragion di stato* can sometimes mean the law of the state, as compared and contrasted to the laws of nature, of war, of the political community. But it can also mean the business of politics: in Renaissance Italian the word *ragione* refers to a business enterprise, and to the embodiment of that enterprise in an account book. Thus the term *ragion di stato* would have had contemporaries thinking of politics as a business, just like the banking business in which the Medici had made their money. It is this last meaning which eventually gave rise in authors like Botero to an idea of *ragion di stato* as the rational choice made by politicians to maximize their power.[39] *Ragion di stato* corresponded to Machiavelli's concept of *necessity.*[40]

Thus, when Machiavelli used the phrase *l'arte dello stato,* he meant something very close to *ragion di stato:* he meant the business of politics.

{ 47 }

And just as ordinary business is conducted in terms of profit and loss, so politics is conducted in terms of gaining or losing power. A businessman is constrained both by the law and the need to maintain a reputation for fair dealing if he is to stay in business; rulers are not similarly constrained. But there *is* a constraint if they are concerned about their reputation in the long run. Machiavelli did not simply have a maximizing view of power; he advocated a preoccupation with glory as well as mere success. Glory is compatible with lying and murdering on occasion, but not with destroying a republic and murdering one's fellow citizens, as Agathocles had done in Syracuse.[41] The highest form of glory was attained by those who, like Romulus, used power to create the conditions for freedom.[42]

Machiavelli thus combined a political analysis which was value-free—one must pay attention to what works—with a nostalgic evocation of those forms of behavior which used to win immortal glory, whether the conquests of Hannibal or Junius Brutus's sacrifice of his sons. The inevitable consequence was that there were moments when Machiavelli's power analysis came into conflict with his value system, and he made clear that the reader faced a difficult choice.

One of the key purposes of reason of state theorists was to appear to extend this conflict (by insisting that Christian moral values had an ultimate authority) and then to turn around and claim to eliminate it (by insisting that godly policies were always in the best interests of the ruler). Thus we find a pair of sermons preached by the royalist and Anglican Robert South in 1659 and 1660, the first entitled *Interest Deposed, and Truth Restored,* the second *Ecclesiastical Policy the Best Policy: Or, Religion the Best Reason of State.* This two-step—"interest deposed" followed by "religion the best reason of state"—was absolutely characteristic of conservative reason of state theorists. Machiavelli's approach was very different: he confined the conflict within a narrow and carefully defined field, but having done so he made no attempt to eliminate it. What we will be looking at in this chapter is one such conflict.

I want to turn from Machiavelli to two texts that are often said to have been influenced by him, and that were written when the full impact of his ideas had begun to be felt across Europe, but when the terms "interest" and "reason of state" had yet to become an automatic part of political discourse:

these texts are Spenser's *A View of the Present State of Ireland,* which is dated 1596, but which was evidently begun in 1590 (it was not published until 1633; its composition is roughly contemporary with that of the second half of *The Faerie Queen,* the first three books of which appeared in 1590, the last three in 1596); and a contemporary text, also about Irish politics, Richard Beacon's *Solon His Follie* (published in 1594). Spenser directly referred to Machiavelli, while Beacon quoted him without naming him, calling him "a learned writer" and "a subtile writer."[43] There was nothing novel about their interest in Machiavelli. Herbert, writing just before them, had quoted him repeatedly, though he named him only when he criticized him. Otherwise he called him simply "that Italian," *ille Italus.*[44] Thus Herbert, or the person who copied his manuscript, added a marginal reference to chapter 5 of Machiavelli's *Prince* against this passage in which he predicted that, if the Irish do not learn obedience,

> some king of England and Ireland, of great prudence and power, prompted by political considerations and designs, will disperse that entire race [the Gaelic Irish] and will extirpate all the inhabitants there who have lapsed into the habits and customs of the Irish [as the Old English had done].
>
> The distinguished Italian has made a most acute and perceptive observation: if a state which is accustomed to live by its own laws and customs comes into the power of someone who thinks it should not be destroyed then he must expect that it will destroy him. For always at a time of rebellion it will have a place of refuge, namely those ancient ordinances of its own. These can never be consigned to oblivion either by the passage of time or by the conferring of benefits, and whatever one might do or provide for, if the inhabitants are not divided up and scattered, those institutions never pass from their memory, and they will immediately return to them at every turn of events.
>
> This stubbornness of mind is a leprosy. Once it has struck deep roots no elixir, no lotion, no skill cures it.[45]

Machiavelli had been writing about republican cities, and had surely admired such stubbornness of mind; repurposed for the circumstances of Elizabethan rule in Ireland, his warning of the difficulty of trying to rule a conquered city like Pisa (or indeed Florence in 1512) became an argument for dispersing and extirpating an entire society. As we shall see, chapter 5 of *The Prince* was not the only text readers of Machiavelli had in mind when advocating such policies.

Let me first give an example of the intertextual presence of Machiavelli in the two texts with which I am primarily concerned. Both Spenser and Beacon talk about the need to establish a perfect commonwealth. Beacon's theme is the restoration of the commonwealth of Ireland, and he begins and ends with references to a commonwealth's "first perfection," while Spenser wants a new institution and writes of "that perfect establishment and new commonwealth" which he is proposing.[46] When I noticed this language of perfection I was a little puzzled. Who would imagine that Ireland had ever had or ever would have a perfect constitution? The answer is simple: this is Machiavelli's language. According to Machiavelli the goal of restoration is always the recovery of a lost perfection (a view particularly appropriate, in his mind, in the case of Rome), and the words *perfetto* or *perfezione* occur eight times in the second chapter of the *Discourses,* and then again in the title to the third chapter. The role given to the word "perfect" in these Elizabethan texts has nothing to do with Ireland and everything to do with Machiavelli.

For Spenser and Beacon the *Discourses* represented a handbook on how to remake a political system and reestablish it on new foundations, and their attention focused particularly on Machiavelli's discussions of how the Romans had governed their empire—a question of obvious relevance to Elizabethan readers of Machiavelli living in Ireland.

Spenser's and Beacon's texts reflected a moment of crisis in the affairs of Ireland. Both were convinced that power was slipping away from the authorities, that the Old English (the descendants of medieval English settlers, who had generally remained Catholic) had formed an alliance with the Gaelic Irish, and that resistance and disorder would inevitably turn into sedition and rebellion—or had already so turned, for by 1596, when Spenser finished *A View,* the Nine Years' War had begun. Both were satisfied that merely going on as before, with occasional military campaigns and token surrenders, would not do. The English were, they acknowledged, losing a long, drawn-out guerrilla war.[47] The character of that war had been neatly summarized by Thomas Churchyard in 1579, describing the tactics employed by Sir Humphrey Gilbert during the First Desmond Rebellion

(1569–1573): "when soeuer he [Gilbert] made any ostyng, or inrode, into the enemies Countrey, he killed manne, woman, and child, and spoiled, wasted, and burned, by the grounde all that he might: leauyng nothyng of the enemies in saffetie, whiche he could possiblie waste, or consume."[48] Gilbert's goal was to starve the enemy into submission.* He took hostages (whom he did not hesitate to kill if their relatives rebelled), and he deliberately sought to instill terror:

> His maner was that the heddes of all those (of what sort soeuer thei were) whiche were killed in the daie, should bee cutte of from their bodies, and brought to the place where he incamped at night: and should there bee laied on the ground, by eche side of the waie leadyng into his owne Tente: so that none could come into his Tente for any cause, but commonly he muste passe through a lane of heddes, whiche he vsed *ad terrorem,* the dedde feelyng nothyng the more paines thereby: and yet did it bryng great terrour to the people, when thei sawe the heddes of their dedde fathers, brothers, children, kinsfolke, and freendes, lye on the grounde before their faces.[49]

That such methods were necessary Spenser and Beacon did not doubt; but they had come to the view that what was required was a much more systematic program to transform Irish society and the Irish state.

Spenser, to his credit, offered a sophisticated analysis of Irish history and culture. The Irish, the Scots, and many of the ancient Britons he believed, following William Camden, to be descended from the warlike Scythians. Spenser is sometimes accused of being some sort of racist; but his key point was that the British and the Irish were descended from the same stock, and he wanted to hammer home the military capacity of the Irish, symbolized by their Scythian origins.

In England, Spenser argued, the character of the Saxons was transformed by the Norman Conquest. A disorderly and rebellious people were slowly civilized by a ruler who settled among them, brought with him a new ruling class made up of his fellow countrymen, and, with all severity, imposed upon them new laws. Ireland was thus to be considered as equivalent in many

---

* As Machiavelli had written, "It is better to overcome the enemy with hunger than with steel." Machiavelli, *The Art of War,* in *The Chief Works* (1989), 2:718.

ways to England before the Norman Conquest, for the English had never carried out a thorough conquest of Ireland, bringing the whole island under their complete control. In effect, the medieval conquests merely saw an English beachhead established; the Gaelic Irish simply retreated to areas outside English control. Over time the Old English had been corrupted, and become no better than the Gaelic Irish. In insisting that the Conquest was a true conquest, Spenser was going against the standard English view of English history which maintained that there had been constitutional continuity from time immemorial; he was doing so in order to insist that Ireland needed to be conquered as if for the first time. The English must now play the role in Ireland that the Normans had played in England.

Spenser's vision of what must follow is horrifying: the result of Irish resistance will be widespread famine, vast numbers of deaths, and in the end unconditional surrender. The Gaelic Irish must be transported from their present locations to new ones and new English settlers brought in. The clan system must be extirpated. The native inhabitants must be required to change their names, their clothes, their haircuts, their customs, and their language. They must be forcibly assimilated. New laws must be imposed upon them requiring (as in Anglo-Saxon England) collective responsibility, so that communities can be punished for the misbehavior of individuals. But martial law and extralegal force will also be necessary.

Only slowly and over several generations could one hope to move toward a truly English system of law. Such cruelty might be dreadful in the short term, but in the long run it would make possible an ordered, peaceable, and prosperous society. Spenser's key term for his long-term objective is "civility," "sweet civility."[50]

While Spenser focuses fairly narrowly on Ireland, Beacon deals with the issue of constitutional reform in general, constantly turning to Ireland as a particular example of a wider theme. In many respects his recommendations coincide with those of Spenser, although he emphasizes the role of persuasion alongside force, does not mention the possibility of famine, and does not advocate enforced transportation.

An extensive literature has grown up around these two texts, which are obviously fundamental for two overlapping enterprises: the study of Irish history under Elizabeth, and the study of Spenser and his poetry. In addition Markku Peltonen has presented Beacon as the best exemplar of what he calls an Elizabethan "classical republicanism," which has naturally led to the question "Is Spenser too a classical republican?," so that these texts have also been caught up in the wider literature on Renaissance republicanism.[51]

In my view these three literatures have failed to address adequately the relationship between these two texts and Machiavelli. Everybody knows that there are implicit and explicit references to Machiavelli in the texts; nobody has grasped the way in which these two texts struggle to come to terms with their Machiavellian inheritance. The two texts, I will suggest, have very different relationships to Machiavelli. Beacon is a mere borrower or recycler (despite the claims frequently made on his behalf), but Spenser really has been deeply influenced by Machiavelli, and is engaged in a sustained repurposing.

Commentary on the influence of Machiavelli has been constructed around what Clare Carroll has called "the Janus face of Machiavelli," the two faces being those of *The Prince* and the *Discourses,* empire and republic, but we shouldn't assume that Machiavelli always looked two-faced to Elizabethan readers, any more than he saw himself as two-faced (or, indeed, than he was two-faced on the reading I have proposed above).[52] Both *The Prince* and the *Discourses* had plenty to interest Elizabethan soldiers and administrators as they struggled with the task of governing Ireland, and the points at which they overlapped were as important as the points on which they differed. Moreover, as we shall see, both implied that politics should be understood not simply in terms of a binary division (despotism or liberty, coercion or co-option) but in terms of a trio of options (despotism, liberty, and—between the two—civility, the good government which leaves men wishing for no further liberty).

Machiavelli devoted a chapter of *The Prince* and several chapters of the *Discourses* to the question of how one should govern conquered territories.[53] He recommended that the new ruler should move to his new territories and establish colonies there—both Beacon and Spenser favored new English colonies (or, as they were called, plantations) in Ireland, and both wanted a powerful lord deputy who could in some measure substitute for the absence of the queen herself.[54] One of the consequences of the absence of the queen was that the Irish settlers wrote about the state as an abstraction in a way that Machiavelli never did. Thus Spenser wrote of those clergy who were "in high place about the state," by which he did not mean near the prince, but near the seat of government.[55]

In *The Prince* Machiavelli discussed the failure of the French to establish a secure base in Italy—the king failed to live there, failed to establish colonies, and failed to make the right alliances in the Italian political system. On the other hand, the French monarchy had successfully integrated Brittany, Burgundy, Gascony, and Normandy by respecting local laws and customs—which, fortunately, were not so different from those of France. In the *Discourses* Machiavelli outlined two alternative policies: one can either rule newly conquered territories through local elites to whom one leaves considerable freedom, or one can get a real grip, as David did when he made the poor rich and the rich poor.[56] The same choice applied if conquered territories rebelled. Once the rebellion had been put down, the rebellious cities must either be generously forgiven or whole communities be extirpated.[57] Halfway measures must be avoided at all costs.

What Machiavelli always had in mind was the conquest of a relatively highly urbanized society which in many respects shared a common culture and religion with its conquerors. When he turned briefly to consider a conquest by alien forces, it was the French in Italy to whom he turned his attention. He would have had to look to the Roman Empire—to the conquest of Germany, for example—to find examples of a centralized state coming up against a largely pastoral and in many respects tribal society, or to the conquests of the Ottomans to find examples of monotheistic rulers whose religion differed from that of their subjects. Machiavelli wasn't interested in these examples because they weren't relevant. He had nothing to say about the establishment of strongholds in hostile territory, about the need to have defensible roads, or about a warfare in which the enemy was often indistinguishable from the civilian population—subjects on which Spenser was an expert. And, of course, he had nothing to say about the Christian wars of religion, which still lay in the future.

Thus, although Spenser and Beacon could find plenty of food for thought in Machiavelli, Machiavelli's interests and theirs diverged, and their own texts were bound to be only partly Machiavellian in character. One passage in Machiavelli was, however, central to their thinking—and needs, I would argue, to be at the heart of any interpretation of their work. In book 1, chapter 25 of the *Discourses* Machiavelli argued that anyone who wanted to reform a republic needed to keep the semblance (he called it the shadow) of old forms in order to win popular support, even though beneath that semblance the realities might have been utterly transformed. But any new ruler who wanted to establish an absolute power, which is always a form of tyranny, should change everything. In the next chapter he described how rulers have sought to do this: making the rich poor and the poor rich, destroying old cities and building new ones, and making it clear that all wealth and power derive from them alone. The best example of this was Philip of Macedon, who moved whole populations as shepherds move their flocks. Such methods were cruel and inhuman, and no one should have been willing to engage in them—better be out of politics than to be such a ruler. But if you were not going to do the right thing, then you must do the wrong thing without compromise. Most men opted for something in between, which was disastrous. Machiavelli went on in the next chapter to discuss the case of Giovanpagolo Baglioni, the tyrant of Perugia, who had not balked at incest but had passed up the opportunity to kill Pope Julius II, who had come to depose him and had entered the city unarmed, proving that men "do not know how to be entirely bad or perfectly good."[58] The murder of Julius might have had the appearance of being an evil action, but in truth it would have been an admirable deed. Baglioni needed to be very bad in order to be very good. The policies of Philip of Macedon were different: Machiavelli was not pretending to condemn them while actually advocating them; his condemnation was unambiguous.[59]

Or was it? For when the Romans under Camillus defeated the rebel Latins in 389 BCE they showed favor to some cities, but others they destroyed, scattering their peoples, ensuring that thereafter they could do no harm.[60] Such behavior met with Machiavelli's unconditional approval; it should have been imitated by the Florentines after the rebellion of Arezzo in 1502. Machiavelli, it turns out, has no principled objection to inhuman methods, at least when used selectively. Indeed he insisted that such policies are absolutely necessary. In his mind, perhaps, there was a distinction between inhuman methods used to ensure the survival of a republic and the same methods used to establish a tyranny; here, it would seem, it is the ends which justify the means.[61]

Machiavelli presented a simple choice: one must aim to establish a republic or a monarchy founded in popular consent, one in which the outward appearance of old forms is maintained (as, to turn from the *Discourses* to *The Prince,* the French had done in Brittany, Burgundy, Gascony, and Normandy); or one must establish a tyranny. So too when facing rebellion, one faced a straight choice between generous and inhuman methods. In principle, having established an effective tyranny one might go on to turn it into a republic; but Machiavelli insisted that the type of person who willingly establishes a tyranny is unlikely to want to establish a good government, and the type of person who aims to establish a good government is unlikely to be able to bear acquiring the ignominy of being a tyrant. In Rome it was accident, not design, which had turned a tyrannical monarchy into a free republic.

Applied to Ireland, the lessons of these chapters were clear. First, the introduction of English institutions, laws, and customs to Ireland must necessarily seem a form of tyranny to the Gaelic Irish, since they were incompatible with preserving even the semblance of the old forms. Such changes could only be introduced through the use of overwhelming force. To this use of force there could be no alternative: the old forms (at least as they were understood by the English) were simply incompatible with security of property and the person, and led inevitably to disorder; they provided no basis for a civilized society. Consequently the English government must rule tyrannically over the Irish. But as far as the Old English and the more recent settlers were concerned, one *might* seek to bring about reforms that preserved the appearances of *their* old order. On the other hand, if one thought (as Spenser did) that the Old English had effectively thrown in their lot with the Gaelic Irish, then they too must be handled tyrannically. Machiavelli had insisted that at all costs one must avoid falling between the two approaches, which is precisely what English policy had so often involved.

As Spenser says,

> the longer that goverment thus contynueth, in the worse case will that Realme bee; for yt is all in vayne that they nowe stryve and endeavor by faire meanes and peaceable plotts to redres the same without first

removinge all those inconveniences, and newe framinge (as yt were in the forge), all that is worne out of fashion: for all other meanes wilbe but lost labor, by patchinge up one hole to make many; for the Irish doe strongly hate and abhor all reformacon and subjeccon to the Englishe, by reason that, having bene once subdued by them, they were thrust out of all theire possessions. Soe as nowe they feare, that yf they were againe brought under, they shoulde likewise be expelled out of all, which is the cause that they hate Englishe government . . . : therefore the reformacon must nowe be with the strength of a greater power.[62]

Spenser's and Beacon's tracts represent an attempt to think about the Irish situation through the categories established by these three chapters of the *Discourses* and chapter 5 of *The Prince.* Spenser held that straightforwardly tyrannical policies must be employed—including the hallmark of such policies, the forced transportation of whole populations. He understood perfectly that such policies are cruel and inhuman, but believed there was no alternative if Ireland was to be brought securely under English control. And, just as the Norman Conquest led eventually to a moderated monarchy in England, if the Irish were successfully forced into adopting the English language, English customs, and English laws it might be possible eventually for them to benefit from an English standard of security, prosperity, and political participation—although, as Machiavelli had stressed, the reform of a corrupt people must involve an extended use of force over more than a generation so that Spenser can have had no expectation of living to see this happy outcome.[63]

The methods proposed by Spenser are truly horrific, as Machiavelli had said they must be. Machiavelli's own advice, in book 1, chapter 26 of the *Discourses,* was that one should never engage in such methods but rather abandon politics altogether. Spenser, we might well think, should have left Ireland and returned to England if he really thought English rule in Ireland required such methods; indeed, he should never have gone to Ireland in the first place, since his vast estate in the plantation of Munster had been carved out by the displacement of the Gaelic-speaking Irish. It's easy to say this. But an independent Catholic Ireland would necessarily have been an ally of Spain, and a staging post for a Spanish invasion of England. Machiavelli did not have to think about the consequences of religious division in Europe, but the English did. Spenser could claim to be acting out of necessity—and in doing so he would have been following Machiavelli's own example. This indeed was Spenser's defense: "Therefore by all meanes it must be fore-seene and assured, that after once entring into this course of reformacon, there bee afterwardes no remorse or drawinge backe for the sight of any such ruefull obiect as must therupon followe, nor for compassion of their calamities, seeinge that by no other meanes it is possible to recure them, and that theis are not of will, but of verie urgent necessitie."[64]

Spenser has been accused of being caught in logical tangles and beset by contradictions, of being in bad faith;[65] but, set against its Machiavellian background, the *View* appears a coherent and consistent work. Where Spenser differed from Machiavelli was in his conviction that a tyrannical rule could, over time, turn into something much more benevolent, a conviction grounded in his assessment of the beneficial consequences of the Norman Conquest. In that respect he was a lot more optimistic than Machiavelli was prepared to be, or perhaps one should say he was willing to think in a much longer time frame.

But the fact that Spenser was coherent and consistent does not mean that he was right. As he finished *A View* he was waiting for the Earl of Essex to be put in charge of Irish affairs; and indeed, Essex was soon to command the largest English army ever to have been deployed in Ireland, an army far larger than Spenser had thought necessary. Yet the whole enterprise was a disastrous failure. Spenser had gone to some trouble to think about the char-acter of guerrilla warfare, but he had hopelessly misjudged the relative ad-vantages of English and Irish troops, and he had massively overestimated English military competence. When his policies were put to the test they failed dismally.

Beacon's case is more puzzling, for he tried to find a route between tyr-anny and moderated monarchy (for which the Machiavellian term was *principato civile*). On the one hand, he emphasized that a total reform of the Irish state was necessary, "nothing els, but a thorough and absolute mu-tation and change, of auncient lawes, customes and manners of the people, and finally of the commonwealth it self into a better forme of governement"— this was Spenser's argument.[66] But on the other hand, Beacon argued that "it was best rather to frame the laws to the subiect and matter than to frame the whole society to meet the laws"—where Spenser had argued the exact opposite, the Irish must be new framed in the forge to fit English institutions—and Beacon concluded his treatise by saying that the Irish state should be reformed in order to remake it what it once was and not something radically different. On the one hand, he suggested such a reform could be achieved peaceably, "without bloodshed and spot of tyranny or cruelty"; "the people conquered" should "be drawn and enticed by little and little to embrace the manners, laws and government of the conqueror." But on the other hand, he "confessed that where *sanandi medicina* may not prevail there *execendi* is rightly used"—strong medicine indeed.[67] And he reserved his highest praise for Sir Richard Bingham, who had not hesitated to execute captured rebels who it was thought might be freed by their allies without wasting time on legal formalities.[68] Thus, where Machiavelli had laid out two alternative policies and insisted one must choose between them, Beacon flip-flopped between the two, which was precisely, in Machiavelli's view, the worst of all policies.

Beacon's equivocations are not only displayed in his discussion of Ireland; they are the necessary consequence of his approach to monarchy. Machiavelli had acknowledged the existence of moderated, law-governed monarchies, and thus he had distinguished three forms of political life: tyranny or absolute rule, the *principato civile* (moderated monarchy, or *regno moderato*), and *vivere libero* (republican rule—though, as we have seen, few republics, in his view, measured up to the ideal).[69] Beacon elaborated on Machiavelli's account of France, so that France became for him the absolute model of a *principato civile*:

> The king of *France* hath reserved vnto himselfe a kingly name, stile, honors, authority, and commandement over the Senate, and to assemble them for the affaires publicke, and a sole absolute and royall authority over the armie for making or finishing the warres, lastly an authority for the levieng and receiving of the revenews belonging to the crowne, but the execution of lawes he leaveth to the Senate, and Iudges, who governe by such lawes as respect a popular liberty and free estate, in the making of which lawes, the people have also their voices, like as in popular estates, where the people holde the soveraity and commaundement; so as by this forme of governement as well to the king, and the nobles, as also to the people, such power is graunted, with so iust and

equall proportion, as either the dignitie of the one, or the liberty of the other may iustly require; in the well tempering wherof, all the skill, arte, and pollicie of governement is wholy contained.[70]

Beacon here makes a crucial, un-Machiavellian move, for Machiavelli never claimed that political liberty could be found in a Renaissance monarchy.[71] Thus Beacon claimed to find "liberty" where Machiavelli had seen only security; and where Machiavelli had praised the Roman republic as a mixed form of government, Beacon substituted the French monarchy.

Beacon's admiration for limited monarchy certainly went beyond anything in Machiavelli, but if he elided the distinction between free states and monarchies, he also elided the equally Machiavellian distinction between moderated monarchy and tyranny. Thus, when it comes to reform, Machiavelli's distinction between republics and moderated monarchies on the one hand and tyrannies on the other is transformed into a distinction between popular states and monarchies:

> It seemeth also requisite, that so often as the subiect or matter of this reformation commeth in question, that we make a difference in the manner of reforming of a free and popular estate, from the Monarchy; for in this one, we shal wisely make a thorough alteration and change, without leaving any resemblaunce or shadow thereof; but in the other, we are to chaunge the substaunce, leaving in the place onely a shadowe and resemblance of that which is chaunged, for the better contentment of the people; for they discerne all things by the outward sence, and not by the sounde discourse of reason, iudging thinges to be such as they seeme to be in outwarde appearance.[72]

Like Machiavelli, Beacon here rejected any attempt to find a middle way between conservative and radical reformation; but in expounding the choice he opted firmly for radical reformation, failing to mention to his reader that Machiavelli associated this with tyranny, with cruelty so dreadful that no one should be willing to undertake it; so the reader is left at a loss when Beacon tries to undo this choice by advocating a conservative, incremental reform.

How are we to make sense of the confusions in Beacon? One answer is that he is trying to put a favorable gloss on the policies he proposes. His spokesperson in the dialogue, Solon, remarks that the use of "faire promises and sweete wordes" by a ruler "is rightlie tearmed pollicie, but in private persons the same is not unjustly condemned by the name of deceite."[73] Beacon may have allowed himself a certain latitude in the use of sweet words; but I am inclined to the view that Beacon was trying to find a middle way precisely where Machiavelli insisted no middle way could be found; although Beacon argued that in Ireland the queen could tax without consent and exercise arbitrary power whenever she chose, still he wanted to pretend the Irish could have the best form of mixed government, and that they ought to be content to call this liberty.

Peltonen has presented Beacon as the exemplary exponent of a new republicanism, one which adapted Machiavelli's ideas to fit with the institutions of limited monarchy.[74] Peltonen is well aware that Beacon slid back and forth between discussing reform and discussing conquest, but he fails to recognize that in doing so Beacon slid back and forth between advocating a *principato civile* and advocating tyranny. He carefully explains Beacon's exposition of the choice between cautious and radical reform, but fails to note that Machiavelli associated the latter with inhuman tyranny. Thus Peltonen takes Beacon at face value, while a comparison between Beacon's text and Machiavelli's ought to have made it clear to him that Beacon's concept of monarchy was carefully constructed to elide the distinctions between liberty and monarchy and between *principato civile* and tyranny, just as the whole argument of Beacon's text elided the distinction between reforms introduced by persuasion and reforms introduced by overwhelming force.

Of course, Beacon was under no obligation to slavishly follow Machiavelli; but he did need to address the charge that the sort of reforms he wanted could not be achieved without the disastrous tyranny that Machiavelli regarded as utterly contemptible. Spenser read his Machiavelli, adopted Machiavelli's tripartite conceptual scheme, and accepted the consequences, although it must be said that—like Machiavelli in *The Prince,* but not the *Discourses*—he carefully avoided using the word "tyranny" (his only mention of it is a reference to the "tirannous rule" of Harold Godwinson).[75] In closely following Machiavelli he was implicitly accusing those like Beacon who sought a middle way of bad faith, and this—far more than the charge of bad faith directed against Spenser—seems to me a charge well made.

What then to make of Peltonen's claim that Beacon is a republican author who aims at liberty, or Andrew Hadfield's claim that Spenser too is really a republican?[76] Neither Spenser nor Beacon wanted to pursue in England policies remotely like those they wanted to adopt in Ireland. And, as the Romans showed, one can have freedom at home and servitude in one's colonies and subject states. Moreover, both envisaged a distant future where Ireland would become another England and benefit from its own form of limited monarchy. But there is an important difference between them: Beacon claimed that there was liberty to be found within a Renaissance monarchy even where the monarch laid claim to an absolute sovereignty; Spenser made no such claim. When he refers to "liberty" the term almost always had negative connotations: "lewd libertye" he called it; "As yt is the nature of all men to love libertye, so they become flatt libertynes, and fall to flatt licentyousnes"; the unruly people attack the laws, we are told, "as most repugnant to ther liberty and naturall fredome, which in ther madnesse they effect"; those who "loke after liberty" want to "shake of[f] all goverment."[77] Instead of liberty Spenser aims at "civility"—a term which Beacon never uses, but which Spenser uses ten times. "Sweete civilitie" he calls it, and his text opens by proposing to reduce the Irish, "that salvage nation to better goverment and civillity."[78] In Spenser's term "civility" we can hear, I think, an echo of Machiavelli's *vivere civile;* unlike Beacon, who constantly elides distinctions which Machiavelli had thought fundamental, Spenser makes Machiavelli's conceptual scheme his own.[79] The best one can hope for under a Renaissance monarchy is not liberty but sweet civility.

Should we prefer the un-Machiavellian moderation of Beacon, or the more-than-Machiavellian extremism of Spenser, who was prepared to be "entirely bad"? Speaking as an intellectual, I have to admit, I prefer Spenser's rigor to Beacon's confusion and equivocation; Spenser at least leaves us free to reach the conclusion Machiavelli recommended (though not, as we have seen, consistently) to his readers in such cases, that if this is what the exercise of power demands then one should have nothing to do with it. If Beacon is the best example of classical republicanism before the English Civil War, then he isn't a very impressive example. According to Peltonen, Beacon exhibits "a genuine," a "fully-fledged Machiavellian conception of politics."[80] This seems to me wrong. Beacon recycles Machiavelli all over the place; but there is a difference between recycling someone's language and thinking as they do. For better or worse, Spenser had fallen far further under Machiavelli's influence than Beacon had; he understood perfectly well that where there is despotism there can be no liberty.

But as a human being I have to prefer the moderates to the extremists. Indeed, we should not allow ourselves to become insensitive to the sheer horror of Spenser's text.* Nor, as David Edwards has argued, was it without influence. In October 1597 Essex was given overall charge of the Irish war. A year later, as he prepared to go with an army to Ireland, starving refugees were flooding into the Pale, producing, in Edwards's words, "such a huge increase in crime that the gaols were full to bursting. In order to prevent the system from breaking down . . . the Elizabethan government decided to attach commissions of gaol delivery to commissions of martial law. By this means, the martial law commissioners were required to empty the gaols by killing all the incarcerees, for the gaols were 'now very much pestered with a great number of prisoners, the most part whereof are poor men.' They had to execute everyone, the innocent along with the guilty, who had been imprisoned pending trial."[81] What a wonderful logic this is. The prisons are overcrowded (that is what the word "pestered" means); the prisoners are a

---

* One of my students, whom I asked to give a seminar presentation on *A View*, said she wished she had never read it, and I can understand why. Here, for example, is Irenius's account of the outcome of the war that he wishes to see fought in Ireland: "The end I assure mee will be verie shorte, and much soner then cann bee, in soe great trouble (as yt semeth) hoped for, although there should none of them fall by the sword, nor be slaine by the soldier, yett thus beinge keepte from manurance, and theire cattle from runinge abroade, by this hard restrainte, they would quicklye consume themselves, and devoure one an other. The proof whereof I saw sufficientlye ensampled in those late warrs in Mounster; for notwithstandinge that the same was a most ritch and plentyfull countrye, full of corne and cattell, that you would have thought they could have beene hable to stand longe, yett eare one yeare and a half they weare brought to such wretchednes, as that anye stonye herte would have rewed the same. Out of everye corner of the woode and glenns they came creepinge forth upon theire handes, for theire legges could not beare them; they looked Anatomies [of] death, they spake like ghostes, crying out of theire graves; they did eate of the carrions, happye wheare they could find them, yea, and one another soone after, in soe much as the verye carcasses they spared not to scrape out of theire graves; and if they found a plott of water-cresses or shamrockes, theyr they flocked as to a feast for the time, yett not able long to contynewe therewithall; that in a shorte space there were none almost left, and a most populous and plentyfull countrye suddenly lefte voyde of man or beast: yett sure in all that warr, there perished not manye by the sworde, but all by the extreamytie of famyne which they themselves hadd wrought" (101–102). Spenser had seen this, and he wanted to see it again.

nuisance; the rule of law is inconvenient; and the solution is obvious: kill them all. These are Spenser's policies in practice, and no beautiful poetry, no intellectual rigor can excuse their horror. Lord Grey's massacre of the troops—Spanish, papal, and Irish—who had surrendered at Smerwick in 1580 was regarded by contemporaries, and by Spenser, as a straightforward act of war, however horrifying it may seem to us. But the massacre of refugees, imprisoned only for trying to feed themselves, was no straightforward act of war, and cannot be justified by appealing to the norms of the day. We may wonder whether even Machiavelli would have excused it.

Felix Raab, writing in 1964, described Spenser's *A View* as demonstrating "the influence of Machiavelli at every turn."[82] He was right, and right to use the word "influence"; we really can't do without it, despite our best efforts. In 1966 Skinner argued that it was virtually impossible to show the influence of one author on another; in 1969 he thought it was not only difficult but nearly always pointless to do so; by 2002 he thought it was occasionally worth the trouble, and indeed his "Classical Liberty, Renaissance Translation, and the English Civil War," first published in that year, is a study in the role of certain Roman texts in legitimizing and hence bringing about parliamentary resistance to Charles I—it is a study in influence.[83] We might well ask, what would be the point of reading and writing if books have no influence? But if Skinner was wrong to reject the category of influence, he was also right to find it deeply problematic, for the relationship between one author and another is never a straightforward one of dependence—even translators remake the texts they claim to follow. Making, remaking, and unmaking shade into each other; quotations are repurposed; something new is constructed out of the lumber inherited from the past.

My argument here has not been that Machiavelli was responsible for Elizabethan policy in Ireland; indeed, he directly warned against the sorts of policies that Spenser advocated. We may think that it was Spenser's Irish experiences which made him into a man of blood; in 1587 he became a planter in Munster, at a time when there was endemic and mortal violence between planters and their Gaelic-speaking neighbors, violence in which Spenser was caught up along with everyone else. This was the world in which the argument of *A View* took shape.

But—and it is a big but—from 1572 until let us say 1740, when Frederick the Great and Voltaire published their *Anti-Machiavel*, it was almost impossible to think about power except in terms derived directly or indirectly from Machiavelli. And sometimes thinking with the text of Machiavelli in hand went beyond mere recycling, for every now and again by reading we change how we think, and indeed who we are. This is what happened to Spenser when he read Machiavelli. He chose to ignore Machiavelli's warnings, and identified with those who were prepared to be entirely bad, those who were prepared to destroy whole cultures and transplant whole societies. Lord Grey of Wilton's measures toward the Irish resistance, bloodthirsty as they seemed to contemporaries and to us, were no longer enough for him. And there can be no doubt that in reaching this conclusion he found comfort in the text of Machiavelli. Thinking with Machiavelli (if I may echo the title of Stuart Clark's *Thinking with Demons*) often involved reaching conclusions Machiavelli himself had not reached, conclusions from which he himself had recoiled in horror. Skinner argued that the meaning of a text is to be found in its author's intentions; but the text that is received by a reader is often quite different from the one intended by the author, and this is what happened in the case of Spenser and Machiavelli.[84]

So let us leave the last word to Machiavelli:

> Those ways are cruel, and contrary not only to all civil, but to all Christian, and indeed humane conversation; for which reason they are to be rejected by every body, for certainly 'tis better to remain a private person, than to make ones self King, by the calamity and destruction of his people. Nevertheless, he who neglects to take the first good way, if he will preserve himself, must make use of this bad; for though many Princes take a middle way betwixt both, yet they find it extream difficult and dangerous; for being neither good nor bad, they are neither fear'd nor belov'd, and so unlikely to prosper.[85]

How clever Spenser must have thought he was being when he finally understood the futility of the middle path, the path that all around him were advocating; but we can only agree with Machiavelli, who would have regarded him as cruel and inhuman. We can only wish Spenser had chosen differently. We can only wish he had read his Machiavelli more carefully. For if Machiavelli understood power, he also understood the evil uses to which it can be put; Spenser, unfortunately, embraced evils that Machiavelli, even Machiavelli, found repugnant.

A

TREATISE

OF

Human Nature :

BEING

An ATTEMPT to introduce the experimental Method of Reafoning

INTO

MOROL SUBJECTS.

by David Hume Esqr.

*Rara temporum felicitas, ubi fentire, quæ velis ; & quæ
fentias, dicere licet.* TACIT.

VOL. I.

OF THE
UNDERSTANDING.

LONDON:
Printed for JOHN NOON, at the *White-Hart,* near
Mercer's-Chapel, in *Cheapfide.*

MDCC XXXIX.

Title page from David Hume, *A Treatise of Human Nature* (8°) (1739).

3

Happiness: Words and Concepts

What do we want for ourselves? Happiness. What do we want for our loved ones? Happiness. What do we do in our quest for happiness? We acquire property, we accumulate savings—or at least we hope to do so. If all else fails, we buy lottery tickets. We know perfectly well that money can't buy happiness; but how can anyone be happy without security, and how can anyone be secure without money? If we know money can't buy happiness, we also believe that with a bit more money we would be a good deal happier.[1] Quite apart from buying happiness, money feeds our self-esteem; Adam Smith thought this was our primary reason for seeking to better our condition.* And we need to put our money in a vault, we need to be able to defend ourselves against those who want what we have got, we need to put a wall around our happiness. Pleasure, profit, and power (or happiness, wealth, and security) have become the three things which we, as individuals, as communities, and as states, pursue without limit and without end. When it comes to these three goods we have great difficulty in saying "enough is enough" for the simple reason that it is hard to identify any point at which we can safely say that we have enough and to spare.

The relationship between profit and wealth is straightforward: profits turn into wealth. So too, in principle, power produces security—though power may also provoke hostility and resistance. But the relationship between pleasure and happiness is more puzzling. In modern usage happiness

---

* The word Smith actually uses in *The Theory of Moral Sentiments* (see the epigraphs to this book) is not "self-esteem" but "vanity." Since this vanity is the primary factor driving economic growth, this is a striking example of "private vices, publick benefits" and demonstrates that Smith's core argument retains a Mandevillian character. Even if the desire for self-betterment is "calm and dispassionate," even if it meets with the approval of our fellow citizens, it remains a vice, and corresponds to what Rousseau calls *amour propre*, the pernicious form of self-love.

is a state of mind, while pleasure is an experience. You can seek out pleasurable experiences, but you cannot choose happiness in the way that you
can choose to listen to a favorite piece of music, confident that it will give
you pleasure. You can hope for happiness, and set in place some of its preconditions, but you cannot plan for it or make it happen. Very often you discover to your own surprise that you are happy—happiness can creep up on
you unawares. You can say "I never realized how happy I was," but not "I
never realized how much pleasure that gave me."[2]

These ways of distinguishing between pleasure and happiness, if they
seem right to us, would have puzzled any eighteenth-century author, for they
seem to have regarded the relationship between happiness (of which the antonym was misery) and pleasure (of which the antonym was pain) as so
straightforward that they rarely felt any need to comment on it. "Everyone
agrees," according to Jean Pestré in Denis Diderot and Jean le Rond
d'Alembert's *Encyclopédie,* "that happiness *(bonheur)* is identical with pleasure."[3] Voltaire thought the difference between happiness and pleasure
was essentially one of duration: pleasure is short-lived, happiness lasts
longer, prosperity longer still—these are experiences, while felicity is an
attitude of mind.[4] Thomas Newman devoted a sermon to the theme
"Happiness Not in a Life of Pleasure," but by "pleasure" he meant only the
baser pleasures of wine, women, and song, which he felt sure must cloy
after a time.[5] A stronger claim is made by Laurence Sterne in the first of
Yorick's sermons. In life, Sterne says, we make various attempts at finding
happiness—in physical pleasure, in wealth, in social standing, and so
forth—all of which prove in the end delusory. True happiness is only to
be found in heaven; for happiness to count as happiness it must endure.[6]
As far as Diderot was concerned, what Sterne was talking about was not
happiness or felicity, but beatitude.[7]

Unlike Sterne, most authors believed in the possibility of happiness here
and now. David Hume wrote that happiness "implies ease, contentment, repose, and pleasure; not watchfulness, care, and fatigue," but he saw no need
to unpack the concept of "contentment," even though he had himself gone
through an extended period of mental distress.[8] Alexander Pope agreed:

O Happiness! our Being's End and Aim!
Good, Pleasure, Ease, Content! whate'er thy name . . .[9]

The general view was that happiness was the goal of human existence, and pleasure was either an essential part of happiness, or the very essence of happiness—clearly contentment and repose are themselves pleasurable, and watchfulness, care, and fatigue are themselves painful.

The classical intellectual tradition which regarded pleasure as the only motive for all human behavior was Epicureanism, and the key figure in making Epicureanism intellectually respectable within Christian culture was Pierre Gassendi, who wrote a long essay in Latin on happiness *(felicitas)* in his posthumous *Survey of the Philosophy of Epicurus* (1659).* But Gassendi was too good an Epicurean to offer an account of happiness as involving the unending pursuit of pleasure. Following Epicurus, he accepted both that we necessarily seek pleasure and flee pain and that the highest good to which we can aspire is tranquility (ἀταραξία, *ataraxia,* or contentment). Pleasure is something we experience; tranquility is a state of mind which is always associated with an experience of pleasure, or at least freedom from pain, but it isn't simply to be identified with pleasure. Thus we can have pleasure without tranquility but not tranquility without pleasure.

In thus identifying two goals, one superior to the other, Gassendi made a distinction that seems rather obvious, but which also exposed Epicureanism to the charge of inconsistency. In the eighteenth century the distinction was still made—thus Diderot and Voltaire both presented felicity (or contentment) as something different from and superior to happiness. You can envy someone's good fortune *(bonheur);* you can take it from them and enjoy it yourself; you cannot rob them of their contentment, although if you deprive them of the source of their pleasures they may well cease to be contented. Just as I have distinguished between pleasure, an experience, and happiness, a state of mind, so these French authors made the same distinction between pleasure and happiness *(bonheur)* on the one hand and felicity or contentment on the other.[10] We thus encounter a fundamental difference

---

* Gassendi's Latin text was translated into French in the seventh volume, published in 1678, of Louis Bernier's *Summary of the Philosophy of Gassendi* (where *felicitas* is translated as *félicité*), and this particular volume was translated into English in 1699 under the title *Three Discourses of Happiness, Virtue, and Liberty.*

between eighteenth-century French and modern English: we standardly translate *bonheur* as "happiness," but in key respects the modern English word "happiness" is closer in meaning to the eighteenth-century French *félicité*. Matters become more complicated when we turn from modern English to early modern English. For this crucial distinction, between a pleasurable experience and a pleasurable state of mind, was expressed, not as a distinction between pleasure and happiness/*félicité* but (insofar as it was expressed at all) as a distinction between pleasure and contentment. In English the standard philosophical view, which was derived from Thomas Hobbes via John Locke, held that happiness was simply to be equated with an unbroken sequence of pleasures. Happiness is pleasure uninterrupted; moreover, there is no need to ask a happy person if they are also contented— of course they are. In such accounts tranquility, contentment, or felicity appeared momentarily, only to disappear again; nobody knew quite what to do with them. This was the necessary consequence of a theory of the mind which insisted that our feelings are simply a reflection of our experiences, complicated only by the fact that past experiences shape how we respond to present experiences. The experience of pleasure must automatically produce the feeling of happiness (though what once gave me pleasure may cease to do so; a book I once liked may cease to please me after I have met the author).

In French, too, the distinction between pleasure and tranquility was deeply problematic. Take, for example, the article in the *Encyclopédie* on happiness *(bonheur)* by Jean Pestré: Pestré distinguishes happiness from pleasure by defining happiness as a state where one experiences intermittent pleasures and no suffering. Pleasure cannot be continuous, but happiness can be. As for tranquility, for Pestré that is not a form of true happiness, but something less than happiness, a miserable happiness—he may here have been following William Wollaston, whose *The Religion of Nature Delineated* had been translated into French in 1726 and who had defined indolence (which is what Pestré has in mind when he discusses tranquility) as negative happiness—and so not happiness at all.[11] But by using the word "tranquility," which Wollaston had avoided, Pestré has mounted a direct attack on traditional Epicureanism.

It is presumably this difficulty about the relationship between happiness and tranquility that led Diderot to omit any mention of tranquility in his article "Epicuréisme" (Epicureanism): his view (in this article Diderot speaks in the person of Epicurus, so that "his view" here means both Diderot's and Epicurus's, or at least Epicurus's as interpreted by Diderot) was that happiness *(bonheur)* was the goal, the only goal, of our existence.[12] In 1763 Beccaria's associate Pietro Verri described pleasure, which was for him but happiness by another name, as "the only universal law, which is always obeyed by creatures capable of sensation."[13]

Verri was wrong. Some individuals, now as then, have their minds set on other objectives—the salvation of their souls, a cure for cancer—but in Western democracies these noble ends are the goals of individuals and of nongovernmental organizations (be they churches, charities, or university laboratories); the goals of democratic states are the happiness, wealth, and security of their members. The separation of church and state, first turned into an institutional principle in the U.S. Constitution, has meant that states that were once Christian and promulgated a view on how souls could and should be saved now pursue fundamentally utilitarian objectives.[14] Our societies have become pluralist not only in religion but also in the absence of any generally accepted hierarchy of goals, statuses, or occupations. We leave individuals to find their own ways, to decide for themselves what works best for them, what will give them most satisfaction. In the old societies of Europe and the Americas—the societies that crumbled and collapsed one by one, from the Revolution of 1688 in England right through to the fall of the Iron Curtain in 1991—states offered a particular vision of a social order within which individuals would be assigned their places. Now, beyond the protection of certain rights (to property, to free speech, to the vote), they don't.*

---

* It would be wrong to think that happiness has been a generally accepted objective since the eighteenth century: Methodism in England and the Second Great Awakening in America, for example, offered a quite different scheme of values. Nor are secular values, even in the public sphere, unopposed at present. The major surviving area of contention is over the right to life. Abortion, euthanasia (and in some circumstances gene modification procedures) are issues which continue to pit religious against secular values—but suicide, which was once illegal in all Christian societies, is now legal everywhere.

Happiness, wealth, and security have, as we have seen, a peculiar feature in common: they can be pursued without end or limit; indeed, according to their inner logic they *should* be pursued without end or limit. It is true that one can try to establish limits. The United Kingdom's Naval Defence Act 1889 stated that the British Navy should be larger than the next two largest navies taken together. That would be big enough, it was held, to deal with all possible eventualities. Fortunately, it was quite easy to establish how many battleships other powers had; in nuclear warfare the doctrine of mutually assured destruction was not similarly clear cut because the quantity and quality of the other side's missiles was always open to debate. In business there is no natural limit of even this sort; companies must always keep trying to grow, and investors must always keep trying to get richer even if at the very same time they are giving much of their money away to charitable causes. Just as some species of shark can't stop swimming or they will die, so no business in a competitive marketplace can have as its goal simply to stand still. So too with pleasures: a lover of wine will always have new wines to taste, a lover of opera new performances to attend, a collector of stamps new stamps to buy, a bibliophile new first editions to hunt down.

Happiness, it may be argued, is different from pleasure, because being happy involves being contented with what you have. To be constantly in pursuit of something you can never catch up with is, it would seem, a form of madness. Perhaps so, but we have built this madness into the very structure of our lives, for every society aims at economic growth, and consequently every society encourages the endless accumulation of wealth, which everyone recognizes is simply a means—so that the presumption would seem to be that the good things that one can buy with money obey the same logic of unending accumulation or limitless pursuit that wealth itself obeys.[15]

This logic was first clearly formulated by Thomas Hobbes in *Leviathan* (1651). In chapter 11 of that extraordinary book he makes a claim which would have shocked any philosopher between Socrates and Niccolò Machiavelli:

> The Felicity of this life, consisteth not in the repose of a mind satisfied. For there is no such *Finis ultimus,* (utmost ayme,) nor *Summum Bonum,*

(greatest Good,) as is spoken of in the Books of the old Morall Philosophers. Nor can a man any more live, whose Desires are at an end, than he, whose Senses and Imaginations are at a stand. Felicity is a continuall progresse of the desire, from one object to another; the attaining of the former, being still but the way to the lat[t]er. The cause whereof is, That the Object of mans desire, is not to enjoy once onely, and for one instant of time; but to assure for ever, the way of his future desire. And therefore the voluntary actions and inclinations of all men, tend, not onely to the procuring, but also to the assuring of a contented life; and differ onely in the way: which ariseth partly from the diversity of passions, in divers men; and partly from the difference of the knowledge, or opinion each one has of the causes, which produce the effect desired.

So that in the first place, I put for a generall inclination of all mankind, a perpetuall and restlesse desire of Power after power, that ceaseth onely in Death. And the cause of this, is not alwayes that a man hopes for a more intensive delight, than he has already attained to; or that he cannot be content with a moderate power: but because he cannot assure the power and means to live well, which he hath present, without the acquisition of more. And from hence it is, that Kings, whose power is greatest, turn their endeavours to the assuring it at home by Lawes, or abroad by Wars: and when that is done, there succeedeth a new desire; in some, of Fame from new Conquest; in others, of ease and sensuall pleasure; in others, of admiration, or being flattered for excellence in some art, or other ability of the mind.

Competition of Riches, Honour, Command, or other power, enclineth to Contention, Enmity, and War: Because the way of one Competitor, to the attaining of his desire, is to kill, subdue, supplant, or repell the other. Particularly, competition of praise, enclineth to a reverence of Antiquity. For men contend with the living, not with the dead; to these ascribing more than due, that they may obscure the glory of the other.[16]

Let me summarize the claims Hobbes is making here:

1. There is no greatest good which all men pursue, not even (as the Epicureans taught) tranquility.
2. Men differ in their priorities, and not just because some are foolish and others wise.

3. Desires can never be satisfied, for one follows another in an endless succession—which makes tranquility unattainable.[17]

4. In order to attain our desires we have need of what Hobbes calls "power"—"riches, honour, command"—and status ("praise"); these are examples of power, for power is anything which enables us to attain our desires.

5. In pursuit of our desires we find ourselves in competition with each other, and competition results, as Hobbes goes on to say, in a war of all against all, unless we establish a ruler capable of imposing peace.

Hobbes is often read (as indeed he wanted to be read) as if he is describing universal features of the human condition. So it is worth pausing to remark that an absolutely key word in the long passage I have quoted is "competition," for "Competition enclineth to Contention, Enmity, and War." If one wanted to sum up the argument of *Leviathan* in a single phrase it would be that human beings need to escape from a state of nature in which they are in remorseless competition. We take the idea of competition so much for granted, in our post-Hobbesian world, that it comes as something of a shock to discover that the word is first used in its modern sense in 1600, and that when Hobbes used it in *Leviathan* it was very much a word of the times, one that had come increasingly into prominence.[18]

This book is about the intellectual and social world that Hobbes maps out here, the world of competition, in which many of us still live, and from which our political communities are unable to escape. Some argue that our insatiable appetites no longer pay off in the way they once did. Happiness, we are told, is relative, and increased inequality leads to diminishing happiness.[19] Power, it is claimed, is not what it was.[20] The economy has grown, but, since the 1970s, median incomes in the United States have stagnated.[21] We need to find other ways of pursuing happiness. But try as we might we find it hard to break the link that we have forged—the "mind-forg'd manacle"—binding wealth and power to happiness.

Hobbes's fundamental assumption is that human beings pursue pleasure and flee pain; that they are motivated by their passions, not by reason; and that they seek to accumulate power, wealth, status, friends, and other goods to ensure future pleasures and to protect themselves against the assaults of others. Hobbes rarely uses the word "happiness," but he is writing about the pursuit of happiness, and the consequences that follow from it.[22] Later authors were to insist that competition need not be destructive in the way that Hobbes assumes it must be—that competition between states can lead to a balance of power, which provides mutual security, and that competition for wealth can lead, thanks to the invisible hand of the market, to an increase in prosperity for all.[23] But to a very large extent they were prepared to accept Hobbes's basic assumptions, that we all pursue pleasure and flee pain, and that we differ only in the ways we evaluate pleasure and pain and in the strategies we adopt to maximize pleasure and minimize pain. Machiavelli is a proto-Hobbesian thinker. Locke, Hume, Smith, and Jeremy Bentham are, broadly speaking, post-Hobbesian thinkers, and the Constitution of the United States is a post-Hobbesian constitution. Insofar as our own moral, political, and economic theories derive from this Enlightenment tradition, we all live in a Hobbesian world.

In modern scholarship discussion of the goods for which demand is insatiable belongs to different disciplines—to moral philosophy, to psychology, to economics, to politics. But, as Hobbes saw, they are inescapably intertwined, rooted in a culture of self-gratification and competition. In the scholarly literature on Smith, the relationship between his moral philosophy (which is partly about seemingly altruistic behavior) and his political economy (which is entirely about selfish behavior) is known (or perhaps it would be more accurate to say, used to be known) as the Adam Smith Problem, but the Adam Smith Problem is merely one manifestation of a whole series of such problems: in Hobbes's case, the problem is how to turn conflict (or competition) into cooperation; in Locke's, how to reconcile the sensationalist epistemology of the *Essay Concerning Human Understanding* with the divinely ordained natural law of the *Two Treatises of Government;* in Jean-Jacques Rousseau's, how to choose between the good man and the good citizen.[24] Such tensions between self and society only come into existence when people are thought of as individuals, not as members of a corporate community, and society is thought of as an informal or unregulated association, with no imposed organization, something distinct from and prior to a corporate community or a commonwealth.[25]

Are we moderns peculiar in seeking happiness? That depends on what you mean by happiness. Ancient Greek moral philosophers all agreed that civilized human beings seek *eudaimonia,* often translated as happiness. But they meant something different by *eudaimonia* from what we mean by happiness.[26] Thus Aristotle held that a child could not have *eudaimonia;* only an adult could. We say that a parent who stays in an unhappy marriage for the sake of the children is sacrificing their happiness; but for Aristotle, *eudaimonia* was not a state of mind or a feeling; you had *eudaimonia* if you were the best you could be; thus, for him a soldier fighting and dying bravely on the battlefield was attaining *eudaimonia,* not losing their chance of finding happiness. For Aristotle, *eudaimonia* was an achievement—the achievement, for example, of an athlete who beats their previous best time, or a mathematician who comes up with a new proof. Realizing our potential gives us a good feeling; but it is the achievement that counts, not the feeling, and you could not call someone who had a misplaced sense of their own abilities and attainments "happy" any more than you could admire a cook who kept burning the cakes—even if they had a great time mucking about in the kitchen. For Hobbes, on the other hand, no one can be a judge of someone else's happiness; happiness is the purely subjective condition of getting what you, at this moment, want. There is no arguing with someone who believes themselves to be happy (just as, we would normally acknowledge, there is no arguing with someone who says they find an experience—being tickled, perhaps, or eating oysters—pleasurable or yucky).

Hobbes and many of his contemporaries were greatly in debt to the philosophy of the Epicureans, which they knew about, above all, through reading Lucretius's great poem *De rerum natura.*[27] The Epicureans accepted that we all aspire to *eudaimonia,* but unlike Aristotle they placed *eudaimonia* in a state of mind combined with a state of body. As we have seen, they held that the body needs to be free of pain, and the mind needs to achieve a state of tranquility, what Hobbes calls "repose of mind," so that it neither feels deprived nor fearful: this is *ataraxia,* or equanimity. The Epicureans may agree with us that happiness is a state of mind or a feeling, but in their view there is only one state of mind that counts as happy. The elation a chess player gets after winning a hard-fought game is not true happiness, even if she feels great; she really shouldn't care whether she wins or

loses; she should prepare for defeat even when winning. Thus the Epicureans agreed with the Aristotelians that there is a *summum bonum,* a single
greatest good to which all should aspire.

Cicero, in his *Tusculan Disputations,* attacks Epicurus for inconsistency:
if happiness depends on physical pleasure it lies outside the philosopher's
control; if it is the same as tranquility then you can be happy *(beatus)* while
being tortured on the rack.[28] His conclusion is that the wise man is always
virtuous, and the virtuous man is always happy; happiness depends solely
on tranquility, and tranquility upon virtue; you can indeed be happy while
being tortured. Thus there was general agreement that, as Seneca put it,
"everyone wants to live happily *(beate).*"[29] But Seneca agreed with Cicero:
only the virtuous are happy, and the happy man can remain happy no matter
what the circumstances.

With this Greek and Roman tradition behind him, Augustine took it for
granted that the answer to the question "Do you think that there is anyone
who does not in every way will and desire a happy life *(vita beata)?*" was
obvious: "Clearly, every human being wills that."[30] But he also thought it
uncontroversial to conclude that only the good could be happy.

Hobbes was therefore right to think that there was something radically
new in the approach he was taking.[31] What was new was the relativistic view
that we are each entitled to determine for ourselves what happiness consists
in. I am terrified of heights, so I can't imagine how anyone can take delight
in hanging from a rope over a sheer drop on a mountainside, or from jumping
out of an airplane, even if wearing a parachute. Mountaineers and parachut-
ists seek happiness in different ways from me, and there is no more to be
said. The logical development of this mode of thought is Bentham's claim
that push-pin is as good as poetry.

What was also new was the idea that we are involved in an endless quest
that can end only in death. Aristotle thought that, provided nothing too
dreadful happened to someone, you could say that they had achieved *eudaimonia* if they became a certain sort of person. Epicurus thought that once
you achieved *ataraxia* you could hold on to this state of mind. Hobbes
thought that human beings are endlessly "in pursuit of their Passions": they
can never arrive at their goal, or achieve what they have set out to achieve;
tomorrow the athlete will try to run faster, the merchant will try to make more

money, the mathematician to solve an even more difficult problem. We are in pursuit of something which we can never grasp and make our own, except fleetingly, "for one instant of time."

You may have noticed a certain slipperiness in the vocabulary I have used. We have seen that Hobbes writes of felicity, not happiness, and that he uses power in a very broad sense; throughout his work he takes great care to construct his own made-to-measure vocabulary. But there is a larger problem here regarding the complex relationship between words and concepts. A striking example of this is provided in an essay by Phil Withington entitled "The Invention of Happiness."[32] Withington starts with the perception that the first translation of Thomas More's *Utopia* (1551) does not use the word "happiness," but that it occurs frequently when the work is retranslated in 1684, and he traces with care the shifting meaning of the word ("hap," "happy," and "happiness" originally refer to luck or fortune) and the growing frequency of its use to conclude that happiness is an invention of the sixteenth and seventeenth centuries: "The invention of happiness was a protracted rather than a sudden affair that involved, at heart, the transformation of the word from a term of hap into one of art. It is here that the antecedents of our modern preoccupations with the happiness industry and happiness by design lie." In other words, happiness became a personal goal and a policy objective.[33]

This is elegant research, but perhaps it misses the point. The first question to be asked is whether the *concept* of happiness is present in More's Latin. The word "happiness" may not be in the first translation of *Utopia*, but "felicity" is, and *felicitas* is there in the Latin. Through the late sixteenth, seventeenth, and eighteenth centuries, in English (unlike French), "happiness" and "felicity" were regarded as virtually synonymous (as Withington recognizes): "felicity and happiness," "happiness and felicity," "happiness or felicity," and "felicity or happiness" occur altogether more than seven hundred times in Early English Books Online and in more than four hundred texts in Eighteenth Century Collections Online.[34] Thus one has to wonder whether "happiness" is an early modern invention, or indeed an invention of the English language: in Latin a similar shift in meaning from "lucky" to "contented" had occurred with *felix/felicitas,* and a movement in the same direction occurred in French with *heur/bonheur,* though as we have seen it did not go quite so far. What happened in early modern England was simply that "happiness" steadily overtook "felicity" as the term for the concept they both referred to.[35] Between 1550 and 1600 "felicity" occurs twice as frequently as "happiness," but between 1650 and 1700 "happiness" occurs twice as frequently as "felicity": this is part of a general move toward a less Latinate English prose.

What is important for our present purposes is that happiness as a personal goal and a policy objective did not have to be "invented." In Latin, *felicitas,* in Italian, *felicità,* and in French, *félicité* could serve to refer to the accomplishments of art as well as the rewards of fortune. The emperors of Rome celebrated *felicitas publica* on their coinage to congratulate themselves on their own good government. More's character Raphael in *Utopia* expounds on Plato: "tuus censeat *Plato* respublicas ita demum futuras esse felices, si aut regnent philosophi aut reges philosophentur, quam procul aberit felicitas si philosophi regibus nec dignentur saltem suum impartiri consilium?" (translated in 1684 as "your Friend *Plato* thinks that then Nations will be happy [*felices*], when either Philosophers become Kings, or Kings become Philosophers. No wonder if we are so far from that Happiness [*felicitas*], if Philosophers will not think it fit for them to assist Kings with their Councels.")[36] The *Vocabolario degli accademici della Crusca* (1612) quotes Dante's *Convivio* (ca. 1305): "Scienzia è ultima perfezione della nostra anima, nella quale sta la nostra ultima felicità" (Knowledge is the utmost perfection of our soul, in which lies our ultimate felicity) and a collection of aphorisms compiled by Niccolò Arrighetti: "Felicità si è un' atto, che procede da perfetta virtù dell' anima, e non del corpo" (Felicity is a condition which derives from the perfection of the soul, not of the body).[37] Along the same lines, in 1606 the *Thresor de la langue francoyse* offered *félicité* as a translation of *summum bonum.*[38] "Happiness" as a personal goal or policy objective was thus not invented; rather, it was simply (at least in its early usages) "felicity" relabeled.

Translations of *Utopia* reflect this shift in an acute form: *felicitas* occurs seventeen times in More's Latin (and *beatitudo* once), while "felicity" occurs thirteen times in the translation of 1551 (by Ralph Robinson), seventeen times in the revised edition of 1639, and not at all in the new translation of 1684 (by Gilbert Burnet); "happiness" occurs not at all in 1551 or 1639, but nineteen times in 1684.[39] Seen in this context, Hobbes's use of "felicity" rather than "happiness" appears slightly old-fashioned, but then Hobbes still belonged to a predominantly Latin-reading and -writing intellectual culture.

The substitution of one word for another does not necessarily indicate conceptual change, but conceptual change did indeed take place.[40] If we turn to *felicitas* / felicity / happiness in More's *Utopia*, what we find is the classical Greek concept of *eudaimonia* translated into Latin and then English.[41] The majority of the Utopians (evidently Epicureans), we are told, identify felicity with pleasure, but by pleasure they mean only that pleasure that is good and honest; their views are scarcely distinguishable from the views of the minority (evidently Aristotelians and Stoics) who identify *eudaimonia* / *felicitas* / felicity / happiness with virtue. In the words of the translation of 1684, the minority "do not place Happiness in all sorts of Pleasures, but only in those that in themselves are good and honest: for whereas there is a Party among them that places Happiness in bare Vertue, others think that our Natures are conducted by Vertue to Happiness, as that which is the chief Good of Man. They define Vertue thus, that it is a living according to Nature; and think that we are made by God for that end: They do believe that a Man does then follow the Dictates of Nature, when he pursues or avoids things according to the direction of Reason."[42] Thus, no matter what philosophical sect they belong to, the Utopians' conception of happiness is objective, not subjective, and they all believe in the *summum bonum*, even if they disagree on how to define it. The word "felicity" in the first translation or "happiness" in the later one means something quite different from what "felicity" means in Hobbes; what is significantly new in the seventeenth century is not the word "happiness" but the Hobbesian conception of it, which marks a radical break with the past. Hobbesian happiness is not just subjective, rather than objective. It can only be pursued; it can never be attained.

I will now turn to three pre-Hobbesian texts to show the emergence of this new conception of happiness. I won't go so far as to claim that they are the first texts of their sort, but they must surely be among the first; nor do I claim that the new value system they reflect is peculiarly English, though I suspect it first emerged in England. In 1639 Robert Crofts published a book entitled *The Terrestriall Paradise, or Happiness on Earth,* the first sentence of which is "All men naturally desire happines. All their plots, purposes, and endevours aime at this end only." Augustine would have agreed. But Crofts was sure that what he had to say (and the way in which he went about saying it) was new: "Although it be truly said that no new thing, can be said or written which hath not been (to the same effect) before; yet may it be said of this Treatise in generall (as well of the composition thereof) that the same is new, in as much as never any man (that I can reade of) hath written any Book of this subject, Namely, the enjoying of earthly happinesse freely and cheerfully (though in the good use therof) and with a heavenly minde: But of the contempt thereof many Bookes have been written."[43]

Hobbes's redefinition of felicity in *Leviathan* (which goes beyond anything to be found in Crofts, for there are no "heavenly minds" in *Leviathan*) could only make sense, indeed, within a wider culture which was already accustomed to self-gratification and competition being presented as social norms. Hobbes's readers had to recognize their own motives and behavior in his account of human psychology or his argument stood no chance of convincing them.

The first example I want to give is the *Loose Fantasies* of Kenelm Digby.[44] The *Loose Fantasies,* unpublished until the nineteenth century, were drafted by Digby during a weeklong break on the island of Milos in the course of a privateering expedition conducted through the Mediterranean in 1628; a postscript was written, apparently later during the same expedition, calling for the manuscript to be burned if Digby was killed in action.[45] It tells the story of Digby's love for his childhood sweetheart, Venetia Stanley, whom he had secretly married (despite knowing that she was reported to have had affairs with other men) in 1625; his mother and his friends strongly disapproved of the match. Digby insists that his love for Venetia is based on her extraordinary qualities, including her ability to be a true friend (a quality at this time usually regarded, by men, as beyond the capacity of a woman).[46] With her he is seeking his happiness, a word that runs right through the text (while the word "felicity" never appears).[47] Love, he has his alter ego say in a dialogue with a friend who has been trying to warn him off his liaison with

Venetia, "is the true happiness that a wise man ought to aim at." It is, in other words, the *summum bonum,* and lovers act "according to the prescripts of nature and reason"—we are still discussing the *eudaimonia* of the ancient Greeks. But Digby's argument quickly shifts to a much more radical subjectivism:

> I conceive that all men naturally desire to live happily, as being the greatest blessing this life can afford us; but in the chase of this state most men steer different courses, and the greatest part lose it in seeking it.* . . . And when the world shall know how little I value their censures, I believe they will soon grow weary of persecuting me with them . . . because I know that he is not happy or unhappy that is thought so, but he only that feeleth and thinketh himself so . . . I love [Venetia] because she is she, and I am I.† . . . while it remaineth in controversy what is best for a man to do, let him in the mean time do what at least pleaseth him most: and for my part, I can never deem those humours very vain that are very pleasing (since content is the true seasoning of all other blessings, and that without it they are all nothing) nor guide my actions by other men's censures . . . thus I shall be free from the servitude that most men live in, who are more troubled by the opinion of evils than by their real essence; and then the world shall see that my happiness and content is not proportioned to the estimation that they make of it, which will soon be forgotten and vanish away; but to what I truly enjoy and feel in myself, which will remain with me for ever . . . then I will entreat them to think of me as I do of others; which is, that no man of a competent understanding and judgment is to be lamented or pitied for finding any means, whatsoever it be, to please and satisfy himself.[48]

Thus, although Digby echoes Epicurus and Aristotle, although he carefully pays his respects to the long tradition which claims that there is one highest good and that reason should guide our choices, in the end his account of happiness is radically subjective, and deliberately opposed to a

---

* "Chase" is, of course, a synonym for "pursuit" (a word we will turn to later), but Digby thinks of happiness as a stable state—not, as in Hobbes, a fleeting moment.

† This is an echo of Michel de Montaigne, "On Friendship," in *Oeuvres complètes,* ed. Maurice Rat (Paris: Gallimard, 1962), 187.

conventional notion of honor ("the opinion of evils"): different people pursue different ends, and each is entitled to please and satisfy himself, or indeed herself (as Digby makes clear when he criticizes the double standard in sexual morality). Happiness is simply a sensation of true enjoyment that we feel in ourselves. There is in the end no arguing with someone who says, "But this [whatever it happens to be] makes me happy." For happiness is a feeling, and all of us throughout our lives chase after that feeling. (Hobbes and Digby later became friends, for they recognized that they had much in common.)

Digby's argument in favor of his love for Venetia is identical to the argument put forward by the chief male protagonist, Giovanni, in John Ford's *'Tis Pity She's a Whore* (1633). Giovanni is in love with his sister Annabella, and is determined to have sex with her, despite the censure of public opinion:

> Shall a peevish sound,
> A customary forme, from man to man,
> Of brother and of sister, be a barre
> Twixt my perpetuall happinesse and mee?[49]

Digby's text was written for his own eyes only; after Venetia's death in 1633 it became one of many memorials to her memory, and it always accompanied him on his travels. Let us turn from Digby's loose (i.e., immodest) and private fantasies to a perfectly orthodox pair of Calvinist sermons preached in 1619 by a London clergyman.[50] The preacher, Thomas Cooper, took as his text Mathew 16:26—"For What shall it profit a man though he should win the whole world, and lose his owne soule?"—and his theme is the very simple and obvious one that those who seek worldly happiness will find they are denied the happiness of heaven. What is important for my present purposes, though, is the way in which Cooper conceives of worldly happiness. It involves, he says,

> an vnsatiable desire of earthly things, teaching vs thereby, that naturally the minde of man, as it is immortall and not to be fadomed; so it is restles and neuer satisfied. And therefore affecteth vnmeasurably the things of the world: gladly would engrosse and appropriate all things to it selfe. It cannot brooke a share in it[s] happines, it endures not to be stinted, and measured therein. So saith the spirit. The eye is not satisfied with

seeing, nor the eare with hearing [Eccles. 1:8], and therefore much lesse the minde. So is the practise hereof discouered: They ioyne houses to houses, and land to land, till there be no place; and the reason hereof is added, that they may liue alone vpon the earth [Isa. 5:8]: And the generall conditions of all estates discouers no lesse; no man is contented with the place and calling wherein God hath placed him, euery one aymes at the highest; subiection is a burthen and disgrace, and soueraignty tickles with the conceit of deity; where the soule finds no rest in God, how can it be but restles in hawking after shadows? . . . this thirst of earthly things puffeth vp, and bewitcheth the minde with a false conceit of happinesse, and excellencie. As if this were the onely happinesse to engrosse and compasse all, that we may liue alone vpon the earth; that none may share with vs; none may controule vs . . . Miserable men that seeke for happinesse in sinfull vanitie and changeablenesse, and can finde this their onely content to be restlesse in the pursuit of what they cannot compasse; or what they compasse, increaseth their miserie.[51]

What Cooper denounces as sin (while declaring that it is natural to fallen humankind) is exactly the condition described by Hobbes as the state of nature, in which, to quote Cooper, "an vnsatiable desire of earthly things, possesseth euery man naturally." Here we find that everyone is in competition with everyone else, that everyone aspires to be superior to his fellows, that everyone is "restlesse in the pursuit of what they cannot compasse." In Hobbes's view there is nothing that can be done about this other than to regulate conflict and impose peace; even under the rule of the strongest monarch, each and every individual will continue to be restless, insatiable, competitive, vainglorious.

Cooper was not alone in presenting sinful man in these terms. Thus the learned Puritan preacher Robert Bolton, in *A Discourse About the State of True Happinesse* (1611), attacked the reprobate for being willing to sacrifice everything in "the pursuit of worldly happinesse."[52] Such happiness was unattainable because pleasures

cannot possibly fill the vnlimited desire of the soule. For although the treasures, the greatnes, the delights of all men liuing, were in the present possession of one: yet somewhat besides, and aboue all this, there would still bee sought, and earnestly thirsted for. Nay, it is certaine, if one man were not onely crowned with the soueraignty of all the kingdomes of the earth, but besides, were made commander of the motions of the sunne, and the glory of the starres; yet the restlesse eye of his vnsatisfied vnderstanding, would peepe and prie beyond the heauens, for some hidden excellencie and supposed felicity, which the whole compasse of this created world cannot yeeld. So vnquenchable is the thirst of mans soule.[53]

What was new in Bolton and Cooper was not the notion that sin involves insatiable desires; Augustine had said as much. Bishop John Jewel, for example, in the Elizabethan homilies to be read in churches, had remarked that "it is commonly sayde, *A drunken man is always dry,* and, *A gluttons gutte is neuer filled.* Unsatiable truely are the affections & lustes of mans heart."[54] Nor was it new to claim that what motivates all human beings all the time is the quest for happiness; again, Augustine had said as much. What was new was the recognition that in a society where everyone has insatiable desires, everyone is in competition with every one else, and this competition potentially results in a war of all against all. As Cooper put it, worldly happiness "cannot brooke a share in it[s] happines." What was new was the scaling up of the idea of insatiable desire, so that it was now thought of as the fundamental characteristic not just of a few individuals, but of mankind in general, and consequently of whole societies. Thus Cooper emphatically states that *no man* is contented, and *every one* aims at the highest; and Bolton's *one* restless, unsatisfied man turns out to be mankind in general. The Greeks and Romans had assumed that human beings are naturally sociable; even Augustine, when he compared kingdoms to robber bands, acknowledged that "in thefts, the hands of the vnderlings are directed by the commander, the confederacie of them is sworne together, and the pillage is shared by the law amongst them."[55] Now it was being claimed that human beings are naturally unsociable, unsuited to confederacy, averse to obedience.

This paradigm of inexorable conflict, of monopolistic ambition, is inseparable from the shift to a subjective notion of happiness. As long as happiness is defined objectively, as identical to or largely overlapping with virtue, conflict between individuals pursuing happiness will be the exception, not the rule. But as soon as it is defined subjectively, as being whatever people want, then they will quickly find that their wants bring them into competition with each other and that they can only get what they want by depriving others. If *you* want to drink the river dry, and *I* want to drink the river dry, then each of us intends that the other should go thirsty. Only if what each wants is unique (as in the case of true love, "because she is she, and I am I") or available in unlimited supply (you can be courageous and I can be courageous too) will such conflict not arise.

Thus Hobbes's account of the condition of humankind, and of their endless pursuit of happiness, can be understood very straightforwardly as corresponding to contemporary Calvinist accounts of fallen human nature; the only difference is that Hobbes was unconcerned with heavenly happiness, while Bolton and Cooper hoped to turn their audiences' minds to heavenly things. Though one cannot help but notice that, for all his theological orthodoxy, Cooper went to great lengths to explain how Christians can, without feeling guilty, engage in what were generally regarded as wicked activities ("As vsury, Monopolies, letters of mart, trading with Infidels and Idolaters; tentering and burnishing our wares, by pressing, sliking,* and keeping in and storing our commodities; changing of our callings, etc."). He was keen to reassure his readers that there are plenty of legitimate reasons for wanting to get rich.[56] Bolton would have been shocked by such arguments. He had nothing but contempt for those who "spend their best thoughts all their life long, in proiecting and contriuing, as though they were borne to aduance themselues, and not to honour God in their callings."[57] Cooper sought an accommodation with commercial society, while Bolton straightforwardly opposed it.

Digby and Hobbes, in presenting a new, subjective form of happiness, were not starting from scratch; rather, they were legitimizing precisely the attitudes and values that were being denounced from the pulpits of Stuart England. It used to be fashionable to say that Hobbes reflected the values of a new commercial society.[58] The similarities between his view of natural man and Bolton's and Cooper's accounts of the sinful, commercialized world they preached against provides some support for that view.

But you did not have to listen to Calvinist sermons to come across what we might term a Hobbesian account of human nature, an account which

---

* *Oxford English Dictionary Online,* http://www.oed.com, s.v. "slicking": making sleek or smooth.

stressed that competition is remorseless and inescapable; all you had to do was read Machiavelli.[59] It was Machiavelli, not Augustine or Hobbes, whom Sir William Drake had in mind when he noted in his commonplace book (in 1640 or soon thereafter) that

> man is created with those desires that are infinite and insatiable to desire all things but is so limited that he can attain but few things, so that there being no proportion between the power of getting and the will and desire of getting, there grow a secret dislike of what a man enjoys; hence proceeds a change of a man's condition, for desiring other men's estates and endeavouring to get them and others loathe to lose what they have already, they proceed to quarrels and divisions.

And again, apparently some years later, but once again with Machiavelli in mind, "God hath created man in such a sort that they can desire everything but not attain to it, so that the desire of getting being greater than the power to get, thence grows the dislike of what a man enjoys; hereupon arises the change of states, for some men desiring to have more and others fearing to lose what they have already, they proceed to war and destroying one another."[60]

The central feature of any modern commercial society is competition; earlier commercial societies went to great lengths to restrain competition through guilds, corporations, apprenticeships, and even monopolies. One of the things that most alarmed Bolton and Cooper about the society they lived in was that people thought they could up and change their occupations whenever they felt like doing so. In other words, there was increasingly a free market in labor. Within such a competitive society individuals were free to behave like Machiavellian rulers, to pursue their own interests convinced that everyone else would be doing exactly the same.[61] This new world, which brought into existence the new language of competition, is one we still live in today. We may wish we could turn back the clock—those who advocate "virtue ethics" think we must—but market societies have their own logic, and that logic, first described by Hobbes, is the logic of endless pursuit.[62]

AN
ESSAY

CONCERNING

Humane Understanding.

In Four BOOKS.

Writtten by *JOHN LOCKE*, Gent.

The Second Edition, with large Additions.

Quam bellum est velle confiteri potius nescire quod nescias, quam ista effutientem nauseare, atque ipsum sibi displicere ! Cic. de Natur. Deor. *l.* 1.

LONDON,

Printed for **Awnsham** and **John Churchil**, at the *Black Swan,* in *Pater-Noster-Row,* and **Samuel Manship,** at the *Ship* in *Cornhill,* near the *Royal Exchange,* MDCXCIV.

Title page from John Locke, *An Essay Concerning Humane Understanding,* 2nd ed. (2°) (1694).

4

Selfish Systems: Hobbes and Locke

In the conclusion to book 1 of *A Treatise of Human Nature* (1739), David Hume described how getting caught up in philosophy made him miserable and unsociable. Abstruse thinking seemed to be merely a way of torturing the brain; if he published, he knew he would face nothing but "dispute, contradiction, anger, calumny and detraction." Yet,

> Most fortunately it happens, that since reason is incapable of dispelling these clouds, nature herself suffices to that purpose, and cures me of this philosophical melancholy and delirium, either by relaxing this bent of mind, or by some avocation, and lively impression of my senses, which obliterate all these chimeras. I dine, I play a game of back-gammon, I converse, and am merry with my friends; and when after three or four hour's amusement, I wou'd return to these speculations, they appear so cold, and strain'd, and ridiculous, that I cannot find in my heart to enter into them any farther.[1]

Hume expected us to recognize at once the pleasures of conversation and backgammon; but he had great difficulty identifying the pleasures of philosophy. He struggled to understand why he should "strive against the current of nature, which leads me to indolence and pleasure." And yet he found that after a few hours of pleasure-seeking,

> I cannot forbear having a curiosity to be acquainted with the principles of moral good and evil, the nature and foundation of government, and the cause of those several passions and inclinations, which actuate and govern me. I am uneasy to think I approve of one object, and disapprove of another; call one thing beautiful, and another deformed; decide concerning truth and falshood, reason and folly, without knowing upon what principles I proceed. I am concern'd for the condition of the learned world, which lies under such a deplorable ignorance in all

these particulars. I feel an ambition to arise in me of contributing to the instruction of mankind, and of acquiring a name by my inventions and discoveries. These sentiments spring up naturally in my present disposition; and shou'd I endeavour to banish them, by attaching myself to any other business or diversion, I *feel* I should be a loser in point of pleasure; and this is the origin of my philosophy.[2]

Note that the series of sentiments he refers to here—curiosity, uneasiness, concern, ambition—are what drive him back to the study of philosophy. And so the circle is squared: philosophy causes him pain, yet he pursues it because he is convinced that if he abandoned it he would be a loser in point of pleasure. Curiosity, uneasiness, concern, ambition: these drive him ever onward into further speculation, although he knows they have no end and can never be satisfied. And so he finds he has ventured himself "upon that boundless ocean, which runs out into immensity."[3] The boundless ocean, in Hume's text, is the ocean of philosophy; but it is also the ocean of those pleasures which, unlike the pleasure we take in conversation and backgammon, are inextricably tangled up with the painful awareness that we can never fully satisfy them, the pleasures of curiosity, concern, and ambition—pleasures that are always accompanied by uneasiness.

It is worth noting that curiosity and ambition had once been vices, since they tie you to this world and distract your attention from the next. Augustine had been particularly scathing about curiosity, which he had described as "a certaine vayne and curious itch . . . which is masked vnder the title of *Knowledge* and *Learning*."[4] Hobbes was one of the first to turn curiosity into an admirable quality, identifying it as the source of all knowledge of causes.[5] Ambition had similarly been regarded as a vice, identified with pride and vain glory. "Love and Ambition," said one of John Fletcher's characters, "draw the devills coach."[6] It is only in the 1660s that the phrase "laudable ambition" began to be commonplace, but for Pufendorf in 1673 ambition was still "the most terrible of evils."[7] Thus when Hume identifies his motivations as being curiosity and ambition he is relying on a transvaluation of values where these sometime vices had fairly recently been reconfigured as virtues— Enlightenment virtues, we might say, the virtues of the new world in which power, pleasure, and profit have become legitimate aspirations. Strikingly, curiosity and ambition are still vices in John Locke up until *Some Thoughts Concerning Education* (1693), when they are transmuted into virtues.[8]

Even the phrase "I am concerned," meaning "I am troubled or distressed," is comparatively modern: the *Oxford English Dictionary (OED)* gives 1674 as the first usage of "concerned" in this sense.[9] As for "uneasiness," the word had come into prominence, as we shall see, with the second edition (1694) of Locke's *Essay Concerning Humane Understanding.* Thus when Hume describes his motivations in the *Treatise* as being ones of curiosity, uneasiness, concern, and ambition, it is natural for us to read him as referring to universal aspects of human psychology—and indeed they seem universal to us because we still share much of Hume's understanding of human motivation. But in fact what we have here is a characteristically Enlightenment language, a language in which insatiable passions have been transformed from vices into virtues.

One of the great things about Hume is that he paints a wonderfully complex picture of the varied pleasures that motivate us in life. Even the virtues are motivated by pleasure. Benevolence, for example, is "sweet, smooth, tender, and agreeable." And these feelings are communicated to bystanders, "and melt them into the same fondness and delicacy."[10] Hume takes it for granted (if he can be said to take anything for granted) that "The chief spring or actuating principle of the human mind is pleasure or pain," and that we are very bad at deferring gratification; what motivates us is what pleases us right now.[11] Curiosity, concern, and ambition pay out now, not just in some distant future which I may never live to see; right now I begin to imagine the pleasures I will derive from reaching my goal, and (by a wonderful alchemy) imaginary pleasures are real pleasures.

There is another remarkable alchemy constantly at work in Hume's world: your pleasures become my pleasures, and your pains become my pains, just as "in strings equally wound up, the motion of one communicates itself to the rest; so all the affections readily pass from one person to another."[12] Hume's appeal to mechanical and physical metaphors (the chief spring, the strings equally wound up) is not coincidental, for the assumption is that pleasures and pains serve as causal mechanisms and provide the only possible explanations for human behavior. This view that we are motivated only by pleasure and pain goes back to the Epicureans, although the mechanical imagery is new, a by-product of the mechanical philosophy of the seventeenth century.

◌•••◌•••◌•

It was a fundamental concern of philosophers such as Francis Hutcheson, Hume, and Adam Smith to find a route between the benevolent philosophy of Lord Shaftesbury and the selfish philosophy of Bernard Mandeville.[13] Naturally they placed their own efforts in the context of a longer history, and in this chapter I am going to discuss two key moments in that history, the philosophies of Hobbes and Locke. According to Hutcheson, Hobbes, following the Epicureans, held that "all the Desires of the human Mind, nay of all *thinking Natures,* are reducible to *Self-Love,* or *Desire of private Happiness:* That from this Desire all Actions of any Agent do flow."[14] Hobbes's view, Hutcheson complains, can never account for what he calls "the principal Actions of human Life," such as friendship, generosity, and compassion.[15] Hutcheson's view of Hobbes is identical with that of Bishop Joseph Butler, who held that according to Hobbes "only the love of power, and delight in the exercise of it" can explain benevolence—an explanation which, Butler insisted, was no explanation at all.[16]

Hume, however, had a quite different view of Hobbes. It is true that he attributed to him "the selfish system of morals" and a "libertine system of ethics," but he insisted that this was entirely compatible with an account of human beings as being capable of benevolence.[17] Hume's defense of Hobbes was necessary because his position and Hobbes's were not that different: Samuel Johnson said that Hume was a man without principle, but "If he is any thing, he is a Hobbist," and there's a certain amount of truth in this.[18] This is what Hume said:

> An *Epicurean* or a *Hobbist* readily allows, that there is such a Thing as Friendship in the World, without Hypocrisy or Disguise; tho' he may attempt, by a philosophical Chymistry, to resolve the Elements of this Passion, if I may so speak, into those of another, and explain every Affection to be Self-love, twisted and moulded[, by a particular turn of imagination,] into a Variety of Shapes and Appearances.[19] But as the same Turn of Imagination prevails not in every Man, nor gives the same Direction to the original Passion; this is sufficient even according to the selfish System to

make the widest Difference in human Characters, and denominate one Man virtuous and humane, another vicious and meanly interested.[20]

A similar disagreement runs through the modern literature, for some insist that Hobbes's moral philosophy is egoistic, while others (currently the majority) deny this strongly. The question of whether Hobbes is or is not an egoist depends partly on how one defines egoist, and (some would argue) partly on which text one regards as the best exposition of Hobbes's views.

What I want to argue here is that Hobbes does indeed think that friendship, benevolence, charity, pity, compassion, and so on are forms of self-love, "twisted and moulded" by a particular turn of imagination into a variety of appearances. In arguing that Hobbes is an egoist I want to find a middle position between a hard-line definition of egoist, which would hold that people never act to benefit others (this is Bernard Gert's definition), and a soft-line definition of egoist which would hold that people only act to benefit others when they do so to satisfy some sentiment of their own, such as sympathy, pity, or benevolence (this is Thomas Nagel's definition).[21] That Hobbes meets this baseline definition of egoism there would seem to be no doubt; he says, for example, "by necessity of Nature, every man doth in all his voluntary Actions intend some good unto Himself."[22] The first sort of egoism few people would defend—Mandeville is the only obvious exception.[23] The second is Hume's view. Hobbes's position, I will argue, lies between the two: he is more of an egoist than Hume, but less of an egoist than Mandeville. Butler was wrong to think that Hobbes holds that human beings only help each other out of love of power and their delight in the exercise in it; but Hume was right that they only act to help each other as a result of a particular turn of imagination, a turn which does not correspond to what we now normally mean when we refer to sympathy, benevolence, or pity. Nor does it correspond to what eighteenth-century philosophers meant when they used these terms (which they carefully distinguished one from another).

John Aubrey tells a story which helps to identify Hobbes's in-between position:

> He was very charitable *(pro suo modulo)* to those that were true objects of his bounty. One time, I remember, going in the Strand, a poor and

infirm old man craved his alms. He, beholding him with eyes of pity and compassion, put his hand in his pocket, and gave him 6d. Said a divine (that Dr Jasper Mayne) that stood by—"Would you have done this, if it had not been Christ's command?"—"Yea," said he.—"Why?" quoth the other.—"Because," said he, "I was in pain to consider the miserable condition of the old man; and now my alms, giving him some relief, doth also ease me."[24]

Here we find Hobbes feeling pain because he has imagined the suffering of the old man; he acts to relieve the old man not in order to relieve the old man's suffering, but in order to relieve his own suffering caused by his own imaginary experience. Sympathy is a precondition for this action, but he does not act out of sympathy, but rather for purely selfish reasons; nevertheless he can only relieve his own suffering by acting to benefit someone else. So Hobbes has acted to benefit someone else, but only out of self-love. What has motivated his action is his imaginary experience of someone else's suffering.

Now, this would be a position between hard egoism and soft egoism—let's call it firm egoism. But, actually, Hobbes's standard position goes further than this. His claim is that we only identify in this way with someone else if we think there is some prospect of the same thing happening to us. So we must not only imagine the other person's suffering; we must recognize that suffering as suffering we might experience ourselves. Thus we do not feel sympathy when a wicked person is punished because we do not regard ourselves as wicked (Hobbes takes it for granted that we tend to think well of ourselves) and do not expect the same thing to happen to us; but we do experience sympathy when we see someone experience poverty and disease because we can easily imagine ourselves being put in the same position. Let us call this position tough egoism. Where firm egoism requires a single act of imagination (I have to imagine your sufferings so that they become in some measure my own) tough egoism requires a double act (I must both imagine your sufferings, and imagine circumstances in which I would suffer in the same way). Only then can I properly identify with you, so that acting to relieve your sufferings becomes a way of relieving my own. We need not puzzle over where this tough egoist position comes from. It comes from Aristotle, who defines pity in *The Art of Rhetoric* as "a certain pain occasioned by an apparently destructive evil or pain's occurring to one who does not deserve it, which the pitier might expect to suffer himself or that one of his own would"; this was a book that Hobbes had adapted and translated in 1637.[25] The conclusion that pity is a form of fear *for ourselves* was standard in seventeenth-century accounts.

Hobbes outlines this tough egoist position over and over again. The examples which follow all come from well-known texts, except that a few come from Hobbes's critique of Thomas White's *De mundo*, a text written in 1643 but not published until 1973, and one which has not, as far as I know, been previously used in this context. Here, for example, is what he has to say about pity and compassion: "*Pity* is *Imagination* or *Fiction* of *future* Calamity to our *selves*, proceeding from the Sense of *another* Mans Calamity. But when it lighteth on such as we think have not deserved the same, the Compassion is greater, because then there appeareth more Probability that the same may happen to us: for, the Evil that happeneth to an innocent Man, may happen to every Man. But when we see a Man suffer for great Crimes, which we cannot easily think will fall upon our selves, the Pity is the less."[26] He would say exactly the same thing in *Leviathan:* "*Griefe,* for the calamity of another, is Pitty, and ariseth from the imagination that the like calamity may befall himselfe, and therefore is called also Compassion, and in the phrase of this present time a Fellow-Feeling."[27]

Tom Sorell has produced a number of criticisms of Butler's famous critique of Hobbes.[28] One is that for Butler to be right when he says that for Hobbes fear and compassion are essentially the same, Hobbes would have to be saying that whenever we feel pity we are not merely imagining that something dreadful could in principle happen to us, but we are expressing the belief that there is a real prospect of that thing happening to us. As it happens, Hobbes says exactly that.

Here is an example of tough egoism being used to explain an apparent oddity in human behavior, what we would call schadenfreude:

Divers other Passions there be, but they want Names: whereof some nevertheless have been by most Men observed: For Example; from what Passion proceedeth it, that Men take *pleasure* to *behold* from the Shore the *Danger* of them that are at Sea in a Tempest, or in Fight, or from a safe Castle to behold two Armies charge one to another in the Field? It is certainly, in the whole Summ, *Joy;* else Men would never flock to such a Spectacle. Nevertheless there is in it both *Joy* and *Grief:* for as there is Novelty and Remembrance of our own Security present, which is *Delight:* so there is also *Pity,* which is Grief: But the Delight is so far predominant, that Men usually are content in such a Case to be Spectators of the Misery of their Friends.[29]

No one, as far as I can tell, has noticed that what Hobbes is doing here is discussing a very famous—famous then and famous now—passage in Lucretius's *De rerum natura,* the proem to book 2. Here is Thomas Creech's translation:

> Tis pleasant, when the Seas are rough, to stand
> And view anothere's danger safe at Land;
> Not 'cause he's troubled, but tis sweet to see
> Those cares and Fears, from which ourselves are free:
> Tis also pleasant to behold from far,
> How troops engage; secure ourselves from war.[30]

Francis Bacon had offered a Christianized paraphrase in his essay "Of Truth" (1625):

> The Inquirie of *Truth,* which is the Loue-making, or Wooing of it; The knowledge of *Truth,* which is the Presence of it; and the Beleefe of *Truth,* which is the Enioying of it; is the Soueraigne Good of humane Nature. The first Creature of God, in the workes of the Dayes, was the Light of the Sense; The last, was the Light of Reason; And his Sabbath Worke, euer since, is the Illumination of his Spirit. First he breathed Light, vpon the Face, of the Matter or Chaos; Then he breathed Light, into the Face of Man; and still he breatheth and inspireth Light, into the Face of his Chosen. The Poet, that beautified the Sect, that was otherwise inferiour to the rest, saith yet excellently well: *It is a pleasure to stand vpon the shore, and to see ships tost vpon the Sea: A pleasure to stand in the window of a Castle, and to see a Battaile, and the Aduentures thereof, below: But no pleasure is comparable, to the standing, vpon the vantage ground of Truth:* (A hill not to be commanded, and where the Ayre is alwaies cleare

and serene;) *And to see the Errours, and Wandrings, and Mists, and Tempests, in the vale below:* So alwaies, that this prospect, be with Pitty, and not with Swelling, or Pride. Certainly, it is Heauen vpon Earth, to haue a Mans Minde Moue in Charitie, Rest in Prouidence, and Turne vpon the Poles of *Truth.*[31]

The passage was famous precisely because its egoistic account of human motivation was regarded as shocking, and Bacon had done his best to remind his readers of it without endorsing its solipsism; Hobbes, on the other hand, intensified what Lucretius had said by suggesting (as Lucretius did not) that we might take pleasure in the sufferings of our friends.

And here is what Hobbes has to say about gifts and benevolence: "For no man giveth, but with intention of Good to himselfe; because Gift is Voluntary; and of all Voluntary Acts, the object is to every Man his own Good; of which if men see they shall be frustrated, there will be no beginning of benevolence, or trust; nor consequently of mutuall help; nor of reconciliation of one man to another; and therefore they are to remain still in the condition of *War.*"[32] Note that benevolent actions are intended to result in benefit to oneself.[33]

And here is what he has to say about charity: "There is yet another Passion sometimes called *Love,* but more properly *good Will* or *Charity.* There can be no greater argument of a man, of his own power, then to finde himself able not onely to accomplish his own desires, but also to *assist* other men in theirs: and this is that conception wherein consisteth *Charity.*"[34]

And of society in general, "All Society therefore is either for Gain, or for Glory, *(i.e.)* not so much for love of our Fellowes, as for love of our Selves."[35]

Hobbes is so explicit and repeats himself so frequently on these matters that I find it a little difficult to understand how the view that Hobbes is not an egoist can have possibly gained traction, let alone have become the dominant view in the scholarly literature.[36] Let me take a couple of examples of where my opponents go wrong.

As support for his view that Hobbes is not an egoist, Bernard Gert cites Hobbes's claim that "no man is tyed by any Compacts whatsoever to accuse himself, or any other, by whose dammage he is like to procure himselfe a bitter life, wherefore neither is a Father oblig'd to bear witnesse against his Sonne, nor a Husband against his Wife, nor a Sonne against his Father;

nor any man against any one, by whose meanes he hath his subsistance; for in vain is that testimony which is presum'd to be corrupted from nature."[37] It should be evident in this example that Hobbes is not talking about bonds of altruistic affection, but about financial dependence and about the capacity of those with whom we live in daily contact to procure for us a bitter life.

Tom Sorell argues, "Instead of denying that there is such a thing as benevolence or charity, Hobbes denies that benevolence ever operates outside one's inner circle of family and friends."[38] Yet although Hobbes recognizes that "men are presumed to be more enclined by nature, to advance their own children, than the children of other men . . . because it is always presumed that the neerer of kin, is the neerer in affection"; he goes on to say "and 'tis evident that a man receives alwayes, by reflexion, the most honour from the greatnesse of his neerest kindred," so that care for our kindred is self-interested, just as friendship is.[39]

Hobbes would have thought it simply wrong to assume that where we practice benevolence or charity it follows that we have admirable motives, and that the benevolent and charitable are therefore morally superior. He insists that it is patently false that the virtuous have more friends than the wicked, and points to Caesar as an example of a morally flawed individual who "won glory through gifts, help, and forgiveness"—acting not altruistically but in order to build himself a power base. By contrast Cato, who was morally admirable, excelled in that he obeyed the law, not in that he helped others.[40]

Sorell also argues that Hobbes's metaphor of life as a race in which every individual strives to come first is perfectly compatible with a desire to see one's relatives and friends do better than others, if not better than oneself.[41] Now, this is certainly true, but we still need to think of relatives and friends, as Hobbes does, in instrumental terms, and this means realizing that there is more than one type of race. If I am a member of a cycle team in the Tour de France I want the other members of my team to do well because they will spell me, support me, and come to my assistance. There's nothing altruistic about my dismay if a member of my team crashes out of the race; having a strong team is a key ingredient in the pursuit of victory. So, too, a partner in a law firm will want to be more successful than the other partners, but even a partner on maternity leave, watching the competition from the sidelines, will still benefit if members of her own firm outperform competing firms. Partners will thus help each other because their welfare is bound up together.

I will concede that Hobbes occasionally—and mainly in *Leviathan*—offers formulations that appear to imply altruism. Thus he offers these two definitions:

> Desire of good to another, [is] BENEVOLENCE, GOOD WILL, CHARITY. If to man generally, GOOD NATURE.

And,

> Love of persons for society, [is] KINDNESSE.[42]

But it turns out as you read further that people's desire of good to another is never altruistic, that people don't really love society, and that people aren't really capable of desiring good to men generally. It is true that Hobbes recognizes that some virtues which advance peace are to be classified as "moral," but it is important to recognize here, first, that advancing of peace is in each person's interests and, second, that in a well-ordered society such virtues will be rewarded with honor and reputation, which are in themselves a form of power.

Moreover, a key piece of evidence regarding Hobbes's views has been overlooked. When he came to translate *Leviathan* into Latin these two key passages evidently concerned him. The first appears truncated:

> Alii bonum Cupere, *Benevolentia* vel *Charitas.*

There is no longer any concession that we might desire good to mankind in general. And the second simply disappears (along, it should be added, with a series of further definitions of "love").[43] If the English *Leviathan* is the key text for those who want to argue that Hobbes was no egoist, then the Latin may be read as Hobbes's own response to that possible reading. Consider, for example, his shifting definition of a law of nature, about which Noel Malcolm has this to say:

> It is hard to understand why Hobbes should have wanted to alter his general definition of a law of nature from "a Precept, or generall Rule, found out by Reason, by which a man is forbidden to do, that, which is

destructive of his life, or taketh away the means of preserving the same; and to omit, that, by which he thinketh it may be best preserved" to the abbreviated version in the Latin text, where a man is merely forbidden to do "that which will seem to him to tend to his disadvantage." Here one must doubt whether Hobbes was alert to all the implications of what he was writing.[44]

Those—and Malcolm is one of them—who want to deny that Hobbes was an egoist must indeed doubt that Hobbes had grasped the implications of what he had written; but it seems more likely that he had deliberately adjusted his argument to make absolutely clear that he was propounding an uncompromising form of egoism.[45]

So although Hobbes occasionally uses language which describes the outward appearances of human behavior rather than the inner mechanisms which cause that behavior, he is, I would argue, indisputably an exponent of a tough egoism. Moreover, he is a much more sophisticated exponent of egoism than has generally been recognized. Thus Butler claimed to refute the notion that we can be motivated solely by the pursuit of pleasure by pointing out that telling us that we should pursue pleasure doesn't actually give us any guidance on what to do until we know what our own particular tastes are. Thus playing golf may give *you* pleasure, but it doesn't follow that *I* should play golf, as I may find hitting a small ball with a stick pointless and boring. Pleasure is thus something one only experiences as a side effect of doing something one has some other motive for doing. You can't aim at it directly. This is how Hume puts the argument:

> Nature must, by the internal Frame and Constitution of the Mind, give an original Propensity to Fame, 'ere we can reap any Pleasure from it, or pursue it from Motives of Self-love, and a Desire of Happiness. If I have no Vanity, I take no Delight in Praise: If I be void of Ambition, Power gives me no Enjoyment: If I be not angry, the Punishment of an Adversary is totally indifferent to me. In all these Cases, there is a Passion which points immediately to the Object, and constitutes it our Good or Happiness; as there are other secondary Passions which afterwards arise, and pursue it as a Part of our Happiness, when once it is constituted such, by our original Affections. Were there no Appetites of any Kind antecedent to Self-love, that Propensity could scarcely ever exert itself;

because we should, in that case, have felt few and slender Pains or Pleasures, and have little Misery or Happiness, to avoid or to pursue.[46]

Now, Butler and Hume were not to know it, but Hobbes says exactly the same thing in the manuscript critique of *De mundo:* "it is clear that anyone's happiness consists in what he finds good: no-one finds something good for which he has no appetite. So he who has nothing to seek after enjoys no happiness."[47]

Or again, a major concept in recent discussions of happiness is what has been termed the hedonic treadmill.[48] For example, I get a big pay increase. For several months I feel prosperous and happy. And then my increased salary becomes the new normal; I no longer feel good about it; I begin to feel once again that I need to be paid more, that I have wants I can't satisfy, that I am constrained by my income. Hobbes understands this perfectly:

> Seeing all *Delight* is *Appetite,* and presupposeth a *further* End, there can be *no Contentment* but in *proceeding:* and therefore we are not to marvel, when we see, that as Men attain to more Riches, Honour, or other Power; so their Appetite continually groweth more and more; and when they are come to the utmost Degree of some Kind of Power, they pursue some other, as long as in any Kind they think themselves behind any other: of those therefore that have attained to the highest Degree of Honour and Riches, some have affected Mastery in some Art; as *Nero* in Musick and Poetry, *Commodus* in the Art of a Gladiator; and such as affect not some such Thing, must find Diversion and Recreation of their Thoughts in the Contention either of Play or Business: and Men justly complain of a great Grief, that they know not what to do. *Felicity* therefore, by which we mean continual Delight, consisteth *not* in *having* prospered, but in *prospering.*[49]

It follows from this account that pleasure for Hobbes is fundamentally imaginary or fictional; our pleasure lies in a construction of the future, not in an experience of the present.

⋄⋄⋄

So Hobbes is an egoist who thinks that every affection is, as Hume puts it, a form of self-love, "twisted and moulded." It *might* be thought that one reason why he holds this peculiar view of human nature (as it seems to most of those who have tried to rescue him from the charge of egoism) is that his conceptual tools for thinking about human behavior are very different from ours. Thus one might note that Hobbes never uses the word "sympathy," which is of such fundamental importance for the moral philosophy of Shaftesbury, Hutcheson, Hume, and Smith.* Indeed, the *OED* assures us that it is only from 1662 that the word "sympathy" is used to mean "The quality or state of being affected by the condition of another with a feeling similar or corresponding to that of the other; the fact or capacity of entering into or sharing the feelings of another or others; fellow-feeling."[50]

But, first, as we have seen, Hobbes does in *Leviathan* use the term "fellow-feeling," which the *OED* regards as a synonym for sympathy, in the relevant sense. He calls fellow-feeling "the phrase of this present time" (and because it is a peculiarly English expression, he drops this whole clause from the Latin translation of *Leviathan*).[51] In fact the term "fellow-feeling" first appeared in the 1580s and was common from the 1600s onward, so to use it in 1651 was not to respond to the latest fashion. Second, look at how, in *De homine,* Hobbes defines "compassion" as being feeling another's pain and suffering with him.[52] "Compassion" is thus a synonym for "sympathy." And last, the *OED* is simply wrong in what it says about sympathy as meaning sharing the feelings of another. For what one regularly finds in the half century before the publication of Leviathan is that "fellow-feeling" and "sympathy" are tied together in a single phrase: "sympathy and fellow-feeling," "fellow-feeling or sympathy," and so on—there are no fewer than ninety-three occurrences of sympathy and fellow-feeling, linked together, in Early English Books Online (EEBO) from 1586 to 1651. So "fellow-feeling" and the new meaning of "sympathy" come in together in the 1580s (the *OED*

---

* Locke, too, avoids the word, complaining that its meaning is rarely clear. John Locke, *An Essay Concerning Humane Understanding* (London: Basset, 1690), 253. But it plays a central role in Thomas Nettleton's elaboration of a Lockean moral philosophy: "This *Sympathetic Sense,* or Feeling, . . . is the Foundation of all those social Affections of Kindness, Benevolence, Compassion, Gratitude, Parental and Filial Affection, Friendship, Love to ones Country, &c. which are as necessary to maintain Societies, and uphold Communities, as the private and selfish Affections are to preserve and support every individual Person." Thomas Nettleton, *Some Thoughts Concerning Virtue and Happiness: In a Letter to a Clergyman* (London: Batley, 1729), 39–40. Remarkably, and surely deliberately, Mandeville never uses the word.

has 1578 for the first use of "fellow-feeling" in the sense of "sharing in the feelings of others").[53] Here are both terms at work together in 1658 in a sermon by Nehemiah Rogers: "Saint *Austin* defineth *Mercy* [*misericordia*] to bee *a fellow feeling in our hearts of anothers misery:* And *Gregory* saith, it hath the denomination and Etimology *a misero corde,* from a miserable and woefull heart; because as often as wee behold a man in misery, the minde (through commiseration being touched with griefe at his misery) doth, as it were, *Cor miserum facere,* vexe and torment the heart with a sympathy and a fellow-feeling of his misery."[54] Hobbes uses only one of these terms, but he could have used either or both. He understands perfectly what the terms refer to; but, unlike Rogers, he believes compassion, pity, sympathy and fellow-feeling are all self-interested emotions.

So why did Hobbes not become the first Enlightenment moral philosopher, if we understand sympathy as being the core principle in Enlightenment moral philosophy? One answer to this question is that Hobbes confused what Bernard Gert has called tautological egoism with psychological egoism.[55] Of necessity, my motives in acting must be *mine;* and one of the satisfactions I get in acting freely is the knowledge that I am doing what I want to do. In that sense, all my actions refer to myself; but that does not necessarily mean, as Hobbes perhaps thinks it does, that it follows that all my actions must be intended to increase my own pleasure or power.

Alternatively, Hobbes needs psychological egoism for his political philosophy. He needs most people to act out of selfish interests or there will be no state of nature; and he needs people to be profoundly reluctant to die or there will be no right to self-preservation. As he himself says, "if we could suppose a great Multitude of men to consent in the observation of Justice, and other Lawes of Nature, without a common Power to keep them all in awe; we might as well suppose all Man-kind to do the same; and then there neither would be, nor need to be any Civill Government, or Commonwealth at all; because there would be Peace without subjection."[56] The claim that the generality of human beings are psychological egoists is thus foundational for his whole system, and Hobbes sees no reason to imagine that a minority of human beings are fundamentally different from all the rest.

But I think these answers aren't really answers at all, for they simply amount to new ways of stating the question. Hobbes confuses tautological egoism and psychological egoism because he finds both plausible; and he believes in the state of nature and the social contract because he really does believe that left to themselves people are more likely to attack each other than to help each other, particularly if they are strangers with no preexisting ties of association. Hobbes, who never refers to the parable of the Good Samaritan, cannot imagine fellow-feeling between strangers: "The Affection wherewith Men many times bestow their Benefits on *Strangers,* is not to be called Charity, but either *Contract,* whereby they seek to purchase friendship; or *Fear,* which maketh them to purchase peace."[57] When Hobbes, according to Aubrey's story, gave alms to an infirm old man, that man was not, in Hobbes's eyes, a stranger, but rather a possible future version of himself. We might compare Hobbes's account of why he had given him alms with François de La Rochefoucauld on pity (in *Maxims,* 1665): "Pity and Compassion is frequently a Sense of our own Misfortunes, in those of Other Men. It is an *Ingenious Foresight* of the *Disasters* that may fall upon us hereafter; we Relieve Others, that they may Return the like, when our Own Occasions call for it; and the Good Offices we Do Them, are, in Strict Speaking, so many Kindnesses done to Our Selves Before-hand."[58]

So, too, when Hobbes (again, according to Aubrey) tried to found a free school in Malmesbury, where he had been born and raised, he was trying to benefit other little Hobbeses; he was giving himself a gift not in advance, but in arrears. This capacity of compassion to look to a real past and an imaginary future was captured by Pierre Nicole: "For there is in the sentiments of Compassion for others some secret reflections upon our selves, by which we look upon our selves either as having suffered the same evils, or as being liable to suffer them."[59] Moreover, on both occasions Hobbes was displaying his superfluity of resources, and thus confirming to himself his sense of his own power (for Hobbes uses "power" to refer to anything which enables one to satisfy one's desires, so that money is power, and so is friendship).[60]

Here I think there is a genuine difference between Hobbes's world and the world of the eighteenth-century Enlightenment. Hobbes cannot imagine that we might feel compassion for a stranger. I don't want to claim that he was entirely typical in this, merely that sympathy for strangers was much more common in the eighteenth century than in the seventeenth.[61] A striking example of seventeenth-century sympathy is provided by Miranda in *The Tempest* (fictional sympathy of course, but the audience presumably found it credible). Her response to the shipwreck brought about by her father's magic is quite different from that of Lucretius or of Hobbes; indeed, it seems entirely possible that Shakespeare, who appears to have been familiar with Lucretius, was here deliberately responding to Lucretius's famous proem to book 2 of *De rerum natura*.[62] This is what she says:

> If by your art, my dearest father, you have
> Put the wild waters in this roar, allay them.
> The sky, it seems, would pour down stinking pitch,
> But that the sea, mounting to the welkin's cheek,
> Dashes the fire out. O, I have suffer'd
> With those that I saw suffer! A brave vessel,
> Who had, no doubt, some noble creature in her,
> Dash'd all to pieces! O, the cry did knock
> Against my very heart! Poor souls, they perished.
> Had I been any god of power, I would
> Have sunk the sea within the earth, or ere
> It should the good ship so have swallowed and
> The fraughting souls within her.

Miranda's words are, as Prospero notes, an expression of "The very virtue of compassion in thee."[63]

But Prospero himself is not so easily moved. In this, I suspect, he is more typical of the age. The biblical injunction, after all, was to love thy neighbor as thy self, and even the obligations to neighbors were coming under growing strain.[64] Seventeenth-century English men and women lived in a world of narrow loyalties. It is true that Hobbes belonged to what would soon be called the republic of letters and traveled widely; but his emotional ties were only to his close associates.

We can immediately in this respect contrast Hobbes with Hume, who wrote, "For supposing I saw a person perfectly unknown to me, who, while asleep in the fields, was in danger of being trod under foot by horses, I shou'd immediately run to his assistance; and in this I shou'd be actuated by the same principle of sympathy, which makes me concern'd for the present sorrows of a stranger. The bare mention of this is sufficient."[65] Hume's example was carefully chosen. Unlike Lucretius's shipwreck (or Mandeville's thought experiment of being forced to watch a pig eat a baby while being prevented from intervening), there is something he can do.[66] For the imaginary Hume, unlike for the Good Samaritan, intervention is easy—there are no noisome wounds to bind up, there is no need to spend money, a journey will not be interrupted. But when Hume wrote "The bare mention of this is sufficient" he assumed too much. A Hobbesian would only intervene if he could either imagine being in the stranger's situation—but perhaps he is very far from being the sort of person (a laborer or a tramp) who would fall asleep in a field—or if he could persuade himself there was some prospect of reward or repayment, in whatever form. Hume assumed we all recognize a bond of common humanity, while Hobbes denied that such a bond exists.

In 1761 Hume wrote a letter of introduction for James Macpherson to the publisher William Strahan. "As he is an entire Stranger in London," said Hume, "you will naturally of yourself be inclind to assist him," thus paying Strahan a neat compliment.[67] Hume went on to assure Strahan that Macpherson was a person of integrity, which was very far from the truth, since he was the author of *Ossian,* an elaborate forgery which Macpherson claimed to be a translation from Gaelic oral traditions. Hume assumed that all Strahan would want in order to decide to help Macpherson was an assurance that no harm would come to him as a result; to suggest that Strahan would only help a stranger if he hoped to benefit himself by so doing would have been to insult him.

Hunt as you may, you will never find Good Samaritan passages like these in Hobbes; and this, I think, is not because Hobbes was peculiar, although he may have been a bit old-fashioned. When he calls fellow-feeling "the phrase of this present time," he is acknowledging a new emphasis on sympathy, fellow-feeling, and humanity. A contemporary (William Whately, 1640) praised "The vertue of humanity, that is, of being ready to shew love to man, as he is man, and because he is a man, one made after Gods owne image, and proceeding out of the same common roote. We all met in *Adams* loynes, and in *Noahs;* let us therefore do good even to strangers. This good will which is communicated to such, savours least of self-love, and of self-respect [i.e., self-interest], and is therefore the more to be commended. It tends to the uniting of the common body of the world together, and to make all mankind happy."[68]

Hobbes explicitly denied that *by nature* we are capable of loving human beings in general: "For if by nature one Man should Love another (that is) as Man, there could no reason be return'd why every Man should not equally

Love every Man, as being equally Man"—which he thinks human beings evidently do not do.[69] But he does appear to acknowledge that one might *learn* to feel benevolent toward other human beings in general, for in *Leviathan* he defined "*Desire* of good . . . to man generally" as "GOOD NATURE."[70] Hume was convinced that all of his readers will think of themselves as good-natured; Hobbes assumed that he and his readers would agree that good-natured people are the exception, not the norm.

If sympathy, humanity, and good nature had only a liminal existence in Hobbes, emphasis on them was to grow and grow, and was marked, for example, by the shift in the meaning of "humane" to mean "kind" rather than "civilized." Hume's moral philosophy differs from Hobbes's partly because eighteenth-century gentlemen and -women were much better than seventeenth-century gentlemen and -women at experiencing and expressing sympathy. There is nothing surprising about this: they had been trained in it by the novel, the theater, and the paintings of the day.[71] This isn't because novels, plays, and paintings necessarily specialize in evoking sympathy; rather, in the eighteenth-century these art forms were reconstructed to encourage a sympathetic identification with others as part of the enterprise of forming a new polite, enlightened, society—novels, plays, and paintings taught people how to be "sentimental" (in the new language of the day).* What is, perhaps, puzzling is the difficulty Enlightenment theorists had in acknowledging the extent to which human motivations and behavior might differ from one society to another.[72]

If the term "fellow-feeling" was not really a term of the present time, the word "selfish" *was.* (Let me remark in passing that Hobbes never encountered the words "egoist," "egotist," "altruist," or "hedonist," which are all later inventions.) In EEBO, "selvish" appears in 1628, and there are two isolated occurrences of "selfish" in 1632, but from 1641 the word enters common discourse.[73] "Self-interest" became commonly used at the same time. Atti-

---

* "What, in your opinion, is the meaning of the word *sentimental,* so much in vogue among the polite. . . . Every thing clever and agreeable is comprehended in that word. . . . I am frequently astonished to hear such a one is a *sentimental* man; we were a *sentimental* party; I have been taking a *sentimental* walk." Lady Bradshaigh to Samuel Richardson, 1749, quoted in the *OED Online,* "sentimental," published 1912.

tudes that had once seemed normal had begun to seem selfish, and the new word marked this shift in values. The earliest occasion I can find of someone using the word "selfish" in the context of Hobbes's philosophy is William Lucy in 1663: "To use the Phrase of the time," he said, "this Gent. is very *selfish*."[74] Hobbes himself used "self-interest," but not until 1682; in *Leviathan,* and only in *Leviathan,* he used "self-love," but with the traditional negative connotations.[75]

For us it seems impossible to imagine a world in which "selfish" is not a marker of vice and "altruistic" is not a marker of virtue. Thus Thomas Nagel says of Hobbesian man, "He is susceptible only to selfish motivation, and is therefore incapable of any action which could be clearly labeled moral. He might, in fact, be best described as a man without a moral sense."[76] But when Hobbes first formulated a philosophy which took self-interest for granted, he had little sense, I think, that what he had to say was particularly shocking; after all, Christianity was standardly interpreted as a system of future pleasure and pains in which a rational person would (if grace permitted) always choose heaven and seek to avoid hell. Even Bishop Butler thought that, in the long run, duty and interest are perfectly coincident, which on Nagel's account would mean that he lacked a moral sense. In *Leviathan,* however, Hobbes already felt obliged to make occasional concessions to the new (and in his view peculiar) preoccupation with benevolence and selfishness as polar opposites. These concessions are, on my reading, merely tokens; they do not represent a fundamental shift away, on his part, from an egoistic mode of thought.

There is a further reason why Hobbes saw individuals as inherently selfish. In order to understand how human beings would behave in a state of nature he thought you only had to look at how states behave toward each other, for states are still in a state of nature. "That *Man to Man is an arrant Wolfe* . . . is true . . ." he says, "if we compare cities [among themselves]."[77] Thus Machiavellian power politics and reason of state theory underpinned his account of human nature. It is true that human beings pursue pleasure and states do not, but in Hobbes the concepts of power and pleasure are inseparable, for pleasures of the body pall, and the only enduring pleasure of the mind lies in the imagination of power.

The scholarly consensus that Hobbes was not an egoist requires us to believe that he not only thought human beings are not always motivated by pleasure but also that they are not always engaged in the pursuit of power as a means to future pleasure. The scholars may perhaps be right about human beings; they are not right about Hobbes.

But *are* they right about human beings? I've gone to some lengths to argue that Hobbes was what I have called a tough egoist most of the time and a firm egoist all the time not just because I think it matters for the understanding of Hobbes. For if the scholars are wrong about Hobbes, it raises the possibility that they are also wrong about human nature—that they underestimate the extent to which human motivations and behavior may vary from one society to another. It is true that Hobbes's contemporaries rejected his arguments, but it was his atheism, his materialism, and his determinism, and not his egoism, that made his views unacceptable. Psychological egoism, as restated by Locke, provoked no general outcry.[78]

Hobbes assumed that we seek the most favorable balance of pleasure (both of the body and of the mind) and displeasure (displeasure of the body being pain, and of the mind being grief); we are motivated by what Hobbes called the appearance of pleasure and displeasure, which might be different from an objective calculation of the likelihood of experiencing pleasure and displeasure. We don't always make rational choices. In the first edition of the *Essay,* which appeared in 1689, Locke took exactly the same view. Locke replaced Hobbes's determinism with a limited and cautious defense of the freedom of the will. And he unhesitatingly rejected Hobbes's tough egoism. "Love and Hatred," he writes, "to[ward] Beings capable of Happiness or Misery, is often the Pain [changed to "Uneasiness" in the fourth edition, 1700] or Delight which we have in their very Being or Happiness. Thus the Being and Welfare of a Man's Children or Friends, producing constant Delight in him, he is said constantly to love them."[79] Nevertheless, Locke remained a psychological egoist.

Shorn of Hobbes's atheism, materialism, determinism, and egoism, the claim that good and evil are simply pain and pleasure, and that reason is subordinate to the passions, became respectable—or at least almost respectable. And as a consequence, for many authors it became, as we shall see in Chapter 9, self-evident that human beings pursue happiness, and can do no other. But in the second edition of the *Essay,* which appeared in 1694,

Locke took a very different view, one that revised the whole relationship between pleasure and motivation. In 1689 he believed that one could be motivated by the consideration of future happiness, including another person's happiness, which could in itself be a source of delight. His argument in 1694 was that what motivates us is uneasiness, not the prospect of future pleasure:

> The chief, if not only spur to humane industry and action is uneasiness. For whatsoever good is propos'd, if its absence carries no displeasure nor pain with it; if a Man be easie and content without it, there is no desire of it, nor endeavour after it; there is no more but a bare *Velleity*, the term used to signify the lowest degree of Desire, and that which is next to none at all, when there is so little uneasiness in the absence of any thing, that it carries a Man no farther than some faint wishes for it, without any more effectual or vigorous use of the means to attain it.[80]

Thus from 1694 onward, Locke held that what motivates the will is not the prospect of pleasure but the presence of uneasiness (or mental pain). The change in his view took place as a result of a correspondence with William Molyneux in 1692, and it should now be apparent why in *Some Thoughts Concerning Education* Locke regarded curiosity and ambition as virtues and not, as he previously had done, as vices. Curiosity and ambition were now sources of uneasiness which motivate human beings to pursue knowledge and glory; these goods in themselves were, in Locke's new view, no longer capable of motivating human beings to action.[81] Locke explained his thinking very clearly by his account of the thought processes of someone who drinks too much:

> Let a Drunkard see, that his Health decays, his Estate wastes, Discredit and Diseases, and the want of all things, even of his beloved Drink, attends him in the course he follows; yet the returns of uneasiness to miss his Companions, the habitual thirst after his Cups at the usual time drives him to the Tavern, though he has in his view the loss of health and plenty, and perhaps of the joys of another life; the least of which is no inconsiderable good, but such as, he confesses, is far greater than the tickling of his palate with a glass of Wine, or the idle chat of a soaking Club. 'Tis not for want of viewing the greater good; for he sees, and acknowledges

it, and in the intervals of his drinking hours, will take resolutions to pursue the greater good; but when the uneasiness to miss his accustomed delight returns, the great acknowledged good loses its hold, and the present uneasiness determines the will to the accustomed action, which thereby gets stronger footing to prevail against the next occasion; though he at the same time makes secret promises to himself, that he will do so no more; this is the last time he will act against the attainment of those greater goods. And thus he is from time to time in the State of that unhappy complainer, *Video meliora proboque Deteriora sequor;* which sentence, allowed for true, and made good by constant Experience, may in this, and possibly no other way be easily made intelligible.[82]

Locke's shift in position meant that he no longer held that we seek pleasure and avoid pain; rather, we always try to relieve present uneasiness or mental pain. Human beings are, he now argued, primarily pain avoiders, not pleasure seekers: "Whilst we are under any uneasiness, we cannot apprehend our selves happy, or in the way to it; pain and uneasiness being, by every one, concluded, and felt, to be inconsistent with happiness, spoiling the relish even of those good things we have; a little pain serving to mar all the pleasure we rejoyced in. And therefore that, which of course determines the choice of our *will* to the next action, will always be the removing of pain, as long as we have any left, as the first and necessary step towards happiness."[83] It is important to see what Locke gained here, and what he lost. He gained an account of human behavior which recognized the reality of weakness of will; but he lost any ability to describe rational action as involving a trade-off between pleasures and pains. As far as Locke was now concerned pain, even the slightest pain, always trumps pleasure.

This has very remarkable consequences.* It means that happiness consists first and foremost in being free of pain. It seems to imply that if I am

---

* Locke's doctrine of uneasiness was developed by Benjamin Franklin to prove that there is no such thing as virtue or vice: "For since *Freedom from Uneasiness* is the End of all our Actions, how it is possible for us to do any Thing disinterested?—How can any Action be Meritorious of Praise or Dispraise, Reward or Punishment, when the natural Principle of *Self-Love* is the only and the irresistible Motive to it?" Benjamin Franklin, *A Dissertation on Liberty and Necessity, Pleasure and Pain* (London: s.n., 1725), 17. (Franklin later disowned this privately printed pamphlet.) The notion that moral action must be "disinterested" was a new one, a response to the claim that all human behavior is

concerned with the welfare of others I should always give priority to relieving any uneasiness they may feel—not only any physical pain, but also any anxiety—ahead of giving them pleasure or happiness. And that I should avoid any action which increases the happiness of several people if it makes any one person uneasy, because an increase in happiness, even for a majority, cannot outweigh an increase in uneasiness, even for one person.

But it also means that nagging, unfulfilled desire, what Locke calls "fantastical uneasiness (as itch after honour, power, or riches, &c.)" is needed if human beings are to escape from indolence. The itches after honor, power, or wealth are what he calls "irregular desires" inculcated by fashion, example, and education, which become natural to us through custom.[84] But these desires, which are irregular from the point of view of the individual because they create an unease that can rarely be satisfied, are regular from the point of view of the society because they encourage industry and other public goods. Consequently they are heavily reinforced by public opinion.

This is how curiosity and ambition come to be reclassified as virtues. If we refuse to reclassify these qualities as virtues, then we have to face up to Mandeville's paradox: private vices can have public benefits, while private virtues have public drawbacks. If we follow Locke and decide that these vices are really virtues, then we enter a Freudian world in which the social order depends on our acquiring anxieties that will always haunt us, itches that can never be soothed—at least not in this world. But this, too, is Mandeville's world, for Mandeville regards morality as an invention constructed to benefit society, an invention which, willy-nilly, we are trained to internalize and regard as natural. The later Locke and Mandeville fundamentally agree in their account of human motivation, even if they disagree as to the language to be used in describing it.

---

selfish. In the seventeenth century, "disinterested" normally meant impartial; for an early example of its use in opposition to psychological egoism, see "Whether any Love be without self interest," in Eusèbe Renaudot and Théophraste Renaudot, *A General Collection of Discourses of the Virtuosi of France, Upon Questions of All Sorts of Philosophy, and Other Natural Knowledg,* trans. G. Havers (London: Dring and Starkey, 1664), 74–77. For the French original, see Eusèbe Renaudot and Théophraste Renaudot, *Recueil général des questions traitées es conférences du bureau d'adresse, sur toutes sortes de matières; par les plus beaux esprits de ce temps* (Paris: Chamboudry, 1656), 210–219.

What I am suggesting is that in 1689 Locke's account of psychology and morality was a watered-down Hobbesianism, but by 1694 it was well on the way to being Mandevillian. A few years later, in 1711, Shaftesbury attacked Hobbes's philosophy as self-refuting: in advocating virtue, Hobbes was acting contrary to his own principles. But Shaftesbury's real target was his tutor, Locke, who in Shaftesbury's view had reduced morality to custom and convention, thus denying that there was such a thing as virtue at all.[85] Locke, I would argue, had also grasped a much more insidious paradox than either of these: in order to be happy as individuals we need society; and in order for society to flourish, we must constantly devise new ways of making ourselves uneasy and anxious. Thus Hume's private paradox—that he does philosophy in order to be happy, despite the fact that it keeps making him unhappy—turns into a more general paradox: the pursuit of happiness involves adopting values and ways of life which ensure that we never attain the very happiness that we seek. The means and the ends cannot be reconciled, and no Hobbesian sovereign can come to our rescue and force them into alignment. These clashes, between the individual and society, and between short-term and long-term outcomes, lie at the very heart of the Enlightenment paradigm, and will remain with us as long as we live in a world of scarcity, as long as wisdom lies in learning how to defer gratification until tomorrow—for, as we all know, tomorrow never comes.

PENSEES
DIVERSES,
Ecrites à un
DOCTEUR DE SORBONNE,

A l'occafion de la Cométe qui parut
au mois de Decembre 1680.

A ROTTERDAM,
Chez REINIER LEERS,
M. DC. LXXXIII.

Title page from Pierre Bayle, *Pensées Diverses* (12°) (1683).

5

Utility: In Place of Virtue

Bernard Le Bovier de Fontenelle began his 1724 essay on happiness by saying that everyone talks about happiness but no one thinks about it; despite the philosophers having discussed it at length, they have had nothing useful to say.[1] "This significant term," wrote Adam Ferguson in 1767, "the most frequent and the most familiar in our conversation, is . . . the least understood."[2] In 1773 Jean-François de Saint-Lambert introduced the posthumous edition of Helvétius's poem on happiness with the words, "Everybody aspires to happiness; but people don't reflect on happiness. They pursue it without ceasing; but they make little effort to learn how to acquire it."[3] In 1778 Guillaume Dubois de Rochefort described happiness as "a shadow that cannot be seized, a cloud that dissipates as soon as you look at it."[4] There is something about the subject which was and still remains resistant; "men are only unhappy because they are ignorant," wrote Paul Henri Thiry d'Holbach; "they are only ignorant because everything conspires to prevent them from acquiring enlightenment."[5] But the type of knowledge required for happiness was and still is difficult to identify.

I want to begin with Ferguson's remark that the term happiness is "the most frequent and the most familiar in our conversation." Ferguson was born in 1723, by which point the word "happiness" had become commonplace. The claim that it was "the most frequent and the most familiar" was, however, something of an exaggeration, at least in print if not in conversation—from 1660 to 1720 "happiness" and "virtue" were roughly equally frequent, but after 1720, when the incidence of "happiness" peaked (and briefly overtook "pleasure"), "virtue" overtook "happiness," and "happiness" slowly declined.[6] In French the word *bonheur* was ten times as frequent in 1760 as in 1620, and by the time of the French Revolution, when its incidence peaks at the same level as "happiness" had been at in England in 1720, it was almost as frequent as *vertu*, a word which was in

{ 115 }

steady decline from 1640 to 1740. Roughly speaking, England had a century when the use of the word "happiness" was on the rise, from 1620 to 1720, while in France there were two long secular upswings, from 1620 to 1700 and then again from 1740 to 1790.

There were two advantages of identifying happiness with pleasure, as nearly everyone did: first, it made the pursuit of pleasure an automatic mechanism, bringing human behavior within a mechanistic account of nature.[7] Thus Richard Cumberland's translator, John Maxwell, complained that "the Epicurean Scheme . . . makes the whole Man to be only a corporeal Engine."[8] (Of course, this isn't true of Epicurus or even of Hobbes, neither of whom had a mechanical philosophy; and it isn't an unmitigated benefit if, like the materialist followers of Locke, you want to retain some account of human free will.)[9]

Second, it enabled one to acknowledge that, since different people have different pleasures, there is no *summum bonum*—for Epicurus and Pierre Gassendi, tranquility had been the *summum bonum*. It is the subjective nature of pleasure that John Locke, like Thomas Hobbes, wanted to emphasize, that

the various and contrary choices, that Men make in the World, doe not argue, that they do not all chuse Good; but that the same thing is not good to every Man. . . .

§. 35. The Mind has a different relish, as well as the Palate; and you will as fruitlesly endeavour to delight all Men with Riches or Glory, (which yet some Men place their Happiness in,) as you would to satisfie all Men's Hunger with Cheese or Lobsters; which, though very agreeable and delicious fare to some, are to others extremely nauseous and offensive: And many People would with Reason prefer the griping of an hungry Belly, to those Dishes, which are a Feast to others. Hence it was, I think, that the Philosophers of old did in vain enquire, whether *Summum bonum* consisted in Riches, or bodily Delights, or Virtue, or Contemplation: And they might have as reasonably disputed, whether the best Relish were to be found in Apples, Plumbs, or Nuts; and have divided themselves into Sects upon it. For as pleasant Tastes depend not on the things themselves, but their agreeableness to this or that particular Palate, wherein there is great variety: So the greatest Happiness consists, in the having those things which produce the

greatest Pleasure, and the absence of those which cause any disturbance, any pain, which to different Men are very different things.[10]

Note that Locke makes no distinction between pleasure and happiness—
happiness is just reiterated pleasure. But he prefaces his remarks with a
caveat: "Were all the concerns of man terminated in this life." He goes on to
reinforce this restriction:

> If therefore Men in this Life only have hope; if in this Life they can only
> enjoy, 'tis not strange, nor unreasonable, they should seek their Happiness
> by avoiding all things that disease them here, and by preferring all that
> delight them; wherein it will be no wonder to find variety and difference.
> For if there be no Prospect beyond the Grave, the inference is certainly
> right, *Let us eat and drink,* let us enjoy what we delight in, *for to morrow
> we shall die.* This, I think, may serve to shew us the Reason, why, though
> all Men's Wills are determined by Good, yet they are not determined by
> the same Object. Men may chuse different things, and yet all chuse right.[11]

Locke is therefore very careful to fit his account of happiness within a
Christian framework; there is of course a *summum bonum,* which is salvation. You need to turn to authors such as François de La Rochefoucauld,
Bernard Mandeville, Voltaire, and Denis Diderot to have the same point
made without this restriction in favor of religious faith: "Every one places
his good where he can," says Voltaire, "and has as much of it as he can, in
his own way, and in very scanty measure. Castor loved horses; his twin
brother, wrestling."[12] That single word "scanty" conceals a whole argument, for it implies that, to paraphrase Mick Jagger and Keith Richards,
"We can't get no satisfaction"—an issue which doesn't arise if you think that
there will be endless happiness in heaven.

The first person after Hobbes to focus on the fact that pleasure is in short
supply was Pierre Bayle. In 1697 Bayle published his *Historical and Critical Dictionary,* a strange and peculiar beast. It was originally intended to
be a compendium of factual errors, but at his publisher's behest Bayle agreed
to make it more user-friendly by including philosophical discussions to supplement the lists of errors.[13] Still, few concessions were made to any user.

Articles you might expect to find—on Plato, for example, or Cicero, or René Descartes—simply aren't there, while long dissertations are devoted to the most obscure and insignificant figures. Nor can one ever quite predict where a particular topic will be discussed, although marginal cross-references sometimes help one find one's way. There is nothing so useful as a subject index; the first readers must have read here and there at random, so it may have been quite some time before anyone noticed, very near the end, the entry for Xenophanes.[14]

Bayle knew almost nothing about Xenophanes, but in the notes he took a remark by Meric Casaubon about Xenophanes as an excuse to discuss whether there is more good or evil in the world. He starts with moral good and evil and has little difficulty in showing that there is more evil than good; after all, most people are going to hell, and only a few will be saved. If God is engaged in a war with Satan, then it is evident that he is losing, not winning, that war. It follows that those who put their hope in heaven are betting against the odds and are likely to be disappointed. Having argued that the doctrine of divine omnipotence is at odds with the facts as reported by Christian believers, Bayle turns to physical good and evil, and he argues that evil generally outweighs good. His conclusion, which is also expounded in his article on the Manichees, is that if God is good, then the world is not fully in his control; there is evil at work in the world, and indeed evil has the upper hand.

Bayle's article on Xenophanes marks an important turning point in modern philosophy, for it led Gottfried Wilhelm Leibniz to invent the term "theodicy" in 1710.[15] Clearly if Bayle was right, God was—at least as far as human beings are concerned—either ill-willed or inadequate; Leibniz's reply was to attempt to prove that this is the best of all possible worlds. God has done everything that could be done to ensure our happiness, and thus he is neither evil nor inadequate.

Bayle's argument depended on a peculiar sort of mental arithmetic, for it required his readers to balance pains against pleasures. Pains are usually much more acute than pleasures, so a minute's pain can outweigh a week of pleasure: "If we had a Scale adapted to weigh both a Disease of 15 days, and the Health of 15 years, we should observe the same difference that we find in the Balance betwixt a Bag of Feathers and a piece of Lead." Thus "the good things of this life are a less Good than the evil things are an Evil," and this is true not just for physical pain and pleasure, but also for mental delight and mental distress.[16] (We have seen that Locke, too, had come to hold this view in the second edition of the *Essay Concerning Humane Understanding* in 1694; Bayle gave Locke's word "uneasiness" a more prominent place in the second edition of the *Dictionary,* but it was already present in the first.)[17]

In general, if they had the choice, human beings would not live their lives over again—an argument which implies that a rational person would prefer to end his life now rather than continue with it any longer. What matters in making such judgments is not the objective balance between good and evil, but our subjective experience. Bayle notes that "to make a Man pass for less happy than unhappy, it is sufficient that he is afflicted with three Evils for thirty Felicities which he enjoys, if those three Evils, as little in themselves as you please, give him more disturbance than thirty good things, as great in their own nature as you please, afford him Pleasure."[18]

Bayle is the inventor of the idea of a felicific or hedonic calculus.* Earlier theorists had assumed that everyone wanted to avoid pain and seek pleasure; but Bayle went further; he turned pleasure and pain into entries in an account book (William Wollaston actually referred to "the foot of the account," which we would call the bottom line) so that one can reach a final balance in which the relative proportions of pain to pleasure can be assessed.[19] We are to be deemed happy if the accounts show a profit, miserable if they show a loss.

With the felicific calculus came three presumptions which are not stated explicitly by Bayle but which are implicit in his account. We may call these presumptions the hedonic test, the hedonic obligation, and the duty/interest junction principle. The hedonic test is the claim that our only purpose in life is to experience happiness, and so a life is only worth living if it is pleasurable: this is the upshot of Bayle's "Xenophanes." The hedonic obligation is the claim that if someone is concerned about the welfare of others, that concern will show itself in an attempt to increase their happiness, and thus to make their life worth living. From this follows the principle of utility, that

---

* The term "hedonic calculus" apparently originates in 1878, and "felicific calculus" in 1918; neither term was used by Jeremy Bentham or John Stuart Mill, but there were equivalent terms: "moral arithmetic" and, in Cesare Beccaria's usage, "political arithmetic."

moral action consists in seeking the greatest happiness of the greatest number (or, in the alternative, egalitarian reformulation of Pietro Verri, the greatest happiness, distributed as equally as possible).* And finally, if our only purpose in life is to experience happiness, then the only circumstance in which we will be concerned about the welfare of others is one in which their interests and ours coincide—the duty / interest junction principle.

If the hedonic obligation and the duty / interest junction principle are implicit in Bayle, they had been explicit in Cumberland's *On the Laws of Nature* (1672), and it was presumably from Cumberland that they were adopted by John Gay.[20] Writing his "Preliminary Dissertation Concerning the Fundamental Principle of Virtue or Morality" in 1731 (shortly after the publication of Cumberland in English translation, a translation which included extensive notes drawn from Wollaston's *Religion of Nature*), Gay was able to define happiness or misery as the sum total of all our individual pleasures and pains, and to argue that only the prospect of happiness can create an obligation: "Obligation," he says, "is the necessity of doing or omitting any action in order to be happy."[21] (Compare Hobbes's account, in the Latin *Leviathan,* of a law of nature as obligating a person not to do "that which will seem to him to tend to his disadvantage.") Thus we must tot up pleasures and pains in order to establish whether or not we are obliged to act in a certain way.

Happiness was now not a distinct type of pleasure, but simply a surplus of pleasure over pain. Gay had entirely accepted the terms of discussion as established by Bayle and Wollaston. He assumed that God must intend the happiness of human beings, and that their happiness is to be identified with a surplus of pleasure. Gay argued from God's wish to ensure our happiness as a species to the individual's obligation to seek the happiness of his fellow human beings. We can be sure that God will reward those who seek the happiness of others, and society also has an interest in ensuring that making others happy is the best route to our own individual happiness. Thus we

---

* Pietro Verri, *Meditazioni sulla felicità* (s.l.: s.n., 1763), 17–18. The principle is not new in the Enlightenment. It is formulated by Ligurio in Niccolò Machiavelli's play *Mandragola*, act 3, scene 4: "io credo che quello sia bene che facci bene ai piú, e che i piú se ne contentino" (I believe that that is good which does good to the greater number, and which gives satisfaction to the greater number).

can have no goal other than private happiness; merit consists in taking an indirect route to our own happiness by way of the happiness of others.

This route is reinforced by the law of esteem, which rewards those who promote the happiness of others by raising their status in their community and punishes those who act to the detriment of others by lowering their status.[22] The very idea that public opinion functions as a sort of law, rewarding behavior of which it approves and punishing behavior of which it disapproves, was also an innovation of Pierre Bayle's, one that dates back to his *Diverse Thoughts on the Comet* of 1682—it's crucial to Bayle's argument that atheists are subject to effective restraints on their behavior even if they do not believe in heaven and hell.

Louis-Jean Levesque de Pouilly's *Theory of Agreeable Sentiments* (1747) is, like Leibniz's theodicy and Gay's "Preliminary Dissertation," a reply to Bayle: "The heart of every man, to use a Cartesian expression, is a sort of vortex, the center of whose motions is its own personal happiness." Those who sacrifice their lives for others gain such exquisite if brief pleasure from their actions that "it is very possible that these illustrious persons may have been more happy in their death, than they would have been had they enjoy'd life longer."[23] Thus Levesque de Pouilly accepts that we pursue our own happiness even when we do so by advancing the happiness of others. Moreover, he turns from psychology and morality to theodicy: he claims that God has constructed the universe in such a manner that our pleasures and pains are precisely those required to further our welfare. Here he is arguing against Bayle, who had claimed, surely rightly, that there is much more pain in the universe than can be strictly necessary. Adam Smith admired Levesque de Pouilly's book, and echoed his argument in the sixth edition of *The Theory of Moral Sentiments*, saying that nothing was more "sublime" than "the idea of that divine Being, whose benevolence and wisdom have, from all eternity, contrived and conducted the immense machine of the universe, so as at all times to produce the greatest possible quantity of happiness."[24] Smith thereby aligned himself with Leibniz against Bayle.

Two years after Levesque de Pouilly, Pierre-Louis Moreau de Maupertuis published an influential discussion of happiness; in 1772 Saint-Lambert thought Fontenelle and Maupertuis the only authors on the subject before

Claude Adrien Helvétius who were worth acknowledging.[25] It was presumably from Bayle (although he never mentions him) that Maupertuis got the key arguments of his essay on morality. Maupertuis argues that pleasures and pains should be assessed in terms of their intensity and duration. There is, he claims, a fundamental lack of symmetry between pleasure and pain: pleasures get weaker the longer they last, while pains become more intolerable. It is not surprising then that pain outweighs pleasure in the course of our lives; and that suicide would be an attractive option if we did not have the prospect of eternal happiness in the next life. Maupertuis's solution to the problem posed by Bayle is thus salvation: only a life after death can balance the hedonic accounts.[26] (You might think that this argument was already implicit in the argument of the second edition of Locke's *Essay,* which implies that we can never attain but can only pursue happiness.)

Thus the period between 1672 and 1776, when Jeremy Bentham published *A Fragment of Government,* saw the emergence of what we may call a proto-utilitarianism.[27] From the publication of Bayle's *Dictionary* onward this proto-utilitarianism was inseparably bound up with the theodicy question, and even those who argued against Bayle did so by accepting the terms of debate which he had established. When Cumberland's treatise was finally translated into English in 1727, it had to be brought up to date by introducing material which took account of the intellectual revolution brought about by Bayle: a discussion proving God's goodness was added, and so too was Wollaston's account of how we can add and subtract happiness as if we were balancing an account book. It's not coincidental that John Gay's "Preliminary Dissertation" of 1731 was first published as a preface to William King's *Essay on the Origin of Evil.* Three questions were now thought to be inseparable: Can we be happy? Does morality consist in making people happy? Is God good? In moral philosophy this period saw the formulation of the hedonic calculus and of the principle of utility, and in law and politics of the duty/interest junction principle.

Strikingly, for the most part these early proto-utilitarian debates did not address directly questions of government or legislation: it is the divine economy which was in question, not the difference between good government and bad. They discussed God's government of the universe, but not the government of the state; the law of esteem, but not actual legislation.

Cumberland, writing after Hobbes but before Bayle, was a partial exception among these thinkers. Cumberland was clear that the sole purpose of government is to enable people to be happy, but he preached passive obedience, and denied that the people had any right of resistance against a government which oppressed them. He thus stopped well short of making the legitimacy of government depend on its success in fostering the happiness of its subjects.

Bayle's theodicy problem, and its associated question of whether life is on balance happy or miserable, continued to be of considerable importance later in the century. It runs through Voltaire's *Candide* (1759), where Martin is Bayle's spokesperson and Pangloss is Leibniz's.[28] And it explains the peculiar way in which Voltaire raises the issue of suffering in his essay on happiness ("Heureux") for Denis Diderot and Jean le Rond d'Alembert's *Encyclopédie* (1765). The issue is one which he says he doesn't want to discuss, but which he wants his reader to think about. Voltaire evidently wanted us to think about the fact that to a considerable degree our happiness is outside our control because it depends on our temperament; moreover, some are simply doomed to misery: "There are dogs that we caress, comb, and feed with biscuits, and to which we give pretty females: there are others which are covered with the mange, which die of hunger; others which we chase and beat, and which a young surgeon then slowly dissects, after having driven four great nails into their paws. Are these poor dogs responsible for whether they are *happy* or *unhappy?*"[29]

Voltaire is thus still debating the question raised by Bayle: Would a benevolent deity have made a universe like this? This question is addressed directly in his essays "All Is Well" (1764) for the *Portable Philosophical Dictionary* and in the posthumous "Of Good and Evil, Physical and Moral" from *L'opinion en alphabet,* where he argues that God is no more concerned with our suffering than he is with that of a dove torn in pieces and eaten while still alive by a falcon.[30] But Voltaire's continuing preoccupation with evil was a little old-fashioned, and not unconnected to his own experience of life; the atheists such as d'Holbach and Diderot on the one hand, and the advocates of theism or deism, such as Leibniz, Jean-Jacques Rousseau, and Smith on the other, were generally agreed that there was plenty of happiness available to human beings, if they only knew where to look for it. Saint-Lambert mocked Maupertuis for thinking that happiness was in short supply; he was, he tells us, simply miserable because he did not get the recognition he thought he deserved.[31] A key question was whether as-yet-unfulfilled desires should be regarded as painful or pleasurable: Maupertuis held them to be painful, while Verri (like Hume) thought that hope was a source of endless pleasures—pleasures no less real for being imaginary.[32]

The chief voice raised against the developing consensus that pleasure and happiness are the same thing was that of Adam Ferguson, whose *Essay on the History of Civil Society* appeared in 1767. Ferguson, who had been chaplain to the Black Watch, a famous Scottish regiment, and had experience of battle, insisted that one could be happy even though one experienced far more pains than pleasures; indeed this is the situation in which most people find themselves. Happiness, he argues, lies in striving, not in succeeding. One can enjoy the hunt even if the deer escapes and one returns home, cold, hungry, and exhausted, with nothing to show for one's efforts: "What we call pleasure or pain occupies but a small part of human life, compared to what passes in contrivance and execution, in pursuits and expectations, in conduct, reflection, and social engagements." Happiness is "to be found only in the qualities of the heart," not in a series of sensations; and we make a fundamental mistake when we think that success is what we are after, when it is the enterprise itself which offers us the prospect of happiness. Above all, Ferguson speaks for a warrior ethos: happiness requires courage: "courage, and a heart devoted to the good of mankind, are the constituents of human felicity."[33]

Moreover, Ferguson complained that the developing consensus was fundamentally individualistic and placed human beings in competition with each other for success, wealth, and pleasure.* "In pursuit of happiness," he writes, "we engage in those scenes of emulation, envy, hatred, animosity, and revenge, that lead us to the highest pitch of distress." We are made, rather, to live in a community, and we are happiest when helping others. Modern individualism is a great source of unhappiness: "To the ancient Greek, or

---

* On his tomb at St. Andrews, Ferguson's children claimed that he was "unseduced by the temptations of pleasure, power, or ambition"—in other words, he carefully avoided the competitive and insatiable appetites.

the Roman, the individual was nothing, and the public every thing. To the modern, in too many nations of Europe, the individual is every thing, and the public nothing."[34]

Ferguson believed that the interests of the individual and of society are easily reconciled, but it is not through the duty / interest junction principle; rather, it is in the discovery that true happiness is to be found in engaging one's heart to the community, and by making strenuous efforts to exercise one's talents and virtues. The greatest source of unhappiness, in this scheme of things, is idleness, which leads to ennui. The great general Ambrogio Spinola, Ferguson tells us, was told that Francis Vere had died of having nothing to do. "That was enough," he said, "to kill a general." But it is not just generals who die of enforced idleness, Ferguson assures us, but also sailors and politicians: "Such men do not chuse pain as preferable to pleasure, but they are incited by a restless disposition to make continued exertions of capacity and resolution; they triumph in the midst of their struggles; they droop, and they languish, when the occasion of their labour has ceased."[35]

At this point we find ourselves turning from the question of private happiness to the question of public happiness: the two have been inextricably linked in Ferguson's insistence that true happiness is to be found in public service. In English the phrase "public happiness" was rare until Charles I introduced it into political debate early in 1642.[36] In 1601, John Croke, the Speaker of the House of Commons, said, "If a question should be asked, What is the first and chief thing in a Commonwealth to be regarded? I should say, religion. If, What is the second? I should say, religion. If, What the third? I should still say, religion."[37] Croke was on safe ground: no one listening would have dared disagree with such admirable sentiments. In his world, piety was bound to be more important than happiness.

And of course such a value system is unquestionably true if you accept a certain number of elementary propositions: if you believe that the salvation of a human being's soul is their most important concern; if you believe that the church and the political community are one corporate body; and if you believe that God rewards faithful and God-fearing communities and punishes those who stray from the truth. In 1601 these propositions were accepted (with some modest variations between Catholic and Protestant states) by every state in Europe. Charles I would certainly not have wanted to argue that one could have public happiness without true religion, and these propositions still provided a rationale for the expulsion of the Huguenots from France in 1685. Thus we find the future archbishop of Canterbury, John Tillotson, arguing in a sermon published in 1671, that "it concerns every one to live in the Practise of Religion and Virtue; Because the publick happiness and prosperity depends upon it."[38]

In England the founding texts for an alternative viewpoint are those of Benjamin Hoadly, later bishop of Winchester, who went on to provoke the Bangorian Controversy in 1717 (so named because at the time Hoadly was the bishop of Bangor) through his radical reinterpretation of the biblical verse "My kingdom is not of this world" (John 18:36). As early as 1705 Hoadly was arguing that the end of government is "the public Happiness of Mankind" (without any reference, even implicit, to the practice of religion and virtue—in this respect he went well beyond Cumberland), and that governments that failed to serve this end could be resisted; and he repeated this argument over and over again throughout his long and distinguished career.[39] By the time Adam Smith came to publish *The Theory of Moral Sentiments,* the view that the sole purpose of government was to promote the public happiness had come to seem entirely uncontroversial: "All constitutions of government," Smith writes, "are valued only in proportion, as they tend to promote the happiness of those who live under them. This is their sole use and end."[40]

In Italian the key text in this shift from theodicy to politics was Lodovico Muratori's *Della pubblica felicità oggetto de' buoni principi* (1749); in French it was the Genevan Jean-Jacques Burlamaqui's *Principles of Politic Law,* which was first published in 1751 and rapidly went through numerous editions and translations; Burlamaqui, in emphasizing happiness, was surely influenced by Cumberland, who had been published in a French translation by Jean Barbeyrac in 1744, but, unlike Cumberland, Burlamaqui recognized a right of resistance.[41] It is Burlamaqui's influence we see in Louis de Jaucourt's 1757 entry under "Gouvernement" in the *Encyclopédie* of Diderot and d'Alembert: "The best of governments is that which makes the greatest number of people happy. No matter what the form of the government is, the duty of whoever is in charge of it, no matter what the nature of their authority is, is to work to make their subjects happy, in procuring for them on one hand the conveniences of life, security and tranquility; and on the other all the means which might contribute to making them virtuous."[42] Even for Jaucourt, then, the government is obliged to make its subjects virtuous, but this is simply an aspect of the greater goal of making them happy. The purpose of government is not the salvation of souls but the happiness of all the members of the society—what Diderot called *l'utilité générale*.[43]

A year later Helvétius published *De l'esprit* in which he argued that virtue consists in seeking to bring about the happiness of others, and restated the greatest happiness principle as the foundation of all morality. But now existing governments came under direct fire for failing to make their subjects happy, and the result was a cultural crisis: Helvétius himself came under sustained attack, but so too did the Encyclopédistes, who were known to share many of his views.

Thus the foundations of a coherent utilitarianism were laid: moral action and good government both aim at the same end, that of making people happy; where government is well-conducted, the pursuit of personal happiness and of public happiness will coincide so that virtue and self-interest will be one and the same thing. Burlamaqui inspired the Encyclopédistes; they inspired Helvétius; Helvétius inspired Cesare Beccaria; and Beccaria inspired Bentham.

"Happiness is a new idea in Europe," said the Jacobin leader Louis-Antoine-Léon Saint-Just, speaking on behalf of the Committee of Public Safety to the National Convention in 1794.[44] But happiness certainly wasn't a new idea. There are three ways of interpreting Saint-Just's highly condensed statement—all, I suspect, correct. First, happiness was a fundamentally new idea, since, in France at least, its key role in political theory had only been explicit since 1751. Second, happiness was a new idea *in Europe:* the American Declaration of Independence had declared there was a right to pursue happiness. Only now was Europe catching up with America. And, third, what was new in 1794 was the idea that one could make a nation happy by confiscating the wealth of counterrevolutionaries and redistributing it to deserving patriots: happiness had become the official goal of a bloody revolution.

Saint-Just was a much more helpful guide in another speech he made ten days later. There he distinguished between two ideas of public happiness: the revolutionary idea, which stressed virtue and hard work, and the aristocratic idea, which was based on living off the surplus product. The happiness the revolution offers, he said, is not that of Persepolis but that of Sparta.[45] Thus, for Saint-Just there were two competing ideas of public happiness, one synonymous with frugality and the other with luxury, one revolutionary and the other (seen from the perspective of the Terror) counter-revolutionary. Both ideas were already present in Jaucourt's brief article for the *Encyclopédie*—on the one hand virtue, on the other the conveniences of life.

The classic presentations of the first idea are to be found in Rousseau and in Helvétius. Helvétius believed that interest rules all human conduct, all intellectual life, and all social structures. Moral reform thus requires a transformation in social and political structures in order to reorientate people's interests; and the vices we complain about now ought to be interpreted not as vices but as functional modes of behavior within a corrupt political and social system: "The vices and the virtues of a people are always a necessary consequence of their legislation."[46] So for Helvétius questions of moral philosophy were inseparable from questions of political philosophy, and any attempt to improve people's behavior must develop into a struggle to bring about a revolutionary transformation in social and political structures. Where previous theorists had been primarily concerned with the happiness of individuals, Helvétius's primary concern was the happiness of whole societies.

Helvétius propounded a systematic egalitarianism: differences in intellectual and physical capacity are, he held, the result of environmental factors, not of any difference in underlying nature between human beings. Helvétius's goal was the destruction of despotism (like Montesquieu, he pretended to be writing about oriental despotism, but expected everyone to understand—and indeed everyone except the lazy censor who approved his book for publication did understand—that he was writing about the French monarchy), for in despotic societies the interests of the individual and the community never coincide; despotic societies may be tranquil but they are never happy; and his admiration was reserved for those societies, such as Sparta, which have been characterized by poverty not wealth, and where the interests of the individual have been aligned with those of the society as a whole.[47]

Courage is only to be found in poor nations, never in rich ones. And it is poor, virtuous, warrior nations which are the happiest: although the most virtuous individuals aren't necessarily the happiest, the most virtuous nations inevitably are. (It is evident that Helvétius admired many of the qualities later admired by Ferguson, but Ferguson could not accept that those qualities could best be defended by arguing from utilitarian premises.)

It is a small step from Helvétius to Beccaria's *On Crimes and Punishments* (1764). Beccaria rigorously applied Helvétius's egalitarian principles, insisting that there should be the same punishments for lords and peasants, generals and grunts. He regarded the art of punishment as lying in the infliction of the minimum of pain required to alter people's behavior, and the goal of legislation as being the creation of a society which is as happy as is possible. Implicitly, Beccaria's new legislative order required a new political order, in just the same way that Helvétius's new moral philosophy required a new political order.

The alternative view to that of Helvétius was presented by the Marquis de Chastellux in *On Public Happiness* (1772).[48] Chastellux was a friend of Voltaire, and like Voltaire he was prepared to defend prosperity and even luxury. He argued that there were two ways of measuring public happiness. First, imagine a one-crop economy. Then happiness depends on how far agriculture is capable of producing more than is needed to reproduce those who work in agriculture. This surplus can take the form of luxuries or of leisure; either way, it represents the material basis of happiness. Of course, by imagining a one-crop, cashless economy, and by ignoring the question of property in land, Chastellux carefully avoided having to discuss the relationship between landlord and tenant, employer and employee, town and country. His model society is one of peasant proprietors, yet the surplus they produce is potentially the basis for social differentiation and exploitation, as well as for leisure and luxury. But one will look in vain in Chastellux for any hint of what Karl Marx will do with the idea of a surplus.[49] His ideal society is England, where agricultural labor is highly productive and where the laborers have a high standard of living—high enough, he says, to make their lives happy (or rather, remarked Voltaire in a marginal note in his copy of the text, tolerable).[50]

Chastellux's second objective measure of happiness is population growth, which will only take place where there is a surplus produced beyond what is necessary to reproduce the existing population. In essence, Chastellux identified happiness with the standard of living: an improvement in the standard of living, or a voluntary decision to forgo such an improvement in order to have more leisure, must generally correlate with an increase in happiness.[51]

Of course, Chastellux's central problem was that he had no way of measuring standards of living over time. But he was confident that there could be little aggregate happiness in societies founded on slavery, and he criticized all those who praised Sparta by pointing to the horrendous mistreatment of the helot population. War was inevitably destructive of happiness (despite what Helvétius had said), but Chastellux hoped that warfare was becoming less destructive and less frequent over time, and he felt sure that modern history was the history of a major improvement in standards of living and in happiness.

Thus Chastellux, who advocated economic growth and approved of luxury, and Helvétius, who advocated the military virtues and admired frugality, stand for two different moral, social, and political aspirations. It is important to note that Chastellux was concerned with the standard of living of the population as a whole, and nowhere supported gross inequality or economic exploitation, but Saint-Just was right: there was a fundamental choice to be made between Voltaire and Rousseau, Chastellux and Helvétius, Georges Danton and Maximilien de Robespierre.

The evolution in the concept of happiness that we have tracked so far has thus been from theodicy to politics, from private to public, from morality to economics. Saint-Lambert, in his introduction to Helvétius's poem on happiness, does not only complain about Maupertuis's inability to have fun; he also complains that Fontenelle's essay on happiness tells us what makes Fontenelle happy, but tells us nothing about how to spread happiness more generally through society.[52] But there were two distinct answers to the question of how to spread happiness more widely: either revolution or economic growth.

I want to leave the insoluble question of public happiness there, and end this chapter by turning back in time to the "Discourse on Happiness" written by Émilie du Châtelet. Du Châtelet, who translated and wrote a commentary on Isaac Newton's *Principia* and translated Mandeville, probably began the essay in the 1730s, when she and Voltaire were a couple, and ended it in

1748.[53] It was a gift for her lover, Jean-Francois de Saint-Lambert, who years later would write the introduction to Helvétius's poem on happiness. Du Châtelet followed the majority in holding that "there is nothing more to do in this life than to procure for ourselves agreeable sentiments and sensations" and in rejecting the classical insistence on self-control (which was, in effect, a euphemism for virtue): "The moralists who say to men, curb your passions and master your desires if you want to be happy, do not know the route to happiness." As for Bayle's insistence that there is more unhappiness than happiness in life, she replied that she did not have an instrument with which to weigh happiness, but she knew unhappiness draws attention to itself while happiness is usually concealed and private. She was unique in insisting that we owe most of our happiness not just to our hopes, but to our illusions: "Far then, from seeking to make them disappear by the torch of reason, let us try to thicken the varnish that illusion lays on the majority of objects." Illusion is "involved in all the pleasures of our life, and provides the polish, the gloss of life."[54]

Du Châtelet wrote only for a narrow group—people of quality, those who were born with a fortune already made (even Voltaire could not be counted among such people) and who were prepared to respect all the social proprieties—which would certainly exclude a Diderot or a Rousseau. Most important, of course, was that she wrote from her experience as a woman. And so the one passion she rejected above all others was ambition, not because it can never be satisfied, but because it makes us dependent on others: "If we value independence, the love of study is, of all the passions, the one that contributes most to our happiness. This love of study holds within it a passion from which a superior soul is never entirely exempt, that of glory. For half the world [i.e., for women], glory can only be obtained in this manner, and it is precisely this half whose education [has] made glory inaccessible, and [has] made a taste for it impossible." And she went on, "Undeniably, the love of study is much less necessary to the happiness of men than it is to that of women. Men have infinite resources for their happiness that women lack." In the case of men, it turns out, ambition is not always unsatisfied. "But women are excluded, by definition, from every kind of glory, and when, by chance, one is born with a rather superior soul, only study remains to console her for all the exclusions and all the dependencies to which she finds herself condemned by her place in society."

And yet the key to happiness is to pay no attention to such exclusions: "one must allow oneself to desire only the things that can be obtained without too much care and effort . . . the happiest man is he who least desires to change his rank and circumstances"; having said which, she immediately turned to praise the pleasures of gambling for high stakes, which offered the exciting prospect of a radical change in circumstances, whether for better or for worse.[55] In her own case, her vast losses at the table led to her expulsion from court in 1747 and Voltaire's with her, for he had rashly muttered that she was playing with cheats.[56]

It is easy to see how the contradictions of her position as a brilliant, ambitious woman are played out in du Châtelet's text. It would be easy to think, then, that her views on happiness are no longer ours. But she speaks for the future, not the past, when she says, "I have said that the more our happiness depends on us, the more assured it is; yet the passion that can give us the greatest pleasures and make us happiest, places our happiness entirely in the hands of others. You have already gathered that I am speaking of love. This passion is perhaps the only one that can make us wish to live, and bring us to thank the author of nature, whoever he is, for giving us life." And by love she means sexual intimacy; she has known close friendship, and (unlike Michel de Montaigne, for example) she rejects it as too peaceful and too weak: "Only lively and agreeable feelings make one happy; why then forbid oneself love, the most lively and most agreeable of all?"[57] Plenty of previous authors had described what it was like to be in love; and we have seen that Kenelm Digby already thought that love was the true source of happiness. The claim was soon to become commonplace.

Keith Thomas's Ford Lectures entitled *The Ends of Life* begin with a chapter on "Fulfilment in an Age of Limited Possibilities"—note the stress on the word "Limited."[58] His book has a good deal to say about friendship, though almost nothing about love or even happiness. His emphases are the right ones if you want to understand early modern society, and in writing a book about power, pleasure, and profit, those three unlimited aspirations, I know I am going against the grain of early modern life as most people experienced it almost all the time, for most people had little power, little experience of happiness, and no prospect of prosperity. But for the intellectuals of the eighteenth century this began to look like an indictment of contemporary society; if God had created human beings so that they might be happy, why was happiness in such short supply?

The resulting tension between the limited and the unlimited is perfectly expressed in du Châtelet's text. She insists, as she was bound to, that happiness lies in reconciling oneself to the limited possibilities of one's station in life. But she also admits that she longs for glory, that she dreams of "the plaudits of posterity, from which one expects more justice than from one's contemporaries." She insists that happiness lies in independence, but she resolves to entrust herself to love, even though she expects no happy ending. Du Châtelet's views on the ends of life are not consistent or coherent; but I happen to think that she understood happiness—its contradictions and its possibilities—far better than Fontenelle or Maupertuis, Beccaria or Bentham.

This chapter was originally a lecture given in an Oxford University building called The Examination Schools. This magnificent building, completed in 1882, is contemporary with the foundation of the first women's colleges at Oxford (1879, 1886). Du Châtelet wrote in a draft of her preface to Mandeville (ca. 1738), "If I were king I would establish colleges for women."[59] (Under the Salic Law, France could only be ruled by a man, so there was no point in du Châtelet asking what she would do if she were queen.) In imagining a society in which women could have ambitions just like men, she looked to the future.

A

D E F E N C E

OF THE

CONSTITUTIONS OF GOVERNMENT

OF THE

UNITED STATES OF AMERICA.

By JOHN ADAMS, LL.D.

AND A MEMBER OF THE ACADEMY OF ARTS AND SCIENCES
AT BOSTON.

All nature's difference keeps all nature's peace.   POPE.

L O N D O N:

PRINTED FOR C. DILLY, IN THE POULTRY

M.DCC.LXXXVII.

Title page from John Adams, *A Defence of the Constitutions of Government of the United States of America* (8°) (1787).

6

The State: Checks and Balances

The state matters. It fights wars. It collects taxes. It puts people in prison. It provides welfare. It regulates, manages, controls, and punishes. It speaks for us, to us, and about us. Does the state make you feel secure, or does it scare you? Do you love it or hate it? Does your government make you feel proud or ashamed? Do you feel that it represents you and your concerns? Your answers to these questions may change depending on who is in power, but they also depend on whether you think of the state as benevolent or hostile. This isn't just a left/right issue, since many anarchists and libertarians agree in their dislike of the modern state. What no one can doubt is that the role of the state has grown and grown, and, despite strenuous efforts to reverse the trend, shows little sign of diminishing. According to the Organisation for Economic Co-operation and Development, 18 percent of all employees in the United States are in the public sector, compared to 22 percent in Canada and the United Kingdom, and 36 percent in Norway.[1]

The truth, though, is that most of us hardly think about the state at all. Like the blind men and the elephant, we concentrate our attention on bits of the whole, and have no sense of how the bits fit together to make one vast creature. Sometimes it seems almost indecent, a tinge paranoid, to suggest there is such a thing as the state. After all what does the National Health Service or Obamacare have to do with the police, or primary school education with customs and excise, or immigration with bridge building? And within a federalist system there is not one state, but many—not only the different states of the confederation, with their taxes, courts and prisons, but federal, state, county and municipal police forces, so that instead of there being one unified state there are lots of states and statelets. It's because we don't see the state as a whole that it manages to grow even when we think it's shrinking: under Margaret Thatcher taxation as a proportion of gross domestic product (GDP) did not fall, it rose; and in the U.S. government debt has risen, not fallen, under the last four Republican presidents.

This elephantine state is very largely the creation of the eighteenth century, although it had been pioneered on a smaller scale by the seventeenth-century Dutch: in Great Britain, national debt went from 0 to 250 percent of GDP between 1690 and 1820 (compare the present figures of 82 percent in the United Kingdom and 104 percent in the United States).[2] In 1764 David Hume wrote, "We have always found, where a government has mortgaged all its revenues, that it necessarily sinks into a state of languor, inactivity, and impotence." A few years later, when the debt-to-GDP ratio was 150 percent, that fate seemed to be fast approaching; as Hume noted, "It will be found in the present year, 1776, that all the revenues of this island, north of Trent and west of Reading, are mortgaged or anticipated forever."[3] In order to service the debt, government revenues increased ten times between 1715 and 1815 (or roughly five times, allowing for inflation).[4] The army increased in size by a factor of seven; average annual expenditure on the army and navy in wartime nearly tripled between the War of the Spanish Succession and the American War of Independence.[5] As a percent of GDP, government revenue went from 10 percent to (in the first decades of the nineteenth century) 20 percent—above the level of Portugal or Japan in 1965, or the United States in 2000, and much higher than the level in the United Kingdom in the decades before the First World War.[6]

Debt and taxation on this scale made the survival of the political system entirely dependent on commercial prosperity and the economy entirely dependent on the state's ability to service its debts; debts and taxes played a key role in binding state to nation and nation to state, in creating that peculiar amalgam, the nation-state. Nations aren't just, in the famous phrase, imagined communities, they are also (or they were, before the globalization of financial networks in recent years) networks of economic interdependence.[7]

Eighteenth-century Britain thus followed the Dutch republic in becoming a society in which the interests of the state and of the nation had become inseparably intertwined through a national debt which could only be serviced through high levels of taxation, and which could not be repudiated because if the nation was the debtor, the citizens were the creditors—the left hand was lending to the right hand.[8] It is at this point, when for the first time they began to aspire to draw upon the whole resources of the nation, that governments began to worry about national prosperity and economic growth. Gregory King, in 1696, set out to calculate the economic wealth of the nation in order to assess its capacity to bear taxes and fund the war against France. He went so far as to estimate the total population of rabbits, hares, and wildfowl—now to be thought of not just as wild creatures or as game, but as much a part of the national wealth as cows or sheep.[9]

This transformation of the state was accompanied, naturally, by a transformation in ways of thinking about the state and how to curb its power. At this point I want to make an important distinction, because this chapter is concerned with what we *might* call metaphors—metaphors which compare the state to a machine, for example, or to the solar system. I want, therefore, to start by saying that the word "metaphor" is an obstacle to thinking about this subject. If I talk about a grassroots political movement, "grassroots" is a metaphor or a turn of speech, and nothing more than that. What we are concerned with here are analogies that are tools for thinking, analogies that are conceptual machines.

Thus, social Darwinism takes a set of conceptual tools from Darwinism, such as survival of the fittest, or adaptation, and applies them in a new context. Such tools sometimes work in the new context, and sometimes they don't—sometimes their claims to provide new insight are fraudulent. But in principle they work (or fail to work) in two distinct ways: first, they provide new interpretations of what is actually going on; and second, they foster certain types of behavior. Take, for example, the idea, to which we will return in Chapter 7, that money and goods circulate through the economy: "circulation" here is a metaphor, but it makes possible a new understanding of how the economy (as we call it) functions. Moreover, once you have the concept of circulation it is clear that the speed at which goods circulate is crucial. If there is one annual autumn harvest for grain, then it takes up to a year for that grain to be distributed to its final consumer, and up to a year for the revenue from it to be realized by its final vendor. But a glove maker can buy leather, make gloves, sell them, and buy more leather in the course of a week; moreover, if he buys his leather on credit he can buy more leather before he has yet sold the gloves made with the previous lot of leather. Credit can thus speed up circulation, which makes possible increased production. This changes the whole understanding of the role of debt: debt (previously, as we have seen identified with sin) can, it turns out, be a good thing, for it can help to expand the economy in just the same way that an influx of gold or silver would result in increased economic activity. Thus a new conceptual tool, the idea of circulation, leads to a new analysis of how the economy works, and this in turn fosters different behaviors on the part of both creditors and debtors. The idea of circulation in part results from a new, commercialized economic order; but it also plays a role in creating that new order.[10]

⦿⦿⦿

In this chapter I am concerned with the application of mechanical conceptual tools to politics in the eighteenth century. What made this application seem viable was the notion that politics could, to quote David Hume, be reduced to a science—that competing interests in a political system could be compared to competing forces in a mechanical system, and that different arrangements of interests would have predictable results, just as different mechanical systems work in predictable ways.[11] This particular application of a scientific model to politics took place within a larger project of constructing new human sciences. The subtitle of David Hume's *Treatise of Human Nature* (1738), for example, was *An Attempt to Introduce the Experimental Method of Reasoning Into Moral Subjects.* Most of the time when he applies this method (and "experimental" here means using history and other types of experience as a laboratory for constructing, testing, and revising theories) he doesn't use mechanical conceptual tools, but these tools are particularly prominent when he and his contemporaries come to think about politics.

Before I go any further it would be helpful to distinguished three types of machine. First, there are machines like clocks, whose moving parts push and pull on each other through direct contact. These machines began to be thought of as particularly important for understanding nature in the seventeenth century with the rise of the mechanical philosophy, and having been used as paradigms for the interpretation of nature they naturally became paradigms for the interpretation of social institutions.[12] Thus John Adams wrote to James Sullivan in 1776, "Upon my Word, sir, I have long thought an Army, a Piece of Clock Work and to be governed only by Principles and Maxims, as fixed as any in Mechanicks, and by all that I have read

{ 138 }

in the History of Mankind, and in Authors, who have Speculated upon Society and Government, I am much inclined to think, a Government must manage a Society in the Same manner; and that this is Machinery too."[13] And he goes on to give as an example of the working of this machinery the Harringtonian principle that power always follows property.

Second, and my order here is chronological, there comes the Newtonian account of the forces at work in the solar system (the centripetal force of inertia counteracted by the centrifugal force of gravity) and in collisions between bodies. The solar system is not a mechanical system in the sense that a watch is; but we call Newton's theories "classical mechanics," so we need to be aware here of an ambiguity of terminology. It has often been said that the eighteenth-century developed a Newtonian theory of politics. Thus Montesquieu says of monarchy, "It is with this kind of government as with the system of the universe, in which there is a power that constantly repels all bodies from the centre, and a power of gravitation that attracts them to it. Honor sets all the parts of the body politic in motion; by its very action it connects them, and thus each individual advances the public good, while he only thinks of promoting his own particular interest." This is an invisible hand argument.[14] And at the federal convention to write the U.S. Constitution, John Dickinson "compared the proposed National System to the Solar System, in which the States were the planets, and ought to be left to move freely in their proper orbits." James Madison replied that the reverse was true: that "to recur to the illustrations borrowed from the planetary System, This prerogative of the General Govt. is the great pervading principle that must controul the centrifugal tendency of the States; which, without it, will continually fly out of their proper orbits and destroy the order and harmony of the political system."[15]

Third, there are machines that involve feedback mechanisms, machines which are in some sense self-regulating or self-governing. There were few such machines in the eighteenth century—two striking examples are the fantail windmill, invented in 1745, and the centrifugal governor, invented by James Watt in 1788. Crucially, in the third quarter of the eighteenth century a series of theorists began to identify self-equilibrating mechanisms in the economy, and it was therefore natural to begin to look for such mechanisms, which we might call imaginary machines, in political systems as well. (Adam Smith, as we will see in Chapter 7, described theoretical systems as "imaginary machines.")[16] Hume invented the modern theory of the balance of trade in 1752; in 1741 he had written of English politics as involving the nation "fluctuating" between support for government and opposition, implying perhaps a self-correcting mechanism.[17] Next, Anne-Robert-Jacques Turgot developed a sophisticated account of the way in which markets establish an equilibrium between prices, wages, profits, interest rates, and other factors. Thus, he wrote in a letter to Hume in 1767, "if we increase one of the weights [if wages go up, for example], it is inevitable that there will result a movement in the entire machine which will tend to re-establish the former balance."[18] And Smith provided the classic formulation of what we now call the market mechanism (he does not use the word "mechanism" himself—the term "market mechanism" dates to 1918—but he would have acknowledged that the market was an imaginary machine) in *The Wealth of Nations* (1776). The whole point of the market mechanism is not that it is a machine but that it is self-regulating or self-stabilizing—that it is a feedback system. Modern economics, as much as modern natural science, is thus dependent on a new understanding of the possibilities of physical systems, though imaginary machines need not abide by identifiable physical principles; indeed gravity, as theorized by Newton, was purely fictional in that no known mechanical system could replicate its working.

These three very different types of machine—the clock, the Newtonian solar system, the fantail windmill—provide three very different conceptual tools for political analysis and for constitutional reform. And, in line with what I said earlier, I would claim that they not only result in different interpretations of what is going on in political systems but also modify the behavior and goals of politicians.

Benjamin Constant pointed out in 1816 that the Greeks and Romans had no conception of freedom from the state, which he thought the peculiar marker of modern liberty.[19] The English Civil War was fought to curb the power of the state, at that time identified with the monarchy. In the early years of the eighteenth century the emphasis was still on curbing the power of the executive; this had still been a major concern in the standing army debates at the very end of the seventeenth century; it was indeed still Tom

Paine's concern in *Common Sense,* the text that more than any other inspired the American Revolution.

But as debt and taxation rose, the key issue for many became limiting the power not of the executive but of the legislature. Notoriously, Hume approved of Robert Walpole's policy of buying votes in the commons by distributing government pensions, since it helped redress the growing imbalance between legislature and executive; in Hume's view it was the executive that now needed protecting from an overweening legislature, and, following on from the arguments of Hume and Jean-Louis de Lolme, this was a central concern of the authors of the American Constitution.[20]

Thus it was not until the eighteenth century that the idea took hold that we need to be protected not just from the executive but also, and more urgently, from our own representatives, and indeed even from ourselves. John Adams coined the phrase "the tyranny of the majority" in 1788; that same year James Madison wrote, "Had every Athenian citizen been a Socrates, every Athenian assembly would still have been a mob."[21] In the United Kingdom this way of thinking still seems a little peculiar, for it stands in direct opposition to the sacred doctrine of the sovereignty of Parliament, by which is normally meant the sovereignty of the elected chamber. Much of *our* political thinking is, I fear, still stuck in the seventeenth century.

In the United Kingdom we do not talk much about the British Constitution, even though the concept of a "constitution" is, as we shall see in Chapter 7, an English invention. In recent years historians of political thought from Britain and the Commonwealth have had little to say about the history of constitutional theorizing. The situation is quite different in the United States, where every educated person knows about the Founding Fathers, everyone reads the *Federalist Papers,* or at the very least *Federalist Nos. 10* and *51,* and everyone knows that the principle of the separation of powers goes back to Montesquieu. More sophisticated people know that the major intellectual source for the *Federalist Papers* is David Hume.[22] In the United Kingdom, by contrast, we often seem to forget that we have a constitution at all, because we have come to think of the prime minister, the cabinet, and the House of Commons (which embody "the close union, the nearly complete fusion of the executive and legislative powers") as the efficient part of the constitution (to use Walter Bagehot's terminology), the rest being largely window dressing.[23] Very few people actually read Hume,

Montesquieu, or the *Federalist Papers*. In the Oxford World Classics series, Montesquieu's *Spirit of the Laws* does not appear; Hume's essays are abridged; and the *Federalist Papers* were only added to the series in 2008.

But I will now argue that eighteenth-century British constitutional theorizing deserves to be taken seriously if we want to understand political liberty, and particularly that peculiar type of liberty that marks the moderns off from the ancients, the liberty that results from restricting the power of the state. That liberty has always been precarious—and is a liberty newly endangered in the age of the internet, when the U.K. government can access metadata on every email I have sent in the last twelve months and find out which websites I have visited.[24] Why would we want to be protected from our own government? For the simple reason, to quote Hume, that

> Political Writers have establish'd it as a maxim, That in contriving any System of Government, and fixing the several Checks and Controuls of the Constitution, every Man ought to be suppos'd a *Knave*, and to have no other End, in all his Actions, than private Interest. By this Interest we must govern him, and by means of it, make him co-operate to public Good, notwithstanding his insatiable Avarice and Ambition. Without this . . . we shall in vain boast of the Advantages of any Constitution, and shall find, in the End, that we have no Security for our Liberties or Possessions, except the Good-will of our Rulers; that is, we shall have no Security at all.[25]

And indeed it is important to recognize that many eighteenth-century Englishmen had no security at all, despite habeas corpus and their other rights at law, for able-bodied men could at any moment be seized by the press gang unless they managed to fight them off. Even blind musicians were seized, so that they could provide music at sea. Hume wrote,

> Authority, in times of full internal peace and concord, is arm'd against law. . . . Liberty, in a country of the highest liberty, is left entirely to its own defence, without any countenance or protection: The wild state of nature is renew'd, in one of the most civiliz'd societies of mankind: And great violence and disorder, amongst the people the most humane and the best natur'd, are committed with impunity; while the one party pleads obedience to the supreme magistrate, the other the permission of fundamental laws.[26]

When we want to talk about limiting the powers of the state we quickly find ourselves discussing "checks and balances," a phrase popularized by John Adams in 1787, but the words "check" and "balance" had been commonplace in political discussions for a long time.[27] It is often supposed that "checks and balances" refers to some feature of clockwork mechanisms. It doesn't, and nor do either of its parts. The word "check," we are told, comes from chess, which is true, and sometimes the word implies the exercise of a veto, as a check in chess is a veto on the king staying where he is. But I think the paradigm use of checking is in riding. "Check" and "bridle" often go together, as do "check" and "curb."[28] "Check and controul" is David Hume's favorite phrase, and a rider uses the bit and reins to check and control his horse. At any rate, whether check is or is not a metaphor from riding, there is nothing necessarily mechanical about checking and controlling.

The word "balance" would seem more straightforward: it obviously refers to a pair of scales in balance, and this is sometimes absolutely explicit. Thus Jonathan Swift:

> The true meaning of a Balance of Power, either without or within a State, is best conceived by considering what the nature of a Balance is. It supposes three Things, First the Part which is held, together with the Hand that holds it; and then the two Scales, with whatever is weighed therein. Now consider several States in a Neighbourhood: In order to preserve Peace between these States, it is necessary they should be formed into a Balance, whereof one or more are to be Directors, who are to divide the rest into equal Scales, and upon Occasions remove from one into the other, or else fall with their own Weight into the Lightest. So in a State within it self, the Balance must be held by a third Hand; who is to deal the remaining Power with utmost exactness into the several Scales. Now, it is not necessary that the Power should be equally divided between these three; For the Balance may be held by the Weakest, who by his Address and Conduct, removing from either Scale and adding of his own, may keep the Scales duly poised.[29]

The balance in a pair of scales is neutral: if you raise one pan and lower the other they will stay in equilibrium, but they will not return to their original positions; and if you add the slightest amount to one pan the scales will tip until they hit a stop. One may contrast this to a boat; if someone rocks the boat it will quickly return to its original position, floating flat on the water, because it is designed to displace more water when heeled over to one side, so that it is self-stabilizing. We need to distinguish this sort of resilient mechanism from a feedback mechanism: the boat doesn't alter its shape to compensate for being rocked; it is simply designed to bring itself back onto an even keel. If the boat heels over because it is out of trim, on the other hand, you have to get it back into trim if you want it to float right, and you do this by moving ballast, cargo, or passengers; this is the same as adding more weight to one of the pans of a balance. Trimming involves a deliberate rather than an automatic feedback process.

One can see political thinkers trying to take these four types of equilibrium into account. Thus James Harrington used the term "libration" for a neutral balance and "overballance" for scales that have tipped; Adams insisted that the British Constitution was resilient, that it is to say was self-stabilizing, while Paine had insisted that it wasn't: the smallest discrepancy between the forces would destroy the balance and lead to an overbalance. Paine would have agreed with Montesquieu's Usbek, in the *Persian Letters* (1721), who maintained that monarchy "is a state of violence, and always falls into a Despotical Government or into a Republic. The Power can never be equally divided between the Prince and the People: the equilibrium is too difficult to preserve: the Power must diminish on one side, while it increases on the other: but the advantage generally happens on the side of the Prince, who is at the head of the Armies." Finally, George Savile, Marquis of Halifax's *The Character of a Trimmer* (1688) is about the need to trim the boat, to ensure that the forces are made equal.[30] So really we need to distinguish four balances: the libration or tippy balance; the overbalance; the stable balance; and the trimmed balance.

The standard view of the British Constitution was that there was one balance—that between monarchy, aristocracy, and democracy, or between king, lords, and Commons—but a number of checks (the royal veto on legislation, the dissolution of Parliament, the civil list; the Commons' right to refuse supply, impeachment, motions of no confidence, and so on). The idea of a balance enforced by a mutual capacity to prevent the other agents from doing as they pleased goes back to Polybius, and was then taken up by Niccolò Machiavelli. The British Constitution was described as balanced by the king in 1642, and the army in 1647 claimed to be a "checke and ballance" (in the singular) to the Presbyterian parliament.[31] It was generally accepted that the theoretical balance of legal powers had to correspond to a deeper set of social forces. Thus John Trenchard wrote that "this Ballance [the British Constitution] can never be preserved but by an Union of the natural and artificial Strength of the Kingdom, that is, by making the Militia to consist of the same Persons as have the Property; or otherwise the Government is violent and against Nature, and cannot possibly continue, but the Constitution must either break the Army, or the Army will destroy the Constitution."[32]

So the big question is whether there is anything new about eighteenth-century ways of discussing checks and balances which differs from the long tradition from Polybius to the Civil War of discussing mixed constitutions. The answer is yes.

If one office is set to regulate and check another, then it becomes in the interests of an officeholder to expose poor performance in his opposite number. The principle is already to be found in Machiavelli, who says that in a mixed system of government the different parts check each other (*l'uno guarda l'altro; Discourses on Livy*, 1.2). In *Leviathan* Hobbes states that the best form of government is one "where the public and private interest are most closely united."[33] It is taken up by Hume, and becomes the core principle of *Federalist No. 51*. When Hume states that it is a maxim established by political writers that every man is to be supposed a knave, he was simply echoing Machiavelli, as he was when he argued that knavish individuals can be successfully controlled by exploiting their self-interested behavior.[34]

What was new was the claim that self-interest is the sole principle on the basis of which governments must be constructed. The duty / interest junction principle in this extended form does not seem to have been clearly stated until the second half of the seventeenth century, and we can be sure it does not go back much before then (at least in English), for the simple reason that discussion of interests was rare before 1640. The duty / interest junction principle is merely a subprinciple within a larger claim that human behavior is predictable, and that what shapes behavior is the framework of incentives and disincentives within which people operate. Hume famously summed this up with the claim that politics can be reduced to a science: If behavior can be predicted, then institutions can be thought of as mechanisms which reliably elicit certain sorts of behavior. Institutions can thus be approached as problems in technical design, as engineering projects. In 1698 John Trenchard expressed this view as follows: "A Government is a mere piece of Clockwork, and having such Springs and Wheels, must act after such a manner: and therefore the Art is to constitute it so that it must move to the public Advantage." The secret is "to make the Interest of the Governors and Governed the same, . . . and then our Government would act mechanically, and a Rogue will as naturally be hang'd, as a Clock strike twelve when the Hour is com [*sic*]."[35] Thus the duty/interest junction principle follows from the reduction of politics to a science; what makes both possible is the interpretation of the state as being a machine like a clock. In insisting that politics was about the calibration of interests, and not about the selection of virtuous leaders, Trenchard and Hume were trying to change the fundamental nature of political argument, and to transform the way in which politicians fashioned themselves before the public.

The state was thus now frequently referred to as a machine, and the constitution was described as a system. I want to pause over this word, "system."[36] The word was first made popular at the beginning of the seventeenth century by the Calvinist theologian and polymath Balthasar Keckermann, and then by Galileo in his *Dialogue Concerning the Two Chief World Systems* (1632), though Galileo was already writing about systems in his *Sidereus nuncius* (1610). When Lucretius wrote of the *machina mundi* he did not mean the machine of the universe—in classical Latin a *machina* need not have any moving parts, and its key characteristic was simply that it was a bulky object. In the Middle Ages the movement of the heavens was compared to a clock; but it was assumed that the sublunar world was much too messy to be likened to clockwork, and clocks were not yet called machines. By the mid-seventeenth century, however, with the distinction between the sublunar and supralunar worlds breaking down as a consequence of Copernicanism, the "Engine of the World" (to quote Walter Charleton) or the "System of the Universe" (to quote Ralph Cudworth) had become to be thought of as an interlocking system, like a clock, and clocks were now called machines.[37]

Clock metaphors naturally played a powerful role in discussion of other systems, including political systems. When in 1729 Bishop Joseph Butler wanted to explain the nature of a system, it was to a clock that he naturally turned. Butler treated "system," "economy," and "constitution" as synonyms, and to these we might add "machine."[38] When Hume wanted to summarize Lord Shaftesbury's arguments for a divine creator, he happily substituted the word "machine" for Shaftesbury's preferred word, "system," so that Cleanthes in the *Dialogues Concerning Natural Religion* says, "Look round the world: contemplate the whole and every part of it: you will find it to be nothing but one great machine, subdivided into an infinite number of lesser machines, which again admit of subdivisions, to a degree beyond what human senses and faculties can trace and explain. All these various machines, and even their most minute parts, are adjusted to each other with an accuracy, which ravishes into admiration all men, who have ever contemplated them."[39] Both system and machine in the relevant senses are new terms in the mid-seventeenth century.

But when Henry St. John Bolingbroke invented modern constitutional theorizing in the years between 1727 and 1735—at the very same time Butler was emphasizing the importance of systems and constitutions—he, unlike Butler, had in mind something other than clockwork. He defined the constitution as "that Assemblage of Laws, Institutions and Customs, derived from certain fix'd Principles of Reason, directed to certain fix'd Objects of publick Good, that compose the general System, according to which the Community hath agreed to be governed." The constitution was "a noble and wise System, the essential Parts of which are so proportioned, and so intimately connected, that a Change in one begets a Change in the whole." Bolingbroke seemed to be referring to the move from Ptolemaic astronomy to Newtonian astronomy when he said the monarch "can move no longer in another Orbit from his *People*, and, like some superior Planet, attract, repel, influence, and direct their Motions by his own. He and They are parts of the same System, intimately join'd and co-operating together, acting and acted upon, limiting and limited, controuling and controuled by one another."[40]

In a clock, each bit of the mechanism acts only on those with which it is in contact; the hands, to take an obvious example, are acted upon, but they do not act upon any other part; force travels through the system from the spring or the pendulum to the hands, and not in the opposite direction; one could not possibly say that a change in one bit of the mechanism begets a change in the whole, though it may affect the ability of the whole to tell the right time. So what sort of system did Bolingbroke have in mind? The answer, I think, has to be the Newtonian account of the working of the solar system, in which every body *does* act upon every other.

You might think that in the Cartesian system every particle is in effect connected to every other particle, but according to René Descartes's fourth rule of impact a larger body which is at rest will never be moved by a smaller body no matter how fast the smaller body is traveling; so in the Cartesian system it is not the case that a change in one body always results in a change in all the other bodies. In the Newtonian system, on the other hand, action and reaction are equal and opposite, and gravity is a reciprocal attraction, so that any alteration in one body has consequences for all the other bodies.

Bolingbroke knew quite a bit about Newton and may well have devised this way of thinking for himself; but it is worth noting that there is a possible source for his systemic analysis in a poem with annotations by the Newtonian scientist John Theophilus Desaguliers entitled *The Newtonian System of the World, the Best Model of Government,* published in 1728. There Desaguliers gives a basic account of the Newtonian system, including the principle of mutual interaction, and takes it as a model for praise of the British government.

This Newtonian rather than mechanical account of systemic interaction is to be found in Madison's famous *Federalist No. 51:*

To what expedient, then, shall we finally resort, for maintaining in practice the necessary partition of power among the several departments, as laid down by the Constitution? The only answer that can be given is, that as all these exterior provisions are found to be inadequate, the defect must be supplied, by so contriving the interior structure of the government as that its several constituent parts may, by their mutual relations, be the means of keeping each other in their proper places. . . . the great security against a gradual concentration of the several powers in the same department, consists in giving to those who administer each department the necessary constitutional means and personal motives to resist encroachments of the others. The provision for defense must in this, as in all other cases, be made commensurate to the danger of attack. Ambition must be made to counteract ambition. The interest of the man must be connected with the constitutional rights of the place.[41]

At first sight it may sound as if Madison is just restating the duty / interest junction principle, but he is doing, I think, much more than that. As each constituent part counteracts the others, the mutual relations between them must shift and vary; the result will be what we may call a variable geometry of force against force, and in this variable geometry any alteration to one part will have effects for all the others. Madison, I would submit, has in mind a Newtonian system. More than that, the Founding Fathers could not have come up with the constitutional system they proposed had they not had in mind a system of variable geometry, a very different sort of machine from a clock.

So far, then, we have identified two new methods of analysis: the duty / interest junction principle, which is associated with checks and balances, and the Newtonian interactive system, in which each part acts on every other part. I want to turn now to the third type of mechanism, the feedback system. In 1743 Edward Spelman, in the introduction to a translation of Polybius on mixed government, published the first systematic defense of political parties to appear in English. Before Spelman, the consensus was that parties were unnecessary, since there was only one common interest. Where there were two parties there must be at least one faction. Spelman disagreed.

Spelman maintained, "In all free Governments there ever were, and ever will be Parties," and that party conflict is not a consequence but a precondition of liberty. The cities of ancient Greece were divided into supporters of aristocracy and democracy, but "it was not the Existence of the two Parties I have mentioned, that destroyed the Liberties of any of those Cities, but the occasional Extinction of one of them, by the Superiority the other had gained over it: And, if ever we should be so unhappy as to have the Ballance between the three Orders [i.e., king, lords, and commons] destroyed; and that any one of the Three should utterly extinguish the other Two, the Name of a Party would, from that Moment, be unknown in England, and we should unanimously agree in being Slaves to the Conqueror."

Party thus becomes a crucial mechanism for checking the power of government: "But, whatever may be the Success of the Opposers, the Publick reaps great Benefit from the Opposition; since This keeps Ministers upon their Guard, and, often, prevents them from pursuing bold Measures, which an uncontrolled Power might, otherwise, tempt them to engage in: They must act with Caution, as well as Fidelity, when they consider the whole Nation is attentive to every Step they take, and that the Errors, they may commit, will not only be exposed, but aggravated."[42]

Spelman also provides a subtle account of party and of how parties operate, distinguishing sharply between the motives of a party's supporters, who want to see certain policies adopted, and its leaders, who want power. The thirst for power provides the leaders with a stronger incentive than any disinterested concern for the public good, and opposition provides a training ground for future rulers. There thus exists an inherent tension between a party's leaders and its followers, for the leaders have an incentive to sacrifice their principles to attain power, while the followers, who will never be rulers, have an interest in seeing the powers of government restrained. A simple confirmation of this theory in Spelman's view is the complete failure of the political elite to repeal the Septennial Act of 1716 (which extended the maximum life of a parliament from three to seven years) and institute annual elections: although the whole nation would benefit from such a measure, and although the population as a whole would support it, politicians as a class have an interest in limiting the electorate's ability to control their actions.

A similar account appears in Jean-Louis de Lolme's *Constitution of England* (1771 in the original French), for Lolme argues that politicians rely on popular support to give them access to power, but as they acquire power and status—as they are promoted, for example, from the House of Commons to the House of Lords—the people cease to trust them and become convinced that their interests are no longer at one with those of their rank-and-file supporters.

Spelman's and Lolme's accounts of the conflict of interest between parties and their leaders are an elegant development of the duty / interest junction principle, but Spelman's account of the role of the opposition in improving the quality of the government is something quite different. What he is discussing here is a feedback mechanism, where opposition causes a government to modify and trim its policies, just as the wind catching the fantail of a windmill turns it and points it into the wind. The process described by Spelman and Lolme, the new balance between politicians and public opinion, is one of constant fluctuation around an equilibrium: government provokes opposition, opposition moves into government, and government provokes opposition. The process is never at rest, but is constantly self-stabilizing. It implies, in fact, the idea of a dynamic rather than a static equilibrium.

Indeed, any careful formulation of the claim that the people control their representatives through elections involves an appeal to a feedback mechanism. It is also worth stressing, if we are to understand the novelty of the intellectual tools I am describing here, that Harrington and Marchamont Nedham, who seem in so many respects to be the founders of the modern republican tradition, had been systematically opposed to feedback mechanisms. They wanted a wholesale rotation or revolution in elected representatives at every election rather than seeing elections as an opportunity to assess the performance of the people's representatives, rewarding the good and punishing the bad. And they wanted political discussions to take place in secret, as in Venice, not in public, thus preventing the emergence of any informed public opinion. Their assumption was that any passage of time, any intervention of outside influence, represented an opportunity for corruption, while for later theorists time provided scope for correcting mistakes and adjusting to developments, and outside influences served to steer the legislature in the right direction.

We can see the new, contrasting conception best in a passage from Lolme:

As the Representatives of the People will naturally be selected from among those Citizens who are most favoured by fortune, and will consequently have much to preserve, they will, even in the midst of quiet times, keep a watchful eye on the motions of Power. As the advantages they possess will naturally create a kind of rivalship between them and those who govern, the jealousy which they will conceive against the latter, will give them an exquisite degree of sensibility on every increase of their authority. Like those Machines which discover the operations of Nature, while they are yet imperceptible to our senses, they will warn the People of those things which of themselves they never see but when it is too late;

and their greater proportional share, whether of real riches, or of those which lie in the opinions of Men, will make them, if I may so express myself, the barometers that will discover, in their first beginning, every tendency to a change in the constitution.[43]

The representatives thus serve as a thermostat, firing up or damping down public opinion depending on the presence or absence of a threat to liberty and property. Again, the process involves constant movement, as representatives compete simultaneously for power and public support, but as long as the circuit of election, representation, sensitivity, publicity, and new elections is unbroken, the mechanism to check power will continue to function. Lolme, we have seen, likens the representatives to barometers, not thermostats, for like barometers they act on men's minds. But while a barometer changes one's behavior, encouraging one to set to sea or carry an umbrella, one's resulting behavior does not in itself affect the weather. In politics, by contrast, the acute sensitivity of the elected representatives actually serves to change the political situation as a result of the information being fed back to the public in the same way that a thermostat serves to change the temperature in the room by supplying information to the furnace. What Lolme is describing is a self-regulating system, and it is because his understanding of politics reaches this level of sophistication that we find him in later editions of his book criticizing Adam Smith's view that a standing army is not a threat to liberty if the sovereign is the supreme commander and the social elite supply the officer caste: "The author we are quoting has deemed a government to be a simpler machine, and an army a simpler instrument, than they in reality are." It is only when we see that Lolme understands England's constitutional machinery to be self-stabilizing that we can understand just how far from simple he thinks it is. We can also recognize why he was in a good position to identify and admire Smith's "very great abilities."[44]

In this chapter I have argued that eighteenth-century political theorists had three paradigmatic machines in mind when they tried to analyze politics: the clock, the Newtonian solar system, and the market mechanism. Each of these had important implications for how they understood politics, and for the goals they set themselves. Clock mechanisms were used to argue that politics is not about virtues (which are always going to be unreliable) but interests (which are entirely predictable). The Newtonian system was used to conceive of a machine in which every part interacted with every other part, and which would therefore respond flexibly to change over time, making it potentially exceptionally resilient. And the market mechanism was used to argue that politicians and parties have to sell themselves to the people, and consequently have to respond to popular demand, so that public opinion becomes the great guiding force in politics. We still rely on these three mental machines to explain how governments can be made to serve the purposes of the governed, and not their own. We, throughout the democratic world, owe what liberty we have to the application of these imaginary machines in the construction and administration of political institutions. And we need to think about the history and character of these machines if we are to ask ourselves—as I think we should—if our inherited institutions are adequate to the challenges they now face.

THE

THEORY

OF

MORAL SENTIMENTS.

By ADAM SMITH,
Professor of Moral Philosophy in the
Univerſity of Glasgow.

LONDON:
Printed for A. Millar, in the Strand;
And A. Kincaid and J. Bell, in Edinburgh.
M DCC LIX.

Title page from Adam Smith, *The Theory of Moral Sentiments* (8°) (1759).

7

Profit: The Invisible Hand

Adam Smith, in *The Theory of Moral Sentiments* (1759), explains that people overestimate the pleasure that wealth will bring to them:

> And it is well that nature imposes upon us in this manner. It is this deception which rouses and keeps in continual motion the industry of mankind. It is this which first prompted them to cultivate the ground, to build houses, to found cities and commonwealths, and to invent and improve all the sciences and arts, which ennoble and embellish human life; which have entirely changed the whole face of the globe, have turned the rude forests of nature into agreeable and fertile plains, and made the trackless and barren ocean a new fund of subsistence, and the great high road of communication to the different nations of the earth. The earth by these labours of mankind has been obliged to redouble her natural fertility, and to maintain a greater multitude of inhabitants. It is to no purpose, that the proud and unfeeling landlord views his extensive fields, and without a thought for the wants of his brethren, in imagination consumes himself the whole harvest that grows upon them. The homely and vulgar proverb, that the eye is larger than the belly, never was more fully verified than with regard to him. The capacity of his stomach bears no proportion to the immensity of his desires, and will receive no more than that of the meanest peasant. The rest he is obliged to distribute among those, who prepare, in the nicest manner, that little which he himself makes use of, among those who fit up the palace in which this little is to be consumed, among those who provide and keep in order all the different baubles and trinkets, which are employed in the oeconomy of greatness; all of whom thus derive from his luxury and caprice, that share of the necessaries of life, which they would in vain have expected from his humanity or his justice. . . . The rich . . . in spite of their natural selfishness and rapacity . . . are led by an invisible hand to make nearly the

same distribution of the necessaries of life, which would have been made, had the earth been divided into equal portions among all its inhabitants, and thus without intending it, without knowing it, advance the interest of the society, and afford means to the multiplication of the species. When providence divided the earth among a few lordly masters, it neither forgot nor abandoned those who seemed to have been left out in the partition. These last too enjoy their share of all that it produces. In what constitutes the real happiness of human life, they are in no respect inferior to those who would seem so much above them. In ease of body and peace of mind, all the different ranks of life are nearly upon a level, and the beggar, who suns himself by the side of the highway, possesses that security which kings are fighting for.[1]

This extraordinary passage is one of three in Smith's works where he refers to an invisible hand. These passages have given rise to an extensive literature, and I want to start by making a number of obvious points which some parts of the literature grasp and some, strangely, show no signs of grasping. First, this is a very serious argument that Smith is presenting, an argument which intends to show that the pursuit of wealth is founded on a fundamental misconception, but we all benefit from that misconception. Second, Smith's argument here is theistic—the "invisible hand" is the hand of nature and of providence—it is providence which has designed a system where people are suckered into creating a wealth from which they personally scarcely benefit, but from which everyone else really does benefit.* And third, it seems perfectly legitimate to look for other arguments which work like this one and call them invisible hand arguments.[2]

Invisible hand arguments (and Smith is not the first to make them; he is merely the first to give us a convenient label for them) reflect a recognition

---

* "The happiness of mankind, as well as of all other rational creatures, seems to have been the original purpose intended by the Author of Nature, when he brought them into existence. No other end seems worthy of that supreme wisdom and divine benignity which we necessarily ascribe to him; and this opinion, which we are led to by the abstract consideration of his infinite perfections, is still more confirmed by the examination of the works of nature, which seem all intended to promote happiness, and to guard against misery." Adam Smith, *The Theory of Moral Sentiments* (London: Millar, 1759), 284.

that what happens in the economy is not obvious or transparent.* Human beings have been trucking and bartering for as long as there have been human beings; and yet the notion that there is something there to study—beyond ethical questions of what constitutes fair dealing, or questions about how to prevent the debasement of the currency, or, later, questions about foreign trade and its contribution to national wealth—is a recent one. The economy is a bit like consciousness or, for that matter, the unconscious: it's always been there, but it was completely invisible until suddenly, somehow it became something inescapable and obvious. The first question I want to address is: What were the preconditions for economics? It is, it should be obvious, a retrospective one. There's a view that there is something inherently illegitimate about such questions, that they are a form of Whig history, but it seems to me that if we can't ask retrospective questions we will end up being unable to ask any interesting "why?" questions at all.[3] Indeed, as we will see, anyone who writes economic history for a period before the eighteenth century (or perhaps the nineteenth) is guilty of anachronism.

The eighteenth century saw the emergence of political economy. But what were the preconditions for political economy? Why did Aristotle not develop any account of the economy (as we call it) as an independent sphere with its own logic and processes? After all, he sought to account for many things that still seem fundamentally important to us—why not for the economy? Why did Nicole Oresme, an extraordinarily brilliant natural philosopher, the first to compare the heavens with a clock, and the author of a treatise on money, not engage in a wider account of economic activity? Why did Copernicus, who wrote an important treatise on monetary reform, not move on from formulating the principle that bad money drives out good to establishing other principles governing economic activity? Why not Jean

---

* In *The Wealth of Nations* Smith effectively defines an invisible hand argument as one in which the selfish actions of individuals have, as an unintended consequence, a social benefit: Adam Smith, *An Inquiry Into the Nature and Causes of the Wealth of Nations*, 2 vols. (London: Strahan and Cadell, 1776), 2:35: "he [the investor] intends only his own gain, and he is in this, as in many other cases, led by an invisible hand to promote an end which was no part of his intention. Nor is it always the worse for the society that it was no part of it. By pursuing his own interest he frequently promotes that of the society more effectually than when he really intends to promote it." For an earlier example, Montesquieu, *The Spirit of Laws*, trans. T. Nugent, 2 vols. (London: Nourse and Vaillant, 1750), 1:36, quoted in Chapter 6 above.

Bodin, or even John Locke? Why is there no way of saying "the economy" in classical Greek, or in classical or medieval Latin—indeed, the *Oxford English Dictionary (OED)* gives 1892 as the first usage of "economy" in the requisite sense, a date which is surely wrong, though as late as the end of the eighteenth century it is difficult (if not impossible) to find "the economy" used as a theoretical abstraction, the nearest equivalent to it being "the national economy."[4]

The first thing to do is ask what sort of preconditions we should be looking for. Should we be looking for economic preconditions—for example, the generalization of market relations—to explain this ever-so-belated occurrence? One can quite see that feudal and slave societies would have no clear conception of the costs of production, but highly sophisticated analysis of the distribution of shares between investors was already present in the work of Leonardo Fibonacci at the beginning of the thirteenth century in Italy; and it is hard to see what more one could need in the way of economic development than the world of the Medici and the Fugger bankers and the double-entry bookkeeping with which they were familiar to generate a theory of economic interaction. I have no doubt that the economy of the eighteenth century was more advanced than the economy of the fifteenth—the emergence of stock markets being an obvious example—but I have difficulty in identifying a crucial economic difference which would have brought the economy out of the shadows into the light in the 1700s and not the 1500s.

Perhaps the preconditions were political? As Hume wrote in 1741, "Trade was never esteem'd an Affair of State, 'till within this last Century; nor is there any antient Writer on Politics, who has made mention of it. Even the *Italians* have kept a profound silence with regard to it; though it has now engaged the chief attention, as well of Ministers of State, as of speculative Reasoners. The great Opulence, Grandeur, and Military Atchievements of the two Maritime Powers, seem first to have instructed Mankind in the vast Importance of an extensive Commerce."[5] The implication seems to be that the speculative reasoners are interested in trade for the same reason as the ministers of state—because of its implications for political power. But it is a puzzle indeed why suddenly the success of the Dutch and English economies should have concentrated people's attention on something that had been important all along. As Hume put it in notes he made as a young man, "There is not a word of Trade in all Matchiavel, which is strange considering that Florence rose only by Trade."[6] Again, there are obvious respects in which the state's relationship to the economy changed between the fifteenth and the eighteenth centuries—in the way in which government debt was funded, for example—but it is hard to see exactly why these should have been revelatory.

In a classic article published in 1969 Moses Finley asked why Aristotle—and the ancient Greeks in general—had no economic theory.[7] The nub of his response was that Greek citizens saw economic activity as something for other—inferior—people, and so, in essence, Aristotle had no economic theory because the Greeks weren't interested in economic activity, and looked down on it. But even if this is true, it won't do for Renaissance Florence. Niccolò Machiavelli, in one of his letters to Francesco Vettori, written just after he had been tortured (it begins with remarkable bravado: "this letter of yours has frightened me more than the rack"), says that he talks and writes about politics, and has no choice but to go on doing so, despite his very recent experience of the nasty consequences that can follow from being thought to have political views, because "Fortune has decided that I must talk about the state—not knowing how to discuss either the silk trade or the wool business, either profits or losses."[8] Florentine citizens were very much interested in discussing the silk trade and the wool business, in profits and losses, even if Machiavelli was not, but they produced no economic theory.

It seems the essential precondition for the emergence of political economy cannot have been economic or political, or even in some broad sense cultural. What we are left with then is the notion that there must have been intellectual preconditions for the emergence of political economy, intellectual preconditions that were not met until the eighteenth century, that were not yet met when a theory of the balance of trade was formulated in England during the 1620s by Gerard de Malynes, Edward Misselden, and Thomas Mun, but were met by the time Richard Cantillon wrote his *Essay on the Nature of Trade in General* around 1730.[9] What sort of preconditions could these have been? The first precondition for political economy, I would argue, is the recognition that any economic theory is going to be a peculiar sort of abstraction, what a Weberian might call an ideal type. No economic theory is going to explain the behavior of every individual, or even of the average individual. Ancient astronomers knew that their theories did not work perfectly—they had to "save" the phenomena. This was not surprising, as their measurements were necessarily imperfect; in principle they were sure the movements of the heavens could be given perfect expression in mathematical terms. The first scientific theory to present itself as a pure idealization is Galileo's account of the behavior of falling bodies, which, he argues, accelerate according to a fixed mathematical ratio—in the absence of air resistance. Cannon balls fly in a parabola, provided they are perfectly round and are not spinning. Thus, in the real world you would never find a perfect example of a falling body or a projectile; always you would find some greater or lesser deviation from a theoretical ideal. In the case of cannon balls, the deviation turned out to be considerable, but Galileo's pupil Evangelista Torricelli insisted this did not matter at all. The theory was sound; it was just that the real world did not match up with the theoretical model. Why it did not match up was an interesting question, but not one that threatened Galileo's theory.[10] This, it seems to me, was a quite new type of knowledge, a theory that was perfectly exact and in some sense true, but must always be inexact in any possible application.

Before you can have a proper political economy you have to have the idea that you can look past various sorts of deviations from the norm in order to find the norm that underlies them. Galileo understood this perfectly, and compared his own work on falling bodies to a businessman working on his accounts—the businessman knows that the goods in his warehouse have to be packed and wrapped, that there will be shrinkage and loss as they make their way to the customer, but he simplifies his calculations by ignoring these factors when he enters five hundredweight of grain or fifty yards of silk into his accounts.[11] So, too, Galileo ignored air resistance when calculating the speed of falling bodies. There's a little puzzle here—Galileo, whose mother dealt in wool, learned about theoretical abstraction from the practices of businessmen and -women, but the principle was applied first in physics, and only much later in economics. The first to fully understand this principle seems to be have been Richard Cantillon, writing in 1730, who consistently appealed to the principles of *caeteris paribus* and "in the long run" in laying out his theory of trade.[12] Clearly this may be an important precondition, but it cannot be the only one we are looking for; if it were Thomas Hobbes, who admired Galileo beyond measure, would have seen the possibility of a theory of the economy.

There's another precondition, perhaps, for the emergence of economics, and that is the notion of circulation. For the first political economists the staple food, grain in western Europe, is the starting point of all economic activity. The division of labor produces specialists—tailors, carpenters, blacksmiths, shoemakers—who exchange their products for food. And this enables farmers to concentrate on the production of food and not waste time on other tasks at which they are not very good. Out of this basic division of labor grows the division between town and country and the exchange of goods between them. And, of course, where goods move, money moves in the opposite direction. Goods and money circulate through the economy; Cantillon was the first to construct an economic theory based on this understanding, and his understanding underpinned François Quesnay's *tableau économique*. But David Hume was convinced that the preoccupation with circulation had originated in England. "There is a word," he wrote in 1752, "which is here in the mouth of every body, and which, I find, has also got abroad, and is much employ'd by foreign writers, in imitation of the *English;* and that is CIRCULATION."[13] "Circulate," "circulation," and so on occur 232 times in the *Wealth of Nations.* For example,

> The industry of Great Britain, instead of being accommodated to a great number of small markets, has been principally suited to one great market [the North American market]. Her commerce, instead of running in a great number of small channels, has been taught to run principally in one great channel. But the whole system of her industry and commerce has thereby been rendered less secure; the whole state of her body politic less healthful than it otherwise would have been. . . . A small stop in that great blood-vessel, which has been artificially swelled beyond its natural dimensions, and through which an unnatural proportion of the industry and commerce of the country has been forced to circulate, is very likely to bring on the most dangerous disorders upon the whole body politic. The expectation of a rupture with the colonies, accordingly, has struck the people of Great Britain with more terror than they ever felt for a Spanish armada, or a French invasion.[14]

There has been some discussion of the metaphor of circulation in political economy, but it has failed, as far as I can see, to distinguish between circular movements of the sort one finds in Ptolemaic astronomy, which can be perfectly represented in mathematical terms, and William Harvey's discovery of the circulation of the blood, which is the identification of a process hidden from view.[15] Nor should all references to blood be assumed to be references to Harveian circulation. Thus Hobbes believed in the circulation of the blood, but when in *Leviathan* he says that commodities nourish the commonwealth, and that this process is "the Sanguification of the Common-wealth," he is referring to the process whereby chyle is turned into blood in the liver and not to Harvey's theory of circulation; and when William Petty says that merchants are "as veins and arteries, to distribute forth and back the blood and nutritive juyces of the Body Politick, namely, the product of Husbandry and Manufacture," he appears to have in mind the Galenic doctrine of the ebb and flow of the blood, not Harveian circulation.[16]

But there is a clear reference to the circulation of money in 1673. Joseph Hill, writing in Holland, said,

> Then we shall lay down this as a fundamental and undoubted Maxim, (which all I think will take for granted) that trade by Sea is the great secular interest of these Provinces, the Maritime especially, by which they most flourish, and without which they cannot subsist. Let Amsterdam and the other Cities be as rich, or richer then they are imagined; yet will they in a few years, if their Trade be obstructed, become as poor as their Neighbours at Gant, or Antwerp. . . . If ever Merchants were, or are in any place of the world, the vena porta (as Bacon stiles them) of any publick body, it is certainly the Belgick.* If they fraight not their Ships, whereby the Marriners may be imployed; if they furnish not the Tradesmen shops, whereby they may follow their Vocations; if they lade not the poor mens backs, whereby their Families may fill their bellies; finally, if they distribute not their Merchandise through the various Seas and Rivers of the Universe: we may linger a while, but it is as impossible we should live long, as for a body deprived of food, whose parts languish for want of nourishment, which should be brought them in the veins, by the bloods regular circulation.[17]

---

* The "vena porta" is the portal vein, which carries nutrients from the stomach to the liver.

The next year we find Richard Haines writing, "what Moneys are given by the Representatives of the Nation to his Majesty, are but like the Moistures drawn up by the Beams of the Sun from the Earth, which soon return down again in showers to refresh the Ground, or like the Blood in its Circulation; for what is carried out of the Countrey goes but into the City, and is there expended again; and forasmuch as it *goes not beyond the Seas,* soon returns again."[18]

These are still metaphors, but by 1679 they were being extended into the notion of the circulation of credit and of goods. We find three people—Slingsby Bethel, Bishop Gilbert Burnet, and the anonymous author of *Popery and Tyranny*—writing of the circulation of money in that year, and thereafter the concept was rapidly adopted.[19] In 1685 Nicholas Barbon, who had studied medicine, wrote, "For the Metropolis is the heart of a Nation, through which the Trade and Commodities of it circulate, like the blood through the heart, which by its motion giveth life and growth to the rest of the Body."[20] The puzzle here is the delay of a generation or so between the general adoption of Harvey's theory of the circulation of the blood and its use first as a metaphor and then as a technical term in discussing economic transactions.

So far, then, I have identified two preconditions: *caeteris paribus* arguments and Harveian circulation of the blood as a model for the circulation of money, credit, and commodities. But an economy is something more than a law-governed abstraction; it is not just a system for the circulation of goods and money; it is an interactive system. From the fourteenth century onward, to go back to Oresme, the movements of the heavens were being compared to the movements of a clock—here was a complicated, interlocking mechanism. Might it have provided an intellectual model for understanding the economy? Evidently there was a temptation to use such images: thus Slingsby Bethel wrote in 1679 that "money is the *primum mobile* which moves the spheres, which are the hearts and hands of men."[21] But this usage shows clearly the limitations of mechanistic thought, since it implies a purely one-way system of causation. No remotely satisfactory economic theory could be monocausal to this degree. The idea of a fully interactive system, which we take completely for granted, is in fact new with Isaac Newton. Before the seventeenth century a system can be, for example, a diagram which lays out a schematic arrangement—Petrus Ramus, the sixteenth-century philosopher, liked to use such schemes or systems, Francis Bacon offered one in *The Advancement of Learning,* and the great *Encyclopédie* of Denis Diderot and Jean le Rond d'Alembert begins with a "Système figuré des connoissances humaines," a diagram of human knowledge.[22] But these systems are static, and they represent a conceptual analysis or a program of teaching and learning. There's a new usage in the title of Galileo's great *Dialogue on the Two Chief World Systems* (1632)—after Galileo it became common to refer to the Ptolemaic, Tychonic, and Copernican systems. But in fact none of these are systems in the required sense.[23]

The Newtonian system is quite different from anything that went before it because if you change the location, velocity, or mass of any planet you immediately alter the movements of all the other bodies in the solar system. We can watch the Newtonian concept of a system travel outward into other disciplines—into Henry St. John Bolingbroke's definition of a constitution, for example, as a system in which a change in one part affects all the other parts.[24] And, of course, Adam Smith was as a young man the author of a history of astronomy—a history of intellectual systems, culminating in the greatest system of all, the fully interactive system of Newton.[25] The word "system" occurs more than two hundred times in the *Wealth of Nations,* but it is important to distinguish its different senses. It is used in essentially three ways: there are systems in the real world, such as the feudal system; there are theoretical systems which misrepresent the world, such as the mercantile system; and there is the system Smith himself advocates, which he calls at one moment "the liberal system," and this system is both normative and descriptive—it describes how markets work in principle, and how they could be made to work in practice.[26] The liberal system is, I will argue, something quite new—a fully interactive system, for which the only possible model is the Newtonian system.*

A crucial feature of the Newtonian system, as opposed to a clock, is that it is flexible: you can calculate what would happen if the mass of Jupiter doubled or quadrupled. If you vary the size of some parts of a clock while leaving other parts unchanged, you simply break it; but if you alter the parameters of the solar system, you won't necessarily destroy it. Newton's

---

* I have discussed systems in Chapter 6.

system may be flexible, but it isn't necessarily stable. Newton believed that the way in which the solar system interacted to create a stable order was evidence of design: the ordering of the planets was the work of God.

An even better system, one might say, would be one that was so flexible that if its order was disturbed it would return to equilibrium—a system of checks and balances (and here I deliberately echo *Federalist No. 51,* which presents the American constitution as a system of this sort).[27] The important word here is "balances." In *The Wealth of Nations* Smith describes Jean-Baptiste Colbert as "a laborious and plodding man of business, who had been accustomed to regulate the different departments of publick offices, and to establish the necessary checks and controuls for confining each to its proper sphere"—checks and controls are static, but a balance implies a constant process of adjustment and self-regulation, like a sailor in a dinghy leaning further out to balance a gust of wind.[28] Balances require some sort of feedback process.

It is a fundamental feature of the market mechanism, as described by Smith, that it contains a feedback loop which makes it self-equilibrating. If profits in one sector of the economy are exceptionally high, investors pile in, supply rises, and prices and profits fall, and the rate of profit eventually settles down close to the rate to be found in other sectors. The classic description of such a system before Smith is Hume's account of the balance of trade.[29] You might easily think that such self-regulating mechanisms in the world of theory must have been modeled on real mechanisms, on real machines, but there is no sign of there being an actual mechanical model of a feedback mechanism which Hume and Smith drew on—the pioneers of feedback equilibrium modeling don't seem to have had any material mechanism in mind. In English the word "equilibrium," by the way, seems first to have been used in this sort of way by Malachy Postlethwayt in his *Universal Dictionary of Trade and Commerce* (1757); strikingly, Smith only uses the word once, and then not to describe his own views on markets and prices, but the mercantilist balance of trade theory to which he is opposed.[30]

This brings us at last back to the invisible hand. Economics depends on what we may call invisible hand arguments. The most elementary example is provided by Adam Smith near the beginning of *The Wealth of Nations,* where he writes, "It is not from the benevolence of the butcher, the brewer, or the baker, that we expect our dinner, but from their regard to their own interest. We address ourselves not to their humanity, but to their self-love, and never talk to them of our own necessities but of their advantages."[31] Arguments of this sort go back to the Jansenist Pierre Nicole in the late seventeenth century.[32] In this simplest version, the people who sell me the makings of my dinner know that their needs coincide with mine—they sell me meat, beer, and bread in order to make money, but they know that I will get a good dinner as a result. They are not motivated by the desire to do me good, but they know that they will be helping me achieve my own purposes. In this elementary case there is something peculiar at work to bring about a coincidence of interests, but that coincidence is not invisible; what is invisible is the mysterious alchemy which prevents the butcher's gain from being my loss, which prevents this encounter being a zero-sum game. How can it be that we both come away from the transaction better off than before we entered into it? Yet clearly we do.

In more complex versions the coincidence of interests may well be invisible. Take the case of the division of labor. A pin manufacturer divides the task of making pins into many subtasks in order to produce pins more efficiently. He hopes for bigger profits, and at first that is indeed what he obtains. But other pin manufacturers copy him, eager to make their own profits. Before long, profits in pin manufacturing are no higher than in other enterprises; the pin manufacturers' gains prove short-lived; but meanwhile competition has driven down the price of pins, and the gain to the consumer proves to be permanent. Moreover, since pins are now cheaper, the demand for them grows, and they are put to all sorts of new uses; as a result more people make a living from pin production, even if the first consequence of the increased productivity of the new manufactory is to throw people in other pin-making businesses out of work. And if demand does not increase to this extent, then consumers will be better off, and will spend more on lace, or gin, creating new jobs as a consequence.

There is no need for the pin manufacturer to grasp this process, and insofar as he does understand it he will surely seek to slow it down and delay it as far as possible; it takes place despite his efforts, and often behind his back. It is built into the logic of competition.[33] There is an invisible hand ensuring that the short-term interests of pin manufacturers coincide with the long-term interests of the nation (which benefits as the economy as a whole grows) and of consumers (who find they can now afford pins). One of the things that makes this hand invisible is, of course, that although in the long term the nation benefits, in the short term there are people who lose their businesses and their jobs because they have failed to adapt quickly enough. This process of creative destruction often makes it difficult to see that the outcome will eventually be beneficial for the nation as a whole, if not for every individual—indeed, without Adam Smith's arguments for a liberal system you simply cannot see that this is bound to be the case.

There is unquestionably something new about invisible hand arguments in the late seventeenth century. Before then the standard assumption seems to have been that social ordering was to be achieved by deliberate action. In *Utopia* (1516) Thomas More pointed out just how complicated social change can be: when arable land is turned over to sheep, farm laborers become unemployed, crime rises, the gallows bend under the weight of dangling men, and society suffers so that a few landlords can get rich. The extension of sheep farming would have had no deleterious consequences if it were labor intensive or if there were other jobs to which displaced laborers could turn. But in the specific circumstances of early sixteenth-century England it had, More believed, disastrous unintended consequences. More, one might think, was on the verge of a proper economic analysis—he even invented the Latin word *oligopolium* (not translated into English as "oligopoly" until 1895) to describe the advantages of landlords.[34] But his only solution to the problem he had identified was to eliminate the pursuit of profit, take control of the economy, and plan for full employment. His ideal, it seems, was a Carthusian monastery. The way to get rid of unintended consequences, he evidently thought, is to eliminate them by planning for every eventuality.[35]

In Utopia there is to be toleration, except for atheists. Atheists, More maintained, because they do not fear God, cannot be trusted and will never make reliable fellow citizens; More is one of the first people to insist on this primarily because the very category of atheist was a new one.[36] The first person to directly attack this view (which was still held by Locke in the *Letter Concerning Toleration* of 1689) was Pierre Bayle in 1682.[37] Bayle pointed out that not all atheists have proved to be wicked in their behavior, and he identified at least two mechanisms that could make atheists potentially good citizens. The first is that atheists, like everyone else, have to get along with their neighbors, and if they behave badly they will experience a whole set of sanctions, from the cold shoulder to the loss of custom and on to blacklisting—their professional, social, and business lives will suffer. They will be punished, as Bayle puts it, by the law of public opinion. This was a quite new conception of how society can impose sanctions and constrain behavior, for this law has no legislator, no courts, no scaffolds. It is enforced by anyone and everyone in the course of daily life.[38]

And there is, Bayle argued, another mechanism also at work: atheists can have principles. Indeed, there have been atheists who have been prepared to die for their beliefs, although they had no hope of reward in another life. Such martyrs, as Bayle called them, are obliged to behave in a principled fashion by their own sense of self-esteem. Public opinion and self-esteem are powerful forces governing behavior, more powerful most of the time than religious belief, which has little effect in persuading people to give up swearing, whoring, and other forbidden activities. And this is because people think only of the here and now, not the distant future—it is precisely in the here and now that public opinion and self-esteem function, which makes them much more effective than the hope of heaven and the fear of hell.

Bayle thus argued that there is no obvious reason why there needs to be an overwhelmingly powerful central authority—a secular or divine Leviathan—maintaining order. People have a remarkable capacity to police each other and even themselves; power can be distributed and dispersed without being weakened or rendered ineffectual.[39]

Bayle's argument chimed with the argument from the self-interest of the butcher, brewer, and baker—the argument I have dubbed the mysterious alchemy argument pioneered by Pierre Nicole. Why, Nicole asked, if human beings are irredeemably corrupt, is social life possible? Because our corrupt motives lead us to behave in ways which have the same effects as virtuous motives would have—the selfish innkeeper feeds us just as well as a benevolent innkeeper would. Bernard Mandeville, a disciple of Bayle's, pushed this argument a step further; a corrupt society, he argues, will flourish in a way that no virtuous society possibly could. A frugal, honest society will be poor and consequently weak; a spendthrift, extravagant, mendacious society will grow rich and powerful—private vices, public benefits.[40] Smith's invisible hand arguments depend on a reworking of this sort of paradox:

selfish behavior within a liberal system proves to be beneficial to the public, while high-minded interference turns out to do more harm than good.

But what, we may ask, is the model for those invisible hand arguments which require a feedback system, a process of equilibration? Smith, for example, explains, "The natural price, therefore, is, as it were, the central price to which the prices of all commodities are continually gravitating. Different accidents may sometimes keep them suspended a good deal above it, and sometimes force them down even somewhat below it. But whatever may be the obstacles which hinder them from settling in this centre of repose and continuance, they are constantly tending towards it."[41] One should not be misled here by the reference to gravity into thinking this is a Newtonian image; the mental model here is one familiar to medieval philosophers. Suppose you drilled a hole through to the center of the Earth and beyond and you dropped a rock into the hole. It would overshoot the center of the Earth and then start falling back to the center again; it would oscillate back and forth until it finally came to rest at the center of the Earth—which, of course, for Aristotelians is also the center of the universe. Smith's language here, of a natural center of repose, is Aristotelian rather than Newtonian.

Or take Hume's classic essay on the balance of trade (1752), the first major exposition of an equilibrium model: "All water, wherever it communicates, remains always at a level: Ask naturalists [i.e., scientists] the reason; they tell you, that were it to be rais'd in any one place, the superior gravity of that part, not being balanc'd, must depress it, till it meets a counterpoize; and that the same cause, which redresses the inequality, when it happens, must for ever prevent it, without some violent, external operation."[42] Hume adopts a hydraulic model for two reasons: the first is that water finds its own level; the second is that if you dam water up, it tries to find a way through, and often succeeds. So too, if you try to run a favorable balance of trade and accumulate specie in one country, the gold and the silver will be smuggled out despite all your rules and regulations. Your dam will leak.

Here we have two models, both of which rely on gravity: the rock which falls and oscillates until it comes to rest, and two tanks of water connected by a pipe in which the water in the two tanks is not initially at the same level. In both cases an equilibrium of forces is established automatically—the idea of an equilibrium is clearly there, even if the word itself is not. But now let us read a bit further in Hume:

The skill and ingenuity of *Europe* in general much surpasses that of *China*,* with regard to manual arts and manufactures; yet are we never able to trade thither without great disadvantage: And were it not for the continual recruits we receive from *America,* money wou'd very soon sink in *Europe,* and rise in *China,* 'till it came nearly to a level in both places. Nor can any reasonable man doubt, but that industrious nation, were they as near us as *Poland* or *Barbary,* would drain us of the overplus of our specie, and draw to themselves a larger share of the *West Indian* treasures. We need have no recourse to a physical attraction, to explain the necessity of this operation. There is a moral attraction, arising from the interests and passions of men, which is full as potent and infallible.[43]

The argument here is simple: gold and silver are expensive in China and cheap in Europe. If there was not such a vast distance between China and Europe, and if there was not a constant supply of precious metals from the New World, the Chinese would buy European gold and silver by trading their own produce and manufactures for them until the price of the precious metals had fallen in China and risen in Europe and they were roughly on a par. Why? Because the interests and passions of men make the pursuit of profit irresistible, sufficiently irresistible at least to ensure that supply and demand will eventually match. This is just another example of the price mechanism; buyers and sellers have no interest in creating an equilibrium, but they do so whether they intend to or not. Hume's balance of trade argument is an invisible hand argument.

Compare it now to the balance of power, which Hume discusses in another essay of the same date.[44] A number of unequally sized powers jockey with each other and form two blocs of alliances. One bloc is bigger than the other. Astute smaller members of the bigger bloc foresee a future in which the bigger bloc gobbles up the smaller bloc, and then the largest member of the victorious bloc turns on its allies and consumes them in turn. The result is a universal empire. They realize that they are only safe if both blocs are of the same size and they tacitly coordinate their actions until this state

---

* From 1760 this reads, "The skill and ingenuity of EUROPE in general surpasses perhaps that of CHINA."

of affairs is achieved. The language of balance of power, which encapsulates this logic, emerged in the 1690s, and became commonplace after the Treaty of Utrecht in 1713, which referred to the need to establish such a balance.[45]

Hume's balance of trade is different from a balance of power because the latter is an outcome deliberately pursued by all the smaller powers if they understand the logic of their situation, while the former is an unintended outcome produced by an invisible hand. This makes it possible, I think, to grasp the nature of invisible hand equilibria. These are equilibria automatically produced by the aggregate actions of individuals, not by the actions of one or two astute individuals, and indeed they are unintended, not intended, outcomes. Even in the case of my buying the makings of dinner from the butcher, the brewer, and the baker, a mutually beneficial outcome depends on their having (in principle at least) other customers to whom they can sell, and my having other sellers from whom I can buy.

Models such as Hume's hydraulic system fail to capture the fact that in society outcomes depend on choices; but models such as the balance of power also fail when it comes to understanding invisible hand equilibria because in such cases the choices are not directed at the outcome. An economic model requires invisible hand equilibria, and an understanding of invisible hand equilibria requires that at least two preconditions be met: first, there must be an understanding of how uncoordinated individual choices can produce results that would seem to require coordination (as with Bayle's law of public opinion); and second, there must be an understanding of how uncoordinated actions can have unintended consequences that are not only orderly, but are superior to the intended consequences (this is the fundamental characteristic of invisible hand arguments). It is not surprising that Hume and Smith have no mechanical model for this system—for, as Hume recognizes, one needs to model not physical but moral forces, and one needs to model rational choices.

Now, it is possible to find mechanical models that model choices—think of a thermostat, for example, or a ballcock—but they involve switches and gauges, and it is hard to identify any pre-Smithian machine that works in such a fashion, except for the fantail on a windmill, which switches the direction in which it turns the mill from clockwise to counterclockwise and back again, and turns it all the more forcefully the further it is from pointing into the wind—the fantail was patented in 1745, but was rare until the end of the eighteenth century.[46] This is why we happily talk about the market mechanism, because we are familiar with self-equilibrating feedback systems, but Smith did not—he could not imagine a mechanism that would serve his purposes. This would not have worried him in that there was no mechanism that could model Newtonian gravity. Smith described scientific theories as mental machines, but mental machines need not operate on the same principles as physical machines; they can, as it were, be fictional machines so long as they successfully model what actually happens.

Here we need a momentary digression. *The Wealth of Nations* is a linguistically conservative text. Smith invents no new technical terms and he even avoids new terms, such as "equilibrium," which are available to him. If he is studying what we would call the economy, he never invents a technical term for the object of his study; his subject is simply "wealth." He uses "political oeconomy," the enterprise he is engaged in, in two distinct senses: "political economy" can stand either for what we would call economic policy (as when he says "the great object of the political oeconomy of every country, is to encrease the riches and power of that country") or for what he calls a "a branch of the science of a statesman or legislator" which is properly concerned with "the nature and causes of the wealth of nations" and we would call the discipline of economics.[47] If you look in the *OED* for words which are said to appear first in *The Wealth of Nations* you will find only five: "derange," "métayer," "unfunded," "reimposition," and "slit-mill," words of no importance for Smith's argument. This is not because lexicographers have not pored over *The Wealth of Nations*—there are more than six hundred quotations from it in the *OED;* it is that Smith never knowingly invented new words. In this respect "competition," "circulation," "system" and "invisible hand" are typical—Smith innovated only through slight adjustments of meaning—and indeed in fifty-eight cases (including "economist" and "market") he is credited (not always correctly) with using words in new senses. Of course, the *OED* may have missed some new words, but if so I have yet to find them. Indeed, it is a striking feature of classical political economy (Smith, David Ricardo, and John Stuart Mill) and of its precursors (William Petty, Nicholas Barbon, Cantillon, James Steuart, and Hume) that its arguments rarely required linguistic innovation.[48] The reason for this is, on reflection, obvious: the political economists were discussing a form of life (to use Ludwig Wittgenstein's phrase) which already existed; and the language required to conduct that form of life consequently already existed.

Much more important is a whole vocabulary that Smith generally avoided using: "selfish," "self-interest," "self-love," and "rapacity" are terms which appear between one and three times each in *The Wealth of Nations,* and never in favorable contexts—one may contrast the passage from *The Theory of Moral Sentiments* with which I began, with its reference to the natural selfishness and rapacity of the rich.* In *The Wealth of Nations* Smith opts for more neutral terms such as "particular interest" and "private interest" (nineteen occurrences, taken together).

Our exploration of the way in which invisible hand arguments can resemble automatic machines, but not machines known to Hume and Smith, is the key, I would argue, to a resolution of the famous Adam Smith Problem, which we begin to see appearing in this issue of vocabulary. "Das Adam Smith Problem" was identified by German scholars in the nineteenth century. They argued that there was a radical difference between the only two books that Adam Smith published in his lifetime: *The Theory of Moral Sentiments* (1759) and *The Wealth of Nations* (1776). *The Theory of Moral Sentiments,* they claimed, was a book which advocated action for the welfare of others, action based on sympathy and benevolence, while *The Wealth of Nations* assumed that human beings are entirely selfish in their behavior. *The Theory of Moral Sentiments* implied a divinely ordained system of values, while *The Wealth of Nations* was implicitly materialist and atheist. The difference between the two works could be explained by Smith's visit to Paris in 1765–1766, where, it was suggested, he had fallen under the influence of Claude Adrien Helvétius.[49] The publication in 1896 of Smith's *Lectures on Justice, Police, Revenue, and Arms* (dating to 1763) eliminated the Adam Smith Problem as originally defined, for it showed that Smith had held the views he had published in *The Wealth of Nations* long before he had gone to Paris; indeed, if we are to believe Dugald Stewart, Smith was already lecturing along these lines early in the 1750s, in which case his economic theory actually predates that of the physiocrats.[50]

---

* In *The Theory of Moral Sentiments* "selfish" and "self-love" each occur thirty-one times, "self-interest" nine times, and "rapacity" only once.

Most scholars now argue that there is no Adam Smith Problem. *The Theory of Moral Sentiments* and *The Wealth of Nations* are different in that one is a work of moral philosophy and social psychology, the other of economic analysis, but the two works fit neatly together, describing the same behaviors and the same society. In particular, the behavior Smith describes in *The Wealth of Nations* corresponds to the behavior he attributes in *The Theory of Moral Sentiments* to a prudent man.* Smith, it must be remembered, uses "sympathy" in a very extended sense: we do not only feel sympathy for someone who has suffered a tragic loss, but also (in Smith's use of the term) for a hardworking businessman who is saving money so that he can invest in his business. Indeed, in *The Theory of Moral Sentiments,* just as in *The Wealth of Nations,* Smith assumes that everyone is engaged in the endless struggle to better their condition.[51]

Another view concedes that the two works do not fit quite so neatly together, for one is about how we ought to behave toward our family, friends, and neighbors (who evoke our benevolent feelings), and the other about how we should interact with strangers we meet in the marketplace (to whom we owe no particular duty of care—caveat emptor is an attitude we can legitimately adopt to strangers, but not to family, friends, and neighbors).

A third approach would be to stress that *The Wealth of Nations* is primarily about government policy toward economic activity and taxation; in matters of government policy it is, to quote Hume, "a just *political* maxim, *That every man must be supposed a knave:* Tho' at the same time, I must own it appears somewhat strange, that a Maxim should be true in *Politics,* which is false in *Fact.*"[52] Human beings are not really utterly selfish, but the legislator should act as if they are.

These various suggestions are helpful, but I would argue that a fundamental difficulty remains, and it is the necessary consequence of Smith's invisible hand arguments, for what matters for the economist and the sociologist are the (often unintended) consequences of our behavior for society as a whole, while what must matter for the moral philosopher is what we intend our actions to achieve and how far we succeed in realizing our objectives. It is this gap between intended and unintended consequences, a gap both central to Smith's theories and to the functioning of modern

---

* See Appendix E in the present volume.

societies, which is at the heart of the Adam Smith Problem and is a genuine problem in the coherence and consistency of Smith's thinking. It is also a problem that bedevils any effort to think about society within the terms established by the Enlightenment paradigm—and, since we continue to think within that paradigm, it is natural that we should wish to minimize the nature and extent of the difficulty. Indeed, the Adam Smith Problem, as I would redefine it, has become so familiar that we now barely notice it: we look out at the world from within the iron cage of Smith's system, and find it difficult to imagine a vantage point from which we could look in on Smith's system from the outside.

The fundamental issue is straightforward. Smith's political economy rejects the idea of a just price and leaves the market to determine what prices should be. As soon as you make this move, you inevitably create a tension between the amoral world of market forces and the moral world of human interactions.* *The Wealth of Nations* establishes the extent to which our choices are constrained by market forces, and these constraints limit our opportunities for admirable moral behavior.[53] Let us consider, for example, a lazy person who owns a pin-making manufactory.† Because he does not supervise his workers properly they will not work as hard as the workers in the manufactory down the road. Occasionally they will be standing around waiting for materials to work on or for tools to be repaired. Completed orders will not be shipped out promptly. Costs will not be controlled, productivity will be low, turnover will be slow. What will happen? Perhaps our lazy entrepreneur will go bust; his business will close and his employees be thrown

---

* Smith writes, "There can be no proper motive for hurting our neighbour, there can be no incitement to do evil to another, which mankind will go along with, except just indignation for evil which that other has done to us. To disturb his happiness meerly because it stands in the way of our own, to take from him what is of real use to him meerly because it may be of equal or of more use to us, or to indulge, in this manner, at the expence of other people, the natural preference which every man has for his own happiness above that of other people, is what no impartial spectator can go along with." Smith, *The Theory of Moral Sentiments* (1759), 180–181 (pt. 2, sec. 2, ch. 2). Yet, indirectly through the market, we constantly hurt our neighbors in these ways with Smith's approval.

† I avoid the word "factory" because Smith was not, in his account of pin making (Smith, *The Wealth of Nations* [1776)], 1:6–7), talking about powered machinery. Watchmaking would have provided him with another example; see Morgan Kelly and Cormac Ó Gráda, "Adam Smith, Watch Prices, and the Industrial Revolution," *Quarterly Journal of Economics* 131 (2016), 1727–1752.

out of work; and the manufactory down the road will acquire his customers. Alternatively he may stumble along, keeping the business going, but only by living modestly himself, and finding himself chronically short of funds for investment and expansion. And, if he is short of funds for investment, he will also be short of funds that he might have chosen to give to charity.

Some entrepreneurs work longer hours, drive harder bargains, and make better profits; others stumble along, more or less keeping up with the competition; others are lazy or good-natured, employing their family and friends on favorable terms, and end up going out of business. Now, in all three cases the market in pins continues to be made as if none of these three people existed: in the longer run the price is set by notional entrepreneurs who have borrowed money and have to pay interest, who run their business with reasonable efficiency, and who expect to live to a certain standard. If a pin-making business will not support such entrepreneurs to the standard they can reasonably expect, then they will close it down and open new businesses that promise to be more profitable. If business is exceptionally good, and they make lots of money, others will crowd in until profits fall to the normal rate. In other words, markets are about aggregates and averages. As far as Smith is concerned in *The Wealth of Nations* it is this "typical" entrepreneur who is the only one who needs to be considered when formulating policy or considering how investments and prices will move. And note that this typical entrepreneur may well be a benevolent pillar of the community—what he chooses to do with his money is, after all, his affair, so long as he keeps generating a return on his investments.[54]

Let us take the case of a benevolent man—Thomas Davison. My interest in him originates in the fact that he owned a copy of Francois Vincent Toussaint's *Les moeurs* (1748) or *Manners* (1749), a book attributed to Diderot when first published and banned in its original language by the French authorities for being irreligious, but one which immediately went through numerous editions—sixteen in French dated 1748 and eight in English between 1749 and 1752.[55] Toussaint wrote that "charity . . . is not a virtue of supererogation. You only satisfy the law of humanity, if meeting a stranger

MANNERS:

Translated from the *FRENCH* of

LES MOEURS:

WHEREIN THE

PRINCIPLES of MORALITY,

O R

SOCIAL DUTIES,

V I Z.

PIETY,	TEMPERANCE,
WISDOM,	LOVE,
PRUDENCE,	FRIENDSHIP,
FORTITUDE,	HUMANITY,
JUSTICE,	&c. &c. &c.

A R E

Described in all their BRANCHES;

T H E

OBLIGATIONS of them shewn to consist in our Nature;

A N D   T H E

ENLARGEMENT of them strongly enforced.

—— *Respicere exemplar vitæ morumque.*
HOR. AD. PIS.

LONDON:

Printed for W. JOHNSTON, in St. *Paul's*
Church-Yard. 1749.

Title page from François-Vincent Toussaint, *Manners* (12°) (1749),
copy originally owned by Thomas Davison.

wounded by robbers, you draw near him to dress his wounds.* The need he has in this case of your succour, is a law, which obliges you to succour him. An indigent person is pressed by hunger; you only pay a debt to nature in relieving his want. The poor are the charge and care of the public: all the superfluity of the rich should go to their subsistance."[56]

Davison seems to have taken these words to heart. In 1754 he founded in Newcastle a hospital for six single women, and in 1755 established a trust to help young men set up in business. His tomb was to be found in or outside St. John's Church, Kirk Merrington:

> Here lies interred the body of Thomas Davison, Esq. third son of Timothy Davison, Esq. of Newcastle, and Beamish in this county, by Elizabeth his wife, daughter of Sir William Blacket, Baronet. He was born on the 15th of May 1675, and died on the 5th of March 1760. He had many more virtues and much fewer foibles than are often found in one man; and though he lived to a great age, he had the uncommon felicity of living universally esteemed and regretted by all who knew him, as well rich as poor. His strict integrity, his unaffected piety, together with a most agreeable and cheerful temper, rendered him truly amiable to the former; his great humanity and most extensive generosity made his life a blessing, and his death an irreparable loss, to the latter.
>
> The following sentences are engraved on his tomb by his own desire:
> Do justly;
> love mercy.
> Walk humbly with thy God,
>   and that will bring thee peace at the last.[57]

Davison was apparently unmarried and childless, and in old age, when his long struggle to better his condition was drawing to an end, he gave away substantial sums to charitable purposes, thus acquiring "the uncommon felicity of living universally esteemed." He had enjoyed the advantages of being wealthy, and now, as he approached the age of eighty, when there was little point in making further investments, he began to enjoy the satisfaction of being benevolent.

---

* Toussaint evidently has the Good Samaritan in mind.

Davison was a small-scale version of entrepreneurs such as Andrew Carnegie, Bill Gates, and George Soros. First, in the spirit of *The Wealth of Nations,* they got rich; and then, in the spirit of (some parts, at least, of) *The Theory of Moral Sentiments,* they gave their money away. Not every individual need perform both parts; but both parts need to be performed if the old and infirm are to be sheltered and the children of the poor are to have opportunities for advancement. The one thing you can't do is be both economically rational and benevolent at the same time. And of course, historically and logically, there is an order that must be respected: prosperity is a precondition for substantial charitable donations, and you can't reverse the order. Carnegie could not have founded libraries without Carnegie Steel, and Carnegie Steel's profits derived partly from union busting.* I don't mean to suggest that Smith held that charitable giving epitomizes virtue or is even a necessary part of a virtuous life; I do mean to claim that he believed that prosperity opens up new opportunities for benevolent sentiments and (seemingly) altruistic actions.

This tension between prosperity and benevolence replicates that between reason of state and conventional morality.[58] Consider the case of the state which switches sides in order to maintain the balance of power. This may well involve breaking treaties, but it would be wrong to describe the action as moral or immoral, for it is simply rational; what is at stake is survival, and safety is the supreme law. And if one small state does not change sides to reestablish the balance, then another must—it really does not matter which one makes the move, as long as someone does. So too an entrepreneur who buys a failing business for less than the value of its assets, makes the workers redundant, and sells the assets at a profit may be described as hard-hearted, but he is simply acting rationally, and can claim that in the long run the resources released will be better employed. Markets are amoral and impersonal in the same way as reason of state is amoral and impersonal.

---

* The same issues arise with tax revenue: only a prosperous economy can generate the taxes required to fund Medicaid and the like, but a prosperous economy requires businesses which engage in cutthroat competition. I won't reiterate here the arguments which demonstrate that a socialist or planned economy is no solution.

But this only takes us from one problem to another. The statesman who tears up a treaty and the entrepreneur who lays off workers both claim to be following a code which trumps conventional morality. Most would now agree that you do not have to be immoral to be a successful entrepreneur, but then morality has been redefined to fit with market values, as we have seen in Smith's account of prudence as a freestanding virtue. Competition, which seeks to put other enterprises out of business, has, partly as a result of Smith's argument, been legitimized: guilds, it must be remembered, existed to limit competition between their members, and in Smith's day lawyers and doctors were forbidden to advertise because members of the liberal professions were not supposed to be in competition with each other. Davison surely dealt with his colleagues with "strict integrity," but strict integrity is compatible with driving hard bargains. And every successful entrepreneur must be prepared to drive hard bargains. There is rarely any place for mercy in business.

Davison, the second surviving son in a very large family, would have had to work hard to make his way in the world. Was it worth it? According to Smith, the struggle to better one's condition is not a rational undertaking—the major benefits flow to society and not to the individual. Economic growth is built on a collective delusion. Smith believes there are two interlocking explanations for this delusion. First, people are competitive. They want to be admired and approved. In general the wealthy are admired and approved, so people pursue wealth not for the sake of money but for the sake of the status that comes with it. They scrimp and save, they work long hours, they fret and worry in the hope that one day they will be successful, rich, and respected—never calculating that the effort they put in costs far more in terms of lost happiness than the rewards they may one day hope to acquire. This failure to calculate is characteristic in fact of what Smith calls, following Plato, the spirited man.[59] Still, even in the short term, such men do have a reward: they are admired for their prudence and hard work even if they never become truly wealthy. In a commercial society hard work itself confers status and esteem; were this not the case commercial societies would be unable to function effectively.[60] Thus the delusion has to be shared by society as a whole, or the individual will be insufficiently motivated to set aside present pleasure for the (often delusory) prospect of future happiness.

Second, there is something else about wealth that makes it attractive and admirable, other than the status it brings. In a feudal society, the great lord has a gang of retainers; he can defend his friends and do harm to his enemies; he can feed his followers and his relatives. But in a commercial society he has no great hall, no feudal army, no private justice. What he has is an elegant carriage, a superior watch, a coat made of silk, a diamond ring from the Indies, a parrot. Those around him admire these trappings of wealth because they exhibit the most exquisite craftsmanship, the most refined taste, the most discriminating consumerism. The wealthy man, if he is civilized and sophisticated, basks in the admiration of others, admiration not just for his success, but also for the good things his success has made it possible for him to acquire.

But does an expensive watch that is right within a minute a fortnight do a significantly better job than one which is right to a minute a day? Surely not. Such objects are "mere trinkets of frivolous utility."[61] There is indeed some additional pleasure in owning a finely made object, the best of its kind, but think of what could have been done with the time in which that money was earned—a country vicar, sitting reading in his garden on a summer's day, with a watch in his pocket that loses a minute or two a day, is far happier than the entrepreneur who occasionally pulls from his pocket an expensive timepiece only to discover that, yet again, the day has slipped away, and his time has not been his own.[62] Thus it would seem that those who pursue wealth do so because they have doubly miscalculated. First, they have overvalued the pleasures that accompany status and luxury, and undervalued tranquility and leisure. And second, they have underestimated the risk that they will never achieve their goals.[63] Even when they do come to enjoy the pleasures of success, few realize that the best thing they can do with their money is give it away. Davison, Smith would have held, would have gotten more satisfaction from establishing charities than from making money or spending it.[64] And Davison would seem to have agreed, for he found peace *at the last.*

Smith tells us, in the passage with which I began, that the miscalculation of those who seek to better their condition is a good thing because it leads to economic growth and population increase. Remember the butcher, the brewer, and the baker: their selfish behavior turns out to be to our benefit. Thus, although there is an Adam Smith Problem—or rather a

market / morality problem—in that sensible people need to compartmen-
talize their thinking and make a sharp distinction between economic and
altruistic behavior, there is, from another viewpoint, no problem in that self-
interested economic behavior benefits everyone, for the butcher, the brewer
and the baker can be described as providing a public service. Moreover,
since self-interested economic motivations (however fallacious the hedonic
calculations on which they are based) are more to be relied on than altruistic motivations it is very fortunate (indeed, it is providential) that private
interest and public interest mesh together in this way.

The issue is well represented by Smith's views on university education.
Smith believed he received an excellent education in Glasgow, but a dreadful
education when he went on to Oxford. In Glasgow professors (including
Smith himself in due course) received much of their income from fees paid
by the individual students who chose to enroll in their classes—no students,
no fees. Professors therefore had a strong financial incentive to attract fee-
paying students. In Oxford there was no incentive of this sort, and instruction was lazy and inadequate. The Oxford system relied on instructors
having a moral commitment to the welfare of their students; the Glasgow
system (while doing nothing to discourage such a moral commitment) relied on self-interest. In Smith's view the Oxford system failed miserably.[65]

It is thus wrong to think that self-interest and benevolence are generally
at odds: a lawyer, a doctor, or a professor who provides good services to customers at a reasonable price is providing a public service just as much as
the butcher, the brewer, or the baker. And, of course, in Smith's world this
is how most services were provided—the state was still small, and the main
nationalized public services (if one can so call them) were the church and
the armed forces. Very few people were in the position of my imaginary
country vicar, or a fellow of an Oxford college, whose income would be the
same no matter how he spent his time. Most were either employed by private enterprises (sometimes on piecework rates) or were themselves, in effect, entrepreneurs. As Cantillon put it, "all the exchange and circulation of
the State is conducted by the medium of these Undertakers."[66] As far as Cantillon was concerned, entrepreneurs were not a peculiar and small group
within society. There were in effect only three economic classes: landlords,
employees, and entrepreneurs. Farmers and butchers, doctors and lawyers,
bankers and authors all fell into this last group.

I have tried to show that whether the Adam Smith Problem exists or not depends upon how you approach it. Yes, self-interested behavior and benevolent behavior are not the same thing and are very often at odds. The successful pin maker must seek to drive his competitors out of business and to make their workers unemployed. But no, self-interested behavior is not immoral (according to Smith), because in market societies the society as a whole benefits from the self-interested behavior of individuals, and indeed their self-interested behavior is often to be preferred over inadequately motivated benevolence. It is thus a good thing, in Smith's view, that we treat "prudence," which is the quality which enables individuals to pursue their own advantage, and encourages them to defer gratification, as a virtue in its own right. The invisible hand turns private interest into public good, and there is no problem after all. Here the comparison between economic behavior and reason of state breaks down, for the statesman who pursues the interests of his state not only finds himself obliged to violate good morals; an outcome that is good for one state is often bad for all the others—there is (except in the special case of the balance of power) no invisible hand at work.

Still, you might say, this way of thinking assumes what it needs to prove. It assumes that economic growth and population increase are inherently good things. But what makes these good? An answer is that they are good from the point of view of political economy, whose purpose is to maximize national wealth—that is to say (before all else, though Smith deals with it last) the resources the state can draw on through taxation in order to engage in warfare. These resources will increase if the population grows while standards of living rise (or at least do not fall). Thus the state's interests coincide with what Smith, in his introduction, calls "the general welfare of the society." But should a person of moral sentiments adopt these values? Might Jean-Jacques Rousseau not be right? Would we not be morally better people, would we not be truly happier if we lived in smaller, poorer societies where we felt strong ties of fellowship with others, where we had a real sense of community?

Smith provides the answer to this question in book 3 of *The Wealth of Nations:* "Order and good government, and along with them the liberty and security of individuals, were," he tells us there, "established in cities at a time when the occupiers of land in the country were exposed to every sort of violence." Later, "commerce and manufactures gradually introduced order and good government, and with them, the liberty and security of individuals, among the inhabitants of the country, who had before lived almost in a continual state of war with their neighbours, and of servile dependency upon their superiors. This, though it has been the least observed, is by far the most important of all their effects. Mr. Hume is the only writer who, so far as I know, has hitherto taken notice of it."[67] The most important effect of commerce and manufactures is thus not wealth or population increase but liberty and security; and liberty and security make possible a happy life, rather than a life blighted by fear and violence, and a virtuous life, rather than a life spent scrambling for subsistence and survival. This is the greatest of all the prestidigitations of the invisible hand of providence: out of the misconceived pursuit of profit there comes the opportunity that each and every one of us who is caught up in the effort to better our condition has to find some measure of happiness and to lead (at least now and again) a life of virtue. The beggar sunning himself by the roadside, who has withdrawn from the struggle to advance himself, is, unlike Smith and his readers, a free rider: he benefits from the liberty and security that commercial society produces, but he no longer contributes to the making of that society.[68]

Thus, as far as individuals are concerned, wealth really is at odds with happiness, and wealth really is in tension with, sometimes at odds with, virtue, while virtue and happiness are generally coincident. Each and every one of us may have to choose between economic interest on the one hand and sentiment and true happiness on the other. But at the same time, quite apart from the fact that commercial society makes prosperity possible, it is commercial society which makes for security, and so makes the lives of happiness and of virtue possible. Consequently, even those who are not taken in by the imaginary benefits of wealth should be glad that others are.* The

---

* This may be compared with the double-truth theory of the Averroists: the philosopher, who knows that religion is an illusion, must be glad, they held, that society as a whole believes in its truth, for this helps ensure good behavior. The early seventeenth-century philosopher and unbeliever Cesare Cremonini hired only pious servants, convinced this would make them less likely to steal from him. Voltaire, in 1770, wrote, "I want my lawyer, my tailor, my servants, even my wife to believe in God, because it means that I shall be cheated and robbed and cuckolded less often. . . . If God did not exist, it would be necessary to invent him." So too Smith, having seen that wealth does not result in happiness,

good society needs economic rationality, even though the good person will not be (or at least will not always be) a rational economic actor. There is a causal chain that links commerce at one end, through liberty and security, to happiness and virtue at the other. Just as Newton's solar system is stable because it has been designed by God, so the tension between the market and morality seems insuperable until you recognize the invisible hand of providence at work.[69] Invisible hand processes are not just some peculiar epicycle within Smith's elaborate system; they are the providential mechanism which reconciles wealth and virtue. Smith would have approved both of Davison's moneymaking and of his charity; and so perhaps must we, but then we approach the question from within Smith's intellectual system, and we do not know how to escape from it.

believes it essential that society as a whole should (mistakenly) believe that it does. If a motive for deferred gratification did not exist, it would be necessary to invent one.

A MODEST
PROPOSAL

For preventing the

CHILDREN

O F

POOR PEOPLE

From being a Burthen to

Their Parents or Country,

A N D

For making them Beneficial to the
P U B L I C K.

By Dr. S W I F T.

Dublin, Printed by *S. Harding*:
London, Re-printed; and fold by *J. Roberts*
in *Warwick-lane*, and the Pamphlet-Shops.
M. D C C. X X I X.

Title page from Jonathan Swift, *A Modest Proposal* (8°) (1729).

8

The Market: Poverty and Famines

This chapter is about what the Irish statesman Daniel O'Connell, speaking in the House of Commons in 1831, called "starvation in the midst of plenty."[1] As he spoke, ships in Irish ports were being laden with grain for export while people died of hunger. There was food in plenty; what the starving lacked was the money to pay for it. What was peculiar to Ireland was not hunger in the midst of plenty, but the absence of effective intervention to prevent hunger intensifying and spreading until it developed into famine.

Such famines had once been commonplace. According to Louis Paul Abeille, writing in 1768, France had often faced the prospect of famine when food supplies were abundant.[2] Writing on the grain trade in 1775, at a time when bread riots ("the flour war") were breaking out across France, Jacques Necker (who would become minister of finance in 1777) stated that his goal was to identify the "sage precautions" which, if adopted by the French government, would ensure that "the cry of famine in the midst of abundance" would no longer be heard.[3] Adam Smith, who consulted Necker's book, was, I will argue, deaf to that cry.

Let us jump ahead, momentarily, from the immediate context of the publication of Smith's *The Wealth of Nations.* Here is a passage from Parson Woodforde's diary for 6 March 1795; Woodforde was dining with three guests and his niece: "For Dinner a Couple of boiled Chicken and Pigs Face, very good Peas Soup, a boiled Rump of Beef very fine, a prodigious fine, large and very fat Cock-Turkey roasted, Macaroni, Batter Custard Pudding with Jelly, Apple Fritters, Tarts and Raspberry Puffs. Desert, baked Apples, nice Nonpareils, brandy Cherries and Filberts . . . Mr. Custance eat [*sic*] very hearty."[4] There was plenty, too, to drink: wines, port, sherries, malt liquors, strong beer, and bottled porter. As Parson Woodforde tucked into his dinner, the poor in his parish were on the point of starvation. They were being supplied with subsidized brown bread, and bread and coal (it was a bitter winter and late spring) were occasionally delivered free to them (paid for by collections in church) on Sundays. In the first months of 1795 there were seventy-two bread riots in England, and this and the next year are years which some would want to call years of famine, though they are perhaps better described, in the words of John Bohstedt, as "years of terrible shortages marked by pockets of starvation."[5]

Hannah More wrote a poem discouraging riots; her views are expressed by Jack Anvil, who resolves,

> So I'll work the whole day, and on Sundays I'll seek
> At Church how to bear all the wants of the week.
> The gentlefolks, too, will afford us supplies,
> They'll subscribe—and they'll give up their puddings and pies.
> *Derry down.*[6]

Though, as we have seen, Parson Woodforde had not and would not give up his puddings and pies.

How should we respond to the juxtaposition of Woodforde's generous dinners and the near starvation of his parishioners? In 1935 his editor John Beresford remarked, "Fortunately for the Poor the fount of eighteenth-century Charity seems to have flowed with generous freedom, and bread and coal were given for many months—Squire Custance and Parson Woodforde each subscribing £10 to the general collection." (Woodforde had an income of £400 per annum.) He describes "the charitable stream" as flowing freely "on all and every occasion of distress."[7] The socialist historian Edward Thompson took a more cynical view, remarking that Woodforde, who suffered horribly from gout, had been "crippled by an excess of rich food" but nevertheless "did not flinch before his continuing duty to his own dinner."[8]

It is no part of the historian's business, it might be argued, to sit in judgment on Parson Woodforde; I would tend to agree. But historians of ideas *are* under an obligation to identify muddled thinking. This chapter is about a striking intellectual failure on the part of Adam Smith: his failure to recognize the possibility of starvation in the midst of plenty. Smith's failure, I will argue, obliges us to question not only the consistency of his ideas, but also his moral judgments. The arraignment of Adam Smith *is,* I submit, part of the historian's business.[9]

The word "system" recurs over and over again in *The Wealth of Nations*—204 times, to be exact. This is because Smith is advocating a system, and at the same time attacking the systems of his opponents (the word "system" runs through the writings of the physiocrats); but it is not immediately apparent that he uses the word in three distinct senses. A system, in the language of Smith's day, can be simply an intellectual structure, a program of knowledge— Francis Hutcheson, for example, had published *A System of Moral Philosophy* in 1749, and Étienne Bonnot de Condillac had published his *Traité des systèmes* the same year (both books were owned by Smith). If the system is too rigid and abstract, its author suffers from an *esprit de système* (a phrase which dates back at least to 1709). Smith originated the phrase "the man of system," at least when used pejoratively: it first appears in the sixth edition of *The Theory of Moral Sentiments* (1790): "The man of system . . . is apt to be very wise in his own conceit."[10]

But a system can also be a mental machine with moving parts, such as the Copernican system (Galileo had written on *the two chief world systems*): in "The History of Astronomy" Smith refers to intellectual systems in natural philosophy as imaginary machines in the mind; because they are imaginary, we cannot be sure that they are correct, and for all his admiration for Isaac Newton, Smith held back from saying the Newtonian system was true—it was merely a very fine act of imagination, a mental machine that perfectly mimicked reality.[11] I don't believe that Smith has anything like the same reservations about the system of free trade; his system is, in his view, not just a good argument, a neat intellectual device, but a true and in some sense a necessary set of claims about what works best. This is partly because it is a form of applied or practical knowledge, but also because it is grounded in certain features of human behavior about which we cannot possibly be mistaken. Gravity is a mental construct; self-interest is a matter of our direct experience.[12]

But if Smith's system is more certain, more incontrovertible than Newton's, it is at the same time (as we saw in Chapter 7) just like Newton's in a crucial respect. In the Newtonian system, as each astronomical body acts on every other astronomical body, if you alter the mass or position or trajectory of one body you alter, perhaps only very slightly, that of all the others.

It is a fully interactive system, although Newton lacked the capacity to model it as such; he struggled with the moon's orbit, which is primarily influenced by the earth and the sun, and this became known as the three-body problem, which was solved by Leonhard Euler and Joseph Louis Lagrange in the decade before the publication of *The Wealth of Nations*. Smith's free market system is a system of this Newtonian sort, though it is not the first economic system in this sense—the credit for that goes to François Quesnay's *tableau économique* of 1758, which Smith so evidently admired. The American constitution is also intended to be a system in this post-Newtonian sense.*

Smith says that what he advocates is the "natural system of perfect liberty and justice" (IV.vii.c.44), "the obvious and simple system of natural liberty" (IV.ix.51)—"system" here is being used, I think, in any one or all three of the senses I distinguished a moment ago.[13] Like Quesnay and the physiocrats, and (Smith implies) like no one else, he advocates "perfect liberty" (IV.ix.38). The physiocrats were primarily concerned to insist on free trade in the products of agriculture, but Smith was the not the first to advocate free trade as a systematic policy; nor the first to write in praise of competition; nor even of the division of labor. As Dugald Stewart put it in his "Account of the Life and Writings of Adam Smith" (1791), "the merit of such a work as Mr Smith's is to be estimated less from the novelty of the principles it contains, than from the reasonings employed to support these principles, and from the scientific manner in which they are unfolded in their proper order and connection."[14] Thus, the secret to understanding Smith is not to look for new words or even concepts but to note what *isn't* there, and what isn't there is a key word for the physiocrats: "equilibrium."

The word "equilibrium" occurs only once in *The Wealth of Nations*, when Smith is outlining a position with which he disagrees. He writes,

---

* The *Oxford English Dictionary* (updated June 2015) gives 1806 for the first use of "system" to mean an "oppressive or stifling . . . impersonal, restrictive organization." Thus "system" used to refer to something one might be trapped within (an "iron cage") was not available to Smith, but an understanding that market economies are inexorable systems was not new; see Richard Cantillon, *Essai sur la nature du commerce en général, traduit de l'anglais* (London: Gyles, 1755), 220–222; and even Sir Thomas Smith, *A Discourse of the Commonweal of this Realm of England*, ed. Mary Dewar (Charlottesville, Va.: Folger Shakespeare Library, 1969), first ed. 1581.

"Nothing, however, can be more absurd than this whole doctrine of the balance of trade. . . . When two places trade with one another, this doctrine supposes that, if the balance be even, neither of them either loses or gains; but if it leans in any degree to one side, that one of them loses, and the other gains, in proportion to its declension from the exact equilibrium. Both suppositions are false" (IV.iii.31). Smith's system is one in constant movement, but one in which (as in the Newtonian system) nothing ever returns exactly to its starting point—unlike Quesnay's model of a fully developed agricultural economy, in which a perfect equilibrium would be achieved. As Andrew Skinner has said, "As befits a writer concerned to address the problems of change, including adjustment to change, Smith's position was also distinctive in that he was not directly concerned with [the] phenomenon even of partial equilibrium. For Smith, the 'natural' (supply) price was, as it were: 'The central price, to which the prices of all commodities are continually gravitating . . . whatever may be the obstacles which hinder them from settling in this centre of response and continuance, they are constantly tending towards it'" (quoting I.vii.15).[15] In the Smithian system all sorts of things are "continually gravitating" or "constantly tending," but nothing ever reaches an end point, a moment of repose, a perfect balance, an equilibrium. In this dynamism Smith is much closer to Richard Cantillon than he is to the physiocrats.[16]

This chapter is concerned with one particular aspect of Adam Smith's dynamic system of liberty: his discussion of what he calls "dearth" and what some call "famine" in book 4, chapter 5 of *The Wealth of Nations,* in the "Digression concerning the Corn Trade and Corn Laws." Smith's views on dearth or famine (I'll use the two words interchangeably for the moment, but it will become apparent that Smith distinguishes sharply between them) are of obvious importance, for they are not only of crucial significance for his whole intellectual system (despite his use of the word "digression," which wrongly implies that they are of merely marginal importance), but through much of the nineteenth century they were used to justify the British government's response to famines in Ireland and India.[17] Let me therefore start by quickly situating my topic within two contexts: first, a historiographical one, and second, the context of the emergence of political economy.

In 1971 Edward Thompson, the author of *The Making of the English Working Class* and perhaps the most important socialist historian writing in English in the twentieth century (a title for which there is rather strong competition), published an essay entitled "The Moral Economy of the English Crowd in the Eighteenth Century" which is a sustained attack on economic reductionism, yet written from a Marxist perspective.[18] Thompson's subject was urban bread riots, and what he set out to show was that eighteenth-century riots over the price of bread were not disorderly, indiscriminate, or indeed violent events. Rioters seized control of bakeries in order to sell bread at what they took to be a fair price, leaving the money collected behind for the baker; similar treatment was handed out to millers, who were forced to sell their flour, and farmers, who were forced to sell their grain.

The mob saw itself as enforcing a right, a right that had once been enforced by the magistrates: the right to have the price of bread, flour, and grain fixed at an affordable level. Since the magistrates had lost the authority to fix bread, flour, and grain prices, the mob now did the job they used to do. Bread riots thus represented a clash between the new values of the free market and the older values of paternalistic and communitarian good government. What was to become the new political economy, which favored competition and profit, clashed with an older set of values which Thompson called a "moral economy," the notion that economic relations should not be determined simply by market forces but should also be constrained by mutually acknowledged moral obligations—the tradition of the just price. Thompson's idea of a moral economy was widely adopted, particularly by those studying peasant societies.[19] He discussed Smith's digression on dearth or famine as the classic example of the new views to which the old moral economy was opposed. Smith stood for everything that the bread rioters were rioting against, for he thought the price of bread should be set by market forces, even if the end result was starvation.[20] His views coincided with the times—the statute against forestalling, or the buying of grain before it was brought to market, was repealed in 1772.

A decade after Thompson's article there appeared Amartya Sen's *Poverty and Famines,* a work which was a significant part of the publication record which won for Sen the Nobel Prize in Economics in 1998.[21] Taking as his major case study the Bengal Famine of 1943 (which he had himself witnessed in childhood), Sen argued that famines could occur not only when there was an absolute shortage of food (what he called FAD, food availability decline), but also when people were unable to access the food that was present (what he called FEE, a failure of exchange entitlements).[22] In Bengal in 1943 the harvest did not fail, but rapid inflation in the cities caused by the introduction of a war economy meant that rural workers were priced out of the grain market. There was grain in plenty, but not for them, and between two and three million died. Sen thus provided a sustained argument explaining how one could have starvation in the midst of plenty.

Sen's basic premise, that there was no shortage of food in Bengal in 1943, has proved highly controversial, but what matters for our present purposes is that it led to a reexamination of Smith's views on famine: Smith, Emma Rothschild argued, was not systematically opposed (as nineteenth-century authors assumed) to government intervention to alleviate famines; in fact, his approach was entirely compatible with steps taken to boost exchange entitlements by creating work or raising wages.[23] Smith may have believed that the market should set the price of bread, but he would have been, could have been, or should have been perfectly prepared to see the exchange entitlements of the poor protected. Rothschild presented a very different Smith from the one described by Thompson.[24]

Thus Smith's views on famine have been, in the course of the last half century, an important text for discussions of the failings of free market economies. Indeed, the discussion of dearth or famine was also a crucial text for the first readers of his book. Free market arguments had been pioneered in France by the physiocrats, whose key policy proposal was the introduction of a free market in grain in an economy where the export of grain was traditionally banned, and where even the sale of grain between different parts of the country was commonly restricted. The new free trade policy was adopted in 1764, but abandoned in 1770 in the light of rising prices, popular protests, and extensive hardship; it was readopted briefly in 1774–1775, and abandoned once again in the face of widespread disorder.[25] Smith was in France from 1764 to 1766, where he became friends with many of the leading free market advocates, including Anne-Robert-Jacques Turgot, and thus he watched the free trade revolution as it happened.* When Smith returned to

---

* What Smith learned from this experiment was, apparently, not that free trade in corn would not work, but that "The laws concerning corn may every where be compared to

Scotland it was to settle down to work on *The Wealth of Nations,* a work he originally intended to dedicate to the intellectual leader of the physiocrats, Quesnay (who died before the book was published). He was certainly aware, when he came to publish, that the free trade revolution had run into insuperable difficulties and he was evidently following developments—in *The Wealth of Nations* he refers to Necker's book of 1775, and he also owned a work published in November 1774.[26] *The Wealth of Nations* was thus conceived, written, and published in the context of French disputes over the regulation of the grain trade, disputes in which the advocates of free trade had ended up on the losing side; Smith's handling of the question of the grain trade was bound to be read in this party political context.

In 1776 grain was also a lively issue in England.[27] At stake was a legal system which provided (except in years of dearth) a bounty for exports of wheat (or "corn," as it was called) combined with duties on imports, the idea being that giving farmers a subsidy for exports and a protected home market would encourage investment in agriculture and expand the area of land under the plow, thus providing greater security and cheaper food in years of bad harvest. There had been harvest crises in 1757, in 1766, and again in 1772–1773; these were accompanied by grain riots, and by a lively pamphlet literature on the laws governing the grain trade.[28] Charles Smith, for example, published *A Short Essay on the Corn Trade* in 1758 and *Considerations on the Laws relating to the Importation and Exportation of Corn* in 1759, in response to the first of these crises—Smith, who is cited by Adam Smith, defended bounties on exports, but attacked the old laws against forestalling, sale by sample, and so forth, while Arthur Young published an expanded edition of his own *The Farmer's Letters to the People of England: Containing the Sentiments of a Practical Husbandman, on . . . the Exportation of Corn* in 1768; *The Expediency of a Free Exportation of Corn at This Time: With Some Observations on the Bounty, and its Effects* in 1770, and *Political Arithmetic: Containing Observations on the Present State of Great*

---

the laws concerning religion. The people feel themselves so much interested in what relates either to their subsistence in this life, or to their happiness in a life to come, that government must yield to their prejudices, and, in order to preserve the public tranquillity, establish that system which they approve of. It is upon this account, perhaps, that we so seldom find a reasonable system established with regard to either of those two capital objects" (IV.v.b.40).

Britain; And The Principles of Her Policy in the Encouragement of Agriculture in 1774 in response to the second and third (Young was a free trader). These are only a sample of a much wider pamphlet literature. These English debates were increasingly carried on with reference to the arguments of the physiocrats. Thus Young apologized for including numerous quotations from French authors in his expanded *Farmer's Letters:* "but the reader will please to consider, that there is at present in France a set of political writers, whose works are really admirable" (he meant the physiocrats).[29]

A free trade policy had opposite implications in France and in England: in France the government had traditionally intervened with the intention of protecting the short-term interests of the consumer; in England the government's policy had been (except in years of harvest failure) to protect the interests of the producer in the conviction that these coincided with the long-term interests of the consumer, even if this meant higher prices in the short term. The view of proponents of free trade was that both systems were defective, but that the French system was far worse than the English.

In Scotland, France, and England, major famines were past history. The last extensive famine in Scotland had been in the 1690s, in France in 1709, and in England famine was virtually eliminated by the early seventeenth century.[30] So Charles Smith, writing in the late 1750s, felt confident that famine was no longer to be feared: "Our agriculture has been so immensely improved by the wise Institutions of Bounties on Corn exported; Commerce is more practiced and better understood; and it may also be reasonably supposed that our Merchants having both more Knowledge and Capital than in former Times, will, by Importations from one Quarter of the World or another, always prevent a Scarcity from becoming intolerable."[31] Subsequent research has shown that this confidence was not misplaced. As a result of improvements in agriculture, it is argued, there was no occasion in Adam Smith's lifetime when two back-to-back harvests were more than 20 percent below the average in yield, and an individual harvest falling more than 20 percent below the average only occurred once every twenty years. Over the previous centuries the difference in yields between good years and bad years had been slowly and steadily diminishing. The weather was much less of a threat than it had once been.[32] Hence Adam Smith's claim that, though drought and rain are the greatest threats to a successful harvest, "But, as corn grows equally upon high and low lands, upon grounds that are disposed to be too wet, and upon those that are disposed to be too dry, either the drought or the rain which is hurtful to one part of the country is favourable to another . . . what is lost in one part of the country is in some measure compensated by what is gained in the other" (IVv.b.6).[33] The result was that there was never such a thing as a true harvest failure.

Charles Smith was also right to think that international markets were becoming steadily more integrated, a process which continued throughout Adam Smith's lifetime, ensuring that supplies were spread more efficiently across the globe, though this integration went into reverse during the French Revolutionary Wars and was not resumed until the age of steam.[34]

This is not to say that bad harvests did not have real consequences; in England, for example, in 1766–1767 the bad harvests and high price of grain and bread resulted in a measurable increase in mortality and fall in conceptions of around 10 percent.[35] This needs to be put in perspective. If in a small town of one thousand people, thirty of them would normally be born and die each year, then thirty-three would have died and twenty-seven been conceived in 1766–1767. The extra deaths and reduced conceptions were generally not due to famine as such but rather to malnutrition and the resulting weakening of resistance to disease; Smith himself acknowledges that "years of dearth . . . are generally among the common people years of sickness and mortality" (I.viii.44).[36] He discussed how the children of the poor tend to die because their parents cannot feed them or care for them properly—in the Highlands of Scotland, he remarked, it was common for a "half-starved" woman to have twenty children, not two of whom survive to adulthood (I. viii.37–38). Smith knew perfectly well that the greatest "inconveniency" of a dearth was an increased mortality among children and the old. Calling this an "inconveniency" is an abuse of language, and it is important to recognize that what Smith calls a dearth can border on what others would call a famine.

There was however a fundamental difference between France and England. In France there was no systematic, universal provision for relief of the poor, so that the increase in mortality and fall in conceptions was steeper in bad years than in England, and in times of crisis the central government was called upon to take action. In England the corn trade was regulated by the government, but poor relief was paid for by a property tax administered at the local level.[37] Since the tax for the relief of the poor fell on the propertied, there was a natural resistance to increasing it in times of scarcity, when many taxpayers might be having trouble making ends meet. Since there was a general understanding that provision must be made for the aged and incapable, and also for those facing particular difficulties—wage workers with numerous children, for example—the solution adopted was to supplement poor relief by various forms of charity.

Thus, when *The Wealth of Nations* was published, parish-based poor relief and local charitable endeavors were intended to address failures of exchange entitlements, while central government sought to prevent food availability decline by encouraging investment in arable farming. This was markedly different from traditional policies, which had seen justices of the peace intervene to force down prices; the mobs studied by Thompson (and referred to by Smith, IV.v.b.8) continued to do this. Smith was straightforwardly opposed to price fixing. Forcing down prices did two things: first, it discouraged those with grain from bringing it to market, and grain merchants from importing from a distance—it thus endangered supply; second, it encouraged consumption, for it made grain more affordable. In both respects, forcing down prices was likely (Smith would have argued) to make a bad situation worse, and turn a dearth into a famine. Intervention of this sort led to FAD and was thus self-defeating.

Another way of combating FEE would have been to use central government, local government, or charitable funds to create jobs. During the *disette,* the dearth or famine, of 1771–1773, the French economist Turgot, who was a free trader and had been appointed intendant of the Limousin, used government funds to feed the impotent poor; but the able bodied poor (including women and children) he set to work on road building so that they could earn a living at a time when many were being thrown out of work. Emma Rothschild thinks that Smith would have approved such projects.[38] To this one can only reply that had he wanted to make such an argument he had an opportunity to do so, and it is an argument he noticeably failed to make.

In his chapter on the wages of labor (I.viii) Smith argues that during dearths demand for labor falls while the supply of labor increases, with the result that wages fall *precisely at the time when the cost of living is rising sharply.*[39] This important argument has not received the attention it deserves, and it is worth noting that it is a remarkable argument. Generally

Smith maintains that a free market will produce the best possible outcomes for the society as a whole—these are his invisible hand arguments. But in this case a free market in labor produces dreadful consequences for a very large section of society. This is the opposite of an invisible hand argument, a malevolent rather than a benevolent design feature of market economies (another well-known example of such a malevolent design feature would be the tragedy of the commons). Geoffrey Brennan and Philip Pettit have invented the name "an invisible backhand" for such design features.[40]

Smith's invisible backhand argument is robust.[41] In times of scarcity, people cut back on their expenditures in order to pay for food; they lay off servants and they spend less on the goods produced by artisans and craftsmen. The artisans and craftsmen first lay off their own journeymen, and eventually they go bust and they too seek employment. The result is that there are more and more people looking for less and less work, and wages fall; indeed, the more food prices rise, the more wages will tend to fall—a scissors effect.[42] What is Smith's response to this state of affairs? Is it to recommend intervention to increase the number of jobs on offer or to raise wages? No. Indeed, legislating to increase wages (as was proposed in 1795) must inevitably have the effect of intensifying the scissors effect by throwing more and more people out of work. Smith merely remarks, "Masters of all sorts, therefore, frequently make better bargains with their servants in dear than in cheap years, and find them more humble and dependent in the former than in the latter" (I.viii.48).

Smith is equally silent on the direct distribution, whether through poor relief or charity, of either money or bread to the poor. The consequences of such actions must be, in Smith's view, that the increased demand would tend to push up prices; so although one group would acquire an enhanced exchange entitlement, others would be forced to cut back on their consumption; meanwhile, higher prices would encourage imports. The overall effect would be to redistribute the suffering caused by dearth, so that more people were adversely affected, but those that were affected were affected less severely; in addition, regions that provided subsidies would receive more supplies than regions that did not.[43]

There is no indication that Smith had a principled objection to subsidizing the poor in this way. He must surely have been aware that such subsidies were common: in Reading in 1757 a subscription was raised to fund subsidized bread for the poor, and the corporation itself donated £21; in Sherbourne in the same year the sale of wheat to the poor was subsidized by subscription at the rate of roughly 40 percent of the market price; one Bristol parish alone supplied twelve thousand pounds of cheap bread that year to seven hundred families.[44] In 1766 Bristol's Merchant Venturers purchased six thousand bushels of wheat in Danzig to ensure supplies while the principal gentlemen of Norwich promised to raise eight thousand pounds to import corn from abroad. It is possible to draw up long lists of members of Parliament who subscribed, usually fifty or a hundred pounds, in 1766. The measures taken in Parson Woodforde's parish of Weston Longville in Norfolk in 1795 were thus entirely conventional. They represent a new moral economy, based on charity, replacing the old moral economy (admired by Thompson) which sought to control prices.

Smith, however, said nothing about charity.* He criticized the poor relief system in *The Wealth of Nations* because it was an obstacle to the free movement of labor: the unemployed were required to seek relief in their parish of origin (I.x.c.45–59). He could equally easily have defended it as a system that protected the unemployed poor in times of hardship, but he failed to do so for what he appears to have thought was a very good reason. The key issue is the role of high prices as a form of rationing. Imagine, Smith said, a ship lost at sea, on which supplies are running low (IV.v.b.3). The captain imposes rationing so that the supplies will last until the ship reaches shore. It would seem obvious from this example that a first mate who starts doling out extra rations may be kindhearted, but his kindness is the sort that kills. The market is, in Smith's view, the best mechanism for deciding how much grain should be consumed because the information available to all the participants in the market taken together is superior to that in the possession of any government apparatchik, no matter how well intentioned. Smith thus assumed that in times of dearth a nation is like a ship: unable to replenish its supplies from abroad, it can only seek to stretch them until the

---

* It is remarkable that even in *The Theory of Moral Sentiments* (1759) the word "charity" occurs only five times. And yet charitable activity was central to the preoccupations of contemporaries; see, for example, Donna T. Andrew, *Philanthropy and Police: London Charity in the Eighteenth Century* (Princeton, N.J.: Princeton University Press, 1989). Smith was also strangely silent on the subject of charity in his conversations with his friends, and he failed to make charitable bequests.

next harvest or, in the case of the ship, the next landfall. The primary function of the market is thus not to provide a remedy for food availability decline (though high prices may encourage imports), but rather to impose a decline in food exchange entitlement—let us call this not FEE (failure of exchange entitlements), but REE (reduction in exchange entitlements). FEE represents famine; REE represents dearth.

Smith's argument then is that the correct response to FAD (food availability decline) is to let the market work: "In an extensive corn country, between all the different parts of which there is a free commerce and communication, the scarcity occasioned by the most unfavourable seasons can never be so great as to produce a famine; and the scantiest crop, if managed with frugality and oeconomy, will maintain, through the year, the same number of people that are commonly fed in a more affluent manner by one of moderate plenty." (IV.v.b.6).* First, the market seeks to eliminate the FAD by increasing the supply of grain. Insofar as that response fails to eliminate the problem, it imposes REE. That reduction is, Smith assumed, absolutely necessary, and Smith was entitled to argue that even in years of bad harvest there was enough food to feed everyone.

But now imagine a first mate who goes to the captain and suggests that the rations be recalibrated; the cabin boys should be given a bit more, and the officers should be given a bit less. Overall consumption will not be altered: there will still be the same overall reduction in exchange entitlement, but the mortality rate among cabin boys may well be lower—though the price for this will be an increased risk of death by starvation or disease among the officers.

In a free market the distribution of the reduction among different sectors of the population is not managed, as it would be on a ship at sea. We may compare Smith's presentation of the argument that the market should be relied on to ration consumption with that of Jean-Antoine-Nicolas Caritat de Condorcet in his *Reflections on the Grain Trade,* a work published the same year as *The Wealth of Nations.* Condorcet and Smith were at one in their support for free trade. But Condorcet acknowledged that there could be unfortunate consequences when those policies were applied: the amount

---

* By corn Smith meant in the first place wheat, but also oats and barley; the convention was that "corn" was used to describe the main grain crop in any region.

the people eat, he remarked, could be significantly reduced for a substantial period of time without any effect *except the destruction of their health* (i.e., without their death from starvation). And this would give time for new supplies to be made available. In the meantime, they would do their best to survive by selling what few possessions they had and by appealing to the rich for charity. In a postscript he expressed concern that he had expressed himself too bluntly; malnutrition, he acknowledged, would mean that many of the young would have their growth permanently stunted, and their fertility might be affected. He had no intention, he insisted, of making light of such terrible suffering; he had seen its consequences, which had often made him shudder; he merely wanted to make clear that no system of intervention in the grain trade would produce better results. The responsibility of the government, he maintained in the main body of the text, was not to provide the able-bodied with charity or food; but it was to ensure that they might find employment at a wage high enough to enable them to purchase food. Thus he approved not only of make-work schemes introduced by the rich to relieve the suffering of their neighbors but also of government intervention to create work and raise wages.[45] Like Turgot, Condorcet wanted a free market in grain (though he conceded that it might sometimes be necessary to make concessions to popular prejudices); but, again like Turgot, he favored intervention in the labor market.[46] The justification for such intervention was simple: although wages were, in general, set at a level which allowed the laboring classes to feed themselves and their families, in years of bad harvest wages fell when they needed to rise. The market didn't work as it should.[47] In Smith there is no expression of unease comparable to Condorcet's postscript, and no acknowledgment that the wealthy and the government had responsibilities toward the poor which would oblige them to intervene—if not in the grain market, then in the labor market.

Still, although Smith did not explicitly advocate the charitable redistribution of resources, one might think that he simply took it for granted that charity was to be admired and encouraged. Remember that in *The Theory of Moral Sentiments* he praised the way in which the rich "are led by an invisible hand to make nearly the same distribution of the necessaries of life, which would have been made, had the earth been divided into equal portions among all its inhabitants."[48] At times of dearth the scissors effect meant that this redistributive process broke down: the proportion of the necessaries of life which fell to the rich increased, while the proportion which fell to the poor declined, and the distribution became far from being nearly equal. So, you might conclude, it may need to be supplemented by charitable giving, because we have an interest in the fortune of others, and their happiness is necessary to our own. In principle, it would seem, Smith ought to have been willing to accept this argument.

However, Smith was soon to claim (in a revised edition of *The Theory of Moral Sentiments*) that nature has wisely inclined us to be more concerned about the welfare of the rich and the powerful than that of the poor and the wretched—which is likely to ensure that those in most need are not going to be the main beneficiaries of our charitable efforts.[49]

And there is a crucial difference between charity in our modern world and eighteenth-century charity. Nowdays we donate to charities which distribute relief in distant continents, and our donations leave us with plenty left over to feed ourselves. But in Smith's world charity was primarily a local undertaking, a redistribution of resources within a community at a time when many people's resources were being stretched. Ferdinando Galiani, in his *Dialogues on the Grain Trade* of 1770 (the most influential attack upon a free market in grain), implicitly addresses this issue. This is what the Marquis, who speaks for the author, says:

> Ah sir, I see that you do not yet know what a famine is. You think a famine is a universal catastrophe. You are mistaken. In a famine everyone suffers as a result of a catastrophe which strikes individuals one by one. During a famine, the rich, the well-to-do do not suffer, and grain merchants even benefit. But all shudder at the sight of the most dreadful spectacle. One sees people dying of hunger. The impact of this is powerful because it is a response to the sight of the most cruel suffering. . . . The catastrophe of a famine strikes a small number, but empathy ensures that all suffer. Even the hardest hearts are touched. One single person dying of hunger in the street makes a whole town full of people who have dined well sad and throws them into a state of despair.[50]

Why, if everyone feels sympathy for the starving, do they not come to their assistance? For a very simple reason: famines take place under conditions of uncertainty, and no one can be sure when they will end. Today a stranger dies. Next week a relative or a friend may go hungry. A month later I too may be starving. My own resources are finite. If I help the stranger now, I may be unable to help my friend next week; indeed, I may be unable to help myself next month. And so I feel sympathy and compassion for the suffering of others, but the worse the famine gets, the less likely I am to come to their assistance. Sympathy is all very well, but it will not break a famine once it has got a grip.

In conditions of dearth, though, charity may well serve to prevent hunger from turning into starvation, and may indeed prevent famine from getting a grip. But for the charity of Parson Woodforde and his fellows there would have been famine in Weston Longville in 1795. The reason for this is simple: although in years of bad harvest the amount of food did not fall greatly below the average, prices were much more volatile.[51] Smith himself provides figures which show that the price of wheat tripled between 1706 and 1709 and halved between 1740 and 1743.[52] Wages for rural workers were set at Michaelmas, just after the main wheat harvest, and long before it was possible to predict just how much prices would rise or fall in the coming year. It was thus perfectly possible for a worker to find that his wages were insufficient to feed a family—yet in his chapter on wages Smith fails to acknowledge this, claiming three times that a floor for wages is set by what he calls "common humanity" (I.viii.16, 24, 28), which is to say that employers intend the wages they pay their employees to be sufficient to keep them (and perhaps also their families) alive. In Smith's England, in the absence of price controls, charity had a crucial role to play in supplementing wages. In years of bad harvest it was charity, not a living wage, which was the natural expression of "common humanity," yet charity is never mentioned in Smith's text.[53]

Smith, instead, addressed himself to the old moral economy of price controls, not the new moral economy of charity and subsidy. He writes,

Whoever examines, with attention, the history of the dearths and famines which have afflicted any part of Europe, during either the course of the present or that of the two preceding centuries, of several of which we have pretty exact accounts, will find, I believe, that a dearth never has arisen . . . from any other cause but a real scarcity, occasioned sometimes, perhaps . . . by the waste of war, but in by far the greatest number of cases, by the fault of the seasons; and that a famine has never arisen from any other cause but the violence of government attempting, by improper means, to remedy the inconveniencies of a dearth. (IV.v.b.5)

The first claim, that dearths arise from real scarcity, reinforces the assertion that REE is necessary.

But Smith goes on in the next paragraph to insist that, no matter how bad the harvest, a dearth never leads to a famine except as a result of pernicious government intervention.[54] He cites the Bengal Famine of 1770 (his source was presumably *The Annual Register* for 1771, a copy of which was in his library at his death) as an example of a government-made famine.* Smith then argues that the only effective preventative of famine and the best palliative for the "inconveniencies" of a dearth is the "unlimited, unrestrained freedom of the corn trade"—the market provides the only effective response to FAD.

There's an obvious puzzle here. Where had Smith read a history or histories of dearth and famine in Europe over the present or previous centuries, a history or histories which provided "pretty exact accounts"? A modern economist would provide a footnote, but footnotes are few and far between in *The Wealth of Nations;* some of Smith's contemporaries helpfully supplied bibliographies, but unfortunately Smith is not one of them. The obvious place to look next is the catalog of Smith's library at his death in 1790. We can find there, I think, the source of his knowledge of the Bengal Famine, and of his argument that true harvest failures are unlikely to occur, and we can also find there most of the books to which he makes explicit reference. Smith cites, for example, Claude-Jacques Herbert's *Essai sur la police générale des grains* of 1753 (I.xi.e.13, I.xi.g.15), an early and influential work advocating free trade in grain, which contains an extended account

---

* In I.viii.26, Smith also presents famine as endemic in Bengal as a result of a general economic collapse caused by the policies of the East India Company. In I.xi.e.23, he acknowledges war and political conflict as causes of famine. These, too, are cases of famine caused by government incapacity or incompetence. It seems misleading to claim, as does Emma Rothschild, *Economic Sentiments: Adam Smith, Condorcet, and the Enlightenment* (Cambridge, Mass.: Harvard University Press, 2001), 73, that "Smith described four different ways in which famines arise," for all famines, on Smith's account, have the same origin.

of the benefits of competition among merchants; there is, as one would expect, a copy in his library at his death.[55]

But I have looked and looked, and I have yet to find there a book which provides "pretty exact accounts" of famines in several major regions of Europe over the preceding 275 years. So far I have found only one book that comes close to filling the gap we have identified. It is a book that is not to be found in Smith's library, but that may explain why (if this is indeed the source on which he relied) he does not describe its argument at all accurately. Behind Smith's appeal to "pretty exact accounts" lies, I suspect, Louis Paul Abeille's *Faits qui ont influé sur la cherté des grains en France & en Angleterre* of 1768.[56] Abeille provides a close study of crisis years in France and England over the previous century, arguing that true food shortages no longer occur and that in years of dearth the problem is now one of poor distribution which is the consequence of mistaken regulation. Abeille is a hard-line free marketeer, and the only person I can find giving a pretty exact accounts of years of dearth, though only in France and England over the course of the previous one hundred years.

To be sure, famine had largely disappeared from France and had completely disappeared from England. But how could Smith be unaware that famines were a recent phenomenon in Ireland, where there had been a major famine in 1740–1741, killing perhaps 10 percent of the population (often through disease, which decimated the undernourished, rather than through sheer starvation), and famines before that in 1720–1721 and 1728–1729? These were real famines—in 1740–1741 there were dead bodies lying unburied in the street where the starving had collapsed for want of nourishment.[57] Smith was a great admirer of Jonathan Swift; there were two copies of Swift's works in his library, both of which included *A Modest Proposal,* published in 1729, a famine year, with its graphic account of how the poor of Ireland were so reduced to the utmost extremes of want that it would be sensible for them to sell their children as livestock to be butchered and eaten:

> I have been assured by a very knowing *American* of my acquaintance in *London,* that a young healthy Child well Nursed is at a year Old a most delicious, nourishing, and wholesome Food, whether *Stewed, Roasted, Baked,* or *Boyled;* and I make no doubt that it will equally serve in a *Fricasie* or a *Ragout.* . . .

A Child will make two Dishes at an Entertainment for Friends and when the Family dines alone, the fore or hind Quarter will make a reasonable Dish, and seasoned with a little Pepper or Salt will be very good boiled on the fourth Day, especially in *Winter*. . . .

I grant this food will be somewhat dear, and therefore very *proper for Landlords,* who, as they have already devoured most of the Parents, seem to have the best Title to the Children.[58]

One thing is immediately apparent to a reader of the *Modest Proposal* and of accounts of the famines of 1720–1721, 1728–1729, and 1740–1741: people did not starve in Ireland because there was no food. They starved because they could not pay for the food that was available in the markets. Swift's modest proposal, after all, is not that they should be given food, but that they should be given an income through the sale of their children. And in the worst years of famine, relief was provided sometimes as soup, but also in the form of money, or delayed collection of rents, or make-work schemes (in one case, the building of an enormous obelisk).[59] With money in their hands, the starving could find food; and, of course, there was nothing preventing the importation of grain into Ireland (from America, for example) should the Irish market be able to bear the cost (which would have been considerable; 1728–1729 and 1739–1741 were years of generalized crisis). These famines were thus classic examples of a failure of exchange entitlements—the problem was not that supplies of food had completely run out, nor that further supplies could not be obtained; the problem was that the poor could not access the supplies that were there or could be acquired because they lacked the resources; and because the poor could not afford to pay the going rate, grain merchants had little incentive to step up supplies— indeed, at the height of the Irish famines, wheat was still being exported to England until the government finally stepped in to halt exports. The situation was simple: had the Irish had more money to spend, more food could and would have been available, and fewer would have died.

I doubt that anyone could give an account of these Irish famines which would plausibly present them as being the result of misconceived government intervention to palliate a dearth. All commentators agree that the striking thing about the Irish famines of the first half of the eighteenth century was how little the government was prepared to do to improve the situation of the starving. What horrified contemporaries was the extent to which a free market operated; the whole point of Swift's *Modest Proposal,* for example, is that the only solution that seems likely to be adopted is a free market solution.[60] It is easy to defend Smith against the charge of *laissez mourir* if one thinks of the English context in which he was writing; it is much harder to defend him against that charge if one imagines he had ever turned his mind to the Irish famines of the eighteenth century.

A number of commentators have claimed that Smith recognized the existence of what they call "real famine" and the need to adopt emergency measures in response to it. Thus Samuel Fleischacker in his *Philosophical Companion* to *The Wealth of Nations* quotes from Smith's *Lectures on Jurisprudence:* "in time of necessity the people will break through all laws. In a famine it often happens that they will break open granaries and force the owners to sell at what they think a reasonable price." But there are three problems here. The first and least is that this passages dates to 1762–1763, prior to Smith's visit to France in 1764–1766. But let us assume that Smith's fundamental views had already taken shape by 1762; there are indeed good arguments that suggest this. That brings us to the second problem: the mature Smith does not deny that there are famines; what he argues is that they are caused by governments, and that the correct response for governments is to stand back and *laisser aller.* What Fleischacker fails to supply is evidence of Smith advocating government intervention. The final problem is that there remains the obvious mistake, as it seems to me, of reading Smith as expressing approval for the actions of food rioters (indeed, Fleischacker himself goes on to acknowledge that breaking open granaries is a poor example of overriding necessity—it is hard to see why he thinks Smith would not have agreed).[61]

Rather, we should place this passage against one of the core arguments of Smith's discussion of dearth in *The Wealth of Nations,* which is that the popular prejudice which blames grain merchants for dearth and justifies the breaking open of granaries is always irrational. Far from forestalling famine, riots exacerbate it, for they lead to the overly rapid consumption of dwindling supplies without the rationing mechanism that the grain merchants, in their pursuit of a profit, enforce. "The popular fear of engrossing and forestalling," Smith writes, "may be compared to the popular terrors and suspicions of witchcraft" (IV.v.b.26). Again, "The laws concerning corn may every where be compared to the laws concerning religion. The people feel themselves so much interested in what relates either to their subsistence in this life, or to their happiness in a life to come, that government must yield to their prejudices" (IV.v.b.40). Governments may thus (as in France) have to ban the export of grain, may even have to stand by while the people break open granaries; but political economists know that such actions are never rational—indeed, that they are self-defeating. For the interests of grain merchants (at least where exports are not in question) are always identical with those of the population as a whole: "The interest of the inland dealer, and that of the great body of the people, how opposite soever they may at first sight appear, are, even in years of the greatest scarcity exactly the same."[62] There is thus no reason to think that Smith thought that "necessity" could be an adequate justification for the breaking open of granaries, any more than it would be justified for the crew to mutiny and throw overboard a captain who sought to ration their supplies of hardtack.

Fleischacker goes on to misinterpret Smith's acknowledgment that there are circumstances in which it may be necessary to restrain the exportation of corn. If all states practiced a free trade in corn, then "the scarcity of any one country," says Smith, would be "relieved by the plenty of some other." But states interfere with the corn trade and bring about famine where no famine need be. Under these circumstances,

> The demand of such countries for corn may frequently become so great and so urgent, that a small state in their neighbourhood, which happened at the same time to be labouring under some degree of dearth, could not venture to supply them without exposing itself to the like dreadful calamity. The very bad policy of one country may thus render it in some measure dangerous and imprudent to establish what would otherwise be the best policy in another. . . . In a Swiss canton, or in some of the little states of Italy, it may, perhaps, sometimes be necessary to restrain the exportation of corn . . . an act of legislative authority which ought to be exercised only, which can be pardoned only in cases of the most urgent necessity. (IV.v.b.39)

Smith's argument here is clear. He does not endorse restrictions on the grain trade as a way of preventing a local dearth from developing, endogenously, into a famine. He only endorses such restrictions as an aspect of international relations, where there is a prospect of one nation, in effect, exporting a famine to its smaller neighbor. Interference with the grain trade does not improve the supply of food to the starving, except where a poorly managed large market is liable to suck all the grain out of a smaller market; only then is interference appropriate. The only other case for interference that Smith acknowledges is where a guild of bakers holds a monopoly over the supply of bread, in which case regulation to prevent them exploiting their position may be necessary (I.x.c.62). Let us go back to the case of Bengal as cited by Smith (IV.v.b.6–7) and as described in *The Annual Register*. Much of the rice crop had failed. Vast supplies held in a granary accidentally went up in flames. The government, facing a situation of urgent necessity, forced the grain merchants to sell at what they thought was a reasonable price. The result was a catastrophe: forced to sell at a loss, the grain merchants ceased to import new supplies. Dearth turned into famine. Fleischacker is quite wrong to state that in cases of urgent necessity Smith favored "the regulation of grain prices."

Smith would seem to have taken his recognition that a Swiss canton or a little state in Italy might represent a special case from Galiani, whose *Dialogues* of 1770 had an enormous success in France because it managed at the same time to be both wickedly funny and at the same time intellectually profound: Voltaire said the book, published anonymously, appeared to have been coauthored by Plato and Molière.[63] Indeed, Galiani's book helped bring about a partial reimposition of restrictions on the grain trade. Smith did not own a copy of Galiani's tract, but he did own a copy of Étienne-Gabriel Morelly's *Refutation,* which, although dated 1770 on the title page, had finally appeared late in 1774, after being held up by the censors. Galiani had used the case of the Swiss canton to argue that the same principle must apply to the frontier province of a great state, and so, by a slippery slope argument, to show that any province might have to introduce restrictions on the free trade in grain. But Smith was having none of it: "In such great countries as France or England" restrictions could "scarce ever" be justified; in such countries there never would be, or to all intents and purposes there never would be, a case of "the most urgent necessity" (IV.v.b39); thus he restated the claims of Herbert, whom he certainly had read, and perhaps of Abeille, whom he may have read. Even in countries which faced urgent necessity, Smith did not advocate a regulation of grain prices, but the much less drastic step of restricting exports.

Let us turn back to Ireland. Smith could have argued that Ireland was not a great country like France or England but rather comparable to a Swiss canton. Better still, he could have argued that the situation in Ireland was to a very considerable degree the consequence of British policy toward Ireland. Smith, indeed, understood this perfectly, and argued that a union with England (which would have established a free trade zone within the United Kingdom of England, Scotland, and Ireland) was the simplest and most effective way to transform the situation of the Irish:

> By a union with Great Britain, Ireland would gain, besides the freedom of trade, other advantages much more important, and which would much more than compensate any increase of taxes that might accompany that union. By the union with England, the middling and inferior ranks of people in Scotland gained a complete deliverance from the power of an aristocracy which had always before oppressed them. By an union with Great Britain, the greater part of the people of all ranks in Ireland would gain an equally complete deliverance from a much more oppressive aristocracy; an aristocracy not founded, like that of Scotland, in the natural and respectable distinctions of birth and fortune; but in the most odious of all distinctions, those of religious and political prejudices; distinctions which, more than any other, animate both the insolence of the oppressors and the hatred and indignation of the oppressed, and which commonly render the inhabitants of the same country more hostile to one another than those of different countries ever are. Without a union with Great Britain, the inhabitants of Ireland are not likely for many ages to consider themselves as one people. (V.iii.89)

So Smith, had he acknowledged the existence of Irish famines, could easily have argued that the cause of those famines was the oppression of the Catholic population by a hard-hearted Protestant aristocracy and the restrictions imposed on the Irish economy by the British government, which insisted on treating Ireland as a colony; but such an argument would have been very different from what he did in fact argue, which was that famines never occurred except as a consequence of government intervention to palliate the consequences of a dearth—even in the case of a Swiss canton or a small Italian state, famine was caused by government intervention in the grain trade, though the government at fault might well be a foreign government. Smith did *not* say that there are some communities whose conditions of life are so adverse that they are stalked by the prospect of famine; nor did he say that responsibility for this state of affairs lies with those in power; nor that such states of affairs can only be alleviated by intervention, whether by government or by charities.

Smith was also well aware that an unbalanced economy cannot be rebalanced quickly or easily. The physiocrats had claimed that a free trade in grain would raise prices for farmers without raising prices for consumers, and that over a short period the new investment released by higher prices would result in increased production. A new equilibrium would be established, they suggested, within sixteen years, at which point landlords would be benefiting from increased rents and consumers from cheaper wheat.[64] Smith surely learned from their failure to foresee just how difficult the transition to free trade would be. He was strongly opposed to the Navigation Acts, but warned about the difficulties of abolishing them:

> To open the colony trade all at once to all nations might not only occasion some transitory inconveniency, but a great permanent loss to the greater part of those whose industry or capital is at present engaged in it. . . . Such are the unfortunate effects of all the regulations of the mercantile system! They not only introduce very dangerous disorders into the state of the body politick, but disorders which it is often difficult to remedy, without occasioning, for a time at least, still greater disorders. In what manner, therefore, the colony trade ought gradually to be opened; what are the restraints which ought first, and what are those which ought last to be taken away; or in what manner the natural system of perfect liberty and justice ought gradually to be restored, we must leave to the wisdom of future statesmen and legislators to determine. (IV. vii.c.44)

Thus Smith could easily have acknowledged the existence of real famines in Ireland; he could have argued that the inclusion of Ireland within a colonial system was the fundamental cause of those famines; and that introducing free trade was no immediate panacea. He didn't. He ignored the famines in Ireland, and insisted real famines did not exist; he presented a free trade in grain as the only solution to dearth, and the only exceptions he recognized were circumstances where other states did not adopt free trade policies or where there was a monopoly affecting the supply of grain, flour, or bread.

Commentators have had difficulty in grasping Smith's argument, I think, because its premise—that all modern famines are government-made—seems to them so implausible that they simply cannot believe that his whole argument relies on it. But it does. Thus Smith insisted that a benevolent nature, under conditions of free trade, would supply an adequate subsistence. Galiani had taken the opposite view; he had argued that it was necessary to ensure that society was never at the mercy of nature and that markets could be ruthless as well as beneficent. Smith's argument ultimately depended on the natural theology which also underpinned his invisible hand metaphor, and indeed his claim that free trade is a "natural liberty."

Smith acknowledged that there were real dearths, but insisted that all famines are government-made. His solution to dearth was to insist on the need for a reduction of consumption, on rationing by high prices. There was an alternative view, that there were plenty of other foods which could be substituted for grain. Thus in 1699 Robert Sibbald published *Provision for the Poor in Time of Dearth and Scarcity.* Sibbald acknowledged that "the Bad Seasons these several Years past, hath made so much Scarcity and so great a Dearth, that for Want, some Die by the Way-side, some drop down on the Streets, the poor sucking Babes are Starving for want of Milk, which the empty Breasts of their Mothers cannot furnish them." Yet he went on to insist that "God hath plentifully provided for the Poor, with what may sustain them in the greatest scarcity and dearth of Victual, if they will put out their hands and take it. And make use of the Art and Industry which is necessary"—they should, he argued, be eating nettles and chestnuts and roasting moles and seagulls.[65] *Yummy.* And, of course, Sibbald was right: in times of dearth the poor substituted rye, barley, and oats for wheat, supplemented by turnips and chestnuts; when they ran out of money they foraged as best they could. But urban communities cannot forage in the way that rural communities can; the only substitutions they can effect are from more expensive market offerings to cheaper market offerings. Their food can only be acquired with cash.*

Smith emphasized neither charity nor food substitution as a response to dearth; rather, he assumed that the working poor could reduce their consumption sufficiently without endangering their own survival. In his library he had a book which laid out this line of thinking clearly and effectively: James Steuart's *Inquiry into the Principles of Political Economy* of 1767. Steuart, like Young and Smith after him, thought that true famines rarely or never occur. Even in 1757, Steuart argued, a year of great scarcity, the importation of foreign grain to London was only sufficient to feed the city for one month; without such imports, London would still have scraped by without a famine. It was equally, Steuart thought, a myth to hold that there were years of abundance when the harvest was three or even five times what the people needed to eat. In reality, the size of the harvest varied within much narrower limits. But, he went on,

> it is far from being true, that the same number of people consume always the same quantity of food. In years of plenty every one is well fed; the price of the lowest industry can procure subsistence sufficient to bear a division; food is not so frugally managed; a quantity of animals are fatted for use; all sorts of cattle are kept in good heart; and people drink more largely, because all is cheap. A year of scarcity comes, the people are ill fed, and when the lower classes come to divide with their children, the portions are brought to be very small; there is great oeconomy upon consumption, few animals are fatted for use, cattle look miserably, and a poor man cannot indulge himself with a cup of generous ale.[66]

Steuart, like Smith, believed it was necessary to face the harsh realities of life. Unlike Smith in *The Wealth of Nations,* he showed that he was fully aware of what dearth means: the portions of the children are very small, the cattle look miserably, and a poor man cannot indulge himself with a cup of

---

* This, I suggest, is the explanation for the puzzling evidence that the demand for wheat was much less elastic in the early modern period than it had been in the medieval; see Bruce M. S. Campbell and Cormac Ó Gráda, "Harvest Shortfalls, Grain Prices, and Famines in Preindustrial England," *Journal of Economic History* 71 (2011), 875–877. The bigger and more highly organized the market in a staple like wheat, the slower and more inefficient it will be in offering cheaper substitutes at times of high prices.

generous ale. There is a certain irony in the fact that Smith, the great theorist of sympathy, does not go so far as to express even this degree of sympathy (or as we would now say, empathy) with the circumstances of the poor in years of dearth. Instead he refers in passing to what he terms "the inconveniencies."

It is useful here to bear in mind the distinction that Smith made in *The Theory of Moral Sentiments* between humanity and generosity: humanity, or fellow-feeling, hardly counted as a virtue in his eyes, though it is an essential prerequisite if we are not to be purely selfish, purely self-interested in our dealings with our friends and neighbors; generosity, self-sacrifice for the benefit of others, really is a virtue.[67] The suffering Galiani described in a town where those who are still well fed are obliged to watch their neighbors starve to death is a suffering induced by humanity or fellow-feeling, but it does not result in generous actions. Smith, while he admires generous actions, does not regard them as obligatory, except in warfare or in response to the generosity of others; for the most part, he urges on us humanity not generosity.

Still, even with this distinction in mind, I do not think we can defend Smith against the charge of a failure of sympathy, of a defect of imagination, of inhumanity. He could have paid attention to Ireland; he could have acknowledged the sufferings of the poor in years of bad harvest; he could have stressed the need for a redistribution of resources, whether through charity or through taxation. He did none of these. When it came to famine, Smith allowed his judgment to be clouded by his dogmatic attachment to the principle of free trade. He became the very thing he would later criticize in the sixth edition of *The Theory of Moral Sentiments;* he became a "man of system."[68]

According to Rothschild, only with the publication in 1800 of Edmund Burke's *Thoughts and Details on Scarcity* (originally written in 1795–1796, when Parson Woodforde was dining well and his parishioners were going hungry) did a mistaken, hard-line, free market reading of Smith become established.[69] Smith, we are to understand, is much to be preferred to Burke, and it is Burke, not Smith, who is responsible for later policies of responding to famines by *laissez mourir*. This, I would submit, is not only a misreading of Smith but also a misreading of Burke.

Burke ran a straightforward free market argument, with one crucial exception. For, unlike Smith, he acknowledged that the wages of laborers might sink so low that it became impossible for them to feed themselves and their families. He was against a minimum wage or controls on the grain market. What, then, was the solution? His answer was charity: "Let compassion be shewn in action," Burke wrote, "the more the better, according to every man's ability." He added, "Without all doubt, charity to the poor is a direct and obligatory duty upon all Christians." And it is this charity which he believed had warded off famine: "Even now [November 1795], I do not know of one man, woman, or child, that has perished from famine; fewer, if any, I believe, than in years of plenty, when such a thing may happen by accident. This is owing to a care and superintendance of the poor, far greater than any I remember."[70]

Why was Burke willing to invoke charity when Smith was not? First, Smith's claim was that free market policies would lead to general prosperity. "The natural effort of every individual to better his own condition, when suffered to exert itself with freedom and security, is so powerful a principle that it is alone, and without any assistance, . . . capable of carrying on the society to wealth and prosperity" (IV.v.b.43). Burke did not believe in general prosperity; he was prepared to acknowledge that poverty was (as he believed) an irremediable aspect of the human condition. So he could acknowledge the need for charity, where Smith could not.

Second, Smith's claim was that the invisible hand, as he called it, ensured that individuals pursuing their own selfish interests served the general good, that there was a natural congruence between market forces and public welfare. His account of how at times of dearth wages are eroded and unemployment is spread simply didn't fit into this story; he made no mention of it in his optimistic account of how the market has only benevolent consequences in the distribution of grain; he couldn't afford to address the issue of exchange entitlements without bringing into question the providential scheme which underpins the whole argument of *The Wealth of Nations*. Smith couldn't face the fact that a benevolent God would not have designed the world in which we find ourselves (which was no problem for Burke, who believed in original sin).

Third, Burke knew that his argument had profound implications for moral philosophy. Samuel von Pufendorf, he remarked, had not fully grasped the extent of the obligation to charity when he described it as a duty of *imperfect* obligation. Burke argued, in response, that one takes pleasure in the fact that one has control over when, where, how, and to whom one exercises charity; but one is *fully* obliged to perform acts of charity.* The obligation is perfect, not imperfect. Turn to Smith's *Wealth of Nations* and you will find no similar emphasis on an obligation on the better off to come to the assistance of their less fortunate neighbors. When Smith writes about sympathy he does not mean the sort of sympathy which leads one to share the sufferings of one's neighbor. Adam Ferguson said that it was by an abuse of language that Smith said that we feel sympathy with the man who pays his bills on time—in other words, we approve of him, we think well of him.[71] I am sure Smith thought well of those who gave money to charitable purposes, but he was far from presenting charity as a perfect obligation (indeed, he claimed that there is no *obligation* to be charitable), far from insisting that generosity (and not merely what he calls "sympathy") is an obligation on those who have resources to spare.[72]

In writing about famine Smith faced a test. He knew the subject was important, and so he gave it considerable thought. But he failed the test, and he failed it not just in one way but in four separate ways. He got his facts wrong: he forgot about Ireland. He got his theory wrong: he failed to recognize that a country is not like a ship at sea because it contains people of widely varied circumstances and conditions. He got his emotions wrong: he failed to empathize with the suffering. And he got his morality wrong: he failed to consider the obligation to charity. Why? Because he was wedded to a system.

Burke, I submit, for all his faults and failings, had a much better understanding of poverty and famine than Smith did. And this may well have had something to do with the fact that Burke was Irish. He was eleven, twelve, thirteen during the dreadful hunger years of 1740–1742, and surely saw the dead and the near dead, "the Roads spread with dead and dying Bodies; Mankind of the Colour of the Docks and Nettles which they fed on; two or three, sometimes more, on a Car going to the Grave for want of Bearers to carry them, and many buried only in the Fields and Ditches where they perished."[73] Just as there is an unspoken, unacknowledged personal experience at the heart of Amartya Sen's great book on famine, so too there must be the very same experience at the heart of Burke's *Thoughts and Details*

---

* Thus agreeing with François-Vincent Toussaint; see Chapter 7.

on Scarcity. Burke had been there; Galiani had been there; unlike Smith, they had seen with their own eyes what Galiani describes:

> The people dying of hunger, who can be seen wandering in the streets, specters, hideous skeletons whose skin is burned red, with bleary eyes and limp hair, covered with sores and vermin; you see them approach you with a shuffling gait, asking in a hoarse whisper and with trembling hand for a piece of bread. And sometimes at the moment you try to help them, you see them fall at your feet and die in the dirt.[74]

IN CONGRESS, JULY 4, 1776.

A DECLARATION

BY THE REPRESENTATIVES OF THE

UNITED STATES OF AMERICA,

IN GENERAL CONGRESS ASSEMBLED.

WHEN in the Course of human Events, it becomes necessary for one People to dissolve the Political Bands which have connected them with another, and to assume among the Powers of the Earth, the separate and equal Station to which the Laws of Nature and of Nature's God entitle them, a decent Respect to the Opinions of Mankind requires that they should declare the causes which impel them to the Separation.

We hold these Truths to be self-evident, that all Men are created equal, that they are endowed by their Creator with certain unalienable Rights, that among these are Life, Liberty, and the Pursuit of Happiness---That to secure these Rights, Governments are instituted among Men, deriving their just Powers from the Consent of the Governed, that whenever any Form of Government becomes destructive of these Ends, it is the Right of the People to alter or to abolish it, and to institute new Government, laying its Foundation on such Principles, and organizing its Powers in such Form, as to them shall seem most likely to effect their Safety and Happiness. Prudence, indeed, will dictate that Governments long established should not be changed for light and transient Causes; and accordingly all Experience hath shewn, that Mankind are more disposed to suffer, while Evils are sufferable, than to right themselves by abolishing the Forms to which they are accustomed. But when a long Train of Abuses and Usurpations, pursuing invariably the same Object, evinces a Design to reduce them under absolute Despotism, it is their Right, it is their Duty, to throw off such Government, and to provide new Guards for their future Security. Such has been the patient Sufferance of these Colonies; and such is now the Necessity which constrains them to alter their former Systems of Government. The History of the present King of Great-Britain is a History of repeated Injuries and Usurpations, all having in direct Object the Establishment of an absolute Tyranny over these States. To prove this, let Facts be submitted to a candid World.

HE has refused his Assent to Laws, the most wholesome and necessary for the public Good.

HE has forbidden his Governors to pass Laws of immediate and pressing Importance, unless suspended in their Operation till his Assent should be obtained; and when so suspended, he has utterly neglected to attend to them.

HE has refused to pass other Laws for the Accommodation of large Districts of People, unless those People would relinquish the Right of Representation in the Legislature, a Right inestimable to them, and formidable to Tyrants only.

HE has called together Legislative Bodies at Places unusual, uncomfortable, and distant from the Depository of their public Records, for the sole Purpose of fatiguing them into Compliance with his Measures.

HE has dissolved Representative Houses repeatedly, for opposing with manly Firmness his Invasions on the Rights of the People.

HE has refused for a long Time, after such Dissolutions, to cause others to be elected; whereby the Legislative Powers, incapable of Annihilation, have returned to the People at large for their exercise; the State remaining in the mean time exposed to all the Dangers of Invasion from without, and Convulsions within.

HE has endeavoured to prevent the Population of these States; for that Purpose obstructing the Laws for Naturalization of Foreigners; refusing to pass others to encourage their Migrations hither, and raising the Conditions of new Appropriations of Lands.

HE has obstructed the Administration of Justice, by refusing his Assent to Laws for establishing Judiciary Powers.

HE has made Judges dependent on his Will alone, for the Tenure of their Offices, and the Amount and Payment of their Salaries.

HE has erected a Multitude of new Offices, and sent hither Swarms of Officers to harrass our People, and eat out their Substance.

HE has kept among us, in Times of Peace, Standing Armies, without the consent of our Legislatures.

HE has affected to render the Military independent of and superior to the Civil Power.

HE has combined with others to subject us to a Jurisdiction foreign to our Constitution, and unacknowledged by our Laws; giving his Assent to their Acts of pretended Legislation:

FOR quartering large Bodies of Armed Troops among us:

FOR protecting them, by a mock Trial, from Punishment for any Murders which they should commit on the Inhabitants of these States:

FOR cutting off our Trade with all Parts of the World:

FOR imposing Taxes on us without our Consent:

FOR depriving us, in many Cases, of the Benefits of Trial by Jury:

FOR transporting us beyond Seas to be tried for pretended Offences:

FOR abolishing the free System of English Laws in a neighbouring Province, establishing therein an arbitrary Government, and enlarging its Boundaries, so as to render it at once an Example and fit Instrument for introducing the same absolute Rule into these Colonies:

FOR taking away our Charters, abolishing our most valuable Laws, and altering fundamentally the Forms of our Governments:

FOR suspending our own Legislatures, and declaring themselves invested with Power to legislate for us in all Cases whatsoever.

HE has abdicated Government here, by declaring us out of his Protection and waging War against us.

HE has plundered our Seas, ravaged our Coasts, burnt our Towns, and destroyed the Lives of our People.

HE is, at this Time, transporting large Armies of foreign Mercenaries to compleat the Works of Death, Desolation, and Tyranny, already begun with circumstances of Cruelty and Perfidy, scarcely paralleled in the most barbarous Ages, and totally unworthy the Head of a civilized Nation.

HE has constrained our fellow Citizens taken Captive on the high Seas to bear Arms against their Country, to become the Executioners of their Friends and Brethren, or to fall themselves by their Hands.

HE has excited domestic Insurrections amongst us, and has endeavoured to bring on the Inhabitants of our Frontiers, the merciless Indian Savages, whose known Rule of Warfare, is an undistinguished Destruction, of all Ages, Sexes and Conditions.

IN every stage of these Oppressions we have Petitioned for Redress in the most humble Terms: Our repeated Petitions have been answered only by repeated Injury. A Prince, whose Character is thus marked by every act which may define a Tyrant, is unfit to be the Ruler of a free People.

NOR have we been wanting in Attentions to our British Brethren. We have warned them from Time to Time of Attempts by their Legislature to extend an unwarrantable Jurisdiction over us. We have reminded them of the Circumstances of our Emigration and Settlement here. We have appealed to their native Justice and Magnanimity, and we have conjured them by the Ties of our common Kindred to disavow these Usurpations, which, would inevitably interrupt our Connections and Correspondence. They too have been deaf to the Voice of Justice and of Consanguinity. We must, therefore, acquiesce in the Necessity, which denounces our Separation, and hold them, as we hold the rest of Mankind, Enemies in War, in Peace, Friends.

WE, therefore, the Representatives of the UNITED STATES OF AMERICA, in GENERAL CONGRESS, Assembled, appealing to the Supreme Judge of the World for the Rectitude of our Intentions, do, in the Name, and by Authority of the good People of these Colonies, solemnly Publish and Declare, That these United Colonies are, and of Right ought to be, FREE AND INDEPENDENT STATES; that they are absolved from all Allegiance to the British Crown, and that all political Connection between them and the State of Great-Britain, is and ought to be totally dissolved; and that as FREE AND INDEPENDENT STATES, they have full Power to levy War, conclude Peace, contract Alliances, establish Commerce, and to do all other Acts and Things which INDEPENDENT STATES may of right do. And for the support of this Declaration, with a firm Reliance on the Protection of divine Providence, we mutually pledge to each other our Lives, our Fortunes, and our sacred Honor.

Signed by ORDER *and in* BEHALF *of the* CONGRESS,

JOHN HANCOCK, PRESIDENT.

ATTEST.
CHARLES THOMSON, SECRETARY.

PHILADELPHIA: PRINTED BY JOHN DUNLAP.

The Declaration of Independence, printed by John Dunlap (broadside) (1776).

9

Self-Evidence

The American Declaration of Independence states, "We hold these Truths to be self-evident, that all Men are created equal, that they are endowed by their Creator with certain unalienable Rights, that among these are Life, Liberty and the Pursuit of Happiness." Scholars used to go to great lengths to track down previous occurrences of the phrase "the pursuit of happiness." In 1936 Herbert Ganter identified five authors who had used the exact phrase before Thomas Jefferson: John Locke (1694), Peter Paxton (1703), William Wollaston (1722), Samuel Johnson (1750), and Oliver Goldsmith (1762), and a further nine who had used very similar phrases.[1] A quick search on Early English Books Online and Eighteenth Century Collections Online enables one to increase this list of five by the addition of no less than 135 names, not including by far the most prolific user of the phrase, Anonymous—a striking example of how digitization has made old-fashioned scholarship irrelevant. Ganter once seemed admirably exhaustive; now he seems simply ill-informed (he had missed the phrase in, for example, Richard Cumberland, Adam Ferguson, David Hume, and Joseph Priestley); and even my present count is very incomplete because internet search engines are far from reliable. What is striking about this long list of names is that it includes authors of every possible opinion. Thus, to take an example almost at random, when a pious and rationalist author, George Anderson, settled down to criticize David Hume at length for his numerous and pernicious errors, it turned out that the one thing on which he and Hume agreed was that "the pursuit of happiness is the main business of life."[2]

The very fact that the phrase occurs so often—and some authors use it several times, and in more than one work—means that the traditional scholarly game of identifying Jefferson's source is pointless. Claims to have identified his source in James Wilson, writing in 1774, or in Jean-Jacques

Burlamaqui (who is cited by Wilson), or in Wollaston, or in Locke are simply wrongheaded. What the new evidence certainly does help one understand is why Jefferson would have thought the idea of a right to pursue happiness was "self-evident." Of course, one could ask who before Jefferson had coupled the pursuit of happiness with the idea of self-evidence; the answer would be Wollaston, and this might support the argument that Wollaston was Jefferson's true source, did we not know that "self-evident" was a late revision to the text of the Declaration of Independence.[3]

But how did this self-evidence come about? The phrase "the pursuit of happiness" first appears, as best we can tell, in 1632; though we have already seen "the pursuit of worldly happiness" being used by Robert Bolton in 1611.[4] If we plot the four or five hundred known occurrences of the phrase "pursuit of happiness" before 1776, the result is a steadily rising curve. Google Books (which can be regarded as a fairly random sample) gives five occurrences in the last quarter of the seventeenth century, thirty in the first quarter of the eighteenth, seventy-two in the second quarter, and 105 in the third quarter; and lots and lots more after 1776.

If we turn to French, we find both *la poursuite du bonheur* and *la poursuite de la félicité* were far from common, and were most frequent in translations of English texts. The standard translation of Jefferson's "pursuit of happiness" into French became *la recherche du bien-être,* but I can't find this phrase before Jefferson is translated. What would seem to be its equivalent is rare in Italian, and I can't find anything in German. The pursuit of happiness is a peculiarly anglophone enterprise; and so you would need to be British (in a broad sense which allows us to think of Jefferson as still British in 1776) to find a right to the pursuit of happiness to be self-evident.

In this chapter I will do four things. First, I will briefly explain why the pursuit of happiness is a right, comparable to life and liberty (something which no one seems to have been able to do). Second, I will explore the question of what is British or anglophone about this right. Third, I will argue that the invention of the social sciences in the Enlightenment has a paradoxical quality, for the new social sciences were prescriptive as well as descriptive. And finally, I will end both the chapter and the book with some general remarks about the Enlightenment paradigm.

❦❦❦

Let us start, then, with the question of how the pursuit of happiness can be a right. It is commonly said that this right was first formulated by Burlamaqui, but Burlamaqui only declares it to be a right of nations, not individuals: nations, he tells us, have the "right of endeavouring to provide for their safety and happiness, and of employing force and arms against those who declare themselves their enemies."[5] It is thus linked to the right of war, a right which, of course, individuals give up on entering civil society. Burlamaqui does not suggest that individuals, even in the state of nature, have a *right* to pursue happiness because they inevitably and automatically are engaged in that pursuit. Happiness is "the ultimate end of man"; it "is not in our own election; it predominates in us, and becomes the primum mobile of all our determinations."[6] Consequently, for individuals the pursuit of happiness is neither a right nor a duty, but a fundamental law of nature, like gravity. What individuals have a right to is *natural liberty,* to dispose of their persons and property "after the manner they judge most convenient to their happiness."[7]

Indeed, "the pursuit of happiness," as a specific phrase, is not in the original French of Burlamaqui, nor in translations of his two key works, though Burlamaqui is often said to be Jefferson's source. Burlamaqui says, for example, that everything we do is "with a view of happiness" and "Such, in effect, is the nature of man, that he necessarily loves himself, that he seeks in every thing and every where his own advantage, and can never be diverted from this pursuit." Thus for Burlamaqui, human beings pursue their interests; happiness is an "internal satisfaction of the soul" which results from success in this pursuit.[8] The phrase "the pursuit of happiness" may seem a small step beyond this, but it turns happiness into something that is endlessly pursued and never fully attained—a Hobbesian view which Burlamaqui is careful to avoid.

Why, then, does Jefferson, in opposition to Burlamaqui, think *individuals* have a *right* to pursue happiness? Clearly there can be no right to happiness, as it is impossible to imagine a society in which there will not be a great deal of unhappiness. So the statement that we have a right to *pursue* happiness must represent a claim that we have a right to certain preconditions which make it possible to pursue, but not necessarily achieve, happiness. What are those preconditions? The most obvious is private property, and it is often said that "life, liberty and the pursuit of happiness" is intended to be in some way equivalent to Locke's phrase in his *Second Treatise of Government,* "life, liberty and estate."[9]

But is that all it means? An article which appeared in Joseph Addison's *Spectator* in 1714, and was probably written by William Bond, perhaps helps us here. The author distinguished two main groups of human beings: those too idle to pursue anything, and those engaged in the "pursuit of happiness." So a right to pursue happiness happiness does not imply a right to be idle. Those who pursue happiness he further divided into four groups: those who seek happiness in (1) wealth, (2) in status or honors, (3) in pleasure, and (4) in religion or virtue. His argument was that whatever form of happiness you aim at, you have to put up with a great deal of inconvenience and suffering on the way; if people would only take proper account of this, virtue would begin to seem a more attractive option than wealth, status, or pleasure.[10]

What is important here, I would suggest, is that these four routes to happiness imply not one but four preconditions: wealth requires the freedoms of the market place; honors require a career open to talents and a public sphere; pleasure requires, among other things, sexual freedom; and virtue requires religious freedom. Placed in this context (and the notion that people pursue happiness by different routes is entirely conventional), the pursuit of happiness may require any of and indeed all of the freedoms of a liberal society. Thus, a right to engage in the pursuit of happiness goes far beyond a right to life, liberty, and property; a civilized monarchy, for example, which will guarantee life, personal liberty, and property, will fail to make honors fully coincident with merit; and one might argue that the unrestricted pursuit of happiness through religion requires the separation of church and state.

The idea that the alternative to the pursuit of happiness is indolence is not peculiar to the *Spectator*—we find it also in Tobias Smollett and William Warburton, and, to take a more obscure example, Wetenhall Wilkes. But the general view, and now I want to move on to my second topic, is Burlumaqui's— that, whether we are energetic or lazy, we have no alternative but to pursue happiness. According to Locke, men are "constant in pursuit of happiness."[11] Peter Paxton, in 1703, wrote that "the pursuit of happiness is as inseparable from the Nature of Man, as the Tendency toward its own Center is to un-thinking Matter."[12] As Thomas Morgan claimed in 1741, "A Man cannot, by any active Power or free Self-Determination, be at Liberty not to desire, chuse and pursue Good, Pleasure, or Happiness; or not reject and fly from Evil, Pain, or Misery: For this is the necessary Law of all animal Nature, both Rationals and Irrationals."[13] David Hume, writing in the person of a Stoic, said that "every Man, however dissolute and negligent, proceeds in the Pursuit of Happiness, with as unerring a Motion, as that which the celestial Bodies observe, when, conducted by the Hand of the Almighty, they roll along the ethereal Plains."[14] Nor was there anything new about this argument, for it derived directly from Thomas Hobbes.

Now it also followed from this that the happiness of others cannot be an immediate motivation of any of our actions. Morgan was very explicit: "No Man can be moved or determined, by the Happiness of another, or by any speculative Appearance of Good, to chuse and pursue a Thing, as his own Good or Happiness, which he does not desire, or feel the Want of."[15] Only a few years later Thomas Rutherforth was arguing that there was "no obligation to virtue unless it [virtue] makes us happy," and that "every man's own happiness is the end which nature teaches him to pursue."[16] In Chapter 5, I quoted John Gay saying much the same thing; and in Chapter 4 we saw Hobbes had said as much in the Latin text of *Leviathan*. And thus happiness came to be acknowledged as our only purpose in existing. According to Robert Clayton in 1740, "Certain it is, that Almighty God has created Mankind for Happiness, and that this is the End of his Being"; and Warburton agreed: "*Happiness* is the *End* of our Creation."[17] Julien Offray de La Mettrie, who did not like to make unnecessary distinctions between humans and other animals, went further and said that happiness was the goal of all creatures.[18]

I want to pause for a moment here, because the account I am giving may seem inherently puzzling. I have quoted lots of anglophones, but also Burlamaqui and La Mettrie. For a moment, let me confine myself to the anglophones. Did all anglophones really think that the pursuit of happiness was inescapable? Adam Smith, for example, ends *The Theory of Moral Sentiments* (1759) by distinguishing between those who place morality in self-love, those who place it in reason, and those who place it in sentiment.[19] What we have here is a very clear account of moral philosophy as a field of disagreement, not agreement. Of course, Smith is right to identify disagreements; but I am right to emphasize the underlying agreement—indeed if there were no underlying agreement, there would be no self-evident truths.

Let's consider Francis Hutcheson, who argues that "there can therefore be no *exciting Reason* previous to *Affection,*" which is equivalent to Hume's statement that reason is "the slave of the passions." Hutcheson is even willing to concede, as compatible with his own views, that "Men are *necessarily* determined to pursue their own Happiness." Even on his own account, self-love and benevolence strictly coincide. He says, "Let the Misery of *excessive Selfishness,* and all its Passions, be but once explain'd, that so *Self-love* may cease to counteract our *natural Propensity* to *Benevolence,* and when this *noble* Disposition gets loose from these Bonds of *Ignorance,* and false Views of *Interest,* it shall be assisted even by *Self-love,* and grow strong enough to make a *noble virtuous Character.*"[20] So benevolence is inseparable from enlightened self-love.

Or let's consider Smith, who regards propriety as a necessary if not a sufficient condition for virtue, impropriety as a necessary if not a sufficient condition for vice. But it is worth remembering the opening passage of *The Theory of Moral Sentiments:* "How selfish soever man may be supposed, there are evidently some principles in his nature, which interest him in the fortune of others, and render their happiness necessary to him, though he derives nothing from it except the pleasure of seeing it." Nothing "except the pleasure of seeing it" means that even benevolent actions contribute to our own happiness. What happens when "we feel for the misery of others"? This is the answer:

> As we have no immediate experience of what other men feel, we can form no idea of the manner in which they are affected, but by conceiving what we ourselves should feel in the like situation. Though our brother is upon the rack, as long as we ourselves are at our ease, our senses will never inform us of what he suffers. They never did and never can carry us beyond our own persons, and it is by the imagination only that we can form any conception of what are his sensations. . . . By the imagination we place ourselves in his situation, we conceive ourselves enduring all the same torments, we enter as it were into his body and

become in some measure [the same person with] him, and thence form some idea of his sensations, and even feel something which, though weaker in degree, is not altogether unlike them. His agonies, when they are thus brought home to ourselves, when we have thus adopted and made them our own, begin at last to affect us, and we then tremble and shudder at the thought of what he feels.[21]

Consequently, our feeling for others is always, before it can be a feeling for them, a feeling for ourselves—this is what Hobbes had argued. It is not surprising that Thomas Reid complained that in Smith "all Our moral Sentiments are resolved into Sympathy so even this Sympathy seems to be resolved into self love, which receives some change in its direction by an operation of the imagination" or that he wrote that "I have always thought Dr Smith's System of Sympathy wrong. It is indeed only a Refinement of the selfish System."[22]

Hume too, like Smith, rejects selfish moral systems, but only in order to insist that moral feelings are always self-interested:

Now where is the Difficulty of conceiving, that . . . from the original Frame of our Temper, we may feel a Desire of another's Happiness or Good, which, by Means of that Affection, becomes our own Good, and is afterwards pursued, from the conjoin'd Motives of Benevolence and Self-enjoyment? Who sees not that Vengeance, from the Force alone of Passion, may be so eagerly pursued, as to make us knowingly neglect every Consideration of Ease, Interest, or Safety; and, like some vindictive Animals, infuse our very Souls into the Wounds we give an Enemy? And what a malignant Philosophy must it be, that will not allow, to Humanity and Friendship, the same Privileges, which are undisputably granted to the darker Passions of Enmity and Resentment?[23]

Thus this anglophone tradition accepts that reason is never in itself a motive to action, and that all our behavior is directed to the satisfaction of our own desires. Morality as it is understood in some traditions—the ability for self-sacrifice, or for doing the right thing simply because it is the right thing to do—becomes, strictly speaking, impossible. Even the minority of moral philosophers who adopted a firmly rationalist position had difficulty avoiding this view. Thus Wollaston argued that we are *obliged* to seek our own happiness, and avoided saying we are *necessitated* to seek our own happiness; but he conceded that every intelligent being may be *supposed* to aim at happiness, which amounts to much the same thing.[24]

And Thomas Reid argued that it was very difficult to achieve happiness by aiming directly at it: "The road to happiness . . . would be found dark and intricate, full of snares and dangers." Duty, on the other hand, is easy to identify. Fortunately, in aiming to do our duty we discover real happiness: "And as no man can be indifferent about his happiness, the good man has the consolation to know, that he consults his happiness most effectually when . . . he does his duty."[25] Thus, once again, duty and interest turn out to be inseparable. The same may be said of Adam Ferguson, who insisted that the problem with those who pursue happiness by competing for wealth and status is not that they have the wrong goal, but that they misunderstand how to achieve it. For Ferguson, as for everyone else, "the happiness of individuals is the great end of civil society"; he simply argued that individuals will be happiest when they prioritize the welfare of their fellow citizens over their own success. Then they will discover that there is no self-sacrifice involved in working for the good of the community, for this is in reality the surest route to personal happiness.[26]

Fortunately (I use the word with a tinge of irony, for there was a good deal of self-deception involved here) it seemed evident to all eighteenth-century anglophone moral philosophers that enlightened self-interest always coincides more or less exactly with true morality. Thus Bishop Joseph Butler, the scourge of Hobbism, insisted that there is "no peculiar Contrariety between Self-love and Benevolence"; indeed, "every particular Affection, Benevolence among the rest, is subservient to Self-love by being the Instrument of private Enjoyment"; benevolence "contributes more to private Interest, i.e. Enjoyment or Satisfaction, than any other of the particular common Affections"—thus benevolence is, paradoxically, particularly self-interested; "Virtue is naturally the Interest or Happiness, and Vice the Misery of such a Creature as Man, placed in the Circumstances which we are [placed in] in this World."[27]

One passage is so famous among Butler scholars that they refer to it as the "cool hour" passage: "It may be allowed, without any Prejudice to the Cause of Virtue and Religion, that our ideas of Happiness and Misery are of all our Ideas the nearest and most important to us. . . . Let it be allowed, though Virtue or moral Rectitude does indeed consist in Affection to and Pursuit of what is Right and Good, as such; yet, that when we sit down in a cool Hour, we can neither justify to ourselves this or any other Pursuit, but from a Conviction that it will be for our Happiness."[28] Indeed, Butler insists that no action contrary to true self-love can be virtuous, and, "It is manifest that, in the Common Course of Life, there is seldom any Inconsistency between our Duty and what is *called* Interest: It is much seldomer that there is an Inconsistency between Duty and what is really our present Interest; meaning by Interest, Happiness and Satisfaction. Self-love then, though confined to the Interest of the present World, does in general perfectly coincide with Virtue, and leads to one and the same Course of Life."[29] This goes, I think, a little further than Locke would have been prepared to go. Locke held that virtuous behavior always produces public happiness; but he did not claim that it nearly always produces private happiness. In any event, Locke and Butler agree that in the long run God will ensure that virtue is rewarded (a view which requires it to be impossible for a good man to find himself in hell, unless hell is only temporary: presumably all conscientious pagans and heretics will be saved).

So we have three arguments that are, among eighteenth-century anglophones, generally accepted: reason is the slave of the passions (here one or two rationalists might disagree); human beings constantly pursue happiness (Reid might have his doubts); but luckily duty and interest are consistently aligned (which is a version of the duty/interest junction principle that I discussed in Chapters 5 and 6, but here the alignment is usually presented as providential).* For those (Bernard Mandeville, David Hume, Jeremy Bentham) who held that the alignment of duty and interest depended on artifice, the key question was whether this alignment had already been achieved at some point in the distant past, or whether it was yet to be achieved and must be achieved in the future.

Why is reason the slave of the passions? The answer is simple: an idea cannot be a motive for action; only a desire or sense of uneasiness can be. This was a fundamentally new claim, one that would have been

---

* Burlamaqui, for example, insists reason is always able to rule the passions; but he defines reason in such a way that it is always at the service of the appetites.

incomprehensible to a Platonist or Aristotelian or Cartesian, but one which was widely accepted after Locke had made a basically Hobbesian psychology respectable. Underlying it was an implicit bias toward materialist—or, more specifically, mechanist—explanations.* If human beings act, it must be because they have been acted upon; actions must originate in passions.† We find this way of thinking even where we might expect not to. Take Lord Shaftesbury, who pioneered the whole effort to escape from the philosophical egoism of Hobbes. Just as Butler turns out to be much more of a philosophical egoist than we might expect, so Shaftesbury turns out to be much more of a mechanist:

> YOU have heard it (my Friend!) as a common Saying, that *Interest governs the World.* But, I believe, whoever looks narrowly into the Affairs of it, will find, that *Passion, Humour, Caprice, Zeal, Faction,* and a thousand other Springs, which are counter to *Self-Interest,* have as considerable a part in the Movements of this Machine. There are more Wheels and *Counter-Poises* in this Engine than are easily imagin'd. 'Tis of too complex a kind, to fall under one simple View, or be explain'd thus briefly in a word or two. The Studiers of this *Mechanism* must have a very partial Eye, to overlook all other Motions besides those of the lowest and narrowest Compass. 'Tis hard, that in the Plan or Description of this Clock-work, no Wheel or Ballance shou'd be allow'd on the side of the better and more enlarg'd Affections; that nothing shou'd be understood to be done in *Kindness* or *Generosity;* nothing in *pure good-Nature* or *Friendship,* or thro any *social* or *natural Affection* of any kind: when, perhaps, the main Springs of this Machine will be found to be either these very *natural Affections* themselves, or a compound kind deriv'd from them, and retaining more than one half of their Nature.[30]

---

* In arguing that it is impossible to prove the existence of an immaterial soul, John Locke, in *An Essay Concerning Humane Understanding* (London: Basset, 1690), 270 (bk. 4, ch. 3, sec. 6), was undoubtedly aware that he was agreeing with Hobbes's reply to René Descartes, published in Descartes's *Meditations on First Philosophy* (1641).

† See, for example, the translation of Louis-Jean Levesque de Pouilly, *Théorie des sentimens agréables* (Geneva: Barrillot, 1747) as *The Theory of Agreeable Sensations,* ed. Jacob Vernet (London: Owen, 1749).

What Shaftesbury argues here is that our motives are not always selfish; but our actions are always governed by our affections; if we act for the welfare of others, it is because our affections prompt us to do so; and it follows necessarily that such actions will contribute to our own happiness as well as to theirs. Since Shaftesbury accepts that our actions are caused by our passions or affections, it is hardly surprising that he accepts a mechanical account of the working of the mind, even while insisting that the machine in question is much more complex than is generally recognized.

What of the second weak point in the trio, the claim that we always pursue happiness? Let me approach this through a letter Adam Smith wrote to the *Edinburgh Review* in 1755–1756.[31] Here Smith lumped all the British moral philosophers together and contrasted them to the Cartesians. The British philosophy (actually he calls it the English philosophy, but he mentions Hutcheson, who was Irish, and certainly intends to include Hume, so I take it he means the anglophone philosophy), he said, was now being taken up in France, and he names Levesque de Pouilly's *Theory of Agreeable Sentiments* (1747) as an example. What do we find if we turn to Levesque de Pouilly (as we did in Chapter 5), who claims, "The heart of every man, to use a Cartesian expression, is a kind of vortex, the center of whose motions is its own personal happiness"? Those who sacrifice their lives for others gain such exquisite if brief pleasure from their actions that "it is very possible that these illustrious persons may have been more happy in their death, than they would have been had they enjoy'd life longer."[32] Thus Levesque de Pouilly accepts the first and the second of our propositions, but he goes on to argue at length that God has constructed the universe in such a manner that our pleasures and pains are precisely those required to further our welfare. Here he is arguing against Pierre Bayle, who had claimed, surely rightly, that there is much more pain in the universe than can be explained by the idea of an omnipotent, benevolent deity.

It seems likely that Smith read this argument with care, for he reproduces it in *The Theory of Moral Sentiments*:

The happiness of mankind, as well of all other rational creatures, seems to have been the original purpose intended by the Author of Nature, when he brought them into existence. No other end seems worthy of that supreme wisdom and divine benignity which we necessarily ascribe to him; and this opinion, which we are led to by abstract consideration of his infinite perfections, is still more confirmed by the examination of the works of Nature, which seem all intended to promote happiness, and to guard against misery.

Again,

> If we consider the general rules by which external prosperity and adversity are commonly distributed in this life, we shall find, that notwithstanding the disorder in which all things appear to be in this world, yet even here every virtue naturally meets with its proper reward, with the recompense which is most fit to encourage and promote it; and this too so surely, that it requires a very extraordinary concurrence of circumstances entirely to disappoint it.[33]

It is true, Smith concedes, that an innocent man may occasionally be convicted of a crime; but this is the equivalent in the social world of an earthquake in the natural world—something so exceptional that it is no reflection on God's benevolence, and need form no part of our own calculations as to how to live our lives.

Levesque de Pouilly and Smith argue from the existence of a benevolent deity to the duty / interest junction principle and back again. "Is" and "ought" happily coincide. What they find in society is what they find in the natural order, and both betray the same *economy*, to use Smith's word:

> Though man, therefore, be naturally endowed with a desire of the welfare and preservation of society, yet the author of nature has not intrusted it to his reason to find out that a certain application of punishments is the proper means of attaining this end; but has endowed him with an immediate and instinctive approbation of that very application which is most proper to attain it. The oeconomy of nature is in this respect exactly of a piece with what it is upon many other occasions. With regard to all those ends which, upon account of their peculiar importance, may be regarded, if such an expression is allowable, as the favourite ends of nature, she has constantly in this manner not only endowed mankind with an appetite for the end which she proposes, but likewise with an appetite for the means by which alone this end can be brought about, for their own sakes, and independent of their tendency to produce it.[34]

Clearly not every moral philosopher was prepared to place God at the center of his arguments in this way; those who were not, such as Hume, had to argue that the coincidence between virtue and interest was either a simple empirical fact about human nature or an artificial consequence of our own social engineering. Either way, their refusal to argue from deistic principles did not lead them to question the duty / interest junction principle, although their account of it certainly became more complicated and sophisticated. Thus, although Hume refused to identify morality with self-interest, he insisted they were nevertheless perfectly aligned. "Having explained the moral *approbation* attending virtue," he wrote, "there remains nothing but to consider briefly our interested *obligation* to it, and to enquire, whether every man, who has any regard to his own happiness and welfare, will not best find his account in the practice of every moral duty." The enquiry could be brief, because the conclusion was obvious: "where is the difficulty of conceiving, that . . . from the original frame of our temper, we may feel a desire of another's happiness or good, which, by means of that affection, becomes our own good, and is afterwards pursued, from the conjoin'd motives of benevolence and self-enjoyment?"[35]

This trio of principles—the constant pursuit of happiness; reason as the slave of the passions; the duty / interest junction principle in its widest form—are not peculiar to the anglophones (we find them, for example, in Cesare Beccaria and Burlamaqui), but I think Smith is right to think that this style of thinking originates among English speakers, and that it is disseminated from English into French—it is worth remembering that Denis Diderot began his life in publishing translating texts from English, and Voltaire's intellectual life was transformed by his visit to England.

If we go back to Levesque de Pouilly we will find that he can't quite commit himself to the view that reason is the slave of the passions in a consistent fashion; he often writes of reason as if it were an independent agent. And, of course, for Cartesians it was an independent agent. For Cartesians, human psychology could not be understood in purely mechanical terms. And Cartesians did not accept the duty / interest junction principle; indeed, Descartes insisted that the universe was not made for man, which was the standard foundation on which the duty / interest junction principle was raised.[36] You need to turn to La Mettrie's *L'homme machine* to find a Frenchman prepared to give full voice to British principles—and he can only do so by adopting a systematic materialism in order to escape the influence of Cartesian dualism.

Writing in 1755 Smith rejects the whole Cartesian tradition of moral philosophy in favor of the anglophone tradition. It is true he goes on to say nice things about Jean-Jacques Rousseau's *Origins of Inequality*, but Rousseau could be read as a sort of Englishman. His philosophy was, Smith maintained, grounded, like so much British moral philosophy, in the rejection of Mandeville. Indeed, Mandeville's slogan, "private vices, public benefits," is only horrifying if you think the fundamental task of moral and social theory is to illustrate and praise the duty/interest junction principle. And if Rousseau thought that in corrupt societies duty and interest rather obviously do not coincide, he also thought that one ought to be able to construct a society in which they did.

Thus, on the one hand, we appear to have arguments that verge on materialism and mechanism; and on the other, arguments that treat the mind as immaterial and free. We have, in short, two competing psychologies—except we should be careful about using that word. None of the British moral philosophers I am talking about uses the word "psychology," although it was already well established. The reason is simple: psychology was generally taken to be synonymous with pneumatology—it was the study of the soul.[37] And our British philosophers were not talking about souls, they were talking about minds.

Minds are peculiar things. You can (in both English and Latin) have something in mind, but your mind itself isn't anywhere. Minds fudge the material/immaterial distinction. An anglophone must find it puzzling that there is no word in French (or German) for "mind."[38] Descartes wrote about the soul, and so (still) did Michel Foucault; Claude Adrien Helvétius wrote about something for which there was and is no word in English: *l'esprit.* Translating the word "mind" in Locke's *Essay Concerning Humane Understanding,* Pierre Coste sometimes used the word *âme* and sometimes the word *esprit;* since the mind is the central topic of Locke's book, it is not clear that its argument can really survive translation into French.[39] La Mettrie, who needed the concept of mind more than anyone, had to make do by redefining the soul as "that part which thinks in us" (i.e., what Descartes had called the *res cogitans*)[40]—but this is at least a more explicit redefinition than is to be found in Coste's Locke.[41]

But the category of "the mind" is not, I think, the only reason for this distinction between the anglophones (and one or two others, such as Beccaria and La Mettrie) and the rest (and I realize that when I say "the rest" there is a bit of a stretch involved—it would take a much longer chapter to establish that the Dutch, the Germans, the Spanish and others were, as I think they were, part of "the rest," but I think my present remarks about Cartesianism could be extended to the followers of Gottfried Wilhelm Leibniz or Immanuel Kant).* What the anglophones crucially had in common was the conviction that moral philosophy can be an empirical science— Hume, for example, writes as an exponent of the experimental method in philosophy.[42] Morgan and Levesque de Pouilly are advocates of what Morgan calls "physico-theology" (Levesque de Pouilly says natural theology is a branch of physics); but even those like Hume, who don't practice physico-theology, assume that empirical enquiry will enable us to identify the underlying order which makes it possible for society to function— "notwithstanding," as Smith puts it, "the disorder in which all things appear to be in this world."[43] This argument, that a study of human beings as they are will enable us to identify their duties, that moral philosophy can be grounded in an empirical sociology and psychology, goes back at least to Richard Cumberland and represents an updating of the traditional natural law view that there are certain moral principles on which all human communities agree. The French skeptics, Michel de Montaigne and Pierre Charron, had mounted a sustained attack on the notion of any such consensus, so the task facing the empiricists was one of accounting not only for the appearance of disorder, but also for the evidence for cultural difference— as manifested, to take an example that could not easily be dismissed as merely barbaric, in ancient Greek infanticide and pederasty. Order must thus be found within these two very different types of disorder. The solution was to move beyond a consideration of particular obligations and prohibitions

---

* See, for example, François-Vincent Toussaint's *Les moeurs* (1748): instincts are there subordinated to reason, the soul to God and the body to the soul. It is reason which "points out true happiness and likewise the means of procuring it." Toussaint's book, which seemed irreligious (because deistic and anticlerical) in France, must have seemed pious to many English readers because it placed God and the soul at the center of moral theorizing.

to the identification of underlying motivations which might, in practice, generate a wide variety of codes and rules.

Of course, you might say that the idea that one can identify moral principles by looking at how societies function goes back to Aristotle and even Plato; but the anglophone Enlightenment approached the question in a way which would have puzzled any classical philosopher. Plato and Aristotle thought that different types of polities foster different characters, and that bad societies produce bad men, but it never occurred to them to claim that the question of what was the best character, or what constituted true virtue, could be an empirical question. The anglophone Enlightenment, on the other hand, had very little to say about the traditional virtues, whether pagan or Christian, or about self-fulfillment; what they wanted to show was that human beings are naturally motivated to behave in ways that serve the interests of society, that they are simultaneously both selfish and sociable. They were thus interested in one system, the mind, which is part of a larger system, the social order. The two systems, they argued, fit neatly one within the other, either because God has constructed them so to do or because human beings have introduced their own devices (such as justice and private property) to ensure that they do. Shaftesbury was the first to stress that (as John Maxwell put it when summarizing Shaftesbury's views) *"The World is a System or Whole, whose Parts are design'd and contriv'd mutually for one another;* which plainly proves it to have been fram'd by *a Being Powerful, Wise, and Good."* Since nature proves God, "All our Knowledge of Natural Religion and Morality, is ultimately resolv'd into our Knowledge of the Frame of Nature."[44]

⋅◦⋅◦⋅◦⋅

"The frame of nature" (the standard translation of the classical Latin *machina mundi*) was, by the time Maxwell used it in 1727, already an old-fashioned way of referring to what was now called "the system of nature" or "the natural system"—phrases which had entered common usage in the 1690s. In 1735 Carl Linnaeus published his *Systema naturae*. As I pointed out in Chapter 8, if we look at early usages of the word system there are three different sorts of usage. First, there are intellectual systems, such as systems of logic or of theology—these are fundamentally static, just like the frame of the universe or Andreas Vesalius's fabric of the human body. This, for example, is the way in which Hume uses the word "system" in his *Treatise of Human Nature*.[45] Second, there are the competing astronomical systems of Tycho Brahe, Copernicus, and Ptolemy, and these, of course, are systems in movement; this naturally leads to the notion of a system as being equivalent to a moving machine, such as a clock. In 1676 Joseph Glanvill described Descartes as having produced "the neatest *Mechanical* System of things that" has "appear'd in the World."[46] As I explained in Chapter 6, in this second sense the terms "machine" and "system" are used more or less interchangeably, and I would argue that you cannot have the idea of a system in this sense unless you already have the idea of a machine as a series of interlocking moving parts—an idea which wasn't clearly formulated until around the year 1600.

Through into the seventeenth century only the heavens were a close-knit, interlocking system; but as the distinction between the sublunary and the supralunary worlds began to break down—finally collapsing with the Newtonian synthesis—the whole of nature began to be thought of as a system, and new abstractions (society, the constitution, the economy) were devised to identify systems within the worlds made by human beings.

What underlies this new preoccupation with systems analysis are four moves that we also see in the scientific revolution. First is the move from Aristotelian qualities to mechanistic quantities. Power, pleasure, and wealth are all talked about as if they can be measured. Shaftesbury is the first, for example, to use the phrase "moral arithmetic," and we have seen Bayle weighing pleasure, and Wollaston entering it into an account book.* Moral arithmetic, said David Fordyce in 1757, "to be able to compute the Rank and Value of every Pleasure," is "the *chief Art of Life*."[47] Similarly, Beccaria wrote about political arithmetic, which again involves computing the values of pleasure and pains.

---

* "THUS have we computed, in the best manner we were able, the Good and Interest of Mankind, by enumerating and casting up all those Particulars from whence, as by way of Addition or Subtraction, that Sum or general Account of Man's Interest or Happiness in Life, is either swell'd or diminish'd: so that the method here taken may perhaps for this reason be call'd a sort of *Moral Arithmetic,* and be said to have an evidence as great as may be found in Numbers, and equal to Mathematical Demonstration." Anthony Ashley Cooper Lord Shaftesbury, *An Inquiry Concerning Virtue: In Two Discourses* (London: Bell, 1699), 196–197.

Second is the move from an Aristotelian structure of causation—formal, final, material, and efficient—to an explanation in terms of the working of laws of nature: thus pleasure, we are repeatedly told, is somehow just like gravity in that it is pervasive and irresistible. As Beccaria puts it, "That force, which continually impels us to our own private interest, like gravity, acts incessantly, unless it meets with an obstacle to oppose it."[48] The task of the legislator is thus to direct and oppose this force, as the architect directs and opposes the force of gravity. Those, like Shaftesbury, who deny that there is only one law at work still accept that a mechanical model is the right sort of model to have in mind.

Third is the move from the bounded to the unbounded. In science, this began with the introduction of the vanishing point to perspective painting; was reinforced by the expansion of the universe required by Copernicanism and by the Cartesian notion that the sun is a star and the stars are all suns; and was confirmed by the Newtonian conception of space as infinite.[49] In politics, it began with Niccolò Machiavelli's admiration for the Roman state as being designed for continuous expansion; in moral philosophy, with Hobbes's account of pleasure as obeying the same logic as power; in economics, with Nicholas Barbon's account of how the demand for the goods of the mind is insatiable.

And fourth, the new systems involve feedback mechanisms. In science the first fully interactive system was Isaac Newton's account of gravity, published in 1687, and it is surely not a coincidence that interactive systems begin to play a much more important role in politics (the balance of power) and psychology (Locke's association of ideas) in the following years.[50] In this respect Hobbes, whose model for the sciences was still, as it had been for Galileo, provided by geometry, belonged to an earlier era, and one sign of this is his belief that order can only be established from outside, by the imposition of sovereign power. Feedback mechanisms made it possible to understand how a system could both be unbounded and orderly at the same time. In the case of the balance of power or the balance of trade, the feedback mechanism serves to establish an equilibrium, and it is these sorts of feedback mechanisms that have caught the attention of historians.[51] But, as we saw when considering the impact of bad harvests on food prices in Chapter 8, not all feedbacks are beneficent: there are hidden backhands as well as hidden hands.

Long before Beccaria and Bentham, justice, to take just one example, began to be thought of as a system for modifying behavior. Shaftesbury held that "a virtuous Administration, and an equal and just Distribution of Rewards and Punishments, is of the highest service; not only by restraining the Vicious, and forcing them to act usefully to Society; but, by making Virtue to be apparently the Interest of every-one, so as to remove all Prejudices against it, create a fair reception for it, and lead Men into that path which afterwards they cannot easily quit."[52]

Thus the intellectual program that led to Helvétius, Beccaria, and Bentham had already been clearly defined by 1711, and had been formulated indeed by someone who was seeking to escape from the principles of Hobbes and Locke, with their stress upon selfish passions, but found himself constantly being drawn back to them. In part authors like Shaftesbury were making concessions to possible Hobbesian or Lockean readers; but more importantly they were conceding their own incapacity to escape the Hobbesian framework, despite their best efforts.[53] They did, however, have an advantage over Hobbes: they could understand how a social process might be self-reinforcing, building upon itself, so that once people had entered upon the right path they would find it harder and harder as time went by to step out of it. They could identify feedback mechanisms.

In the fourth edition of the *Essay Concerning Humane Understanding* Locke added a new chapter, "Of the Association of Ideas" (II.xxxiii). There he argued that we all of us have in our thinking and behavior a touch of unreasonableness so profound that one might properly call it madness. This "disease," as he terms it, does not simply come from self-interest or prejudice. It comes from the fact that once our mind has established and reestablished links between concepts or experiences, those links become unconscious and difficult to break, even if they are profoundly mistaken. This process has advantages: a musician can play a tune she knows well without having to think where to put her hands on the keyboard or which fingers to use. But a mistaken link, once reinforced, becomes robust; our habits sometimes help us, but sometimes they are profoundly detrimental.

Locke stressed that this must lead to a new theory of education: the task of the educator is not just to teach his pupils the right opinions but also to establish the right associations of ideas, the right mental customs and habits. If we go back to Shaftesbury, in the passage I have just quoted, he says that the task of a system of rewards and punishments is to "lead Men into that path which afterwards they cannot easily quit." This is an echo of Locke's claim that "Custom settles habits of Thinking in the Understanding, as well as of Determining in the Will, and of Motions in the Body: all which seems to be but Trains of Motion in the Animal Spirits, which, once set a going, continue on in the same steps they have been used to, which by often treading are worn into a smooth path, and the Motion in it becomes easy, and as it were Natural."[54] Here the actions of the mind alter the mind itself, smoothing a path which at first was rough and rugged. Thus human beings become, often unconsciously, trained to engage in certain sorts of behavior. Changing a pattern of behavior is difficult, just as it is hard to step off the beaten path into the scrubland around it.

We can see the importance of these systems for the training of human beings in appropriate behavior if we read La Mettrie, whose subject is man, and who is therefore peculiarly simpleminded whenever he discusses social systems. Thus he says, "Words, languages, laws, sciences, and the liberal arts were introduced in time, and by them the rough diamond of our understanding was polished. Man has been broke and trained up, like any other animal."[55] Thus human beings, by a peculiar bootstrapping operation, break (as you break a horse) and train (as you train a dog to do tricks) each other. It's this puzzle of how we collectively do something to ourselves individually—polish the rough diamond, beat smooth the path—that the new type of systems theory was designed to explain. So Adam Smith's economic theory does not simply explain why the economy rewards those businesses which improve productivity; it also shows how economic activity serves, through a system of rewards and punishments, to train the individual to engage in certain sorts of behavior—the market economy not only produces profits but also produces *Homo economicus,* and the two processes reinforce each other.

At this point I want to say something that may seem odd but that is, I think, inescapably true, and that is that the various systems that I have been discussing—society, the economy, the state, the constitution, the penal system—are examples of what is called the Tinker Bell effect.[56] That is, they exist only because people believe they exist, and consequently they did not exist before people began to believe in them. (In J. M. Barrie's 1911 novel about Peter Pan, *Peter and Wendy,* Tinker Bell is a fairy who will die if the children stop believing in her.) Nicholas Barbon began his pathbreaking essay on trade, published in 1690, with the complaint that even Machiavelli had not seen that trade was relevant to affairs of state, and that people discuss the interests of particular trades, but up to now have been incapable of standing back and discussing the interest of trade as a whole.[57] Barbon was not simply analyzing the interest of trade but was also creating a new social entity, the trading interest; he was not simply saying that governments need to concern themselves with trade but was also helping to educate the government to understand that one could identify a generalized trading interest.[58] Identifying a trading interest and creating a trading interest are two sides of the same coin. Or take Smith's free market economics: it was not a theory of economic relations in general, but of free market relations in particular; and by theorizing those relations it helped bring them into existence every bit as much as it described them.

The Tinker Bell effect is an extension of the bootstrapping process: if free markets produce and are produced by *Homo economicus,* so, too, political economy comes into existence both as a meditation on the activities of markets and traders and as an attempt to modify and direct those activities. It creates the very thing it describes, just as a Möbius strip turns back on itself.

Margaret Thatcher once said, "There's no such thing as society."[59] What I am saying is that there once was no such thing as society, or the economy, or the state, or the constitution, or, for that matter, religion, and one day there may be no such thing as society, or the economy, or the state, or the constitution, or religion.* This claim may shock, but it should not. After all, John Bossy recommended, in his brilliant essay entitled "Some Elementary Forms of Durkheim," that historians avoid using the word "society" for the world before John Locke—before the Enlightenment—because that world lacked the very concept of society. Religion, it turns out, is another modern concept, as is politics. And Edward Thompson insisted that class is not only a structural relationship but also an experience—that it exists only in and

---

* "Psychology," it may be remarked, is different. A market economy requires people who understand that they are in competition with each other; a religion requires people who make a distinction between sacred and profane, natural and supernatural, and believe that other societies make comparable distinctions. But to discuss Joe's psychology is not to make any claim about Joe's beliefs.

through our own consciousness of it.[60] So too, we might say, the economy exists only in so far as *Homo economicus* exists, and vice versa; and both the economy and *Homo economicus* exist only if agents have some sort of understanding of what the economy is and how it functions.[61]

This sort of argument may seem paradoxical. "Which comes first," you may wonder, "the chicken or the egg?" But that is precisely to miss the point of bootstrapping and the Tinker Bell effect: there are certain types of social activities that exist only because we bring them into existence through our own actions (bootstrapping) and our own beliefs (the Tinker Bell effect). Social conventions, as they establish themselves, are self-reinforcing, so that behaviors create beliefs and beliefs create behaviors, and both bring into existence new structures, which in turn shape behaviors and beliefs. Social systems are socially constructed—on reflection, the point is obvious.[62]

Both behaviors and beliefs have material embodiments; thus an account book results from a certain type of business activity, but it also makes that activity possible; the pulpit in a Calvinist church embodies the belief that salvation comes through hearing the word, and not through participation in the sacraments, but it also makes it possible for the preacher to be heard and to be seen; the guillotine is an icon of the French Revolution because it works fast and efficiently, knows no distinction of rank, and inflicts no pain—since it did not exist, it was necessary to invent it.

Beliefs (about politics, economics, or religion) are inseparable from behaviors, and both are inseparable from the objects that embody those behaviors; the theories we have are constitutive of the activities we engage in and the material tools we use, as well as vice versa. Thus Hume sought to understand morality by studying what people *believed* to be good and bad, right and wrong; but the whole point of his enquiry was to subtly alter people's moral beliefs by explaining them to them and thus to change their behavior; and these new moral beliefs were embodied in new locations—the Bath Assembly Rooms, for example—where a new type of social interaction took place.[63] The Enlightenment played a part in creating the very systems which it claimed to study.

Bootstrapping and the Tinker Bell effect are consequences of the entanglement of thoughts and actions, words and deeds, projects and objects.[64] Take, for example, the ceremony of a birthday cake. One can disassemble it, and say it is made up of an iced cake, some burning candles, and the song

"Happy Birthday," all brought together on a particular day of the year, but then you immediately lose sight of the crucial features that these four have when assembled together—the fact that they constitute a ceremony, a ceremony both of giving and sharing, a ceremony which constitutes a celebration of a person's life and represents a rite of passage. Birthday cakes only exist because people believe in the ceremony of the birthday cake (even if they don't believe that wishes made when the candles are blown out actually come true); and the belief only exists because from earliest childhood we encounter birthday cakes. You can't separate the belief and the cake, nor either of these from the notion that birthdays are occasions for celebration. Beliefs and rituals are entangled with sugar, eggs, and flour in the making of a birthday cake. Analytically we can separate out the different elements that make up the birthday cake ceremony; we can explore their history and the ways in which they change over time.[65] But in real life they are entangled together: the cake is both object and symbol, art and food, given to one person and shared by all. Religion, society, and the economy are like birthday cakes: of course they are real, they exist; but they are also the peculiar products of a particular civilization, and one day they, along with the roadside memorials which in England mark the sites of fatal automobile accidents, will seem as peculiar as the ex-voto objects and paintings that until recently were left in Catholic churches as thanksgivings to saints, or as the now lost virtues of magnanimity and humility—or, indeed, as the very ideas of "virtue" and "vice" themselves.

This book has been about power, pleasure, and profit, three goods which can be pursued without limit. These endless pursuits stepped into a gap opened up by the decline of godliness and of Aristotelian virtue. The long wars of religion, from the Reformation to the Revocation of the Edict of Nantes, had a good deal to do with the decline of godliness, and the Scientific Revolution had a great deal to do with the decline of scholastic philosophy. Commercial society eroded aristocratic values.

What was absolutely crucial, though, for the success of the new culture of pleasure and profit and of instrumental logic were two purely intellectual shifts: first, a redefinition of morality as an interested obligation through the theory of sympathy, and second, the recognition that order can underlie apparent disorder, that checks and balances can work as well or better than deliberate planning and direction, that one can have a constant clash of interests and aspirations without the bloody warfare of a Hobbesian state of nature. Machiavellism, Hobbism, and the cynicism of Mandeville were never likely to become the predominant values of a new, post-Aristotelian culture. Hard-line egoism had to be replaced by something more palatable, and at the same time self-interested behavior had to be shown to be socially beneficial. Both tasks were accomplished by the philosophers of the Scottish Enlightenment; the famous Adam Smith Problem simply reflects the fact that these two tasks were somewhat at odds with each other. The result was not (I would argue) a fully coherent and consistent set of theories in politics, moral philosophy, or economics; but it was a set of theories and values which provided a reasonably stable and persuasive foundation for a new culture, a culture that was rapidly exported not only to England and America but also to France, Germany, and Italy.[66]

Back in 1981, Alasdair MacIntyre popularized the term "the Enlightenment project."* "The Enlightenment" is a problematic term, because it is easy and fruitful to multiply enlightenments. Even if we accept the term "the Enlightenment" (as I do, for want of a better one), the word "project" is surely too strong in that it suggests that people knew where they were going and how they intended to get there; that's not how history works. But I think "the Enlightenment paradigm" can be a useful shorthand for a set of intellectual claims which we have been exploring in this book. It may be helpful simply to list them:

1. In psychology:
   a. Human beings pursue pleasure and flee pain. Pleasure is in short supply and pain is difficult to avoid.
   b. People do not agree on what is most pleasurable, so there is no *summum bonum* or greatest good.
   c. Happiness and success consist in an excess of pleasure over pain (the hedonic calculus).

---

* An alternative term for what we are discussing here would be C. B. MacPherson's term, "possessive individualism."

    d. Knowledge originates in sensation, and the mind works through the association of ideas.

    e. Reason is the slave of the passions.

    f. The passions can be set against each other; some passions have detrimental consequences, while others result in beneficial outcomes.

    g. Reasoning consists of engaging in a cost-benefit analysis; it is instrumental and seeks to maximize benefits and minimize costs.

2. In society:

    a. Human beings constantly pursue their interests.

    b. In pursuit of their interests they interact: there is thus such a thing as "society" which is conceptually prior to the state.

    c. Human beings are naturally sociable in so far as they feel sympathy and pity.

    d. Fortunately, thanks to an invisible hand or to political and social engineering, in pursuing their interests human beings benefit others, thus producing an order which is either spontaneous or at first sight appears to be so.

3. In moral philosophy:

    a. Though human beings are self-interested, it is evident that the welfare of others can be a source of pleasure to them, and the suffering of others can be a source of pain.

    b. Human behavior is thus not narrowly selfish in that we recognize that our happiness is in some measure inseparable from that of others.

    c. The goal of human behavior must be to increase the happiness of the self and others (the hedonic calculus).

    d. The study of how to achieve this is an empirical enquiry, a branch of the social sciences.

    e. Education, public opinion, and the law must be mobilized to reinforce behavior which is beneficial to others and to penalize behavior which is detrimental to others; duty and interest must be brought to coincide.

4. In politics:

    a. Political actors are pursuing their own interests rather than the common good.

    b. Political activity must thus be controlled by checks and balances so that the interests of politicians are brought to coincide with the interest of society at large—the duty / interest junction principle again.

    c. Various institutions make this possible: a free press and public opinion; political parties, elections; a bicameral legislature; the separation of powers.

5. In economics:

    a. An economic system in which individuals pursue their own interests results in public benefits.[67]

    b. This is because markets contain feedback mechanisms and are self-equilibrating, thus leading to an optimum distribution of resources.

    c. Markets lead to an extended division of labor, which leads to increased productivity and greater personal and national wealth.

    d. A commercial society is law-abiding and peaceable, and thus an excellent context in which individuals can pursue happiness, even if the pursuit of wealth is not in itself the best strategy for attaining happiness.

    e. The self-interested pursuit of wealth must sometimes be at odds with our moral obligations to our neighbors.

At each level we find a series of claims that acquire the status of paradigms: they provide a framework for continuing debate and discussion. Each of these levels reflects and depends on the others, and together they make up a resilient, self-confirming system, both in theory and in practice, although the system has internal tensions, as reflected in the Adam Smith Problem. Thus a market economy encourages self-interested behavior, and limited government provides a stable framework for acquisitive behavior. The fundamental claims are that human beings pursue pleasure and the means to pleasure; that well-regulated and prosperous societies can be the outcome of this pursuit; and that education, morality, and the law must be employed to shape and direct this pursuit for the greater good.

    This broad Enlightenment intellectual framework was built up over time. Instrumental reasoning took its inspiration from double-entry bookkeeping. Machiavelli, Hobbes, and Locke played a crucial role in justifying self-interested behavior, but it is only with the development of physiocracy and political economy, and with them of the idea of spontaneous order, that the new arguments began to develop into a coherent, overarching philosophy which covered all aspects of life. As such, the Enlightenment depended on systems thinking, which is a post-Newtonian development of the mechanical philosophy. This Enlightenment framework displaced—or at least everywhere sought to displace—alternatives, such as the classical accounts of virtue and republican liberty, natural law theories of scholastic origin, and the Cartesian attempt to construct a replacement for Aristotle.

It should also be evident that there are strains and tensions within this system. Human beings seems to be very bad at weighing long-term interests against short-term satisfactions: some forget about tomorrow, and sink into indolence and dissipation; others are so obsessed with acquiring the means to future pleasure (such as wealth) that they never actually enjoy themselves. Imaginary pleasures seem to be every bit as important as real pleasures, but if pleasure is imaginary, then it can hardly be the crucial motive for human behavior. Sympathy and imagination may lead to fellow-feeling and compassion, but if human beings are fundamentally selfish, the ties of affection are likely to be narrow and fragile. The pursuit of wealth is not likely to lead to individual happiness, but it has benefits for society as a whole. The division of labor results in specialization which turns work into mind-numbing repetition. A prosperous commercial society may include people who are starving. There is plenty of room for disagreement as to whether human behavior within society provides evidence of a providential design, or rather of our own efforts to tame and civilize ourselves, and for disagreement as to whether materialism can provide an adequate account of all aspects of human behavior.

Thus, within this very broad framework we can find bitter disputes between those who see evidence of a providential order and those who do not; between materialists and those who oppose materialism; between political radicals and political conservatives; between those who emphasize how unfit human beings are for society and those who insist that they are naturally sociable; and so on. These disputes are very important, and as a result of them no Enlightenment thinker provided an uncontested account of the Enlightenment paradigm as a whole. But disagreements among Enlightenment thinkers should not prevent us from seeing that for the most part they take place within this overarching framework and do not throw the framework itself into question. For all their numerous disagreements, Denis Diderot and Paul Henri Thiry, Baron D'Holbach, Voltaire and Edward Gibbon, David Hume and Adam Smith recognized that they had a shared culture (and indeed they met and socialized together).

Alongside this framework, of course, there survived a classical inheritance which continued to be respected; and many individuals and institutions refused to adopt this framework, holding fast to Aristotelian philosophy, Christian theology, and royal absolutism. Enlightenment thinkers thus often sought to present their views in ways which made them seem compatible with more traditional modes of thought, particularly since in many countries those advocating Enlightenment values faced censorship and persecution. Moreover, some individuals were profoundly uncomfortable with this Enlightenment paradigm and sought to destroy it from within by exploiting its internal tensions and contradictions—Rousseau and Kant being the two most significant examples.

Thus the Enlightenment framework was largely invisible to participants, and has been largely invisible to historians. Participants were more concerned with areas of disagreement than of agreement; and historians have often shared many of the assumptions of Enlightenment authors, and have thus regarded them as obviously true, rather than as the result of a complicated historical process of intellectual and cultural transformation. To see the system as a whole you have to be prepared to doubt its founding assumptions; but you also have to be willing to recognize (as opponents of the Enlightenment have generally been unwilling to do) that the system had (and has) considerable coherence and resilience.[68]

By the 1780s there was an emerging Enlightenment consensus, one which inspired the American Constitution. That consensus was destroyed by the French Revolution, which seemed to many the evil and inevitable consequence of the Enlightenment paradigm. This is not the place to write a history of nineteenth-century thought, but religious revivalism, idealism, socialism and Marxism, social Darwinism, the emergence of moral philosophies based on altruism, and (in the twentieth century) Freudianism and postmodernism all represent attacks upon the Enlightenment framework.

But this leads us to a deep puzzle. The Enlightenment framework has resisted all efforts to kill it off. Over and over again garlic and crosses have been held out to defeat it; again and again a stake has been driven through first one and then another vital organ. Yet, vampire-like, it returns to life. When at the beginning of the twentieth century Max Weber described the disenchantment of the world and said that we are trapped within the iron cage of instrumental reasoning, it was Enlightenment values that he was describing. When, at the end of the twentieth century the collapse of European communism seemed to herald a new world order, that order was to be based on Enlightenment principles: free markets, freedom of speech, constitutional government, the separation of religion from the state. When we talk about Western values, the values we have in mind are the values of the American Founding Fathers, which are Enlightenment values. When we describe what is good about our societies and when we criticize their failings, we are mobilizing arguments developed within the Enlightenment paradigm. Weber was right—no matter how we try to escape, we remain within the cage.

Why is this? The answer, I would suggest, is that in the West, Enlightenment values, free markets, and political liberty are intertwined and interdependent. We have constructed a society based on competition between enterprises (the free market) and between individuals (the career open to talents, meritocracy), within a framework of limited government, and the arguments in favor of such a society go back to Adam Smith and his contemporaries. No psychologist now studies Locke as an introduction to psychology; few moral philosophers now describe themselves as utilitarians; but *The Wealth of Nations* is still the founding text of economic theory, and the American Constitution still provides a model that others follow. As long as free markets and limited government continue, Enlightenment values are going to be constantly brought back to life to explain the advantages and to justify the continuance of these institutions. We thus have a striking paradox: Enlightenment values fostered capitalism and political liberty; now it is capitalism and political liberty which sustain Enlightenment values.

The future may be very different. One day robots may do all the hard work, energy may come from sources which make it effectively cost-free, and genetic modification may make disease and pain things of the past. In that world the Enlightenment paradigm, which originates in a recognition of scarcity, in the realization that pleasure and happiness are in short supply but that they matter more than anything else, will come to seem irrelevant. Until then, there is no escape from instrumental reasoning or from the duty / interest junction principle.

{ 247 }

There is, to echo Sigmund Freud, no adequate understanding of civilization which is not also an account of its discontents, just as (as Adam Smith already saw) there is no adequate understanding of economic development which is not also an account of alienation. What the Enlightenment paradigm created was a new type of civilization, and with that civilization came new discontents. This book has sought to show how, in order to understand the construction and consequences of that civilization, we need to study the key transformations which mark the end of the old social and intellectual order and the emergence of the new: the triumph of the idea that power, pleasure, and profit are goods to be pursued without end and without limit, and the development of systems theories to provide the tools with which to understand what happens when people pursue power, pleasure, and profit without end and without limit. But the real transformation was not in the world of ideas; it was in the lives and behavior of people who had come to accept that virtue, honor, shame, and guilt counted for almost nothing; all that mattered was success. Thomas Hobbes summed up the new world that was coming into existence around him—the world we still inhabit—when he compared life to a race: "this *Race* we must suppose to have no other *Goal*, nor other *Garland*, but being formost."[69] (The garland he has in mind is the laurel wreath awarded to victors in the Olympic games in ancient Greece.) Competing is not much of a goal; winning is not much of a garland. There are more important things in life than having lots of money in the bank or a low handicap in golf. Happiness, which so many pursue and some find, is one of them.

I end with a quotation from Adam Ferguson:

We look abroad for a happiness which is to be found only in the qualities of the heart: we think ourselves dependent on accidents; and are therefore kept in suspense and solicitude: we think ourselves dependent on the will of other men; and are therefore servile and timid; we think our felicity is placed in subjects for which our fellow-creatures are rivals and competitors; and in pursuit of happiness, we engage in those scenes of emulation, envy, hatred, animosity, and revenge, that lead to the highest pitch of distress. We act, in short, as if to preserve ourselves were to retain our weakness, and perpetuate our sufferings. We charge the ills of a distempered imagination, and a corrupt heart, to the account of our fellow-creatures, to whom we refer the pangs of our disappointment or malice; and while we foster our misery, are surprised that the care of ourselves is attended with no better effects.[70]

Appendix A

On Emulation, and on the Canon

Unlike philosophers and political theorists, who have often been happy to confine themselves to a study of a canon of classic texts, historians have long had a professional commitment to exploring as wide a range of sources as possible, whether they be hidden in archives or in obscure books. What is often called the Cambridge school of intellectual historians has been particularly associated with an insistence on applying a rigorously historical method to the study of ideas in the past.[1] In recent years they have been joined by literary critics, particularly those practicing the new historicism, who have deliberately sought to juxtapose canonical and noncanonical texts. Edmund Spenser's *A View of the Present State of Ireland* (discussed in Chapter 2), for example, was published long after his death and then quickly forgotten; known only to a specialized community of Spenser scholars, it became a crucial point of reference not only for all students of Spenser but for students of Renaissance literature more generally once it was discussed in Stephen Greenblatt's *Renaissance Self-Fashioning* (1980).[2]

A book which seeks to provide new perspectives on well-worn topics, as the present one does, cannot confine itself to the established canon; it must provide a new approach to classic texts, but in order to do this it needs to place those texts in new contexts. It must juxtapose canonical texts with hitherto obscure texts.[3]

In the epigraphs that open this book, I juxtapose two passages from Adam Smith, passages which suggest a striking continuity between *The Theory of Moral Sentiments* and *The Wealth of Nations*.[4] The first of these passages uses a key word, "emulation."[5] To understand why Smith uses that word we have to turn to relatively obscure texts. The use of that word in this sort of context goes back at least to Roger Coke's *Discourse of Trade* (1670), which describes an emulation (i.e., competition) among producers. Paul Slack has shown that Coke was replied to by Nicholas Barbon and John

Houghton, who picked up his concept of emulation while extending it from producers to consumers, who compete for social status, and they in turn influenced Dudley North.[6] Within a short time the ephemeral works of Barbon and Houghton were forgotten, but it seems likely that Barbon's *Discourse of Trade* (1690), which mentions "emulation," was read by Bernard Mandeville, who laid great stress on consumer emulation in remark M of the *Fable of the Bees* (1714). Mandeville likely also read Dudley North's *Discourses upon Trade* (1691), which draws on Barbon's ideas, though it does not use the word "emulation"; North and Mandeville both write of "spurs to industry." Mandeville was presumably read by James Steuart (*Principles,* 1767, especially, on consumer emulation, book 1, chapter 10), although he does not name him, and certainly by Adam Smith, who does.[7]

Thus we can now trace Smith's argument back through authors with whom Smith was undoubtedly familiar (Mandeville, Steuart) to authors he almost certainly never read (Coke, Barbon, Houghton, North). Coke, Barbon, and company are irrelevant if we want to understand what Smith thought he was doing, though not if we want to understand Mandeville's intentions. But for our present purposes what matters is that Coke, Barbon, Houghton, and North are crucial if we want to understand the first emergence of a theory of economic growth as leading to generalized prosperity or "affluence."

The theory of consumer emulation, as propounded by these authors, served two important purposes. First, it was part of a general defense of what was called "luxury" against a long tradition defending frugality, parsimony, and simplicity and advocating sumptuary legislation.[8] Extravagance, it was argued, led to economic growth, while parsimony must lead to economic contraction. Second, it addressed a specific issue regarding the laboring classes. It was generally claimed that laborers would work only to satisfy their immediate needs for food and shelter and to provide those few extras sanctioned by custom; if they were paid more they would simply work less, so that if production was to be increased wages needed to be lowered.[9] The emulation argument tackled this notion directly, for it claimed that, if exposed to new consumer goods, laborers (just like their social superiors) would want to earn more in order to spend more, so that rising wages for the poorest classes would lead not to idleness and economic contraction but to an increase in industry and so to economic growth.

Here, then, are two texts which mark the emergence of a new understanding of commercial society as being founded in "exorbitant" (indeed insatiable) appetites. For, as Barbon says in his *Discourse of Trade*, "The Wants of the Mind are infinite, Man naturally Aspires, and as his Mind is elevated, his Senses grow more refined, and more capable of Delight; his Desires are inlarged, and his Wants increase with his Wishes, which is for everything that is rare, can gratifie his Senses, adorn his Body, and promote the Ease, Pleasure, and Pomp of Life."[10] First, Barbon, in *A Discourse Shewing the Great Advantages that New-Buildings and the Enlarging of Towns and Cities Do Bring to a Nation:*

> The increasing of the Inhabitants of a City, increaseth the Emulation of the People; and Emulation increaseth Industry; and Industry Riches: There are two great Causes, of Labour and Industry, Necessity for Food and Emulation; The necessity of Hunger makes Men Industrious, but when Hunger is satisfied, Industry is at an end till a new provocation of Hunger makes them work again; and those People that have no other design, but to satisfie that necessity continue always miserably Poor, as it is observed in those that only work from hand to mouth; for Hunger hath Intervalls, and so hath the Labour for it as the Proverb saith, When the Belly is full the Bones will be at rest. But Emulation provoaks a continued Industry, and will not allow no Intervals or be ever satisfied: The Cobler is always indeavouring to live as well as a Shoomaker, and the Shoomaker as well as any in the Parish; so every Neighbour and every Artist [artisan] is indeavouring to out vy each other, and all Men by a perpetual Industry, are strugling to mend their former condition: and thus the People grow rich, which is the great advantage of a Nation: and this benifit ariseth solely from Cities; for in a Countrey Solitude there is little Emulation, for there if a Man be Fed and Cloathed he is a Prince to himself, for there is no body by him that is better Fed and Cloathed.[11]

And second, North, who writes in *Discourses upon Trade:*

> The main spur to Trade, or rather to Industry and Ingenuity, is the exorbitant Appetites of Men, which they will take pains to gratifie, and so be disposed to work, when nothing else will incline them to it; for did

Men content themselves with bare Necessaries, we should have a poor World.

The Glutton works hard to purchase Delicacies, wherewith to gorge himself; the Gamester, for Money to venture at Play; the Miser, to hoard; and so others.

Now in their pursuit of those Appetites, other Men less exorbitant are benefitted; and tho' it may be thought few profit by the Miser, yet it will be found otherwise, if we consider, that besides the humour of every Generation, to dissipate what another had collected, there is benefit from the very Person of a covetous Man; for if he labours with his own hands, his Labour is very beneficial to them who imploy him; if he doth not work, but profit by the Work of others, then those he sets on work have benefit by their being employed. . . .

The meaner sort seeing their Fellows become rich, and great, are spurr'd up to imitate their Industry. A Tradesman sees his Neighbour keep a Coach, presently all his Endeavours is at work to do the like, and many times is beggered by it; however the extraordinary Application he made, to support his Vanity, was beneficial to the Publick, tho' not enough to answer his false Measures as to himself.[12]

It is important to distinguish this theory of consumer emulation, which involves acquisition without limit, not only from competition between producers and nation-states but also from the topic Smith goes on to discuss in the next chapter of *The Theory of Moral Sentiments*, competition or rivalry for place, where he notes that "place, that great object which divides the wives of aldermen, is the end of half the labours of human life; and is the cause of all the tumult and bustle, all the rapine and injustice, which avarice and ambition have introduced into this world."[13] The struggle for place involves a defined set of limited goods: once the alderman's wife has seen her husband elected lord mayor, what else is there for her to aspire to? Moreover, it is essentially conservative: it assumes that the places worth having are predefined. But competition to be the most elegantly dressed of all the aldermen's wives is remorseless and requires an endless succession of new outfits. Such competition brings with it an unending process of economic growth and the constant transformation of both goods and services.

Competition for place has existed as long as there have been places to fill; but consumer emulation, extending down through the social ranks, requires a consumer society. It can occur only where, in Daniel Defoe's words, "every Man [is] busie on the main Affair of Life, that is to say, getting Money," for you have to earn money before you can spend it.[14] It thus implies a free market for producers as well as consumers and a constant interplay between the wants that consumers already know they have and wish to satisfy and the wants that producers and retailers can persuade them that they have, although they were previously quite unaware of the very possibility of having them—wants for beaver hats, for example, or rice pudding, coffee, tea, sugar, calico cottons, pocket watches, barometers, novels, Wedgwood china dishes, Hogarth prints.[15] These are (with the exception of beaver hats) no longer luxuries, but they were once, and consequently they were the focus of the fierce rivalry generated by consumer emulation.

Consumption creates the desire for ever more consumption in a never-ending spiral. Smith, from his vantage point, looking back over time, could see the struggle for place as the most important form of competition, after (presumably) the quest for the bare necessities of food, shelter, and security. We, from our vantage point, can see that those who have struggled to get money so that they can spend it have created far more tumult and bustle in the world over the last two and a half centuries than professors aiming at tenure, councilors hoping to become mayors, or executives aspiring to become chief executive officers. As Smith said, "An augmentation of fortune is the means by which the greater part of men propose and wish to better their condition." Bettering one's condition first and foremost involves getting more money so that one can spend more money.

Appendix B

Double-Entry Bookkeeping

Double-entry bookkeeping no longer shapes our own lives (though spreadsheets often do), so it is easy to miss its importance for people in the early modern period. Today we rely on bank statements to keep track of our finances, but they had to write out their own accounts, and this habitual practice shaped their thinking. For example, the core Protestant doctrine is that believers have Christ's righteousness imputed to them; "impute" is a term from bookkeeping meaning "to bring into the reckoning, enter into the account, charge."[1] Protestant theology was founded on the principle that one could not earn merit which would entitle one to escape hell or purgatory; nevertheless, guided by the language of bookkeeping, theologians and preachers kept undermining this doctrine. Even Calvin, who had insisted that—contrary to the teaching of the Roman Catholics—we cannot make our accounts good with God, had been happy to describe charitable giving as an investment that would be entered in God's accounts and that he would repay with interest.[2] Others extended the account book metaphor to the whole of our dealings with God, for it was universally assumed that God keeps an account book in which he records our sins: they "all remaine scored vp, and being registred in his [God's] booke of accounts, stand in Record."[3] Just as merchants kept their accounts in three books, the memorandum, the journal and the ledger, so too

> God hath a threefold book. The first is his priuate booke Enchiridion, or *vade mecum,* in which onely the names of the elect are written, whom hee knoweth and calleth by their names: whose names hee will not put out of the booke of life, *è libro praesentis iustitiae aut praedestinationis aeternae,* as the Schoolmen distinguish. The second is his booke of accounts and black booke, blurde and blotted with the register of sin, wherein onely the wicked are written, according to that *Dan. 7. The iudgement was set, and the bookes opened.* The third is his vniuersall

common-place booke, wherein both good and bad are recorded, according to that of the Prophet, *In thy book are all my members written:* so that albeit in death there be a dissolution of body and soule, yet in the resurrection there shall bee a restitution and revniting of the same body (in substance though altered in quality) to the same soule, that the ioy of both may be consummated: to which purpose, God is said to write all our members in his booke.[4]

The whole language of redemption was assumed to be drawn from accounting. Thus, while Episcopalians are familiar with a version of the Lord's Prayer in which we ask God to forgive us our trespasses, the Latin text was *dimitte nobis debita nostra,* and this was often translated (perfectly correctly) as "forgive us our debts." A standard handbook of Protestant theology explained that "debts" and "sins" are the same thing (in modern German, *Schuld* means both "debt" and "guilt") and went on to explain the remission of sins: "The Creditor is said to *Remit* the Debtor, when he never requireth the debt of him; but, as if it were paid, crosseth it out of his books of accounts, and punisheth him not: as we may reade in the parable of the King which forgave his servant, who besought him, the debt of ten thousand talents. So God forgiveth us our sins, when he imputeth them not unto us, nor punisheth us for them, and that therefore, because he hath punished them in his Son our Mediatour."[5]

It was thus apparent that imputation "is a word . . . borrowed from *Merchants,* which upon their Book of accounts with a man, enter the Wares which they have had of him, and the price or goods which they are to give in exchange for them: Here faith is as it were, the Ware, Righteousness the Price or Goods to be given for it."[6] And it followed that in the doctrine of the remission of sins, "We have God represented as a great Merchant, with his rich Fund, and his Books of Accompts."[7]

If God keeps accounts, then so must we: "In life; is it not a comfort to a man when he hath been casting up his Accounts and finds that he hath gained in his Trade? you come hither [to Church] in the use of Ordinances, Word, and Prayer, to trade for heaven; now if ye find upon a true account that ye have gain'd in the Trade of godliness, and are *fill'd with the fruits of the Spirit,* will not this be a great comfort to you?"[8] Christians were frequently admonished to enter "the closet of our hearts, where all our bookes of account doe lye" and review their own conduct.[9] For "wee should pre-serue our soules and hearts in a thriuing estate, when wee doe like wise Mer-chants and shopkeepers, examine them and search ouer our consciences (as it were) our bookes of accounts, to see whether wee haue gayned or lost in our spirituall trading, by examining what wee haue receiued, and what we haue layd out."[10] The account book was thus something more than a metaphor: it was an organizing principle through which all human behavior could be interpreted. And that principle was one of endless pursuit, of insatiable acquisition, of limitless aspiration. Double-entry bookkeeping comes, we may say, to substitute itself for virtue.

Appendix C

"Equality" in Machiavelli

Niccolò Machiavelli's analysis of republics in the *Discourses on Livy*, 1.55, depends on two key terms: "corruption" and "equality." The modern literature on Machiavelli has focused on the concept of corruption and has had little to say about "equality."[1] Yet we can hardly understand Machiavelli until we have clarified his use of the term, for in *Discourses*, 1.55, he argued that it is easy to build a republic where there is great equality, and a princedom where there is great inequality, and in a programmatic chapter of the *History of Florence* (3.1) he sharply distinguished between the Roman republic, which began with equality and ended with extreme inequality, and the Florentine republic, which began with inequality, but whose conflicts culminated in a remarkable equality. What sort of equality does he have in mind?

Elsewhere in the *Discourses* Machiavelli distinguishes between three types of equality: equality of wealth, equality of rank (in Sparta, he says, there was equality of wealth but not of rank [1.6]) and what he calls *civile equalità* (1.2, 3.3), civil equality, which requires the rule of law and respect for the rights of others. All three types of equality, it would seem, are to be found in the free cities of Germany and Switzerland; in the early Roman republic there may have been little inequality of wealth, and there may have been civil equality, but there certainly was not equality of rank, for the distinction between patricians and people was a basic fault line in the republic. In Machiavelli's own Florence there was great inequality of wealth, but little inequality of rank and a good deal of civil equality. Of these three types of equality, then, only one would seem to be essential, and that is civil equality; but civil equality, which we tend to take for granted but which frequently broke down in Renaissance Italy, is sufficient, on my reading of Machiavelli, only for an enfeebled republicanism.[2] The true republicanism of early Rome and contemporary Germany is based on subsistence agriculture, not commercial prosperity; it requires both equality of wealth and civil equality.

The key threat to civil equality comes from privatized violence. The free German cities, we are told, seize on every opportunity to kill "gentlemen," who are defined as wealthy individuals who do not personally engage in commerce or agriculture but live off the income from their estates. Gentlemen are particularly dangerous when they have private castles and armed retainers. Killing them is entirely justified, because wherever they are found civil equality ceases to exist. In the "Discourse on Remodeling the Government of Florence" Machiavelli wrote that "in order to have a princedom in Florence, where equality is great, the establishment of inequality would be necessary; noble lords of walled towns and boroughs would have to be set up, who in support of the prince could with their arms and their followers stifle the city."[3]

Book 2 of the *History of Florence* details the extended conflict between the nobles, as Machiavelli calls them there (with their tower houses in the city, capable of defense in time of conflict, their castles and fortified villages in the countryside, and their gangs of armed retainers), and the people, which ended with the complete triumph of the people and the destruction of all castles within twenty miles of the city (2.32).* This victory was the essential precondition for civil equality; unfortunately it was pushed too far and nothing was left of the warrior ethos so essential for a state to defend itself against its enemies (3.1).

This new civil equality simply opened up a new conflict between the people and the plebs, which is the subject of book 3, and culminated in the Revolt of the Ciompi (1378–1382). The government was effectively taken over by the guilds (2.11, 3.12)—that is to say by commercial interests—and the city grew rich. Though at first the guilds provided the organizational basis for a citizen militia, the Florentines soon decided it was preferable to pay others to fight on their behalf. The class conflict between rich and poor created repeated opportunities for constitutional reform, and again and again public-spirited citizens (Michele di Lando, Benedetto Alberti, Veri

---

* Machiavelli's family co-owned a small castle just outside the twenty-mile limit; see William J. Connell, "Dating *the Prince:* Beginnings and Endings," *Review of Politics* 75 (2013), 500–501.

de' Medici) tried to moderate it and generate from it a new sense of the public good. But time and again they failed: Florence failed to develop a constitution which gave adequate expression to the tensions within Florentine society, while at the same time creating an incentive for the conflicting groups to cooperate to the greater good. As a result the Florentines ceased to care greatly about liberty: the prospect of rule by the Duke of Athens in 1342 was met with a firm insistence that the people would always lay claim to liberty (2.34), but by 1397 appeals to liberty fell on deaf ears (2.27; contrast Lucca in 1437, 5.11). Florence had become a city incapable of liberty, but hostile to servitude (2.36, 3.5).

Machiavelli tells readers of the *History* that the character of Florentine society is such that it lends itself to being governed under any type of constitution (3.1); in "A Discourse on Remodeling the Government of Florence" he wrote that Florence kept changing its system of government because "she has never been either a republic or a princedom having the qualities each requires."[4] And yet in the *Discourses* he had claimed that the Tuscan cities were naturally republics (1.55). How is that Florence failed to become a proper republic, despite its "equality," and became politically amphibious, neither free nor enslaved?

Part of Machiavelli's explanation for this lies in Florence's long history of internal division, which originated in the struggle between pope and emperor for control of Italy, a struggle which divided Italy between Guelfs and Ghibellines, a division which ran not only between cities and states but within each city and each state. In Florence the Guelfs were victorious, but they then divided into the factions of the Blacks and the Whites, each faction seeking to monopolize power and drive its opponents into permanent exile. Thus the relatively healthy conflict between classes was overlaid by a deeply unhealthy conflict between factions, and a political culture which aspired to outright victory over opponents developed where what was needed was a willingness to seek compromise and consensus. Machiavelli's complaints about Florentine disunity are directed primarily at these factional conflicts rather than at the class conflicts which he held, it would seem, expressed legitimate political aspirations.

The crucial moment came in 1426, when the wealthy sought to persuade Giovanni de' Medici to join with them in (yet again) reforming the constitution in order to consolidate power in their own hands. Giovanni refused.

He preferred to operate, not openly, but through deception (4.10). He consolidated power, not in the hands of his social group, but in his own private hands, by appealing to the self-interest of individuals, by persuading the Florentines to sell their liberty to the highest bidder (4.27). If the foundations of a sound republic were laid with the elimination of privatized violence, its survival as something more than a facade required that politics should be conducted in public. What the Medici did, however, was privatize politics, and the consequence was that the republic no longer loved all its citizens equally (5.8). A republic, Machiavelli believed, can function with economic inequality and inequality of status: the rich in Florence were used to receiving visits and gifts from those who were seeking their patronage and their votes, just as Roman patricians had received their clients. But Cosimo de' Medici restored selection to office by lot, while controlling which names entered the lottery (7.2). After that, wealth, status, and influence no longer counted for anything; power was exercised entirely behind the scenes by Medici rulers who were citizens in appearance, princes in reality, while nominally the republic was governed by their handpicked agents.

Thus Machiavelli's *History of Florence* is a story of endlessly repeated failure. Florence never developed the institutions required for an authentic liberty, and once politics has been privatized the distinction between liberty and servitude became meaningless. Distinctions of rank, in Medicean Florence, were of little importance, and there was civil equality. But collective allegiances—to the city, to a guild, to a social class—had been dissolved, replaced by an individualist pursuit of self-interest. Liberty was for sale because prosperity, not liberty, was what everyone was after, and prosperity was now sought not collectively and publicly, through a guild, but privately, through backroom deals and confidential agreements. Public life was now a charade which concealed the real business of ruling. The Medici were bankers, and politics had been refashioned in the image of private banking.

Was this failure inevitable? Machiavelli evidently thought not, for in the "Discourse on Remodeling the Government of Florence" he advocated yet another republican constitution, one in which the elite would be represented in a Council of Thirty-Two, a middle group in a Council of Two Hundred, and the citizens as a whole in a Council of One Thousand. Despite the evidence of this fundamentally oligarchic proposal, some scholarship has sought to propose a radical reinterpretation of the *History of Florence,* claiming that Machiavelli had egalitarian and democratic allegiances.[5] The key episode for such an interpretation is the Revolt of the Ciompi, when the urban working class, some of them wage laborers, and others engaged in low-status occupations such as butchering, demanded that power be transferred to them.

This reading (which goes against Machiavelli's explicit statements of hostility to the lower orders and their demands) depends on reading into the text a series of comparisons that Machiavelli never makes. In the *Discourses on Livy* Machiavelli takes the side of the plebs against the patricians; in *The Prince* he urges the ruler to please the people and repress the elite. Surely, then, the argument goes, Machiavelli is on the side of this popular rebellion. There is a central problems with this claim: the rebels were caught in a logic of escalating violence and ever-increasing demands, which meant that it was impossible to reach a settlement with them (3.13, 17). Their demands were such as must endanger all commerce: a halt to the payment of interest and to the enforcement of contracts of debt, for example.

But there is a more fundamental reason. The rebels were, by their own account *servi* (3.13; the word can mean "servants" or "slaves") protesting against their treatment by their *maestri* (3.12, "masters"). In Machiavelli's *Discourses* there are schoolmasters and Masters of Horse, but there are no masters of men, for the simple reason that Roman citizens had no masters—servile work was done by slaves, not servants. Those who propose a protodemocratic reading of the *History* are committing themselves to the view that Machiavelli thought that servants should have power over their masters, employees over their employers. Machiavelli may well have thought, as an anonymous rebel puts it, that we are all alike: "Strip us all naked; you will see us all alike; dress us then in their clothes and they in ours; without doubt we shall seem noble and they ignoble, for only poverty and riches make us unequal."[6] But he was a realist. In ancient Rome the plebs had been free men; in Renaissance Florence they were *servi,* and the commercial life of a manufacturing city required that they remained *servi* if profits were to be made and commerce was to flourish. Machiavelli may have sympathized with the *ciompi* because he well understood that they were men like himself; but it never occurred to him that he needed to show in detail why they were unfit for government. To refer to them as *servi* was sufficient, for everyone understood that *servitú* was the antithesis of liberty, and consequently that a servant could not be a citizen.[7] Machiavelli may have been attached to the idea of equality, at least as he understood the term, but he would have been unable to make sense of the modern idea of democracy. His was a world which took the existence of servitude, whether in the form of slavery, serfdom, or wage labor, for granted.

Appendix D

The Good Samaritan

The parable of the Good Samaritan (Luke 10:25–37) should find a place in any account of the obligation to show kindness to strangers as understood in the early modern period. The story is, in essence, simple: The Good Samaritan comes to the aid of a complete stranger, and Christ tells his followers to go and do likewise. In doing so he radically reinterprets the injunction to love thy neighbor as thyself (Lev. 19:18; Matt. 22:35–40; Mark 12:28–40; Rom. 13:9; Gal. 5:14; James 2:8; 1 John 3:17–19). The parable was well known, and so no one, it would seem, can have doubted that it was both possible and indeed obligatory to feel sympathy with and to come to the aid of strangers. But the situation is not quite as it seems.[1]

First, the obligation to be kind to strangers seemed excessive, and to go well beyond the command to love thy neighbor as thyself. Christ also instructed anyone with two coats to give one away (Luke 3:11), an instruction generally ignored. Charity, it was generally argued, should only go to the deserving poor; preachers, even when preaching on the topic of the Good Samaritan, were quick to insist that alms should never be given to sturdy beggars.[2] Still, it is perfectly possible to find texts in which the obligation to love strangers is stated unequivocally. For example, Henry Hammond wrote in 1659, "Take that for an answer to thy question, Who is thy neighbour, v. 29. For every person that is in want of thy relief, although he be to thee as a Jew to a Samaritan, upon terms of absolute separation and hostility toward thee, must be looked on by thee as the object of thy compassion and mercy, and of any charity of thine of which he is capable."[3] And here is Archibald Symmer in 1629:

> As the Apostle saith: *There is neither Iew nor Greeke, there is neither bond nor free, there is neither male nor female, for ye are all one in Christ Jesus:* so there is neither *American,* nor *Indian,* neither *Barbarian* of *Morocco,* nor Inhabitant of *Monomotapa,* but all are brethren, whom, as we haue

opportunitie, wee must embrace with Charitie; those that are true Saints, with joy for their sanctification; those that are not, in the iudgement of Charitie, with heartie, and earnest supplications to the Lord for their true and timely conuersion.[4]

But for the most part Christ's words were reinterpreted in the light of other texts, particularly Galatians 6:10: "As we have therefore opportunity, let us do good unto all men, especially unto them who are of the household of faith." This *especially* could be made to do a lot of work:

> For if our Love must thus extend to *Enemies,* how much *more* to such as are *friends?* friends to our *persons,* and to our *God* too? The love of *Christ* had *degrees,* & so must *ours.* As the Apostle tells concerning *Christ, he is the Saviour of all,* but *especially of them that believe* (1 *Tim.* 4. 10.) so the same Apostle doth also tell us of *our selves, we must do good unto All men, but especially to them who are of the houshold of faith* (*Gal.* 6. 10.) And even of those that are *faithfull,* a primary care is to be taken for them that are of our *own Country.** . . . But many times our *neerest Countrymen* may become our *worst Neighbours;* and, in respect of their Religion, dwell *farthest off* too. . . . *This* is therefore the firmest Bond whereby to hold us together in peace and love, not that we are of *one Countrey,* but that we are of *one Christ;* And can say of our selves, with better reason, then it was anciently said of the *Lomnini,* That in *all our bodies* there is no more then *one soul.*[5]

Thus the obligation to love strangers was turned into an obligation on the godly to look after each other: "We must (indeed we may and ought to) preserve a Brother before a Kinsman, a Kinsman before a Countryman, a Countryman before an Alien; but yet so that the beams of our Love may scatter themselves throughout the whole World by a general affection to all Mankind. Love seeking not her own, includes every man that issued from *Adam,* especially those of the Christian Profession; and even amongst them the most Eminent and Exemplary for sound Piety and Devotion."[6] And some went even further. John Boys, preaching on the Good Samaritan, did not hesitate to say, "Yet (all other things being alike) wee must affect

---

* In seventeenth-century usage, "country" often means county or locality.

and respect our owne wife before our owne children, our children before kinsmen, our kinsmen before such neighbours as are not of our blood, our neighbours before strangers, and strangers of our owne countrey before forreiners of another nation."[7] In other words, all things being equal, we are under no obligation to show kindness to strangers because we have plenty of obligations which should take precedence over our notional obligations to strangers. Nehemiah Rogers agreed:

If our estate be such that we are not able to relieve all that crave our helpe, (being in the same degree of Poverty and Necessity) than [sic] the nearer any is unto our selves, the more must he be preferred.

Thus our *wives* next our *selves*, and before all other whatsoever, *Ephes.* 5.28.

Then our *Parents*, who are to be preferred before our *children* . . .

After them our *Children* with the rest of our *Family*, 1 *Tim.* 5.8. These are to be relieved before all other, even before those who are virtuous and religious, being not so near unto us in the bonds of Nature.

After these our *spirituall Kindred* must take place and be preferred in workes of *Mercy* before those who are a kin unto us only in the flesh, *Psal.* 16.3. *Rom.* 12.13. Than *they* before any *common friend,* or *Neighbour,* and *these* before *Strangers,* and *Strangers* before *Enemies.*[8]

But the real difficulty with the parable of the Good Samaritan was not that its demands on the faithful seemed excessive—the Gospels are full of excessive demands. The fundamental problem was that the Good Samaritan was presented by Christ as fulfilling the commands of the law. As one Catholic put it, "In this verse is grounded the Catholick doctrine that the Law is observeable, against Hereticks who say it is impossible to be kept."[9] For an orthodox Protestant it was essential to find a way round this, and there was only one solution that would work: the Good Samaritan must stand for Christ, in which case the parable is primarily to be understood as being about the salvation of souls. Thus Martin Luther:

The Samaritane in this place is without all doute our Lord Iesus Christ, who hath declared his loue toward God and men: Toward God, in that he descended from heauen, and was incarnate, and so fulfilled the will of his father: Toward men, for that by and by after baptisme, he beganne to preach, to worke miracles, to heale the sicke, neither was there any worke that he did, which did concerne himselfe onely, but all his workes were directed to his neighbour, being made our minister, when as notwithstanding he is aboue all, and equall to God: but he did all these thinges, for that he knew that they did please God, and that it was the will of his father. . . . This is that Samaritane, who being desired by no prayers, came, & fulfilled the law with his whole heart, he alone hath fulfilled it, which praise none can take from him: he alone hath dese-rued it, and to him onely it appertaineth.

But whereas he is touched with care of the wounded man, hath com-passion on him, byndeth vp his woundes, bringeth him with him into an Inne, prouideth for him, that pertaineth vnto vs. The man which lieth half dead, wounded, beaten, & spoiled, is Adam, yea and all we. The theeues which spoiled vs, wounded vs, and left vs halfe dead, as yet a litle panting, are the Deuels. The horse and his sitter do here fall downe, we are not able to helpe our selues, and if we should be left lying so, we should die, through great anguish and distres, our woundes would become festred, and our affliction miserable and exceeding great.[10]

In this, which became the orthodox interpretation, the parable is no longer to be read as requiring us to show kindness to strangers.[11] As Henry Hol-land put it in 1700,

And here is the great Doctrine of the Parable, Health and Salvation only comes from him: *The Blessed Jesus* himself, the only *Saviour,* the true *Samaritane,* the careful *Keeper,* he comes and relieves us, he comforts and restores us effectually.

He searches our Sores and discovers our Corruption, then he heals and binds up our Wounds.[12]

The result of this orthodoxy was that the Good Samaritan is noticeable for his absence in precisely those places where one might expect him to appear. Thus, in Henry Smith's *The Poore Mans Teares* (1592), an appeal for gen-erous almsgiving to the poor, he does not appear in the eloquent panegyric of charitable action, but only in the peroration, as a type of Christ, who saves us from sin.[13]

There is a simple indicator which allows us to see when the parable of the Good Samaritan began to be interpreted as straightforward advice on how Christians should behave toward those in physical need, as an incitement to charity in a secular context, and that is when we first find someone called a Good Samaritan for coming to the relief of the suffering. In 1691 Lady Mary Ramsey was described as a Good Samaritan for her charity toward injured soldiers.[14] This was followed by *The Charitable Samaritan, or, A short and impartial account of that eminent and publick-spirited citizen Mr. Tho. Firmin who departed this life on Monday Dec. 20, 1697/by a gentleman of his acquaintance.*[15]

Within a few years the Good Samaritan was no longer simply a representation of Christ himself, or of the clergy whose task it was to heal spiritual wounds. In a sermon preached in 1708 entitled *The good Samaritan exemplify'd in the charitable Christian,* the congregation were thus instructed: "no Man of what Calling or Employment, in what State or Condition whatever, can be exempted or excused from following the Example of the Good Samaritan." They were told to "imitate the Active Diligence of the Compassionate *Samaritan,*" told the Good Samaritan should be *"the lively Pattern of our Imitation,"* and called upon "to act the *good Samaritan."* Their task was to "make up and complete the character of the *Good Samaritan."* This language of following, imitating, acting, and making up was new, for the Good Samaritan—now, for the first time—represented a pattern for every Christian; all were now called to "go and do thou likewise." Indeed, the sermon itself was printed and sold "for the benefit of the poor."[16] By the end of the century the Good Samaritan was an emblem for practical assistance to those in need—and so a series of self-help medical texts were entitled *The Good Samaritan.* The Good Samaritan had become a brand.

Appendix E

Prudence and the Young Man

A standard view in the current literature is that the Adam Smith Problem can be ignored because the prudent man described in the 1790 edition of *The Theory of Moral Sentiments* is the rational economic actor required by *The Wealth of Nations.* Since the prudent man is presented as both morally admirable and economically rational, there is no conflict between economic activity and morality in Smith (or, indeed, in the real world of the eighteenth century). This argument is superficially attractive, but on closer examination it proves to be unsatisfactory. For a start, the argument runs in a circle, for in Smith prudence only counts as a virtue because it is economically rational, and it would not count as a virtue if economic rationality was not taken to be a good thing; consequently, one might argue that the absence of a conflict between economic rationality and morality in Smith (if indeed there were no conflict) is the consequence of his tailoring his morality to suit his economics.

But the real problem goes deeper: society benefits when we struggle to better our condition, but we, for the most part, lose out. Our efforts to pursue happiness are self-defeating but socially beneficial. In order to show this I will take the version of the no-Adam-Smith-problem argument presented by Ryan Hanley in *Adam Smith and the Character of Virtue* (2009).[1] Hanley's argument depends on his interpretation of the story of the poor man's son, which comes immediately before the passage with which I began Chapter 7:

> The poor man's son, whom heaven in its anger has visited with ambition, when he begins to look around him, admires the condition of the rich. He finds the cottage of his father too small for his accommodation, and fancies he should be lodged more at his ease in a palace. He is displeased with being obliged to walk afoot, or to endure the fatigue of riding on horseback. He sees his superiors carried about in machines, and imagines that in one of these he could travel with less inconveniency.

He feels himself naturally indolent, and willing to serve himself with his own hands as little as possible; and judges that a numerous retinue of servants would save him from a great deal of trouble. He thinks if he had attained all these, he would sit still contentedly, and be quiet, enjoying himself in the thought of the happiness and tranquillity of his situation. He is enchanted with the distant idea of this felicity. It appears in his fancy like the life of some superior rank of beings, and, in order to arrive at it, he devotes himself for ever to the pursuit of wealth and greatness. To obtain the conveniencies which these afford, he submits in the first year, nay, in the first month of his application, to more fatigue of body and more uneasiness of mind, than he could have suffered through the whole of his life from the want of them. . . . Through the whole of his life he pursues the idea of a certain artificial and elegant repose which he may never arrive at, for which he sacrifices a real tranquillity that is at all times in his power, and which, if in the extremity of old age he should at last attain to it, he will find to be in no respect preferable to that humble security and contentment which he had abandoned for it.[2]

Hanley argues that this is to be understood not as a reflection of the true character of commercial society but as a cautionary tale. The problem with the poor man's son is that he lacks prudence, for a prudent man would have found that individual happiness and the economic activities which benefit society are not mutually exclusive. It should be immediately apparent that Hanley wants to dispute Smith's statement in the passage which immediately follows (and which offers his final judgment on the case of the poor man's son) that "it is well that nature imposes on us in this manner" (a phrase Hanley never quotes). Hanley thinks the poor man's son could have been both moderately happy and moderately successful if only he had been prudent, if he had been a little more moderate in his aspirations.

Unfortunately, prudence is not an option available to the poor man's son, at least in the early stages of his career, for the simple reason that Smith's account of a prudent man in part 6, added in 1790, is of someone who is already wealthy, respected in society, and securely established in his profession:

Security, therefore, is the first and the principal object of prudence. It is averse to expose our health, our fortune, our rank, or reputation, to any sort of hazard. It is rather cautious than enterprising, and more anxious to preserve the advantages which we already possess than forward to prompt us to the acquisition of still greater advantages. The methods of improving our fortune, which it principally recommends to us, are those which expose to no loss or hazard; real knowledge and skill in our trade or profession, assiduity and industry in the exercise of it, frugality, and even some degree of parsimony, in all our expenses. . . . The man who lives within his income is naturally contented with his situation, which, by continual, though small accumulations, is growing better and better every day. He is enabled gradually to relax, both in the rigour of his parsimony and in the severity of his application; and he feels with double satisfaction this gradual increase of ease and enjoyment, from having felt before the hardship which attended the want of them. He has no anxiety to change so comfortable a situation, and does not go in quest of new enterprises and adventures, which might endanger, but could not well increase, the secure tranquillity which he actually enjoys.[3]

The prudent man seeks to preserve his advantages, while the poor man's son has none; the prudent man lives within his income, while the poor man's son is looking for an income; the prudent man experiences secure tranquility, while the poor man's son is in quest of new enterprises.[4] Indeed, we might say that the poor man's son needs—if his business eventually flourishes— to become a prudent man, but we can't argue that if he only he were prudent he would calculate the benefits of deferred gratification differently. For he has to start with rigorous parsimony and severe application, whether he is prudent, greedy, ambitious, or vain, and the fundamental question is whether he will ever find a reward that will properly compensate him for those hard years of toil, particularly as so many hard workers never reach a secure tranquility. Smith's answer when he tells the story of the poor man's son is that he won't, even if he becomes prudent in middle age, but that it is fortunate for us that he overestimates the extent to which money can buy happiness.

Of course you might argue that all the labors of the poor man's son are unnecessary: after all, Smith will shortly tell us that "the beggar, who suns himself by the side of the highway, possesses that security which kings are fighting for." But the beggar's security, in Britain at least, is bound to be short-lived. Come winter, he will need a roof over his head, and food and fuel in store. In January of 1776, for example, the year in which *The Wealth of Nations* was published, Gilbert White recorded "rugged Siberian weather," with the Thames freezing over at London, and temperatures falling as low as zero degrees Fahrenheit. Unlike the beggar, the poor man's son looks to the future; and so he should.

Hanley, however, tries to reinterpret the story of the poor man's son by appealing to another story taken from *The Wealth of Nations,* noting "a young man, who, instead of applying to trade or to some profession, should employ a capital of two or three thousand pounds in the purchase and cultivation of a small piece of land, might indeed expect to live very happily, and very independently, but must bid adieu, for ever, to all hope of either great fortune or great illustration, which by a different employment of his stock he might have had the same chance of acquiring with other people."[5]

"In offering this choice," says Hanley, "Smith suggests that economic growth and personal happiness are not necessarily incompatible, however incompatible the greedy ambition for great wealth and happiness may well be."[6] The young man who opts to invest in land, it would thus seem, has made a prudent choice, one of which Smith (and Hanley) approves. Again, though, Hanley is reading Smith while ignoring what Smith says. Smith surely cannot approve the young man's choice when he has only just said, "To purchase land is every-where in Europe a most unprofitable employment of a small capital." Moreover, it seems that this young man is unlikely to contribute to economic growth at all, for "Such a person too, though he cannot aspire at being a proprietor, will often disdain to be a farmer." In other words, he will find that he does not own enough land to make a living as a landlord, but he will disdain to work the land himself.*

One might think, nevertheless, that the young man has made a good choice. The young man could have spent his capital seeking to qualify as a lawyer and build up a practice, but, Smith tells us, only one in twenty who go down this route succeed in making a living from the law.[7] Better an unprofitable investment in land than to seek fortune and fame ("illustration," Smith calls it) and in the process risk losing everything. And indeed this

---

* Smith frequently uses the word "proprietor" to mean someone whose income comes from rents.

would seem to be quite good advice. The young David Hume, for example, faced a similar set of choices. He was a younger son, and his family was not rich. He tried briefly to become first a lawyer and then a merchant, but at last he opted to abandon the pursuit of wealth. "I went over to France, with a view of prosecuting my studies in a country retreat; and I there laid that plan of life which I have steadily and successfully pursued. I resolved to make a very rigid frugality supply my deficiency of fortune, to maintain unimpaired my independency, and to regard every object as contemptible, except the improvements of my talents in literature."[8] Crucially, Hume, like most intellectuals, avoided marrying. In the end, unexpectedly, he became wealthy through publishing, but, of course, Grub Street was full of promising authors whose talents in literature had led only to penury. He could not have predicted such good fortune when he opted to live off his limited capital.

What would a very rigid frugality mean? Something more penurious than the life of Smith's young man who buys land, for it is essential to grasp that the young man of *The Wealth of Nations* was very far from being a poor man's son. His capital represented ten years' income for a clergyman or solicitor, twenty for a surgeon.[9] Smith immediately goes on to contrast the cost of land in England with America, where fifty or sixty pounds would be sufficient to buy a farm, and where investment in land was highly profitable. In England the young man's income from his farm would have been roughly one hundred pounds per annum, at a time when some said two hundred pounds and others three hundred pounds was the minimum needed to live the life of a gentleman.[10] He would have made about the same amount if he had lent the money to a sound creditor, such as a city, for such loans earned 4 percent.[11]

It is easy to see one simple consequence of this: he would not have been able to afford to buy *The Wealth of Nations*, or at least not without thinking twice. The first and second editions (two volumes in quarto) sold new in leather bindings for two pounds, two shillings (rising to two pounds, fourteen shillings for an elegant binding), dropping to a guinea (one pound and one shilling) for the fourth edition (three volumes in octavo), and to fourteen shillings, one penny for the 1793 Dublin edition. Copies could be obtained slightly cheaper in boards, but secondhand prices held up well: a copy of the first edition, for example, was going for one pound, six shillings in 1793, despite the fact that editions from the third (1784) incorporated the seventy-nine pages of additions and corrections Smith had published as a pamphlet and also had the benefit of an index.[12] Even membership in a circulating library was not cheap, costing a minimum of ten shillings, six pence a year, with rates up to three pounds, three shillings for those wanting to borrow lots of books. (There were twelve pence [or pennies] in a shilling, twenty shillings in a pound.)

We ought also perhaps add to the cost of buying or renting a book the cost of providing light by which to read it. In Edinburgh, for example, there are only seven hours of daylight in midwinter, eight hours in Bristol. A dozen tallow candles (each providing perhaps five hours of light but emitting approximately nine lumens, or 0.75 percent of the output of a one-hundred-watt filament bulb) would have cost seven shillings, so four candles would have added 10 percent to the cost of buying and reading one of the cheaper editions, and a dozen would have added 30 percent. Beeswax candles would have been much more expensive.[13]

Since twelve shillings represented a week's income for a craftsman in London (or thirty pounds a year; an agricultural laborer earned twenty-one pounds), the equivalent to one pound in modern money must be at least one thousand dollars, and our young man who has chosen to invest a capital of $2,500,000 in land would have been living happily and independently on $100,000—a life of comfort, but not of luxury, in a world where books were still luxuries for the wealthy.[14] Against the young man of *The Wealth of Nations*, with his two or three thousand pounds of capital, we should set Thomas Davison's bequest to set the sons of poor men up in business: they were to receive fifty pounds to get them started.[15] The sons of the poor did not have the option of retiring to a country estate, however modest; nor could they go into business without putting their whole capital at risk.

Hume and the notional young man of *The Wealth of Nations* may have made the right choice for their private happiness, but not for the nation's wealth, to which they could expect to contribute little or nothing. Precisely because they had not been imposed upon, as so many are, by nature, which encourages us both to overestimate our chances of success and to exaggerate the happiness that money will buy, they had chosen to be economically inactive. The quest for fortune and fame, from which the young man turns aside, serves the public good, while his chosen life of unenthusiastic farming and modest living has few benefits for any one except himself and his immediate family.

Hanley's attempt to prove that a poor man can pursue wealth and soon find happiness fails. The young man is not poor, which is why he can opt for happiness. The poor man's son is not happy, but is forced to make his way in the world, and, even if successful, will not be secure for many years.

To be prudent, as Smith understands the term, you need to be rich. It is not surprising that Daniel Defoe advises a quite different set of values for the established trader from those he recommends to the young man starting out: "Bold Adventures are for Men of desperate Fortunes, not for Men whose Fortunes are made. . . . He that runs into great Adventures after he has enrich'd himself, seems not to have a true Notion of Trade; or to think it so much a Lottery as he ought to know it is."[16] Even the comparatively advantaged young man of *The Wealth of Nations* has no good choice that he can make, for if he goes into commerce or a profession he risks his capital, and if he lives off his capital he will find himself excluded from polite society and cultural life. For a poor man's son, every option involves risk, and if you have had to make your own way out of poverty then it is rather unlikely that you will know when to relax into ease and enjoyment.[17]

Moreover, there is a further problem about prudence: it assumes that the world stands still. If you are a lawyer or a doctor, secure in your profession, it may well be possible to avoid new enterprises and adventures; and it is lawyers, doctors, scientists, and intellectuals Smith seems to have in mind in his discussion of prudence when he says that "the prudent man does not always think of cultivating the favour of those little clubs and cabals, who, in the superior arts and sciences, so often erect themselves into the supreme judges of merit; and who make it their business to celebrate the talents and virtues of one another, and to decry whatever can come into competition with them."[18] But those engaged in commerce live a very different life from those making a living in the superior arts and sciences, and they often find change forced upon them. In 1792 France and Great Britain began a war which lasted, with only brief interruptions, until 1815. Plenty of merchants suddenly found their ships sunk, their livelihoods destroyed, and were forced to seek new enterprises in the hope of rescuing themselves from catastrophe. And soon after the Napoleonic Wars came the first great disruptive technology, the steam engine, which both created new wealth and destroyed old livelihoods.[19]

The word *hasard* in French, "risk" in modern translations, runs through Richard Cantillon's great *Essay on the Nature of Trade in General* (1755). Thus, "As the Farmers and Masters of Crafts in Europe are all Undertakers working at a risk, some get rich and gain more than a double subsistence, others are ruined and become bankrupt, . . . ; but the majority support themselves and their Families from day to day."[20] For Cantillon, prudence could never be enough; indeed, he never uses the word, for it is an inevitable feature of commercial society that just as some get rich, others will go bust. Cantillon, unlike Smith, had grasped that commercial society involves a constant process of "creative destruction" (in Joseph Schumpeter's phrase) against which even hard work, frugality, and prudence provide no sure defense. He devotes a whole chapter to the inescapable nature of risk:

> The Manufacturer who has bought wool from the Merchant or direct from the Farmer cannot foretell the profit he will make in selling his cloths and stuffs to the Merchant Taylor. If the latter have not a reasonable sale he will not load himself with the cloths and stuffs of the Manufacturer, especially if those stuffs cease to be in the fashion.
>
> The Draper is an Undertaker who buys cloths and stuffs from the Manufacturer at a certain price to sell them again at an uncertain price, because he cannot foresee the extent of the demand. He can of course fix a price and stand out against selling unless he gets it, but if his customers leave him to buy cheaper from another, he will be eaten up by expenses while waiting to sell at the price he demands, and that will ruin him as soon as or sooner than if he sold without profit.
>
> Shopkeepers and retailers of every kind are Undertakers who buy at a certain price and sell in their Shops or the Markets at an uncertain price.[21]

When Smith suggested that prudence is the answer to the contradictions of commercial society, he was thinking of those who have reached the top rungs of the liberal professions, not what he called those engaged in the "mean professions," the professions where one could never attain security.[22]

In other words, he was thinking of the sort of people who could afford to buy his books, for it was they who constituted the constantly repeated "we" of his texts. He was not thinking of poor men's sons and the younger sons of the gentry, men, making their own way in the world, or of importers of brandy, wine, or fine silks, men whose capital was constantly at risk.

The Adam Smith Problem was supposed to be a contradiction between the benevolence of human beings according to *The Theory of Moral Sentiments* and their selfishness according to *The Wealth of Nations.* Adam Smith would have denied that there was such a problem. Selfish people grow the economy, and so benefit everyone. Hardworking, abstemious, prudent people are rewarded. Smith had no doubt that a providential justice was at work:

> If we consider the general rules by which external prosperity and adversity are commonly distributed in this life, we shall find, that notwithstanding the disorder in which all things appear to be in this world, yet even here every virtue naturally meets with its proper reward, with the recompense which is most fit to encourage and promote it; and this too so surely, that it requires a very extraordinary concurrence of circumstances entirely to disappoint it. What is the reward most proper for encouraging industry, prudence, and circumspection? Success in every sort of business. And is it possible that in the whole of life these virtues should fail of attaining it?—Wealth and external honours are their proper recompence, and the recompence which they can seldom fail of acquiring.[23]

Cantillon knew better than this, and so too did Defoe, who had himself gone bankrupt:

> A Tradesman, like a great Tree in a thick Wood, if he falls, he is sure to crush a great deal of the Under-Wood which lies within the Reach of his Boughs and Branches. A young Tradesman miscarries and it reaches but a little Way; a few Creditors are affected and some Hurt is done: But if the overgrown Tradesman falls, he shakes the *Exchange,* as we call it; he dips deep among other Tradesmen; he pulls down here half a Dozen and there half a Score; and they pull down others, and, like rolling Ninepins, they tumble down one another.[24]

Thus Smith failed to acknowledge the amorality of market forces. He identified hidden hands, but not hidden backhands. He failed to recognize that speculators and gamblers, thieves and fraudsters often flourished while people of industry, prudence, and circumspection were broken by forces outside their control. This willful ignorance was the price he paid for ignoring the real Adam Smith problem, which lies in the arbitrary and amoral character of the market as a system for distributing rewards, and the delusory character of many of the rewards that are distributed.* Smith was prepared to acknowledge, at least on occasion, that the rewards are delusory; what he could never accept is that very often they are distributed unfairly.

---

* I do not mean for a moment to suggest that markets are more morally unsatisfactory than other methods of distributing resources; and they are clearly, in economic terms, much more successful than other methods. But Smith relied on the existence of a providential architect to justify a systematic understatement of the imperfections of market systems.

Appendix F

"The Market"

Emma Rothschild writes, "Turgot himself did not use the word 'market' in the abstract sense of 'labour markets' or 'market forces.' For Turgot and Condorcet, as for Smith, the word 'market' had the generally concrete connotation of a particular physical structure, and indeed one which was protected by oppressive government regulations—as when merchants were forced to sell their corn 'in markets.'"[1] Adam Smith may not use the phrases "labour markets" or "market forces," but he certainly does talk of markets in an abstract sense; see, for example, *The Wealth of Nations* (1776), the title of book 1, chapter 3: "That the division of labour is limited by the extent of the market"; 1:57: the relative value of gold and silver is "settled by the market"; book 1:62: "In the market of Europe . . . an ounce of fine gold exchanges for about fourteen ounces of fine silver"; 1:132: "the market rate of interest, or the rate at which people of good credit usually borrowed"; and so on.

The crucial move from a "concrete" to an "abstract" understanding of the market would appear to come in David Hume's essay "Of Money" (1752): "after money enters into all contracts and sales, and is every where the measure of exchange, the same national cash has a much greater task to perform; all commodities are then in the market; the sphere of circulation is enlarg'd."[2] Thus all goods and services exchanged for money (or credit) are "in the market," including labor, and Hume's essay is evidently an analysis of market forces. Richard Cantillon has this understanding of the market, but not this language; Hume would thus seem to be the first to state clearly the modern concept of "the market."[3]

Notes

Computers and the internet are revolutionizing scholarship. Where in the past the scholar had to go to the books, now the books—or, rather, images of them—come to the scholar. The result is that often the first edition of a work has become more accessible—because it is to be found in Early English Books Online, or Eighteenth Century Collections Online, or Google Books, or Gallica (the digital library of the Biliothèque nationale in Paris)—than the modern scholarly editions. I therefore tend to cite first editions, for my own convenience and that of my readers, while occasionally identifying modern editions when they seem to me particularly helpful or where I am relying on editorial scholarship. I give places of publication as they appear on the title page: these are, particularly for French eighteenth-century texts, often fictitious. And I give authors for works that were originally published anonymously if there is no doubt as to who the author was.

I have tried to preserve original spelling and punctuation in quotations, because it is always good to be reminded that the texts we read are survivors from a very different world. For the same reason, I often use early modern translations of classical texts, and contemporary translations of early modern texts. To philosophers who want to get straight to the argument this may seem odd, but even they need to remember that these authors are not our contemporaries.

One of the problems about using internet sources is that the internet expands continuously, and many of the sources on it, such as the *Oxford English Dictionary (OED)*, are subject to continuous revision. In the case of the *OED*, I give the date of the most recent revision accessible to me; in the case of statistics drawn from constantly expanding sources (Early English Books Online, Eighteenth Century Collections Online, and Google Books) I have checked my source during copyediting, so all counts were accurate as of May 2018.

Epigraphs: Niccolò Machiavelli, *Discorsi sopra la prima Deca di Tito Livio,* bk. 1, ch. 37, translated by Edward Dacres in *Machiavels Discourses Upon the First Decade of T. Livius* (London: Paine, 1636), 151; Niccolò Machiavelli, *Discorsi sopra la prima Deca di Tito Livio,* bk. 2, preface, translated by Edward

Dacres in *Machiavels Discourses Upon the First Decade of T. Livius* (London: Paine, 1636), 250; Niccolò Machiavelli, "Tercets on Ambition," translation from *Lust and Liberty: The Poems of Machiavelli,* trans. Joseph Tusiani (New York: Obolensky, 1963), 122; Adam Smith, *The Theory of Moral Sentiments* (London: Millar, 1759), 109–110; Adam Smith, *An Inquiry Into the Nature and Causes of the Wealth of Nations,* 2 vols. (London: Strahan and Cadell, 1776), 1:415.

TO THE READER

1. William Percey, *The Compleat Swimmer* (London: Fletcher, 1658).
2. Walter Charleton, *The Darknes of Atheism Dispelled by the Light of Nature: A Physico-Theologicall Treatise* (London: Lee, 1652), sig. a3r, insists that pleasure and profit are directly opposed to virtue, "since in this life of Sensuality, the Encouragements and Invitations to vice, are both more and stronger, then those to virtue: most certain it is, that very few men would prefer the harsh dictates of Honesty and Right, to those more complacent ones of Pleasure and Profit; if they neither feared the just vindication of an All-observant Deity, nor expected a future Subsistence after Death." For the standard coupling of pleasure and profit in the context of reading, see, for example, Lodovico Guicciardini, *The Garden of Pleasure,* trans. J. Sandford (London: Bynneman, 1573), sig. A4v.
3. For animals too, see, for example, Jean-Jacques Burlamaqui, *The Principles of Natural Law, in Which the True Systems of Morality and Civil Government Are Established* (London: Nourse, 1748), 47.
4. Paul Henri Thiry, Baron d'Holbach, *The System of Nature,* trans. W. Hodgson, 4 vols. (London: The Translator, 1795–1796), 1:262; first published in French in 1770. For the origins of this view in Machiavelli, see Quentin Skinner, *Visions of Politics,* vol. 2, *Renaissance Virtues* (Cambridge: Cambridge University Press, 2002), 212.
5. For Hume's distinctions, see David Hume, "Of the Dignity of Human Nature," in *Essays, Moral and Political,* 2 vols. (Edinburgh: Kincaid, 1741–1742), 1:168–171, rev. in Hume, *Essays and Treatises on Several Subjects. Containing An Enquiry Concerning the Principles of Morals,* 4 vols. (London: Millar, 1753), 1:125–128; David Hume, "Why Utility Pleases," and "Conclusion," part 2, in *An Enquiry Concerning the Principles of Morals* (London: Millar, 1751), 73–104, 187–195; David Hume, "Of Self-Love," in *Essays and Treatises on Several Subjects,* 2 vols. (London: Cadell and Donaldson, 1777), 2:349–356.

6. Thomas Nettleton, *Some Thoughts Concerning Virtue and Happiness: In a Letter to a Clergyman* (London: Batley, 1729), 71–72. Nettleton goes on (with little regard for coherence or consistency) to praise those who give their lives for a friend or their country. For what little is known about Nettleton, see Herbert McLachlan, "Thomas Nettleton, MD, 1683–1741/2," *Transactions of the Unitarian Historical Society* 9 (1947), 21–27; and Brian Michael Norton, "Ancient Ethics and Modern Happiness: A Study of Three Treatises in Enlightenment Britain," *Eighteenth-Century Life* 38 (2014), 54–61. Nettleton's book, expanded in 1736 and revised in 1751, went through a further thirteen editions; see, for example, Thomas Nettleton, *A Treatise on Virtue and Happiness: The Second Edition* (London: Batley and Wood, 1736).

7. Burlamaqui, *The Principles of Natural Law* (1748), 46. Pufendorf had opposed such Hobbesian arguments; see Samuel Pufendorf, *The Law of Nature and Nations,* ed. Jean Barbeyrac, trans. B. Kennett (London: Bonwicke, 1749), 2.3.14, 7.1.2.

8. The *Oxford English Dictionary (OED) Online,* http://www.oed.com, updated January 2018, gives 1628 for the first use of "selfish." *OED Online,* again updated January 2018, gives 1595 for the first use of "self-interest."

9. On Bayle, see David Wootton, "Pierre Bayle, Libertine?," in *Oxford Studies in the History of Philosophy,* vol. 2, *Studies in Seventeenth-Century European Philosophy,* ed. M. A. Stewart (Oxford: Oxford University Press, 1997), 197–226; and the excellent Mara van der Lugt, *Bayle, Jurieu, and the* Dictionnaire Historique et Critique (Oxford: Oxford University Press, 2016). On Hobbes, see Chapter 4 in the present volume. Bayle scholars seem to have become confused over some basic methodological issues. Gianluca Mori, "Persécution et art d'écrire: Strauss, Skinner et Pierre Bayle," in *Leo Strauss: Art d'écrire, politique, philosophie,* ed. Laurent Jaffro, Benoît Frydman, Emmanuel Cattin, and Alain Petit (Paris: Vrin, 2001), 197–219, discusses Quentin Skinner's critique of Strauss in the context of a defense of a Straussian reading of Bayle, but fails to mention that Skinner has no problem with reading Hobbes and Bayle as atheists because that is how contemporaries read them. Quentin Skinner, "Meaning and Understanding in the History of Ideas," *History and Theory* 8 (1969), 33–35, rev. in Skinner, *Visions of Politics,* vol. 1, *Regarding Method* (Cambridge: Cambridge University Press, 2002), 80–82. Skinner's objections are to "esoteric" readings—those which find meanings unavailable to informed contemporaries, not to "between the lines" readings where they are supported by contemporary interpretations. (Van der Lugt, *Bayle, Jurieu* [2016], 5, has read but misunderstood the relevant pages of Skinner, as has Helena Taylor, in *The Lives of Ovid in Seventeenth-Century French Culture* [Oxford: Oxford

University Press, 2017], 146.) However, Skinner fails to acknowledge that the case of Bayle is more problematic than the case of Hobbes because not all contemporaries read him as attacking religious faith. See Pierre Rétat, *Le dictionnaire de Bayle et la lutte philosophique au XVIIIe siècle* (Paris: Les Belles Lettres, 1971); and Elisabeth Labrousse, "Reading Pierre Bayle in Paris," in *Anticipations of the Enlightenment in England, France, and Germany,* ed. Alan Charles Kors and P. J. Korshin (Philadelphia: University of Pennsylvania Press, 1987), 7–16 (both of which were, of course, unavailable in 1969). Nevertheless, it is safe to argue that the *Dictionnaire* was deliberately constructed so as to be open to atheistical readings while throwing the responsibility for such readings onto the reader, not the author. One can see the first glimmerings of this technique in 1683 when Bayle reissued his *Lettre à M.L.A.D.C.* of the previous year as the *Pensées diverses:* the printer advised the reader that the book had not only been expanded, but also subdivided into many sections, so that "readers . . . will be able to linger where they want to, and pick up again where they choose to, without being held up or obliged to read on an on until they finally reach a break." In other words, the book has been redesigned for an active rather than a passive reader, one who will, for example, pick out the discussions of atheism and ignore those of Catholic superstition; meanwhile, the author remained free to claim that any such selective reading was a misreading. The *Dictionnaire* carried this technique to its logical conclusion.

10. It thus excludes topics which would be relevant in other contexts: there is no discussion, for example, of cameralism, on which see Andre Wakefield, *The Disordered Police State: German Cameralism as Science and Practice* (Chicago: University of Chicago Press, 2009).

11. The subject of this book might be termed, following Kant, "unsocial sociability," but although Kant is concerned with insatiable appetites, this book is primarily concerned with selfish systems, and Kant's category, evidently deriving from Hume and from Jean-Jacques Rousseau, refers to systems where there are two competing drives, one sociable and the other competitive. See Amélie Oksenberg Rorty and James Schmidt, eds., *Kant's* Idea for a Universal History with a Cosmopolitan Aim: *A Critical Guide* (Cambridge: Cambridge University Press, 2012); and Istvan Hont, *Politics in Commercial Society: Jean-Jacques Rousseau and Adam Smith,* ed. Belá Kapossy and Michael Sonenscher (Cambridge, Mass.: Harvard University Press, 2015), 13 (which seems to me to elide the differing views of Rousseau and Smith, but of course Hont's whole book is an argument for linking Rousseau and Smith together).

12. Burlamaqui, *Principles of Natural Law* (1748), 48. Hobbes (*Leviathan,* chs. 4 and 5) relies on the same etymology, takes reasoning to be a form of adding

and subtracting, and uses bookkeeping as a paradigmatic case. But he does not say that all reasoning is intended to identify on which side the advantage lies.

13. Charles Taylor, *The Ethics of Authenticity* (Cambridge, Mass.: Harvard University Press, 1992) identifies three malaises of modernity: individualism, instrumental reasoning, and "soft" despotism. I focus on the first two; the third would take the book into the nineteenth century. Both individualism and instrumental reasoning are bound up with the demise of Aristotelianism. On rational choice theory, see Donald P. Green and Ian Shapiro, *Pathologies of Rational Choice Theory: A Critique of Applications in Political Science* (New Haven, Conn.: Yale University Press, 1994). A useful reference point is also Leo Strauss, "The Three Waves of Modernity," in *An Introduction to Political Philosophy: Ten Essays by Leo Strauss,* ed. Hilail Gildin (Detroit: Wayne State University Press, 1989), 81–98. My concern is with the first of Strauss's three waves; the second wave (Rousseau, Kant, and G. W. F. Hegel) lies outside my scope (though I make a few passing references to Rousseau), as does the third (Friedrich Nietzsche). See also part 3 of Strauss's essay "What Is Political Philosophy?," in Strauss, *What Is Political Philosophy? And Other Studies* (Chicago: University of Chicago Press, 1959), 40–55.

14. Jon Elster, *Reason and Rationality,* trans. Steven Rendall (Princeton, N.J.: Princeton University Press, 2008).

15. David Hume, *A Treatise of Human Nature,* 3 vols. (London: Noon, 1739–1740), 2:248. I take this to be Hobbes's view, *pace* Adrian Blau, "Reason, Deliberation, and the Passions," in *The Oxford Handbook of Hobbes,* ed. A. P. Martinich and Kinch Hoekstra (Oxford: Oxford University Press, 2016), 195–220, who, in his discussion of the "scouts and spies" passage, avoids any reference to the role of scouts and spies.

16. David Hume, "Of Some Remarkable Customes," in *Political Discourses* (Edinburgh: Kincaid and Donaldson, 1752), 148.

17. Xenophon, *Hiero,* 7.3; translation from Paul A. Rahe, "Liberty and Property in Classical Antiquity," *Journal of Policy History* 29 (2017), 203.

18. Aristotle, *Ethica Nicomachea,* trans. W. D. Ross (Oxford: Clarendon, 1925), bk. 6, ch. 12.

19. Adam Smith, *The Theory of Moral Sentiments* (London: Millar, 1759), 360. Consequently Smith confuses *phronesis* and *sophia;* see Adam Smith, *The Theory of Moral Sentiments,* ed. Amartya Sen and R. P. Hanley (New York: Penguin, 2009), 474n5.

20. On the history of prudence, see Douglas J. Den Uyl, *The Virtue of Prudence* (New York: Lang, 1991). The redefinition of prudence begins with Hobbes; see

Bernard Gert, "Hobbes and Psychological Egoism," *Journal of the History of Ideas* 28 (1967), 510–512.

21. This is a central theme of Berlin's account of the Enlightenment; see, for example, Isaiah Berlin, "The Counter-Enlightenment," in *The Proper Study of Mankind* (London: Chatto and Windus, 1997), 243–268. For a critique of this essay, see Robert Edward Norton, "The Myth of the Counter-Enlightenment," *Journal of the History of Ideas* 68 (2007), 635–658. I do not think it follows from the view that we are all fundamentally alike that Enlightenment thinkers were necessarily opposed to value pluralism; see Hobbes's "Introduction" to *Leviathan,* and Chapter 3 in the present volume. On the uniformity of human nature, see Henry Vyverberg, *Human Nature, Cultural Diversity, and the French Enlightenment* (Oxford: Oxford University Press, 1989); and Simon Evnine, "Hume, Conjectural History, and the Uniformity of Human Nature," *Journal of the History of Philosophy* 31 (1993), 589–606. Gender, of course, constitutes an obvious mark of difference; see Sara Knott and Barbara Taylor, eds., *Women, Gender, and Enlightenment, 1650–1850* (London: Palgrave Macmillan, 2005).

22. Holly Brewer, "Slavery, Sovereignty, and 'Inheritable Blood': Reconsidering John Locke and the Origins of American Slavery," *American Historical Review* 122 (2017), 1038–1078. For an extended account of Locke's politics, see David Wootton, introduction to John Locke, *Political Writings,* ed. David Wootton (Indianapolis: Hackett, 2003). See also William W. Freehling, "The Founding Fathers and Slavery," *American Historical Review* 77 (1972), 81–93.

23. David Wootton, *The Invention of Science: A New History of the Scientific Revolution* (New York: Harper, 2015).

24. Peter Baehr, "The Iron Cage and the Shell as Hard as Steel: Parsons, Weber, and the *Stahlhartes Gehäuse* Metaphor in the Protestant Ethic and the Spirit of Capitalism," *History and Theory* 40 (2001), 153–169. On our ambiguous relationship to the Enlightenment, see Charles L. Griswold Jr., *Adam Smith and the Virtues of Enlightenment* (New York: Cambridge University Press, 1999), 1–7.

25. I take it that our understanding of ourselves is different from our understanding of nature. Nature is an objective reality outside ourselves; but when we study ourselves and our societies we are studying something we have made, and we alter ourselves and our societies in the act of studying them. People who believe human beings are motivated only by pleasure and profit will behave and think differently from people who believe in virtue, honor, and piety. This follows from the Thomas theorem ("If men define situations as real, they are real in their consequences"), propounded in 1928 by William Isaac Thomas and Dorothy Swaine Thomas and popularized in Robert K. Merton,

"The Self-Fulfilling Prophecy," *Antioch Review* 8 (1948), 193–210. Note that Merton defines self-fulfilling prophecies as false beliefs that come true; but the feedback effect identified in the Thomas theorem occurs with true beliefs as well as false beliefs. See also the discussion of the Tinker Bell effect in Chapter 9.

1. INSATIABLE APPETITES

1. An extensive literature now seeks to argue, against MacIntyre, that virtue ethics was flourishing in the eighteenth century; see, for example, Deirdre N. McCloskey, *The Bourgeois Virtues: Ethics for An Age of Commerce* (Chicago: University of Chicago Press, 2006). There are two problems with the bourgeois virtues: (1) they are instrumental; and (2) they mix and match neatly with the bourgeois vices—for example, industry with avarice, integrity with pride, piety with hypocrisy—so that the virtues can be redescribed as vices, and vice versa. On redescription, see Quentin Skinner, *Reason and Rhetoric in the Philosophy of Hobbes* (Cambridge: Cambridge University Press, 1996), 138–180; and Quentin Skinner, *From Humanism to Hobbes: Studies in Rhetoric and Politics* (Cambridge: Cambridge University Press, 2018), chs. 3 and 5. The bourgeois virtues and the bourgeois vices are fundamentally alike because both encapsulate strategies for success; on Smith's account, though, the world is providentially ordered so that the virtues, not the vices, pay out reliably; see Adam Smith, *The Theory of Moral Sentiments* (London: Millar, 1759), 285–287. Of course, my complaint is not novel, but goes back to Augustine. See Michael Moriarty, *Disguised Vices: Theories of Virtue in Early Modern French Thought* (Oxford: Oxford University Press, 2011).

2. Alasdair C. MacIntyre, *After Virtue: A Study in Moral Theory* (London: Duckworth, 1981), 6–22.

3. Ibid., 35–75.. For the postmodernist attack on the Enlightenment, see, for example, Jean-François Lyotard, *La condition postmoderne: Rapport sur le savoir* (Paris: Éditions de Minuit, 1979). For the claim that we should now should speak of Enlightenments in the plural, not the Enlightenment in the singular, see Roy Porter, *Enlightenment: Britain and the Creation of the Modern World* (London: Allen Lane, 2000), xvii–xviii. For a defense of a unitary view, see John Robertson, "The Enlightenment above National Context: Political Economy in Eighteenth-Century Scotland and Naples," *Historical Journal* 40 (1997), 667–697; John Robertson, *The Case for the Enlightenment: Scotland and Naples 1680–1760* (Cambridge: Cambridge University Press, 2005); and John Robertson, *The Enlightenment: A Very Short Introduction* (Oxford: Oxford University Press, 2015). Where Robertson takes political economy to be the core

of the Enlightenment, I take the central doctrine to be the claim that human beings of necessity flee pain and pursue pleasure, which underlies political
economy as an intellectual system.

4. John Greville Agard Pocock, *Politics, Language and Time: Essays on Political
Thought and History* (London: Methuen, 1971), which is contemporary with
Michel Foucault, "Nietzsche, l'histoire, la généalogie," in *Hommage à Jean
Hyppolite* (Paris: Presses universitaires de France, 1971), 145–172. The meth-
odological issues are discussed at length in David Wootton, *The Invention of
Science: A New History of the Scientific Revolution* (New York: Harper, 2015).
John Greville Agard Pocock, *The Machiavellian Moment: Florentine Political
Thought and the Atlantic Republican Tradition* (Princeton, N.J.: Princeton Uni-
versity Press, 1975), offers a very different grand narrative from the one pre-
sented here because it explores a different paradigm. For critical approaches to
The Machiavellian Moment see Vickie B. Sullivan, "Machiavelli's Momentary
'Machiavellian Moment': A Reconsideration of Pocock's Treatment of the *Dis-
courses,*" *Political Theory* 20 (1992): 309–318; and David Wootton, "From Com-
monwealth to Common Sense," in *Republicanism, Liberty, and Commercial
Society: 1649–1776,* ed. David Wootton (Stanford, Calif.: Stanford University
Press, 1994), 1–41.

5. Georg Wilhelm Friedrich Hegel, *Hegel's Philosophy of Right,* trans. T. M. Knox
(Oxford: Clarendon, 1942), 12–13.

6. For an excellent discussion, see Ada Palmer, "Sketches of a History of Skepticism, Part I: Classical Eudaimonia," Ex Urbe, 11 February 2014, http://www
.exurbe.com/?p=2725.

7. Isaiah Berlin, "The Originality of Machiavelli," in *Studies on Machiavelli,* ed.
Myron P. Gilmore (Florence: Sansoni, 1972), 149–206, repr. in *Against the Current: Essays in the History of Ideas,* ed. Henry Hardy (Oxford: Clarendon, 1979),
25–79, http://berlin.wolf.ox.ac.uk/published_works/ac/machiavelli.pdf. For
Machiavelli as a proto-Enlightenment thinker, see Humfrey C. Butters, "Machiavelli and the Enlightenment: Humanism, Political Theory, and the Origins
of the Social Sciences," in *Florence and Beyond: Culture, Society, and Politics
in Renaissance Italy: Essays in Honor of John M. Najemy,* ed. David S. Peterson
and D. E. Bornstein (Toronto: Centre for Reformation and Renaissance Studies,
2008), 481–498; and Skinner, *Renaissance Virtues* (2002), 160–185. See also Don
Herzog, "Some Questions for Republicans," *Political Theory* 14 (1986), 489:
"How, then, does Machiavelli propose to deal with conflict? In a way strikingly
reminiscent of Bentham and Madison, writers not ordinarily thought of as his
intellectual bedfellows. The Machiavellian legislator tries to ensure that the pursuit of private interest will pay off in public benefits, and even has 'selfishly
ambitious men . . . watch each other in order that lawful bounds may not be

overpassed'" (quoting Niccolò Machiavelli, *History of Florence*, bk. 7, ch. 1, in *The Chief Works and Others*, trans. and ed. Allan H. Gilbert, 3 vols. [Durham, N.C.: Duke University Press, 1989], 3.1337).

8. See the discussion in Russell Price, "The Theme of Gloria in Machiavelli," *Renaissance Quarterly* 30 (1977), 588–631.

9. Or that is how it should be. In *The Florentine Histories*, bk. 1, ch. 39, Machiavelli complains of princes who do not aspire to glory but aim only at wealth and security. Machiavelli also regards literary fame as glorious (*Discourses*, bk. 2, preface), and he perhaps hoped to win that particular form of glory himself; but only a small number aspire to be a famous poet or historian.

10. Hobbes's radicalism is helpfully explored in Richard Tuck, "The Utopianism of *Leviathan*," in *Leviathan after 350 Years*, ed. Tom Sorell and Luc Foisneau (Oxford: Oxford University Press, 2004), 125–138.

11. Thomas Hobbes, *Leviathan, Or, the Matter, Forme, and Power of a Common Wealth, Ecclesiasticall and Civil* (London: Crooke, 1651), 42.

12. Ibid., 26–27.

13. For a striking example of how these layers parallel each other, see Albert O. Hirschman, *The Passions and the Interests: Political Arguments for Capitalism before Its Triumph* (Princeton, N.J.: Princeton University Press, 1977), 30–48, 110–113.

14. Thomas Hobbes, *Humane Nature, or the Fundamental Elements of Policie* (London: Bowman, 1650), 106–107.

15. Ibid., 96–97.

16. Quentin Skinner, "Hobbes and the Classical Theory of Laughter," in *Visions of Politics*, vol. 3, *Hobbes and Civil Science* (Cambridge: Cambridge University Press, 2002), 142–176.

17. Montesquieu, *Lettres persanes*, ed. Catherine Volpilhac-Auger and Jean Ehrard (Oxford: Voltaire Foundation, 2004), 568.

18. Abraham Nicolas Amelot de La Houssaye, *Histoire du gouvernement de Venise* (Paris: Leonard, 1676); Abraham Nicolas Amelot de la Houssaie, *The History of the Government of Venice* (London: Starkey, 1677); David Wootton, "Ulysses Bound? Venice and the Idea of Liberty from Howell to Hume," in Wootton, *Republicanism, Liberty, and Commercial Society 1649–1776*, 341–367; Jacob Soll, *Publishing the Prince: History, Reading, and the Birth of Political Criticism* (Ann Arbor: University of Michigan Press, 2005).

19. In *The Spirit of the Laws* (1748) Montesquieu argued that monarchy requires a special group, the aristocracy, who are uniquely preoccupied with honor; but the *Persian Letters* had demonstrated that such distinctions are unnatural, irrational, and profoundly corrupting. See Christopher Brooke, "Arsehole Aristocracy (or: Montesquieu on Honour Revisited)," *European Journal of Political*

Theory (2018), https://doi.org/10.1177/1474885118783603. Montesquieu provided a theory of monarchy, but not a defense of it. For an interesting attempt to rescue honor for democratic discourse, see Sharon R. Krause, *Liberalism with Honor* (Cambridge, Mass.: Harvard University Press, 2002).

20. Louis Desgraves, Françoise Weil, and Catherine Volpilhac-Auger, *Catalogue de la bibliothèque de Montesquieu à la Brède* (Naples: Liguori Editore, 1999). Amelot is cited in Montesquieu, *The Spirit of the Laws,* bk. 5, ch. 8.

21. Carlo Ginzburg, "Machiavelli, l'eccezione e la regola," *Quaderni storici* 38 (2003), 195–214.

22. Mary Wollstonecraft, *A Vindication of the Rights of Woman* (London: Johnson, 1792); Barbara Taylor, *Mary Wollstonecraft and the Feminist Imagination* (Cambridge: Cambridge University Press, 2003); Lena Halldenius, *Mary Wollstonecraft and Feminist Republicanism: Independence, Rights and the Experience of Unfreedom* (London: Pickering and Chatto, 2015).

23. Hirschman, *The Passions and the Interests* (1977), 9; Herbert Andrew Deane, *The Political and Social Ideas of St. Augustine* (New York: Columbia University Press, 1963), 44–56.

24. Hirschman, *The Passions and the Interests* (1977), 42.

25. See, for example, Niccolò Machiavelli, *Opere,* ed. Corrado Vivanti, 3 vols. (Turin, Italy: Einaudi-Gallimard, 1997–2005), 2:616, 629, 720, 796, 844, 870, 947. Noel Malcolm, *Reason of State, Propaganda, and the Thirty Years' War: An Unknown Translation by Thomas Hobbes* (Oxford: Oxford University Press, 2007), 94, is therefore wrong to think that "interest" is a late-sixteenth-century term, and that it originates in French. But he provides the best brief introduction to reason of state and the literature on it; see 92–105.

26. This is a case where it is essential to distinguish between words and concepts. The concept of interest is central to Thucydides's *Peloponnesian War;* see David Cohen, "Justice, Interest, and Political Deliberation in Thucydides," *Quaderni urbinati di cultura classica* 16 (1984), 35–60; the key term in Greek is ὠφέλειᾰ. Machiavelli knew Thucydides through Lorenzo Valla's translation (see Luciano Canfora, "Tucidide e Machiavelli," *Rinascimento* 37 [1997], 29), where the key terms are *utilis* and *utilitas.* Selections from the Valla translation are reproduced in "Thucydides' Plataean Debate (3.52–68) & Melian Dialogue (5.85–115), with the Latin Translation of Lorenzo Valla, in Stephanus' 1588 Edition, Compared with the Valla MSS," Department of Classics, University of Dallas, http://udallasclassics.org/maurer_files/Valla-Intro.htm. In Hobbes's translation of Thucydides, published in 1629, the word "interest" is used in its modern sense four times, but the key word is "profit." In Smith's translation of 1753, "interest" is used very frequently, and "profit" (in this sense) never. Thus ὠφέλειᾰ, *utilitas, utilità,* "profit" and "in-

terest" are effectively synonyms. Machiavelli also employs the concept of *neces-sità,* but this belongs to a different vocabulary—see Felix Gilbert, "Florentine Political Assumptions in the Period of Savonarola and Soderini," *Journal of the Warburg and Courtauld Institutes* 20 (1957), 206. I owe this note to discussions with Paul Rahe.

27. See, for example, Giovanni Botero, *Della ragion di stato,* ed. Romain Descendre and Pierre Benedittini (Turin, Italy: Einaudi, 2016), 59: "Tenga per cosa risoluta, che nelle deliberazioni de' prencipi l'interesse è quello che vince ogni partito"; J. A. W. Gunn, "'Interest Will Not Lie': A Seventeenth-Century Political Maxim," *Journal of the History of Ideas* 29 (1968), 551–564; J. A. W. Gunn, *Politics and the Public Interest in the Seventeenth Century* (London: Routledge and Kegan Paul, 1969); and David Wootton, "Machiavelli and the Business of Politics," in *Machiavelli's Legacy: The Prince after Five Hundred Years,* ed. Timothy Fuller (Philadelphia: University of Pennsylvania Press, 2016), 92–94. On reason of state in England before the language of interest became fully established, see Noah Millstone, "Seeing Like a Statesman in Early Stuart England," *Past and Present* 223 (2014), 77–127; Noah Millstone, *Manuscript Circulation and the Invention of Politics in Early Stuart England* (Cambridge: Cambridge University Press, 2016). Millstone stresses dissimulation as the key category, but arguably dissimulation was always paired with a concept of "interest," however expressed, and was also always contrasted with "sincerity"—on which, see John Martin, "Inventing Sincerity, Refashioning Prudence: The Discovery of the Individual in Renaissance Europe," *American Historical Review* 102 (1997), 1309–1342.

28. See, for example, Hobbes, *Leviathan* (1651), 96: "Where the public and private interest are most closely united, there is the public most advanced. Now in monarchy the private interest is the same with the public. The riches, power, and honour of a monarch arise only from the riches, strength, and reputation of his subjects." This is an early version of the duty / interest junction principle—on which, see Chapters 5, 6, and 9 in the present volume.

29. Niccolò Machiavelli, *Discourses on Livy,* 1.16, in Machiavelli, *The Chief Works* (1989), 1.235–238.

30. This is, of course, a much debated issue; see, for example, *Hobbes Studies,* ed. K. C. Brown (Cambridge, Mass.: Harvard University Press, 1965), 31–100.

31. *Oxford English Dictionary Online,* http://www.oed.com (first published 1900, and thus surely unreliable).

32. David Hume, "That Politics May Be Reduc'd to a Science," in *Essays, Moral and Political,* 2 vols. (Edinburgh: Kincaid, 1741–1742), 1:27–48.

33. It has been claimed that the ancient Greeks had no concept of power as we understand the term. See Benedict Anderson, *A Life beyond the Boundaries*

(London: Verso, 2016), 114–115; and Benedict Anderson, *Language and Power: Exploring Political Cultures in Indonesia* (Ithaca, N.Y.: Cornell University Press, 1990), 20–22. See also the rebuttal from Colin Wells (letter), *London Review of Books,* 4 February 2016, https://www.lrb.co.uk/v38/n03/letters. It is clear that the Greeks had a concept of power not that different from our own (one need only think of the arguments of Thrasymachus in book one of Plato's *Republic,* or Thucydides's Melian Dialogue in bk. 5 of *The History of the Peloponnesian War*); but Anderson is also right to think that there is something new about discussions of power from Machiavelli onward, particularly in regard to the recognition that, in Anderson's formulation, *"The accumulation of power has no inherent limits"* (his emphasis).

34. For an extended attack, directed ostensibly at the insatiable ambition of Alexander, but really at the emperor Charles V and the Spanish conquests in the New World, see Antonio de Guevara, *Archontorologion, or, The Diall of Princes* (London: Alsop, 1619), 98–104 (first published in Spanish in 1529). On this text, which is from start to finish a lament for a lost world of honor and virtue, see Carlo Ginzburg, "Making Things Strange: The Prehistory of a Literary Device," *Representations* 56 (1996), 12–15.

35. Plutarch, "On the Fortune of Alexander," in *Moralia,* trans. F. C. Babbitt, 15 vols. (Cambridge, Mass.: Harvard University Press, 1936), 4:397.

36. Thus (see above, n. 26), when the Greeks do use a concept equivalent to "interest" it is in the context of warfare, or in a context which denies natural sociability.

37. William Shakespeare, *As You Like It,* act IV, scene 1, line 1900.

38. Nicholas Barbon, *A Discourse of Trade* (London: Milbourn, 1690); Andrea Finkelstein, "Nicholas Barbon and the Quality of Infinity," *History of Political Economy* 32 (2000), 83–102. See also Appendix A in the present volume.

39. Henry St. John Bolingbroke, *The Craftsman,* 13 June 1730; Hirschman, *The Passions and the Interests* (1977), 77; Robert Shackleton, "Montesquieu, Bolingbroke, and the Separation of Powers," *French Studies* 3 (1949), 25–38.

40. Machiavelli, *Discourses,* 1.5, in Machiavelli, *Chief Works* (1989), 1:204–206; William J. Connell, "Machiavelli on Growth as An End," in *Historians and Ideologues: Essays in Honor of Donald R. Kelley,* ed. Anthony Grafton and J. H. M. Salmon (Rochester, N.Y.: University of Rochester Press, 2001), 259–277. Hobbes, by contrast, regards "the insatiable appetite, or *Bulimia,* of enlarging Dominion" as a weakness which can lead to the dissolution of a commonwealth; Hobbes, *Leviathan* (1651), 174.

41. John Bossy, "Moral Arithmetic: Seven Sins into Ten Commandments," in *Conscience and Casuistry in Early Modern Europe,* ed. Edmund Leites (Cambridge: Cambridge University Press, 1988), 214–234.

42. Max Weber, *The Protestant Ethic and the Spirit of Capitalism,* trans. Talcott Parsons (London: Allen and Unwin, 1930); Hirschman, *The Passions and the Interests* (1977), 128–131.

43. Jacob Viner, *Religious Thought and Economic Society: Four Chapters of an Unfinished Work,* ed. Jacques Melitz and Donald Winch (Durham, N.C.: Duke University Press, 1978), 130–140.

44. John Locke, *An Essay Concerning Humane Understanding* (London: Basset, 1690), bk. 2, chap. 20.

45. Hume, *A Treatise of Human Nature,* 3 vols. (London: Noon, 1739–1740), 2:292.

46. Voltaire, *Oeuvres complètes de Voltaire,* ed. Jacques Joseph Marie Decroix, 70 vols. (Kehl, Germany: De l'imprimerie de la Société littéraire-typographique, 1784–1785), 55:372.

47. Berlin, "The Originality of Machiavelli" (1972).

48. Niccolò Machiavelli to Francesco Vettori, 16 April 1527, in Machiavelli, *Chief Works* (1989), 2:1010; for similar passages, see Eugenio Garin, *Dal Rinascimento all'Illuminismo: Studi e ricerche* (Florence: Le Lettere, 1993), 47, 76–77.

49. Francesco Guicciardini to Niccolò Machiavelli, 17 May 1521, in Machiavelli, *Chief Works* (1989), 2:971–973, translation from John M. Najemy, "Papirius and the Chickens, or Machiavelli on the Necessity of Interpreting Religion," *Journal of the History of Ideas* 60 (1999), 664.

50. Chauncey E. Finch, "Machiavelli's Copy of Lucretius," *Classical Journal* 56 (1960), 29–32. On Lucretius in the Renaissance, see Ada Palmer, *Reading Lucretius in the Renaissance* (Cambridge, Mass.: Harvard University Press, 2014).

51. On the Lucretian distinction, see James Warren, "Lucretian Palingenesis Recycled," *Classical Quarterly* 51 (2001), 499–508. On Machiavelli and Lucretius, see Alison Brown, *The Return of Lucretius to Renaissance Florence* (Cambridge, Mass.: Harvard University Press, 2010); and Alison Brown, "Lucretian Naturalism and the Evolution of Machiavelli's Ethics," in *Lucretius and the Early Modern,* ed. David Norbrook, Stephen Harrison and Philip Hardie (Oxford: Oxford University Press, 2016), 69–89. For discussions of this passage, which miss the Lucretian reference, see Niccolò Machiavelli, *Clizia; Andria; Dialogo intorno alla nostra lingua,* ed. Giorgio Inglese (Milan: Biblioteca Universale Rizzoli, 1997), 12–19; and Niccolò Machiavelli, *Teatro: Andria, Mandragola, Clizia,* ed. Pasquale Stoppelli (Rome: Salerno editrice, 2017), 239–240, 255.

52. Hobbes, *Leviathan* (1651), 47.

53. MacIntyre, *After Virtue* (1981), 22.

54. Jonathan I. Israel, *A Revolution of the Mind: Radical Enlightenment and the Intellectual Origins of Modern Democracy* (Princeton, N.J.: Princeton University Press, 2010), summarizes his argument.

55. On the philosophes' attacks on slavery, see Claudine Hunting, "The Philosophes and Black Slavery: 1748–1765," *Journal of the History of Ideas* 39 (1978), 405–418.

56. Voltaire, *Candide and Related Texts,* trans. D. Wootton (Indianapolis: Hackett, 2000); David Wootton, "Unhappy Voltaire, or 'I Shall Never Get Over It as Long as I Live,'" *History Workshop Journal* 50 (2000), 137–155.

57. There are limits to any defense of Voltaire. It would be foolish to defend him against the charge of anti-Semitism, and I would not seek to do so.

58. Ben Rogers, *Beef and Liberty* (London: Chatto and Windus, 2003).

59. Michel de Montaigne, *The Complete Essays,* trans. M. A. Screech (London: Allen Lane, 1991), 956; Voltaire, *Questions sur l'Encyclopédie* (Geneva: Cramer, 1770), pt. 1, 33 (later often included in the *Philosophical Dictionary*); Denis Diderot, *Jacques le fataliste et son maitre,* 2 vols. (Paris: Buisson, 1796), 2:190; David Wootton, "Pierre Bayle, Libertine?," in *Oxford Studies in the History of Philosophy,* vol. 2, *Studies in Seventeenth-Century European Philosophy,* ed. M. A. Stewart (Oxford: Oxford University Press, 1997), 197–226; Baruch Spinoza, *Ethica,* III, appendix, def. 48.

60. Robert Darnton, *The Forbidden Best-Sellers of Pre-revolutionary France* (New York: Norton, 1996); Alan Ryan, *On Politics: A History of Political Thought from Herodotus to the Present* (New York: Liveright, 2012), 359. Contrast the sensible remarks in Berlin, *Against the Current* (1979), 72.

61. Niccolò Machiavelli to Francesco Vettori, 5 January 1513 / 1514, in Machiavelli, *Chief Works* (1989), 2:934–935, translation from Michael Rocke, *Forbidden Friendships: Homosexuality and Male Culture in Renaissance Florence* (New York: Oxford University Press, 1996), 147, with a correction; for the original text, Machiavelli, *Opere* (1997–2005), 2:304. See also Guido Ruggiero, *Machiavelli in Love: Sex, Self, and Society in the Italian Renaissance* (Baltimore: Johns Hopkins University Press, 2006); and Robert Black, *Machiavelli* (London: Taylor and Francis, 2013), 24–29.

62. Jeremy Bentham and Louis Crompton, "Essay on Paederasty," *Journal of Homosexuality* 3 (1978), 389–405; Jeremy Bentham and Louis Crompton, "Essay on Paederasty: Part 2," *Journal of Homosexuality* 4 (1978), 91–107; Jeremy Bentham, *Of Sexual Irregularities, and Other Writings on Sexual Morality,* ed. Philip Schofield, Catherine Pease-Watkin, and Michael Quinn (Oxford: Oxford University Press, 2013). Bentham uses a conventional vocabulary, such as "unnatural," but makes clear that by "natural" he means simply statistically preponderant.

63. For attitudes to sexual relations between males in Machiavelli's world, see Rocke, *Forbidden Friendships* (1996); and Ruggiero, *Machiavelli in Love* (2006).

64. Hume, *Treatise* (1739–1740), 1:204–205.

2. POWER: (MIS)READING MACHIAVELLI

1. On the dating of *The Prince*, see William J. Connell, "Dating *the Prince:* Beginnings and Endings," *Review of Politics* 75 (2013), 497–514. The classic study of the reception of Machiavelli is now Sydney Anglo, *Machiavelli—The First Century: Studies in Enthusiasm, Hostility, and Irrelevance* (Oxford: Oxford University Press, 2005). English-language discussions of Machiavelli, such as *Machiavelli and Republicanism,* ed. Gisela Bock, Quentin Skinner, and Maurizio Viroli (Cambridge: Cambridge University Press, 1990), remain, to a surprising extent, trapped in the tradition established in Hans Baron, *The Crisis of the Early Italian Renaissance: Civic Humanism and Republican Liberty in An Age of Classicism and Tyranny,* 2 vols. (Princeton, N.J.: Princeton University Press, 1955), which concentrated on questions of liberty rather than power and glory. See William J. Connell, "The Republican Tradition in and out of Florence," in *Girolamo Savonarola: Piety, Prophesy, and Politics in Renaissance Florence,* ed. Donald Weinstein and V. A. Hotchkiss (Dallas: Bridwell Library, 1994), 95–105; John M. Najemy, "Baron's Machiavelli and Renaissance Republicanism," *American Historical Review* 101 (1996), 119–129; William J. Connell, "The Republican Idea," in *Renaissance Civic Humanism: Reappraisals and Reflections,* ed. James Hankins (Cambridge: Cambridge University Press, 2000), 14–29; Mark Jurdjevic, "Virtue, Commerce, and the Enduring Florentine Republican Moment: Reintegrating Italy into the Atlantic Republican Debate," *Journal of the History of Ideas* 62 (2001), 721–743; and David Wootton, "The True Origins of Republicanism: The Disciples of Baron and the Counter-Example of Venturi," in *Il repubblicanesimo moderno: L'idea di repubblica nella riflessione storica di Franco Venturi,* ed. Manuela Albertone (Naples: Bibliopolis, 2006), 271–304. See also (though directed at the Cambridge school rather than Baron) John P. McCormick, "Machiavelli against Republicanism: On the Cambridge School's "Guicciardinian Moments," *Political Theory* 31 (2003), 615–643, and Gabriele Pedullà, *Machiavelli in tumulto: Conquista, cittadinanza e conflitto nei "Discorsi sopra la prima deca di Tito Livio"* (Rome: Bulzoni, 2011), esp. 77–80.

2. Edwin A. Greenlaw, "The Influence of Machiavelli on Spenser," *Modern Philology* 7 (1909), 188.

3. Denis B. Woodfield, *Surreptitious Printing in England, 1550–1640* (New York: Bibliographical Society of America, 1973); Peter Samuel Donaldson, *Machiavelli and Mystery of State* (New York: Cambridge University Press, 1988), 86–110; Clifford Chalmers Huffman, *Elizabethan Impressions: John Wolfe and His Press* (New York: AMS Press, 1988).

4. Lisa Jardine and Anthony Grafton, "'Studied for Action': How Gabriel Harvey Read His Livy," *Past and Present* 129 (1990), 30–78.

5. Rory Rapple, *Martial Power and Elizabethan Political Culture: Military Men in England and Ireland, 1558–1594* (Cambridge: Cambridge University Press, 2009), 61, 179.

6. David Beers Quinn, "Renaissance Influences in English Colonization," *Transactions of the Royal Historical Society*, 5th ser., 26 (1976), 84–85. On Spenser, see Stephen Greenblatt, *Renaissance Self-Fashioning: From More to Shakespeare* (Chicago: University of Chicago Press, 1980), 157–192, esp. 184–188. See also the influential studies of Andrew Hadfield: Andrew Hadfield, "Spenser, Ireland, and Sixteenth-century Political Theory," *Modern Language Review* 89 (1994), 1–18; Andrew Hadfield, *Edmund Spenser's Irish Experience: Wilde Fruit and Salvage Soyl* (Oxford: Clarendon, 1997); Andrew Hadfield, "Was Spenser a Republican?," *English* 47 (1998), 169–182, and Edmund Spenser, *A View of the State of Ireland: From the First Printed Edition (1633),* ed. Andrew Hadfield and Willy Maley (Oxford: Blackwell, 1997); page number citations herein are from this edition, but quotations are from the online edition at Scholar's Bank, University of Oregon, https://scholarsbank.uoregon.edu/xmlui/bitstream /handle/1794/825/ireland.pdf, which preserves the original spelling. On Spenser and Machiavelli, see Émile Gasquet, *Le courant machiavélien dans la pensée et la littérature anglaises du XVIe siècle* (Paris: Didier, 1974), 343–353. On Beacon, see Sydney Anglo, "A Machiavellian Solution to the Irish Problem: Richard Beacon's *Solon His Follie* (1594)," in *England and the Continental Renaissance: Essays in Honour of J. B. Trapp,* ed. Edward Chaney and Peter Mack (Woodbridge, England: Boydell, 1990), 153–164; and Anglo, *Machiavelli—The First Century* (2005), 467–476.

7. William J. Connell, "New Light on Machiavelli's Letter to Vettori, 10 December 1513," in *Europa e Italia: Studi in onore di Giorgio Chittolini/Europe and Italy: Studies in Honour of Giorgio Chittolini,* ed. P. Guglielmotti, I. Lazzarini, and G. M. Varanini (Florence: Firenze University Press, 2011), 93–127.

8. The classic discussion is Cecil H. Clough, *Machiavelli Researches* (Naples: Istituto universitario orientale de Napoli, 1967). See also Robert Black, *Machiavelli* (London: Taylor and Francis, 2013), 79–81, 84–86.

9. Andrea Guidi, "Un texte autographe inédit de Machiavel: La *Minuta di provvisione per la restituzione dei beni agli eredi dei Medici e per la riforma dello stato* (projet de décret pour la restitution des biens aux héritiers des Médicis et pour la réforme de l'État), 1512," *Laboratoire italien: Politique et société* 17 (2016), http://journals.openedition.org/laboratoireitalien/973, is instructive.

10. The conviction that *The Prince* must be about Florence can easily lead to the claim that it is either a satire or some sort of trap set for the Medici. See Garrett Mattingly, "Machiavelli's 'Prince': Political Science or Political Satire?," *American Scholar* 27 (1958), 482–491; and Mary G. Dietz, "Trapping the Prince:

Machiavelli and the Politics of Deception," *American Political Science Review* 80 (1986), 777–799.

11. Niccolò Machiavelli to Francesco Vettori, 31 January 1515, in "Familiar Letters," in *The Chief Works and Others*, 3 vols., trans. and ed. Allan H. Gilbert (Durham, N.C.: Duke University Press, 1989), 2:962. I have not been persuaded by John M. Najemy, "Machiavelli and Cesare Borgia: A Reconsideration of Chapter 7 of *The Prince*," *Review of Politics* 75 (2013), 539–556.

12. On the dating, see Black, *Machiavelli* (2013), 129–133.

13. Machiavelli, *Discourses*, 2.22, in *The Chief Works* (1989), 1:389. Erica Benner, *Machiavelli's Ethics* (Princeton, N.J.: Princeton University Press, 2009), 466, mistakenly attributes this passage to Camillus rather than Machiavelli. For essays which provide an account of Machiavelli which fits with the one offered here, and which provide critiques of the prevailing "civic humanist" interpretation, see Vickie B. Sullivan, "Machiavelli's Momentary 'Machiavellian Moment': A Reconsideration of Pocock's Treatment of the Discourses," *Political Theory* 20 (1992), 309–318; Hillay Zmora, "A World without a Saving Grace: Glory and Immortality in Machiavelli," *History of Political Thought* 28 (2007), 449–468; and Mark Jurdjevic, "Machiavelli's Hybrid Republicanism," *English Historical Review* 122 (2007), 1228–1257.

14. Machiavelli, *Discourses*, 2.2, in *The Chief Works* (1989), 1:329.

15. Machiavelli, *Discourses*, 3.5, in *The Chief Works* (1989), 1:428. Despite the title of this chapter, "What Causes a Kingdom to Be Lost by a King Who Has Inherited It," neither of the two examples Machiavelli puts forward, Timoleon or Aratus, was an hereditary ruler; see also *Discourses*, 1.10.

16. Francesco Guicciardini, "Considerations," in *Selected Writings*, ed. Cecil Grayson (Oxford: Oxford University Press, 1965), 92. See also Machiavelli, *Discourses*, 2.2, in *The Chief Works* (1989), 1:328–333; and Marcia L. Colish, "The Idea of Liberty in Machiavelli," *Journal of the History of Ideas* 32 (1971), 323–350. The resistance of a city such as Pisa to Florentine rule arose, Machiavelli may have thought, not from any extraordinary love of liberty but from the harsh conditions imposed by republics on their subjects.

17. William J. Connell, "Machiavelli's Utopia," *Times Literary Supplement*, 2 December 2016, 15–17.

18. Machiavelli, *The Art of War*, in *The Chief Works* (1989), 2:571–572. That Machiavelli is mocking his own reputation for idealistic republicanism here should not surprise us: the character Nicomaco in *Clizia* is evidence enough that he could invite his audience to laugh at him as well as with him. *The Art of War* was written at the exact same time that Machiavelli was making his rapprochement with the Medici, which culminated in his being commissioned in November 1520 to write the *History of Florence* (see Black, *Machiavelli* [2013],

213–214, 223–224, 242); its publication, in August 1521, marks Machiavelli's new-found respectability. It needs to be read in this context, one in which Machiavelli's erstwhile idealism needed to be turned into a joke. It was followed by his *Life of Castruccio Castracani of Lucca,* in which he praises a figure comparable to Agathocles, whom he had condemned in *The Prince,* someone who wants to live and die like Caesar; here too Machiavelli rejects (at least ostensibly) his earlier views. This may also be the context of the Florentine publication of *Utopia,* carried out by Machiavelli's friends, in 1519; the message of More's *Utopia* is that one can have a deep commitment to an ideal, and at the same time recognize that it is completely impractical and, ultimately, irrelevant. If More could advocate communism and go on to serve Henry VIII, so could Machiavelli advocate classical republicanism and go on to serve the Medici.

19. See, in particular, the end of *The Art of War,* in *The Chief Works* (1989), 2:720–724.

20. The "civic humanist" literature on Machiavelli is bedeviled by the notion that he advocated, for contemporary Florence, a citizen army. See, for example, John Greville Agard Pocock, *The Machiavellian Moment: Florentine Political Thought and the Atlantic Republican Tradition* (Princeton, N.J.: Princeton University Press, 1975), 147–148, 76, 200–204; and Quentin Skinner, *Machiavelli* (Oxford: Oxford University Press, 1981), 37. Machiavelli did not so advocate (at least as far as the infantry were concerned), and Allan Gilbert's translation of *ordinanza* (or militia) in *The Art of War* as "citizen army" (in, for example, *The Chief Works* [1989], 2:580, 583, 590, 591, 594) is profoundly misleading. Robert Black, "Machiavelli and the Militia: New Thoughts," *Italian Studies* 69 (2014), 41–50, provides a helpful guide to the literature.

21. I have not, it will be evident, been persuaded by Marcia L. Colish, "Machiavelli's Art of War: A Reconsideration," *Renaissance Quarterly* 51 (1998), 1151–1168.

22. Machiavelli, *The History of Florence,* in *The Chief Works* (1989), 3:1393.

23. In *Discourses,* 2.2, Machiavelli asks why modern peoples are less attached to liberty than the ancients were. He offers two explanations: Christianity, and the destructive consequences of the Roman Empire. But he goes on to describe how liberty leads to wealth, which might be regarded as itself the primary source of corruption. Neither Christianity nor the Empire can explain the love of liberty to be found in the German free cities; the crucial factor, as we shall see, is their lack of engagement in commerce. In *The Art of War* he mentions another factor: the fear of servitude, by which he presumably means enserfment (in *The Chief Works* [1989], 2:624).

24. Quentin Skinner, *The Foundations of Modern Political Thought,* vol.1, *The Renaissance* (Cambridge: Cambridge University Press, 1978), 163, stresses Machi-

avelli's praise of poverty, which Machiavelli himself describes as entirely conventional; Jurdjevic, "Virtue, Commerce, and the Republican Moment" (2001), 729–730, 738–739, presents Machiavelli's conflicting views on poverty and prosperity, but fails to explain how this conflict was reconciled in his own mind. On this issue see also Cary J. Nederman, "Commercial Society and Republican Government in the Latin Middle Ages: The Economic Dimensions of Brunetto Latini's Republicanism," *Political Theory* 31 (2003), 644–663.

25. Machiavelli, *Discourses,* 1.55, in *The Chief Works* (1989), 1:308 (translation adapted); see also *Discourses,* 1.37, 3.25.

26. Machiavelli's birth family was largely excluded by poverty from this commercial society. They lived mainly off the produce of their farm, as is apparent from his father's notebooks; see Catherine Atkinson, *Debts, Dowries, Donkeys: The Diary of Niccolò Machiavelli's Father, Messer Bernardo, in Quattrocento Florence* (Frankfurt am Main: Lang, 2002). His father was excluded because of unpaid taxes from any participation in politics.

27. Jurdjevic, "Virtue, Commerce, and the Republican Moment" (2001), 738. For Savonarola's influence on Machiavelli, see John Humphreys Whitfield, *Machiavelli* (Oxford: Blackwell, 1947), 83–91; and John Humphreys Whitfield, "Savonarola and the Purpose of 'The Prince,'" *Modern Language Review* 44 (1949), 44–59.

28. Quentin Skinner, "Machiavelli's Discorsi and the Pre-humanist Origins of Republican Ideas," in Bock, Skinner, and Viroli, *Machiavelli and Republicanism* (1990), 141; see also Skinner, *Foundations* (1978), 1:170; and Quentin Skinner, "Machiavelli on the Maintenance of Liberty," *Politics* 18 (1983), 3–15. For a contrasting view, see Ernst Cassirer, *The Myth of the State* (New Haven, Conn.: Yale University Press, 1946), 145–148. For a balanced account of the *Discourses,* see Black, *Machiavelli* (2013), 129–176. For history's cycles, see Machiavelli, *Discourses,* 2.5, in *The Chief Works* (1989), 1:339–341.

29. On legitimation, see Quentin Skinner, "Augustan Party Politics and Renaissance Constitutional Thought," in *Visions of Politics,* vol. 2, *Renaissance Virtues* (Cambridge: Cambridge University Press, 2002), 344–367, which is a revised version of a paper first published in 1974.

30. Skinner, "Meaning and Understanding" (1969), 25–27. For an earlier and even stronger statement, see Quentin Skinner, "The Limits of Historical Explanations," *Philosophy* 41 (1966), 199–215; for a critique, see Francis Oakley, "'Anxieties of Influence': Skinner, Figgis, Conciliarism and Early Modern Constitutionalism," *Past and Present* 151 (1996), 60–110; and for a tactical retreat, see Quentin Skinner, *Visions of Politics,* vol. 1, *Regarding Method* (Cambridge: Cambridge University Press, 2002), 75. See also Michael Baxandall, *Patterns of Intention: On the Historical Explanation of Pictures* (New Haven, Conn.: Yale University Press, 1985), 58–62.

31. Ciaran Brady, "Spenser's Irish Crisis: Humanism and Experience in the 1590s," *Past and Present* 111 (1986), 20.

32. T. S. Eliot, *Shakespeare and the Stoicism of Seneca* (London: Shakespeare Association, 1927); repr. in *Selected Essays* (London: Faber and Faber, 1932).

33. Graham Allen, *Intertextuality* (London: Routledge, 2000).

34. See, for example, Carlo Ginzburg, "Machiavelli and the Antiquarians," in *Machiavelli, Islam and the East,* ed. Lucio Biasiori and Giuseppe Marcocci (Cham, Switzerland: Palgrave, 2018), 61–75. David Wootton, "Hume's 'Of Miracles': Probability and Irreligion," in *Studies in the Philosophy of the Scottish Enlightenment,* ed. M. A. Stewart (Oxford: Oxford University Press, 1990), 191–229, runs an argument of this sort.

35. Greenlaw, "The Influence of Machiavelli" (1909), 195–196.

36. Ibid., 199–200. Early English Books Online, https://eebo.chadwyck.com/home, gives 109 hits for "strong medicine" (including variant forms) before 1600, and only eight for Spenser's preferred term, "violent medicine."

37. The translator of Guicciardini's *History,* Geoffrey Fenton, moved to Ireland in 1580, where he served alongside Spenser and advocated plantations and the assassination of rebel leaders. See Andrew Hadfield, "Fenton, Sir Geoffrey," *Oxford Dictionary of National Biography,* https://doi.org/10.1093/ref:odnb/9296.

38. Helpful here is Maurizio Viroli, *From Politics to Reason of State: The Acquisition and Transformation of the Language of Politics, 1250–1600* (Cambridge: Cambridge University Press, 1991).

39. Corrado Vivanti, *Niccolò Machiavelli: An Intellectual Biography* (Princeton, N.J.: Princeton University Press, 2013), 22; David Wootton, "Machiavelli and the Business of Politics," in *Machiavelli's Legacy: The Prince after Five Hundred Years,* ed. Timothy Fuller (Philadelphia: University of Pennsylvania Press, 2016), 92–98; Romain Descendre, introduction to Giovanni Botero, *Della ragion di stato,* ed. Romain Descendre and Pierre Benedittini (Turin, Italy: Einaudi, 2016), xxix–xxxviii.

40. Harvey Mansfield, "Machiavelli on Necessity," in *Machiavelli on Liberty and Conflict,* ed. David Johnston, Nadia Urbinati, and Camila Vergara (Chicago: University of Chicago Press, 2017), 39–57. Gianmatteo Giberti referred to *la necessità delli stati* in 1537; see Susan Brigden, *Thomas Wyatt: The Heart's Forest* (London: Faber, 2014), 338.

41. Victoria Kahn, "*Virtù* and the Example of Agathocles in Machiavelli's *Prince,*" *Representations* 13 (1986), 63–83; David Wootton, introduction to Niccolò Machiavelli, *Selected Political Writings,* trans. David Wootton (Indianapolis: Hackett, 1994), xxi–xxii.

42. Machiavelli, *Discourses,* 1.9, in *The Chief Works* (1989), 1:217–220. See also John Humphreys Whitfield, *Discourses on Machiavelli* (Cambridge: Heffer, 1969), 141–162.

43. Spenser, *A View* (1997), 160; Clare Carroll, "The Text, Its Sources, and Traditions," in Richard Beacon, *Solon His Follie, or, A Politique Discourse Touching the Reformation of Common-weales Conquered, Declined or Corrupted,* ed. Clare Carroll and Vincent Carey (Binghamton, N.Y.: Medieval and Renaissance Texts and Studies, 1996), xxxiv–xxxviii; Richard Becon, *Solon His Follie, or A Politique Discourse, Touching the Reformation of Common-weales Conquered, Declined or Corrupted* (Oxford: Barnes, 1594), 8, 19, 21, 103, 107; Anglo, "A Machiavellian Solution" (1990); Anglo, *Machiavelli—The First Century* (2005), 468–476; Vincent Carey, "The Irish Face of Machiavelli: Richard Beacon's *Solon His Follie* (1594) and Republican Ideology in the Conquest of Ireland," in *Political Ideology in Ireland, 1541–1641,* ed. Hiram Morgan (Dublin: Four Courts, 1999), 83–109.

44. William Herbert, *Croftus, sive, de Hibernia liber,* ed. Arthur Keaveney and J. A. Madden (Dublin: Irish Manuscripts Commission, 1992), 74 (twice), 86, 92, and appendix 3.

45. Herbert, *Croftus* (1992), 87 (with quotation marks around Herbert's paraphrasing of Machiavelli removed).

46. Becon, *Solon His Follie* (1594), 5, 6, 113; Spenser, *A View* (1997), 117.

47. On whether English policies in Ireland were more savage than in other theaters of war, see Neil Murphy, "Violence, Colonization and Henry VIII"s Conquest of France, 1544–1546," *Past and Present* 233 (2016), 13–51.

48. Thomas Churchyard, *A Generall Rehearsall of Warres* (London: White, 1579), sig. Q2r.

49. Ibid., sigs. Q2r, Q3v.

50. Spenser, *A View* (1997), 11, 15, 21 (twice), 54, 61, 65, 68, 119, 156; it seems to me unhelpful to say that Spenser defines civility as "what is English rather than Irish" (Carroll, "The Text, Its Sources, and Traditions" [1996], xxxv); or to simply identify incivility with the alien, as in Patricia Coughlan, "'Some Secret Scourge Which Shall by Her Come unto England': Ireland and Incivility in Spenser," in *Spenser and Ireland: An Interdisciplinary Perspective,* ed. Patricia Coughlan (Cork, Ireland: Cork University Press, 1989), 46–74. Moreover, there must be a strong presumption that Spenser's use of the term is influenced by Machiavelli; see Alberto Tenenti, "'Civilitas' e Civiltà in Machiavelli," *Il pensiero politico* 4 (1971), 161–174.

51. Markku Peltonen, "Classical Republicanism in Tudor England: The Case of Richard Beacon's Solon His Follie," *History of Political Thought* 15 (1994),

469–503; Markku Peltonen, *Classical Humanism and Republicanism in English Political Thought, 1570–1640* (Cambridge: Cambridge University Press, 2004), 73–103; Hadfield, "Was Spenser a Republican?" (1998). For a critique of Peltonen, see Carey, "The Irish Face of Machiavelli" (1999). Rory Rapple, *Martial Power and Elizabethan Political Culture: Military Men in England and Ireland, 1558–1594* (Cambridge: Cambridge University Press, 2009), 250, presents Beacon as "the clearest example we have of a full reception of Machiavelli in Elizabethan England."

52. Clare Carroll, "The Janus Face of Machiavelli: Adapting *The Prince* and the *Discourses* in Early Modern Ireland," in *Circe's Cup: Cultural Transformations in Early Modern Writing about Ireland* (Notre Dame, IN: University of Notre Dame Press, 2001), 91–103.

53. Machiavelli, *The Prince*, ch. 5, in *The Chief Works* (1989), 1:23–24; Machiavelli, *Discourses*, 1.26, 2.21, 23, in *The Chief Works* (1989), 1:253–254, 383–385, 388–392.

54. Ciaran Brady, "Spenser, Plantation, and Government Policy," in *The Oxford Handbook of Edmund Spenser*, ed. Richard A. McCabe (Oxford: Oxford University Press, 2010), 86–105.

55. Spenser, *A View* (1997), 88.

56. Machiavelli, *The Prince*, ch. 3, in *The Chief Works* (1989), 1:12–20; Machiavelli, *Discourses*, 1.26, in *The Chief Works* (1989), 1:253–254.

57. Machiavelli, *Discourses*, 2.23, in *The Chief Works* (1989), 1:388–392.

58. Machiavelli, *Discourses*, 2.27, in *The Chief Works* (1989), 1:401–404.

59. This is misinterpreted in Isaiah Berlin, "The Originality of Machiavelli," in *Against the Current: Essays in the History of Ideas*, ed. Henry Hardy (Oxford: Clarendon, 1979), 57–58; compare Cassirer, *Myth of the State* (1946), 148. Machiavelli's disapproval of Philip of Macedon may be contrasted with his admiration for Severus; see Machiavelli, *The Prince*, ch. 19, in *The Chief Works* (1989), 1:67–76.

60. I am not persuaded by the reading of this passage in Benner, *Machiavelli's Ethics* (2009), 466–468.

61. Machiavelli, *Discourses*, 2.23, in *The Chief Works* (1989), 1:388–392; see also Niccolò Machiavelli, *The Art of War*, in *The Chief Works* (1989), 2:623.

62. Spenser, *A View* (1997), 91–92.

63. Machiavelli, *Discourses*, 1.17, in *The Chief Works* (1989), 1:238–240. In thinking about such questions, in particular in trying to understand the nature of the English monarchy through Machiavelli's categories, Spenser must surely have read with care Machiavelli's account of the *principato civile* (*The Prince*, ch. 9, in *The Chief Works* [1989], 1:39–42) and of France as a *regno moderato* (*The Prince*, ch. 4, in *The Chief Works* [1989], 1:20–23; *Discourses*, 1.16, 58, in *The Chief Works* [1989], 1:235–238, 313–318).

64. Spenser, *A View* (1997), 106.
65. Brady, "Spenser's Irish Crisis" (1986), 36–37; see, in response, Hadfield, *Spenser's Irish Experience* (1997), 63–66. David J. Baker, "Spenser and Politics," in *The Oxford Handbook of Edmund Spenser,* ed. Richard A. McCabe (Oxford: Oxford University Press, 2010), 49–54, also claims Spenser's reading of Machiavelli is confused.
66. Becon, *Solon His Follie* (1594), 19.
67. Ibid., 113.
68. Ibid., 16.
69. For the *principato civile,* see Machiavelli, *The Prince,* ch. 9, in *The Chief Works* (1989), 1:39–42. Although Machiavelli does not use the term *principato civile* in the *Discourses,* he does refer to some nonrepublican governments as having a *vivere civile* (a term synonymous with *vivere politico*); see *Discourses,* 1.9, 19, 26, 58, and 2.19, in *The Chief Works* (1989), 1:217–220, 244–245. For an extended analysis, see Giorgio Cadoni, *Machiavelli: Regno di Francia e "principato civile"* (Rome: Bulzoni, 1974). It is thus wrong to say, per Emanuele Cutinelli Rèndina, *Introduzione a Machiavelli* (Rome: Editori Laterza, 2003), 71, that a *vivere libero* and a *vivere civile* are, even in the *Discourses,* synonymous; rather, *vivere libero* is a subset of *vivere civile.* (I am grateful to Robert Black for discussing this point with me, though he would not agree with the formulation offered here.)
70. Becon, *Solon His Follie* (1594), 62.
71. Hans Baron, "Machiavelli: The Republican Citizen and the Author of 'The Prince,'" *English Historical Review* 76 (1961), 226n1, and Skinner, *Renaissance Virtues* (2002), 199, seem to overextend the possibility of liberty, as Machiavelli understood it, being found within a monarchy: the only clear-cut case is Rome under the kings (*Discourses,* 3.5, in *The Chief Works* [1989], 1:427–428), where a certain liberty was to be found; and Tarquin was expelled because he destroyed that liberty and sought to establish a tyranny. Rome could become a free republic simply by putting consuls in the place of the king; the same could not be said for any Renaissance monarchy (*pace* Hilary Gatti, "'El nome della libertà e gli ordini antiqui sua': The Problem of Liberty in *The Prince,*" in *Machiavelli's Prince,* ed. Nicola Gardini and Martin McLaughlin [Rome: Viella, 2017], 115, which misrepresents *The Prince,* ch. 19).
72. Becon, *Solon His Follie* (1594), 46.
73. Ibid., 11–12.
74. Peltonen, "Classical Republicanism" (1994); Peltonen, *Classical Humanism* (2004), 73–103.
75. Spenser, *A View* (1997), 14.
76. Hadfield, "Was Spenser a Republican?" (1998).

77. Spenser, *A View* (1997), 76, 144, 21.
78. Ibid., 11.
79. Beacon does twice use the word "civil" in a related sense (in the preface to the queen, and on 53 of *Solon His Follie* [1996]), but it seems to me doubly wrong for Carroll, in "The Text, Its Sources, and Traditions," xxxv, to claim that "Starkey's sense [in the *Dialogue between Pole and Lupset*] of civility as citizen government . . . is deployed throughout Beacon's *Solon.*" By "civility" Starkey does not mean citizen government, but *vivere civile;* see, for example, Thomas Starkey, *A Dialogue between Pole and Lupset,* ed. Thomas F. Mayer (London: Royal Historical Society, 1989), 6, 13, 36–37, where civility is taken to be equally compatible with popular and princely government—and, in any case, Beacon does not deploy the concept.
80. Peltonen, "Classical Republicanism" (1994), 472.
81. David Edwards, "Ideology and Experience: Spenser's View and Martial Law in Ireland," in Morgan, *Political Ideology in Ireland* (1999), 153–154.
82. Felix Raab, *The English Face of Machiavelli: A Changing Interpretation, 1500–1700* (London: Routledge and Kegan Paul, 1964), 61–62.
83. See Quentin Skinner, "Classical Liberty and the Coming of the English Civil War," in *Republicanism: A Shared European Heritage,* ed. Martin van Gelderen and Quentin Skinner, 2 vols. (Cambridge: Cambridge University Press, 2002) 2:9–28.
84. Quentin Skinner, "Meaning and Understanding in the History of Ideas," *History and Theory* 8 (1969), 3–53.
85. Machiavelli, *Discourses,* 1:26, translation from Niccolò Machiavelli, *The Works of the Famous Nicholas Machiavel,* trans. H. Neville (London: Starkey, 1675), 297.

3. HAPPINESS: WORDS AND CONCEPTS

1. There are empirical studies which seek to show how far money correlates with happiness, and just how much happiness a pay increase or a promotion will get you. The answer is that we consistently overestimate the extent to which an improvement in our finances will improve our sense of well-being. See Philip Brickman, Dan Coates, and Ronnie Janoff-Bulman, "Lottery Winners and Accident Victims: Is Happiness Relative?," *Journal of Personality and Social Psychology* 36 (1978): 917–927; Daniel Kahneman and Angus Deaton, "High Income Improves Evaluation of Life but Not Emotional Well-Being," *Proceedings of the National Academy of Sciences* 107 (2010), 16489–16493; and Robert Skidelsky and Edward Skidelsky, *How Much Is Enough? The Love of Money and the Case for the Good Life* (London: Allen Lane, 2012). Smith, as we shall see, thought this was unlucky for us, but lucky for our community,

which benefits from the hard work we put in in our misconceived efforts to get ahead.

2. This is not the same claim as Henry Sidgwick's paradox of hedonism, that pleasure is best pursued indirectly, for Sidgwick makes no distinction between pleasure and happiness; nor quite the same as John Stuart Mill's claim, in his *Autobiography,* that if you aim at happiness you will not attain it. Mill distinguishes between pleasure ("the enjoyments of life") and happiness, but he also claims that if you ask yourself if you are happy you will cease to be so—which seems false to me. For a survey of paradoxes involving happiness, see Mike W. Martin, "Paradoxes of Happiness," *Journal of Happiness Studies* 9 (2008), 171–184. Jean Austin, "Pleasure and Happiness," *Philosophy* 43 (1968), 51–62, takes a similar view to mine, while Wayne Davis, "Pleasure and Happiness," *Philosophical Studies* 39 (1981), 305–317, identifies happiness with pleasure.

3. Jean Pestré, "Bonheur," in *Encyclopédie, ou dictionnaire raisonné des sciences, des arts et des métiers,* ed. Denis Diderot and Jean le Rond d'Alembert, 17 vols. (Paris: Briasson, 1751–1777), vol. 2 (1751): "Les hommes se réunissent encore sur la nature du *bonheur.* Ils conviennent tous qu'il est le même que le plaisir, ou du moins qu'il doit au plaisir ce qu'il a de plus piquant & de plus délicieux." Claude Yvon, in the same volume, states that the good *(le bien),* in moral philosophy, was simply pleasure or a cause of pleasure; this was later to be Bentham's view.

4. Voltaire, "Heureux, heureuse, heureusement," in Diderot and d'Alembert, *Encyclopédie,* vol. 6 (1765). This, together with his article "Félicité" (from the same volume), appears in posthumous editions of his *Dictionnaire philosophique.*

5. Thomas Newman, "Happiness Not in a Life of Pleasure," in *Sermons on Happiness,* 2 vols. London: Hett, 1760), 1:99–190. On the different pleasures, see Anonymous, "Plaisir," in Diderot and d'Alembert, *Encyclopédie,* vol. 12 (1765).

6. Laurence Sterne, "Inquiry After Happiness," in *The Sermons of Mr. Yorick,* 2 vols. (London: Dodsley, 1760), 1:1–23.

7. Denis Diderot, "Béatitude, Bonheur, Felicité," in Diderot and d'Alembert, *Encyclopédie,* vol. 2 (1752).

8. David Hume, "The Epicurean," in *Essays, Moral and Political,* 2 vols. (Edinburgh: Kincaid, 1741–1742), 2:103. On his personal crisis, see David Hume, *The Letters of David Hume,* ed. J. Y. T. Greig, 2 vols. (Oxford: Clarendon, 1932), 1:12–18; David Hume, *A Treatise of Human Nature,* 3 vols. (London: Noon, 1739–1740), 1:461–475; John P. Wright, "Dr. George Cheyne, Chevalier Ramsay, and Hume's Letter to a Physician," *Hume Studies* 29 (2003), 125–141; and James A. Harris, *Hume: An Intellectual Biography* (Cambridge: Cambridge University Press, 2015), 35–116. Elie Luzac, *Le bonheur ou nouveau systeme de jurisprudence naturelle* (Berlin: s.n., 1753), 33–34, 57–58, defines contentment as

the belief that there is no way in which one's situation could be improved—a definition which would make it rare indeed.

9. Alexander Pope, *An Essay on Man. Address'd to a Friend. Part I* (London: Wilford, 1733), 61 (epistle 4).

10. Diderot, "Béatitude, Bonheur, Felicité"; Voltaire, "Félicité," in Diderot and d'Alembert, *Encyclopédie,* vol. 6 (1756). Anonymous, "Plaisir," in Diderot and d'Alembert, *Encyclopédie,* vol. 12 (1765), begins: "Le *plaisir* est un sentiment de l'ame qui nous rend heureux du-moins pendant tout le tems que nous le goûtons."

11. William Wollaston, *The Religion of Nature Delineated* (s.l.: s.n., 1722), 26–27.

12. Denis Diderot, "Epicuréisme," in Diderot and d'Alembert, *Encyclopédie,* vol. 5 (1755). Even the word *félicité* only appears once; *plaisir,* on the other hand appears fourteen times, and *bonheur* nine times. A striking contrast is Anonymous, "Volupté," in Diderot and d'Alembert, *Encyclopédie,* vol. 17 (1765), which also discusses Epicurus. This post-Hobbesian reading of Epicurus goes back at least to Samuel Parker in 1678, who reinterpreted Epicurus in the light of Hobbes, although in doing so he was able to draw on a long tradition of attacks on Epicurus.

13. Pietro Verri, *Meditazioni sulla felicità* (s.l.: s.n., 1763), 12. Compare Pestré in "Bonheur": "Tous les hommes se réunissent dans le desir d'être heureux. La nature nous a fait à tous une loi de notre propre *bonheur.* Tout ce qui n'est point *bonheur* nous est étranger: lui seul a un pouvoir marqué sur notre coeur; nous y sommes tous entraînés par une pente rapide, par un charme puissant, par un attrait vainqueur; c'est une impression ineffaçable de la nature qui l'a gravé dans nos coeurs, il en est le charme & la perfection."

14. See David Wootton, introduction to *Divine Right and Democracy: An Anthology of Political Writing in Stuart England,* ed. David Wootton (Harmondsworth, England: Penguin, 1986), 58–77.

15. There are numerous critics of growth, beginning with Rousseau. Key texts are Donella H. Meadows, *The Limits to Growth: A Report for the Club of Rome's Project on the Predicament of Mankind* (New York: Universe, 1972); and E. F. Schumacher, *Small Is Beautiful: Economics As If People Mattered* (New York: Harper and Row, 1973). But so far such views have always been those of a minority, and they have never been adopted by any democratically elected government.

16. Thomas Hobbes, *Leviathan, Or, the Matter, Forme, and Power of a Common Wealth, Ecclesiasticall and Civil* (London: Crooke, 1651), 47–48.

17. Rousseau regarded this condition as intolerable: "Mais l'objet qui paraissait d'abord sous la main fuit plus vite qu'on ne peut le poursuivre; quand on croit l'atteindre, il se transforme et se montre au loin devant nous. Ne voyant plus le

Decade	1601–10	1611–20	1621–30	1631–40	1641–50	1651–60
No. of occurrences	10	86	105	208	415	934
No. of searchable titles	1,732	1,936	2,263	2,086	11,205	7,691
Occurrences per 1,000 titles	5.8	44.4	46.4	99.7	37.0	121.4

pays déjà parcouru, nous le comptons pour rien; celui qui reste à parcourir s'agrandit, s'étend sans cesse. Ainsi l'on s'épuise sans arriver au terme; et plus nous gagnons sur la jouissance, plus le bonheur s'éloigne de nous." Jean-Jacques Rousseau, *Emile ou De l'éducation,* 4 vols. (The Hague: Néaulme, 1762), 1:155.

18. The *Oxford English Dictionary (OED) Online,* http://www.oed.com, s.v. "competition," gives a first usage as 1608, but the entry has not been revised since 1891. The earliest would seem to be in Livy, Lucius Annaeus Florus, and Bartolomeo Marliani, *The Romane Historie,* trans. P. Holland (London: Islip, 1600)— there are a few earlier usages in which the word has a different sense. Its growing popularity is illustrated above in the table of hits in Early English Books Online (EEBO; https://eebo.chadwyck.com/home).

The drop in the decade before *Leviathan* is to be attributed to the changing character of publication with the end of censorship and the outbreak of the English Civil War. "Competition" is followed in 1620 (*OED Online,* again 1891) by the verb "compete." "Competitor" is a sixteenth-century word, but it is not common until the seventeenth century. The obvious synonyms are "rivalry" (*OED Online,* 1598, updated June 2010); "rivality" (*OED Online,* 1528, updated June 2010); "rival" (noun; *OED Online,* 1577, updated June 2010; EEBO, 1567); "rival" (verb; *OED Online,* 1607, updated June 2010; EEBO, 1606); and "rivalship" (*OED Online,* 1604, updated June 2010). Earlier is "emulation" (*OED Online,* 1552, updated 1989; EEBO, 1531).

19. Richard G. Wilkinson and Kate Pickett, *The Spirit Level: Why More Equal Societies Almost Always Do Better* (London: Allen Lane, 2009), 3–14.

20. Moisés Naím, *The End of Power: From Boardrooms to Battlefields and Churches to States, Why Being in Charge Isn't What It Used to Be* (New York: Basic Books, 2013).

21. Robert J. Gordon, *The Rise and Fall of American Growth: The U.S. Standard of Living since the Civil War* (Princeton, N.J.: Princeton University Press, 2016).

22. Donald Rutherford, "In Pursuit of Happiness: Hobbes's New Science of Ethics," *Philosophical Topics* 31 (2003), 369–393. When Hobbes does use the

word "happiness" in *Leviathan* it is always in a religious context, where one might expect "felicity" or "blessedness"—the latter being a word Hobbes never uses. Phil Withington, "The Invention of 'Happiness,'" in *Suffering and Happiness in England 1550–1850: Narratives and Representations; A Collection to Honour Paul Slack,* ed. Michael J. Braddick and Joanna Innes (Oxford: Oxford University Press, 2017), 44.

23. Richard Tuck, "The Utopianism of *Leviathan,*" in *Leviathan after 350 Years,* ed. Tom Sorell and Luc Foisneau (Oxford: Oxford University Press, 2004), 125–138, shows that more of this optimism than one might think is already present in Hobbes.

24. Judith N. Shklar, *Men and Citizens: A Study of Rousseau's Social Theory* (London: Cambridge University Press, 1969). For an account of Rousseau's politics, see David Wootton, introduction to Jean-Jacques Rousseau, *Basic Political Writings,* ed. David Wootton, trans. Donald A. Cress (Indianapolis: Hackett, 2011).

25. Thus Hobbes writes of "individual persons" and of both "society" and "civil society." On "society," see Raymond Williams, *Keywords: A Vocabulary of Culture and Society* (New York: Oxford University Press, 1976); John Bossy, "Some Elementary Forms of Durkheim," *Past and Present* 95 (1982), 3–18; Phil Withington, *Society in Early Modern England* (Cambridge: Polity, 2010), 102–133; and *OED Online,* s.v. "society" (updated September 2009) and "civil society" (updated November 2010), but this last gives a first usage of 1575, while earlier instances, beginning in 1536, can now be found on EEBO.

26. John Ackrill, "Aristotle on Eudaimonia," *Proceedings of the British Academy* 60 (1975), 339–359; Richard Kraut, "Two Conceptions of Happiness," *Philosophical Review* 88 (1979), 167–197; Julia Annas, *The Morality of Happiness* (Oxford: Oxford University Press, 1993). Arthur William Hope Adkins, *Merit and Responsibility: A Study in Greek Values* (Oxford: Clarendon, 1951), establishes a broader context for the understanding of Greek moral philosophy.

27. There has been much work on Lucretius and Epicureanism in the Renaissance; see, for example, Catherine Wilson, *Epicureanism: At the Origins of Modernity* (Oxford: Clarendon, 2008); Alison Brown, *The Return of Lucretius to Renaissance Florence* (Cambridge, Mass.: Harvard University Press, 2010); Stephen Greenblatt, *The Swerve: How the Renaissance Began* (London: Bodley Head, 2011); Ada Palmer, *Reading Lucretius in the Renaissance* (Cambridge, Mass.: Harvard University Press, 2014).

28. In *De natura deorum* (1.95) Cicero invented the term *beatitudo* (derived from *beatus*) to describe the happiness of the gods according to the Epicureans. Thus Diderot, "Béatitude, Bonheur, Felicité," defines *béatitude* as "l'état d'une ame que la présence immédiate de son Dieu remplit dans ce monde-ci ou dans

l'autre; état qui seroit au- dessus de toute expression sans doute, si nous le con-
noissions." The consequence was that in postclassical Latin, *beatus* came to
bear a distinctly religious meaning, and to be translated by words such as
"blessed"—except, of course, when commenting directly on classical Latin
texts; see, for example, Elisabeth of Bohemia and René Descartes, *The Correspondence between Princess Elisabeth of Bohemia and René Descartes,* ed. Lisa
Shapiro (Chicago: University of Chicago Press, 2007), 97. Protestants, perhaps
in order to mark their differences from Catholics, often translated *beatus* as
"happy"; see Craig Muldrew, "Happiness and the Theology of the Self," in
Braddick and Innes, *Suffering and Happiness in England,* 68, 77, 79.

29. Seneca, "De Vita Beata," in *Moral Essays,* trans. John W. Basore, 3 vols. (Cambridge, Mass.: Harvard University Press, 1928–1935), 2:99; and see Descartes
to Elisabeth of Bohemia, 4 August 1645 and 1 September 1645, in Elisabeth of
Bohemia and Descartes, *Correspondence* (2007), 97, 107.

30. Augustine, *On Free Choice of the Will,* trans. T. Williams (Indianapolis: Hackett,
1993), 23 (*De libero arbitrio libri tres,* 1.14).

31. In *Protagoras* Socrates proposed a straightforward hedonism; but he did so only
to tie Protagoras in knots; there is no suggestion that the view he advanced was
one that he found convincing; see Daniel Russell, *Plato on Pleasure and the
Good Life* (Oxford: Oxford University Press, 2005), 239–248. Among the Greek
philosophers, Aristippus seems to have come closest to adopting a systematic
hedonism.

32. Withington, "The Invention of 'Happiness'" (2017), 1–44.

33. Ibid., 44.

34. Ibid., 29–39. In Samuel Johnson's *Dictionary of the English Language* (1755),
each is the first word used in the definition of the other. In French, as we have
seen, *bonheur* and *félicité* were not synonyms—*bonheur* referred to an experience and *félicité* to a state of mind; or, as Jean Féraud, "Bonheur," in *Dictionaire critique de la langue française* (1787–1788) put it, "Ils difèrent, en ce que
bonheur marque proprement l'état de la fortune; *félicité,* l'état du coeur." Similarly, in English "passions" and "affections" were so frequently coupled together
that they were evidently regarded as synonyms; but it is rare to find either coupled with "emotions"—evidence that emotions are indeed a novel category, as
is argued in Thomas Dixon, *From Passions to Emotions: The Creation of a Secular Psychological Category* (Cambridge: Cambridge University Press, 2003);
on the difference between passions and emotions in Hume, see 104–109.

35. Richard Huloet and John Higgins, *Huloets Dictionarie Newelye Corrected*
(London: Marsh, 1572) gives English, French, and Latin equivalents for "felicity"
and "happiness." In French, *heur* (which is a quite different word from *heure*
and means "chance" or "fortune"), and the words derived from it—*bonheur*

(good fortune), *heureté, heureuseté*—developed into a vocabulary for discussing happiness (or something like happiness) earlier than the comparable shift from "hap" to "happiness" in English; but the shift in the meaning of *heur* did not go as far as the shift in the meaning of "hap."

36. Thomas More, *Utopia: Latin Text and English Translation*, ed. George M. Logan, Robert M. Adams, and Clarence H. Miller (Cambridge: Cambridge University Press, 2006), 81-82; Thomas More, *A Fruteful, and Pleasaunt Worke of the Beste State of a Publyque Weale, and of the Newe Yle Called Vtopia*, trans. R. Robinson (London: Vele, 1551), sigs. Fiv(v)-Fv(r): "youre Plato Iudgethe that weale publyques shall by this meanes attayne perfecte felicitie, other [either] if phylosophers be kynges, or els if kynges giue them selfes to the study of Philosophie, how farre I praye yowe, shall commen wealthes then be from thys felicitie, if phylosophers wyll vouchesaufe to instructe kynges wt their good counsell?"; Thomas More, *Utopia*, trans. G. Burnet (London: Chiswell, 1684), 40-41.

37. *Vocabolario degli Accademici della Crusca*, http://vocabolario.sns.it/html/_s _index2.html, s.v. *"felicità."*

38. "Felicité," Dictionnaires d'autrefois, https://artflsrv03.uchicago.edu/philologic4 /publicdicos/query?report=bibliography&head=félicité.

39. Though, as Withington, "The Invention of 'Happiness'" (2017), 39-43, points out, Burnet was particularly keen in his use of the word "happiness" and employed it to translate a wide range of terms in More's Latin.

40. I thus have more sympathy with the argument in Paul Slack, "The Politics of Consumption and England's Happiness in the Later Seventeenth Century," *English Historical Review* 122 (2007), 609-631, than with Withington, "The Invention of 'Happiness'" (2017), which misses the importance of the move from an objective to a subjective conception of happiness—on which, see Bernard Mandeville, *The Fable of the Bees: Or, Private Vices, Publick Benefits* (London: Roberts, 1714), 113-140 (remark N).

41. For evidence that *Utopia* is an engagement with Greek rather than Roman thought, see Eric Nelson, *The Greek Tradition in Republican Thought* (Cambridge: Cambridge University Press, 2004).

42. More, *Utopia* (1684), 115.

43. Robert Crofts, *The Terrestriall Paradise, Or, Happinesse on Earth* (London: Aderton, 1639); Crofts was also the author of *The Lover: Or, Nuptiall Love. VVritten, by Robert Crofts, to Please Himselfe* (London: Meighen, 1638—on which, see Catherine Belsey, "Love as Trompe-L'oeil: Taxonomies of Desire in Venus and Adonis," *Shakespeare Quarterly* 46 [1995], 257-276); *Paradise Within Us: Or, the Happie Mind* (London: Alsop and Fawcet, 1640—on which, see George C. Taylor, "Did Milton Read Robert Crofts' *A Paradice within Us or The Happie Mind?*," *Philological Quarterly* 28 [1949],

207–210); *The Way to Happinesse on Earth: Concerning Riches, Honour, Conjugall Love, Eating, Drinking* (London: G. H., 1641); and a work now lost, *Heaven Within Us, or, Divine Happinesse on Earth* (see Crofts, *Paradise Within Us* [1640], sig. A2v, and pp. 124, 196, and *The Way to Happinesse on Earth* [1641], 131). As the titles imply, Crofts's conception of happiness slips and slides between competing views. But the title of his lost work and the final words of *The Lover* make me wonder if his oscillation between terrestrial and celestial delights may not have been influenced by the Family of Love religious community. In heaven, he writes in *The Lover*, "doth GOD purifie and reduce us to a being supernaturall and deified, vnites and takes the soule into his owne divine nature. . . . hereby the Soule becomes a Part of GOD, and with him and in him, enjoyes all Happinesse; So, as now it may be sayd, to be no more a Soule but GOD himselfe." The phrase "*The Kingdom of God,* is a Paradise *Within Us*" is to be found in a posthumous work of the Familist John Everard; see John Everard, *The Gospel Treasury Opened, Or, the Holiest of All Unvailing* (London: Harford, 1657), 380.

44. Kenelm Digby, *Loose Fantasies,* ed. Vittorio Gabrieli (Rome: Edizioni di Storia e Letteratura, 1968), 216; on Digby, see Michael Foster, "Digby, Sir Kenelm (1603–1665)," *Oxford Dictionary of National Biography,* https://doi.org/10.1093 /ref:odnb/7629; and Joseph Moshenska, *A Stain in the Blood: The Remarkable Voyage of Sir Kenelm Digby* (London: Heinemann, 2016).

45. I say "drafted" because the manuscript was obviously revised later. One evident major revision is in the account of Digby's meeting with a demon who had been conjured by a holy man (74–87). Digby himself participated in such conjuring at some date prior to 1632; see William Lilly, *Mr. William Lilly's History of His Life and Times, From the Year 1602 to 1681* (London: Roberts, 1715), 20, 23. But later he became highly skeptical of claims of demonic intervention; see Sir Kenelm Digby to Thomas Hobbes, 11 September 1637, in Thomas Hobbes, *The Correspondence,* vol. 1, *1622–1659,* ed. Noel Malcolm (Oxford: Clarendon, 1994), 50. The passage seems to have been written at least after 1651, and probably after 1660, as it implies a knowledge of the ideas of Nicolaus Le Fèvre; see Betty Jo Dobbs, "Studies in the Natural Philosophy of Sir Kenelm Digby," *Ambix* 18 (1971), 22–24.

46. Jeremy Taylor, *A Discourse of the Nature, Offices, and Measures of Friendship with Rules of Conducting It* (London: Royston, 1657) is one of the earliest works to stress the possibility of friendship between men and women; see Frances Harris, *Transformations of Love: The Friendship of John Evelyn and Margaret Godolphin* (Oxford: Oxford University Press, 2004). Whatever the men might say, women, of course, had friendships; see Amanda E. Herbert, *Female Alliances: Gender, Identity, and Friendship in Early Modern Britain* (New Haven, Conn.: Yale University Press, 2014).

47. Lawrence Stone, *The Family, Sex, and Marriage in England, 1500–1800* (London: Weidenfeld and Nicolson, 1977), 202, 274, naturally regards Digby as representative of a new view of marriage; but Stone treats the pursuit of happiness as a late seventeenth- and eighteenth-century phenomenon (236), when it is already present in Digby.

48. Digby, *Loose Fantasies* (1968), 143, 144, 155, 156.

49. John Ford, *'Tis Pitty Shee's a Whore* (London: Collins, 1633), sig. B1v. I owe this reference to Stephen Collins.

50. The sermons were actually delivered to the Oundle Grammar School, but Cooper was there as part of a visitation by a London guild, the Company of Grocers, and publication was primarily for a London audience. On Cooper, see Stephen Wright, "Cooper [Cowper], Thomas," *Oxford Dictionary of National Biography*, https://doi.org/10.1093/ref:odnb/6230. Cooper was also the author of *Wilie Beguile Ye, or the Worldlings Gaine* (London: s.n., 1621), which overlaps in part with *The Worldlings Aduenture,* also attacking the "vnsatiable desire of earthly things, [which] possesseth euery man naturally" (10).

51. Thomas Cooper, *The Worldlings Aduenture: Discouering, the Fearefull Estate of All Earth-Wormes, and Men of This World* (London: Redmer, 1619), 4, 11, 50.

52. Robert Bolton, *A Discourse About the State of True Happinesse* (London: Weauer, 1611), 120.

53. Ibid., 9.

54. John Jewel, *The Second Tome of Homilees* (s.l.: Iugge and Cawood, 1571), 205.

55. Augustine, *Of the Citie of God* ([London]: Eld, 1610), 159 (bk. 4, ch. 5).

56. Cooper, *The Worldlings Aduenture* (1619), 66.

57. Bolton, *True Happinesse* (1611), 72. Or consider his complaint, "In this respect then, that the wicked dare enlarge their consciences to the vtmost bounds of any pleasure, gaine or preferment, they haue great aduantage for the ingrossing of all worldly happinesse, and may easily purchase a Monopoly of earthly prosperity" (55).

58. C. B. Macpherson, *The Political Theory of Possessive Individualism: Hobbes to Locke* (Oxford: Clarendon, 1962); the classic rebuttal is Keith Thomas, "The Social Origins of Hobbes's Political Thought," in *Hobbes Studies,* ed. Keith C. Brown (Oxford: Blackwell, 1965), 185–236; but see also Michael Bray, "Macpherson Restored? Hobbes and the Question of Social Origins," *History of Political Thought* 28 (2007), 56–90.

59. Hobbes surely did read Machiavelli. The long-debated question of Hobbes's relationship to Machiavelli and the Machiavellian tradition is transformed by Noel Malcolm, *Reason of State and the Thirty Years' War: An Unknown Trans-*

lation by Thomas Hobbes (Oxford: Clarendon, 2007). Machiavelli, one might add, also preceded Hobbes in implying that there is no *summum bonum.*

60. Kevin Sharpe, *Reading Revolutions: The Politics of Reading in Early Modern England* (New Haven, Conn.: Yale University Press, 2000), 107, 238; Drake apparently had in mind Machiavelli's *Discourses on Livy,* 1.46 ("Li uomini salgono da una ambizione a un'altra; e prima si cerca non essere offeso, dipoi si offende altrui"), but also, surely, the preface to the *Discourses,* bk. 2, in *The Chief Works and Others,* trans. and ed. Allan H. Gilbert, 3 vols. (Durham, N.C.: Duke University Press, 1989), 1:290–291, 321–324. I owe this reference to Sharpe to Blair Worden.

61. Machiavelli expressed this view in what would appear to be one of his earliest surviving texts, *Parole da dirle sopra la provisione del danaio* (1503?)—though some think the text was written much later for inclusion in a history.

62. Rosalind Hursthouse, *On Virtue Ethics* (Oxford: Oxford University Press, 1999). The classic early article is G. E. M. Anscombe, "Modern Moral Philosophy," *Philosophy 33* (1958), 1–19.

4. SELFISH SYSTEMS: HOBBES AND LOCKE

1. David Hume, *A Treatise of Human Nature,* 3 vols. (London: Noon, 1739–1740), 1:467.

2. Ibid., 1:469–470.

3. Ibid., 1:458.

4. Augustine, *Saint Augustines Confessions,* trans. W. Watts (London: Partridge, 1631), 685–686 (bk. 10, ch. 35).

5. Thomas Hobbes, *Leviathan, Or, the Matter, Forme, and Power of a Common Wealth, Ecclesiasticall and Civil* (London: Crooke, 1651), 26; Lorraine J. Daston, "Curiosity in Early Modern Science," *Word and Image* 11 (1995), 391–404; Peter Harrison, "Curiosity, Forbidden Knowledge, and the Reformation of Natural Philosophy in Early Modern England," *Isis* 92 (2001), 265–290. Harrison presents Bacon as a key figure in the revaluation of curiosity—but for Bacon the word always has negative connotations.

6. John Fletcher, "The Island Princesse" (1621), 3.1, in Francis Beaumont and John Fletcher, *Comedies and Tragedies* (London: Robinson and Moseley, 1647), 106.

7. The earliest example in Early English Books Online, https://eebo.chadwyck .com/home, is 1637, followed by 1657, and then thirteen hits in the decade 1664–1673. Samuel Pufendorf, *On the Duty of Man and Citizen According to Natural Law,* ed. James Tully, trans. Michael Silverthorne (Cambridge: Cambridge University Press, 1991), 133. See also William Casey King, *Ambition, a History: From Vice to Virtue* (New Haven, Conn.: Yale University Press, 2013).

8. On curiosity, compare John Locke, *An Essay Concerning Humane Understanding* (London: Basset, 1690), table of contents for bk. 1, ch. 1, sec. 6 ("useless Curiosity") with John Locke, *Some Thoughts Concerning Education* (London: Churchill, 1693), sec. 103 ("Curiosity should be as carefully cherished in Children, as other Appetites suppressed"), and secs. 111, 114. On ambition, compare John Locke, *A Letter Concerning Toleration*, trans. W. Popple (London: Churchill, 1689) ("Pride and Ambition," "Ignorance, Ambition, or Superstition," "Covetousness, Rapine, and Ambition," "Covetousness, Ambition, Discord, Contention") with Locke, *Some Thoughts Concerning Education* (1693), sec. 104 ("Ambition, and the Desire still to get forward, and higher"), where ambition is to be encouraged.

9. *Oxford English Dictionary (OED) Online,* http://www.oed.com, s.v. "concern" (verb), updated September 2015; see also "concern" (noun), sense 4c, also updated September 2015.

10. David Hume, *An Enquiry Concerning the Principles of Morals* (London: Millar, 1751), 192 (sec. 9, pt. 2), 155 (sec. 7).

11. Hume, *Treatise* (1739–1740), 3:201 (bk. 3, pt. 3, sec. 10); see also 1:210 (bk. 1, pt. 3, sec. 9).

12. Ibid., 3:201 (bk. 3, pt. 3, sec. 10).

13. On Archibald Campbell as one of those searching for this elusive middle way, see Paul Sagar, "Sociability, Luxury and Sympathy: The Case of Archibald Campbell," *History of European Ideas* 39 (2013), 791–814; and Christian Maurer, "What Can An Egoist Say against An Egoist? On Archibald Campbell's Criticisms of Bernard Mandeville," *Journal of Scottish Philosophy* 12 (2014), 1–18.

14. Francis Hutcheson, *An Essay on the Nature and Conduct of the Passions and Affections* (London: Smith and Bruce, 1728), 208. Actually, Hobbes rarely uses the word "happiness," but as we have seen ,"happiness" is a synonym for the word he does use, "felicity"; and he only uses the word "self-love" in *Leviathan.*

15. Hutcheson, *Essay* (1728), 209. See also Francis Hutcheson, *Reflections Upon Laughter, and Remarks Upon the Fable of the Bees* (Glasgow: Baxter, 1750), 6.

16. Joseph Butler, *Fifteen Sermons Preached at the Rolls Chapel* (London: Knapton, 1726), 6.

17. Hume, *An Enquiry* (1751), 13; David Hume, *The History of Great Britain*, vol. 2 (London: Millar, 1757), 126–127.

18. James Boswell, *The Journal of a Tour to the Hebrides, with Samuel Johnson, LL. D.* (London: Dilly, 1785), 335. See also Paul Russell, *The Riddle of Hume's Treatise: Skepticism, Naturalism, and Irreligion* (Oxford: Oxford University Press, 2008).

19. The bracketed text was added in 1770.

20. Hume, *An Enquiry* (1751), 13–14.

21. Bernard Gert, "Hobbes, Mechanism, and Egoism," *Philosophical Quarterly* 15 (1965), 341–349; Bernard Gert, "Hobbes and Psychological Egoism," *Journal of the History of Ideas* 28 (1967), 510–512; Bernard Gert, "Hobbes's Psychology," in *The Cambridge Companion to Hobbes*, ed. Tom Sorell (Cambridge: Cambridge University Press, 1996), 157–174; Thomas Nagel, "Hobbes's Concept of Obligation," *Philosophical Review* 68 (1959), 68–83. See also Noel Malcolm, "Hobbes and Spinoza," in *The Cambridge History of Political Thought, 1450–1700* (Cambridge: Cambridge University Press, 1991), 534–535; Gregory S. Kavka, *Hobbesian Moral and Political Theory* (Princeton, N.J.: Princeton University Press, 1986), 29–82; F. S. McNeilly, "Egoism in Hobbes," *Philosophical Quarterly* 16 (1966), 193–206; F. S. McNeilly, *The Anatomy of Leviathan* (London: Macmillan, 1968), 95–136; and D. D. Raphael, *Hobbes: Morals and Politics* (London: Allen and Unwin, 1977), 64–66, 77–80.

22. Thomas Hobbes, *De corpore politico, Or, The Elements of Law, Moral and Politick* (London: Ridley, 1652), 22.

23. See, for example, Bernard Mandeville, *The Fable of the Bees: Or, Private Vices, Publick Benefits* (London: Roberts, 1714), 40: "There is no Merit in saving an Innocent Babe ready to drop into the Fire: The Action is neither good nor bad, and what Benefit soever the Infant received, we only obliged our selves; for to have seen it fall, and not strove to hinder it, would have caused a Pain which Self-preservation compell'd us to prevent" (in the table of contents this section is listed as "Pity no Virtue, and why"). See also Mandeville's account of how people become inured to the suffering of others in *The Fable of the Bees*, 2nd ed. (London: Parker, 1723), 293: "Thus thousands give Money to Beggars from the same Motive as they pay their Corn-cutter [i.e., chiropodist], to walk Easy." Mandeville does not deny that we experience pity; he denies that pity is really altruistic.

24. Thomas Hobbes and John Aubrey, *The Elements of Law, Natural and Politic: Part I, Human Nature, Part II, De Corpore Politico; With Three Lives*, ed. J. C. A. Gaskin (Oxford: Oxford University Press, 1994), 242.

25. Aristotle, *The Art of Rhetoric*, ed. and trans. Hugh Lawson-Tancred (Harmondsworth, England: Penguin, 1991), 163; for Hobbes's version of this passage, see Aristotle, *A Briefe of the Art of Rhetorique* (London: Cotes, 1637), 93–95. I am in debt to Katherine Ibbett, *Compassion's Edge: Fellow-Feeling and Its Limits in Early Modern France* (Philadelphia: University of Pennsylvania Press, 2018), 60–61.

26. Thomas Hobbes, *Humane Nature, or The Fundamental Elements of Policie* (London: Bowman, 1650), ch. 9, sec. 10. Here are two further examples, both modern translations from Hobbes's Latin. On firm egoism: "To grieve because

of another's evil, that is to feel another's pain and to suffer with him, that is to imagine that another's evil could happen to oneself, is called compassion"; Thomas Hobbes, *Man and Citizen: Thomas Hobbes's De Homine,* ed. Bernard Gert (Garden City, N.Y.: Anchor, 1972), translating Hobbes, *De homine* (1658), ch. 12, sec. 10. And on tough egoism: "We also find distressing the evils that befall others, but only if we suppose or believe that similar ones will happen to us as well; otherwise we do not, because mental stress consists in an awareness of our own weakness, not of someone else's"; Thomas Hobbes, *Thomas White's De Mundo Examined,* ed. and trans. Harold Whitmore Jones (London: Bradford University Press, 1976), ch. 38, sec. 7.

27. Hobbes, *Leviathan* (1651), 27.
28. Tom Sorell, *Hobbes* (London: Routledge and Kegan Paul, 1986), 97–100.
29. Hobbes, *Humane Nature* (1650), chap. 9, sec. 19.
30. Titus Lucretius Carus, *T. Lucretius Carus the Epicurean Philosopher: His Six Books De Natura Rerum,* trans. T. Creech (Oxford: Stephens, 1682), 35. Remarkably, this very passage of Lucretius is discussed in the context of an account of his influence on Hobbes without the connection being made to the text of *Humane Nature.* See Ioannis D. Evrigenis, *Images of Anarchy: The Rhetoric and Science in Hobbes's State of Nature* (Cambridge: Cambridge University Press, 2014), 189. For discussion of the passage and its significance for later authors, see Hans Blumenberg, *Shipwreck with Spectator: Paradigm of a Metaphor for Existence* (Cambridge, Mass.: MIT Press, 1997); and Valentina Prosperi, "The Reception of Lucretius's Second Proem: The Topos That Never Was," *Lingue antiche e moderne* 4 (2015), 5–37.
31. Francis Bacon, "Of Truth," *in The Essayes or Covnsels, Civill and Morall* (London: Haviland, 1625), 3–4; I owe this reference to Samuel Zeitlin. Bacon also paraphrases the Lucretian passage in *Of the Proficience and Aduancement of Learning, Divine and Humane* (London: Tomes, 1605), 44.
32. Hobbes, *Leviathan* (1651), 75 (pt. 1, ch. 15).
33. Here are two further examples from *Leviathan:* "When the transferring of Right, is not mutual: but one of the parties transferreth, in hope to gain thereby friendship, or service from another, or from his friends; or in hope to gain the reputation of Charity, or Magnanimity; or to deliver his mind from the pain of compassion; or in hope of reward in heaven; this is not Contract, but GIFT, FREE-GIFT, GRACE: which words signify one and the same thing." Hobbes, *Leviathan* (1651), 66 (pt. 1, ch. 14). "Reward, is either of Gift, or by Contract. When by Contract, it is called Salary, and Wages; which is benefit due for service performed, or promised. When of Gift, it is benefit proceeding from the grace of them that bestow it, to encourage, or enable men to do them service." Hobbes, *Leviathan* (1651), 166 (pt. 2, ch. 28).

34. Hobbes, *Humane Nature* (1650), 109 (ch. 9, sec. 17). Compare Hobbes on friendship (the first three passages are modern translations): Hobbes, *De Homine* (1658), ch. 11, sec. 6, in *Man and Citizen* (1972): "Friendships are good, certainly useful. For friendships, among many other things, confer protection." Hobbes, *De mundo* (1976), ch. 38, sec. 7: "We grieve over the loss of riches and of friends because we feel ourselves deprived of the [power] and of the protection that have raised our hopes of advancement." Hobbes, *De mundo* (1976), ch. 38, sec. 8: "Honours, friendships and riches are parts of [power]." Friendship, he notes, is, like riches and reputation, an instrumental power; Hobbes, *Leviathan* (1651), 41 (pt. 1, ch. 10): "to have servants, is Power; To have friends, is Power: for they are strengths united."

35. Thomas Hobbes, *Philosophicall Rudiments Concerning Government and Society* (London: Royston, 1651), 5–6 (*De Cive*, 1642, ch. 1, sec. 2). See also *Philosophicall Rudiments*, 3 (*De Cive*, 1642, ch. 1, sec. 2): "We doe not therefore by nature seek Society for its own sake, but that we may receive some Honour or Profit from it; these we desire Primarily, that Secondarily."

36. Thus Sharon A. Lloyd and Susanne Sreedhar, "Hobbes's Moral and Political Philosophy," in *The Stanford Encyclopedia of Philosophy*, Spring 2014 ed., ed. Edward N. Zalta, https://plato.stanford.edu/archives/spr2014/entries/hobbes-moral/, note: "The formerly dominant view that Hobbes espoused psychological egoism as the foundation of his moral theory is currently widely rejected."

37. Gert, "Hobbes's Psychology" (1996), 167. Hobbes, *Philosophicall Rudiments* (1651), 31 (*De Cive*, ch. 2, sec. 19); the text has "better," but this is a misprint: the Latin original has *vita sibi acerba*.

38. Sorell, *Hobbes* (1986), 97.

39. Hobbes, *Leviathan* (1651), 101 (pt. 2, ch. 19). Compare Mandeville, *The Fable of the Bees* (1723), 285–286: "What we do for our Friends and Kindred we do partly for our selves: When a Man acts in behalf of Nephews or Nieces, and says they are my Brother's Children, I do it out of Charity; he deceives you; for if he is capable, it is expected from him, and he does it partly for his own Sake: if he Values the Esteem of the World, and is nice as to Honour and Reputation, he is obliged to have a greater Regard for them than for Strangers, or else he must suffer in his Character."

40. Hobbes, *De mundo* (1976), ch. 38, sec. 16.

41. Sorell, *Hobbes* (1986), 97–98.

42. Hobbes, *Leviathan* (1651), 26 (pt. 1, ch. 6).

43. Hobbes, *Leviathan*, ed. Noel Malcolm, 3 vols. (Oxford: Clarendon, 2012), 2:85, 87.

44. Ibid., 1:185–186, 2:198–199.

45. For examples of the sort of interpretation that seems impossible to sustain in the light of the Latin text, see R. E. Ewin, *Virtues and Rights: The Moral*

Philosophy of Thomas Hobbes (Boulder, Colo.: Westview, 1991), 114–117; and David Van Mill, *Liberty, Rationality, and Agency in Hobbes's Leviathan* (Albany: State University of New York Press, 2001), 119–150.

46. Hume, *An Enquiry* (1751), 20–21.

47. Hobbes, *De mundo* (1976), ch. 38, sec. 5.

48. Ed Diener, Richard E. Lucas, and Christie Napa Scollon, "Beyond the Hedonic Treadmill: Revising the Adaptation Theory of Well-Being," *American Psychologist* 61 (2006), 305–314.

49. Hobbes, *Humane Nature* (1650), 39 (ch. 7, sec. 7). See also, in modern translation, Hobbes, *De mundo* (1976), ch. 38, sec. 7: "If happiness consisted in the pleasure of possession, but not in the pleasure of expectation, we would call no-one happy, because everyone despises what he possesses in comparison with what he would like to possess. It is therefore clear that [power] pleases only in relation to the gaining of delights not yet acquired, and that the pleasure derived from [power] . . . consists in the imagining . . . a benefit that has not yet been won . . . those born to riches or to civil power or to honour derive no more pleasure from these things than they derive . . . from possessing arms and feet."

50. *OED Online*, s.v. "sympathy," not updated since 1919.

51. Hobbes, *Leviathan* (1651), 27.

52. Thomas Hobbes, *Man and Citizen* (1972), translating Hobbes, *De homine* (1658), ch. 12, sec. 10.

53. *OED Online*, s.v. "fellow-feeling," updated September 2017.

54. Nehemiah Rogers, *The Good Samaritan; Or An Exposition on That Parable Luke X. Ver. XXX–XXXVIII* (London: Saubridge, 1658), 110.

55. Gert, "Hobbes and Psychological Egoism" (1967), 507.

56. Hobbes, *Leviathan* (1651), 86.

57. Hobbes, *Humane Nature* (1650), 58 (ch. 9, sec. 17).

58. François de La Rochefoucauld, *Moral Maxims and Reflections* (London: Gillyflower, Sare and Everingham, 1694), 70.

59. Pierre Nicole, *Moral Essays*, 3 vols (London: Magnes and Bentley, 1677–1680), 3:42; see also Ibbett, *Compassion's Edge* (2018), 76.

60. In a striking concession, Gert, who denies that Hobbes is a psychological egoist, admits that in Hobbes's view rational human beings would act like sophisticated psychological egoists: "Hobbes's view of rational behavior loosely resembles psychological egoism. He held what may be called 'rational egoism' viz., that the only rationally required desires are those that concern a person's own long-term benefit, primarily their preservation." Gert, "Hobbes's Psychology" (1996), 14. If Hobbes is a rational egoist, his moral philosophy must be grounded in rational egoism. Why, then, would he resist psychological egoism? The psychological egoist can, after all, happily acknowledge that much human behavior

is, in the long term, irrational while defending a rational egoism; but someone who rejects psychological egoism can scarcely hope to justify rational egoism.

61. Ryan Patrick Hanley, "The Eighteenth-Century Context of Sympathy from Spinoza to Kant," in *Sympathy: A History,* ed. Eric Schliesser (Oxford: Oxford University Press, 2015), 171–198. For supporting evidence, see Appendix D of the present volume.

62. On Shakespeare's likely familiarity with Lucretius, see Jonathan Gil Harris, "Atomic Shakespeare," *Shakespeare Studies* 30 (2002), 47–51; Stephen Greenblatt, *The Swerve: How the Renaissance Began* (London: Bodley Head, 2011), 242–243; and Adrian Streete, "Lucretius, Calvin, and Natural Law in Measure for Measure," in *Shakespeare and Early Modern Religion,* ed. David Loewenstein and Michael Witmore (Cambridge: Cambridge University Press, 2015), 131–154.

63. William Shakespeare, *The Tempest,* act 1, scene 2, lines 3–13, 27, in *The Complete Works,* ed. Stanley W. Wells and Gary Taylor (Oxford: Clarendon, 2005).

64. Keith Wrightson, "The Decline of Neighbourliness Revisited," in *Local Identities in Late Medieval and Early Modern England,* ed. Norman L. Jones and Daniel Woolf (Basingstoke, England: Palgrave Macmillan, 2007), 19–49.

65. Hume, *Treatise* (1739–1740), 2:193 (bk. 2, pt. 2, sec. 9).

66. Mandeville, *The Fable of the Bees* (1723), 287–288.

67. David Hume to James Macpherson, 1761, in David Hume, *The Letters of David Hume,* ed. J. Y. T. Greig, 2 vols. (Oxford: Clarendon, 1932), 1:343.

68. William Whately, *Prototypes, Or, the Primarie Precedent Presidents Ovt of the Booke of Genesis* (London: Edwards, 1640), 76.

69. Hobbes, *Philosophicall Rudiments* (1651), 3.

70. Hobbes, *Leviathan* (1651), 26.

71. See, for example, Michael Fried, *Absorption and Theatricality: Painting and Beholder in the Age of Diderot* (Berkeley: University of California Press, 1980).

72. See John Locke, *An Essay Concerning Humane Understanding* (London: Basset, 1690), 15–26 (bk. 1, ch. 3); contrast Mandeville, *The Fable of the Bees* (1723), 255–256 (remark T). Hume's position is, of course, nuanced; see Duncan Forbes, *Hume's Philosophical Politics* (Cambridge: Cambridge University Press, 1975), 107–108.

73. See also *OED Online,* s.v. "selfish," updated January 2018.

74. William Lucy, *Observations, Censures, and Confutations of Notorious Errours in Mr. Hobbes His Leviathan and Other His Bookes* (London: Brooke, 1663), 178.

75. Thomas Hobbes, *An Answer to a Book Published by Dr. Bramhall, Late Bishop of Derry; Called the Catching of the Leviathan* (London: Crooke, 1682), 5; Hobbes, *Leviathan* (1651), 79, 94, 143.

76. Nagel, "Hobbes's Concept of Obligation" (1959), 74.

77. Hobbes, *Philosophicall Rudiments* (1651), sig. A4r.
78. In Chapter 3 I discussed influence, and Quentin Skinner's early resistance to the very idea that one could identify one author as influencing another. One source of Skinner's hostility to the idea of influence was the frequently made claim that Hobbes had influenced Locke's political theory, a claim that Skinner's research supervisor, Peter Laslett, had forcefully (and mistakenly) rejected. See John Locke, *Two Treatises of Government: A Critical Edition,* ed. Peter Laslett (Cambridge: Cambridge University Press, 1960), x, xv, 21, 47, 67–91. Jon Parkin, *Taming the Leviathan: The Reception of the Political and Religious Ideas of Thomas Hobbes in England, 1640–1700* (Cambridge: Cambridge University Press, 2010), 397–402, discusses the charge of Hobbism levied against Locke by contemporaries and provides a valuable corrective to the Laslett view. But Parkin does not explore the relationship between their psychological views, nor does he study the reception of Hobbes's psychology in general.
79. Locke, *An Essay* (1690), 113 (bk. 2, ch. 20, sec. 5).
80. Locke, *An Essay Concerning Humane Understanding* (London: Awnsham and Churchill, 1694), 122 (bk. 2, ch. 20, sec. 6).
81. Locke's new account of motivation dovetails neatly with the account of consumer emulation (rather than utility or pleasure) as a "spur to humane industry" put forward by Nicholas Barbon and Dudley North (see Appendix A). Clothing as provoking emulation is discussed in *Some Thoughts Concerning Education,* so it is possible that a reading of Barbon and/or North played a part in Locke's change of mind. See also Hans Aarsleff, "The State of Nature and the Nature of Man in Locke," in *John Locke: Problems and Perspectives,* ed. John Yolton (Cambridge: Cambridge University Press, 1969), 99–136.
82. Locke, *An Essay* (1694), 135–136 (bk. 2, ch. 21, sec. 35).
83. Ibid., 136 (bk. 2, ch. 21, sec. 36).
84. Ibid., 140 (bk. 2, ch. 1, sec. 46).
85. David Fate Norton, "Shaftesbury and Two Scepticisms," *Filosofia* 19, supplement (1968), 713–724.

5. UTILITY: IN PLACE OF VIRTUE

1. Bernard Le Bovier de Fontenelle, "Du bonheur," in *Entretiens sur la pluralité des mondes* (Paris: Brunet, 1724), 386.
2. Adam Ferguson, *An Essay on the History of Civil Society* (Edinburgh: Millar and Caddel, 1767), 60.
3. Jean-François de Saint-Lambert, introduction to Claude Adrien Helvétius, *Le bonheur, poéme en six chants,* ed. Jean-François de Saint-Lambert (London: s.n., 1772), i.

4. Guillaume Dubois de Rochefort, *Histoire critique des opinions des anciens, et des systemes des philosophes, sur le bonheur* (Paris: Knapen, 1778), vii.

5. Paul Henri Thiry d'Holbach, *Le bon-sens ou idées naturelles opposées aux idées surnaturelles* (London: s.n., 1772), x. That, since human beings necessarily pursue happiness, failure to attain it must be due to error or ignorance had been maintained in Elie Luzac, *Le bonheur ou nouveau systeme de jurisprudence naturelle* (Berlin: s.n., 1753), 90.

6. Based on Google Ngrams (https://books.google.com/ngrams), with upper- and lower-case words added together.

7. Elie Luzac, *L'homme plus que machine* (London: s.n., 1748), sigs. *r–*2v, was happy to defend determinism, but not materialism: he acknowledged that some might regard all determinists as mechanists, but thought the terms should not be regarded as synonymous. Luzac, in his role as printer and publisher, had produced the first edition of Julien Offray de La Mettrie's scandalous *L'homme machine* (1747).

8. John Maxwell, "Of the Imperfectness of the Heathen Morality," in Richard Cumberland, *A Treatise of the Laws of Nature,* trans. John Maxwell (London: Knapton, 1727), lv.

9. On Hobbes's premechanist materialism, see Samantha Frost, *Lessons from a Materialist Thinker: Hobbesian Reflections on Ethics and Politics* (Stanford, Calif.: Stanford University Press, 2008).

10. John Locke, *An Essay Concerning Humane Understanding* (London: Basset, 1690), 125.

11. Ibid., 126.

12. Voltaire, *Questions sur l'Encyclopédie* (Geneva: Cramer, 1770), pt. 3, 86 ("Souverain Bien"); the text is altered from that of Voltaire, *Dictionnaire philosophique, portatif* (London: s.n., 1764), 49. The translation is my own, based on Voltaire, *A Philosophical Dictionary,* 6 vols. (London: Hunt, 1824), 3:354.

13. Pierre Bayle, *Projet et fragmens d'un dictionnaire critique* (Rotterdam: Leers, 1692); Pierre Bayle, *Progetto di un dizionario critico,* ed. Lorenzo Bianchi (Naples: Bibliopolis, 1987).

14. Bayle appears to have an unacknowledged (and unacknowledgeable) source for "Xenophanes" (as was pointed out by the editors of the edition of 1820–1824; see Bayle, *Political Writings,* ed. Sally Jenkinson [Cambridge: Cambridge University Press, 1999], 292), for Vanini attributed the same basic argument to an anonymous atheist in Amsterdam. See Giulio Cesare Vanini, *Oeuvres philosophiques,* trans. X. Rousselot (Paris: Gosselin, 1842), 271–272, translating Vanini, *De admirandis naturae reginae deaeque mortalium arcanis* (Paris: Perier, 1616), 420–421.

15. Gottfried Wilhelm Leibniz, *Essais de théodicée sur la bonté de dieu, la liberté de l'homme et l'origine du mal* (Amsterdam: Troyel, 1710). John Milton, in *Paradise Lost,* 1.26, had already sought to "justify the ways of God to men."

16. Pierre Bayle, *An Historical and Critical Dictionary,* 4 vols. (London: Harper, 1710), 4:3052.

17. In the French, *inquiétude;* see Pierre Bayle, *Dictionaire historique et critique,* 2 vols. (Rotterdam: Leers, 1697), vol. 2, pt. 2, 1256; Pierre Bayle, *Dictionaire historique et critique,* 3 vols. (Rotterdam: Leers, 1702), 3:3041. For this as a translation of Locke's "uneasiness," see John Locke, *Essai philosophique concernant l'entendement humain,* trans. P. Coste (Amsterdam: s.n., 1700), 267. The review of Coste's translation in the *Nouvelles de la République des lettres* (August 1700) stressed the importance of the additions in the second English edition of Locke's *Essay.* Bayle had a high opinion of Locke before 1700, but presumably, as he did not read English, he relied on reviews of the first edition in French and on Locke's own account of his argument in *Bibliothèque Universelle et Historique* 8 (1688) 49–142; it seems unlikely that he would have had knowledge of the revisions in the second English edition before the publication of Coste's translation. But both Locke and Bayle were probably drawing, independently, on Pascal's use of *inquiétude:* see Paul Rahe, *Soft Despotism, Democracy's Drift: Montesquieu, Rousseau, Tocqueville, and the Modern Prospect* (New Haven, Conn.: Yale University Press, 2010), 40–41.

18. Bayle, *An Historical and Critical Dictionary* (1710), 4:3053.

19. William Wollaston, *The Religion of Nature Delineated* (s.l.: s.n., 1722), 27.

20. Cumberland, *Treatise* (1727), ch. 5. Cumberland had previously been available in English in an authorized summary; see James Tyrrell and Richard Cumberland, *A Brief Disquisition of the Law of Nature* (London: Baldwin, 1692), 104–110. He had also been adapted in Samuel Parker, *A Demonstration of the Divine Authority of the Law of Nature and of the Christian Religion* (London: Royston, 1681). There is a striking critique of Cumberland in Maxwell's appendix to the 1727 edition: "The *Law of Nature,* according to this Scheme of it, is an Institution of mere publick *Self-convenience* as the End, and of mere publick *Self-convenience* as the *Means*" (45). And, "This Scheme of the Law of Nature, and its Definition of Good, introduceth an Institution of Morality, not truly moral, but merely politick and prudential" (47). That is, it makes morality indistinguishable from public and personal self-interest.

21. Cumberland, *Treatise* (1727), 189–190; John Gay, "Preliminary Discourse," in William King, *An Essay on the Origin of Evil* (Cambridge: Thurlbourn, 1731), xviii.

22. Gay, "Preliminary Discourse" (1731), xxiii–xxxiii.

23. Louis-Jean Levesque de Pouilly, *Théorie des sentimens agréables* (Geneva: Barrillot, 1747); Louis-Jean Levesque de Pouilly, *The Theory of Agreeable Sensations*, trans. Jacob Vernet (London: Owen, 1749), 219, 93. Unauthorized editions, under the title *Réflexions sur les sentimens agréables*, had appeared in 1736 and 1743.

24. Adam Smith, *The Theory of Moral Sentiments*, 2 vols. (London: Strahan, 1790), 2:117–118. For Smith on Levesque de Pouilly, see Adam Smith, *Essays on Philosophical Subjects*, ed. W. P. D. Wightman, J. C. Bryce, and I. S. Ross (Oxford: Oxford University Press, 1980), 250 (the text is originally from 1755).

25. Saint-Lambert, introduction to Helvétius, *Le bonheur* (1772), iii.

26. Pierre-Louis Moreau de Maupertuis, *Essai de philosophie morale* (Berlin: s.n., 1749).

27. Bentham first uses the phrase "principle of utility" in *A Fragment,* but it was not new with him. It occurs over and over again in Henry Home, Lord Kames's *Principle of Equity* (1760). In the same year in which Hume first uses it (1753) we find Hume's "great principle of utility" attacked: "Utility is his favourite and capital principle, to which he reduces all the several branches of morals." Anonymous, *Some Late Opinions Concerning the Foundation of Morality Examined* (London: Dodsley and Cooper, 1753), 33, 13. On proto-utilitarianism, see Robert Shackleton, "The Greatest Happiness of the Greatest Number: The History of Bentham's Phrase," *Studies on Voltaire and the Eighteenth Century* 90 (1972), 1461–1482; James H. Burns, "Happiness and Utility: Jeremy Bentham's Equation," *Utilitas* 17 (2005), 46–61; Colin Heydt, "Utilitarianism before Bentham," in *The Cambridge Companion to Utilitarianism*, ed. Ben Eggleston and Dale E. Miller (Cambridge: Cambridge University Press, 2014), 16–37; Frederick Rosen, *Classical Utilitarianism from Hume to Mill* (London: Routledge, 2015); and Joseph Persky, *The Political Economy of Progress: John Stuart Mill and Modern Radicalism* (Oxford: Oxford University Press, 2016), 26–41. As Voltaire, *Voltaire's Notebooks*, ed. Theodore Besterman, 2 vols. (Geneva: Institut et Musée Voltaire, 1952), 2:383, 442, notes, "La vertu est ce qui est utile à la société: le vice au contraire." The question of whether Hume is properly described as a "utilitarian" (a term Bentham first used in 1781) is a separate one; see Massimo Reichlin, "Hume and Utilitarianism: Another Look at An Age-Old Question," *Journal of Scottish Philosophy* 14 (2016), 1–20.

28. Voltaire, *Candide and Related Texts*, ed. and trans. D. Wootton (Indianapolis: Hackett, 2000); David Wootton, "Unhappy Voltaire, or 'I Shall Never Get Over It as Long as I Live,'" *History Workshop Journal* 50 (2000), 137–155.

29. Voltaire, "Heureux," in *Encyclopédie, ou dictionnaire raisonné des sciences, des arts et des métiers*, ed. Denis Diderot and Jean le Rond d'Alembert, 17 vols. (Paris: Briasson, 1751–1777), vol. 8 (1765), 195.

30. Voltaire, *Dictionnaire philosophique, portatif* (1764), 53–60; Voltaire, *Oeuvres complètes de Voltaire,* ed. Jacques Joseph Marie Decroix, 70 vols. (Kehl, Germany: De l'imprimerie de la Société littéraire-typographique, 1784–1785), 38:279.

31. Saint-Lambert, introduction to Helvétius, *Le bonheur* (1772), iv.

32. Maupertuis, *Essai* (1749), 16–18; Verri, *Meditazioni* (1763), 29–30.

33. Ferguson, *An Essay on the History of Civil Society* (1767), 61, 77, 80.

34. Ibid., 77, 82.

35. Ibid., 65. Ferguson's views may usefully be compared with those of Gabriel Bonnot de Mably; see Johnson Kent Wright, *A Classical Republican in Eighteenth-Century France: The Political Thought of Mably* (Stanford, Calif.: Stanford University Press, 1997). For a helpful comparison and contrast between Ferguson, Hume, and Smith, see Lisa Hill and Peter McCarthy, "Hume, Smith and Ferguson: Friendship in Commercial Society," *Critical Review of International Social and Political Philosophy* 2 (1999), 33–49.

36. *The Kings Maiesties Answer to the Petition of the House of Commons Sent on Saturday Last, the Nine and Twentieth of This Instant Jan. 1642* (broadsheet) (London: FCIW, 1642).

37. David Scott Kastan, *A Will to Believe: Shakespeare and Religion* (Oxford: Oxford University Press, 2014), 3.

38. John Tillotson, *Sermons Preach'd Upon Several Occasions* (London: Gellibrand, 1671), 147. The term *felicitas publica* appears on Roman imperial coins.

39. Benjamin Hoadly, *A Sermon Preach'd Before the Right Honourable the Lord-Mayor* (London: Childe, 1705), 7, 8, 9, 11.

40. Adam Smith, *The Theory of Moral Sentiments* (London: Millar, 1759), 352.

41. Jean-Jacques Burlamaqui, *Principes du droit politique,* 2 vols. (Amsterdam: Chatelain, 1751).

42. Louis de Jaucourt, "Gouvernement," in Diderot and d'Alembert, *Encyclopédie* (1751–1777), vol. 7 (1757), 790. Similar views (without any reference to virtue) are expressed in André Morellet, *Réfutation de l'ouvrage qui a pour titre Dialogues sur le commerce des bleds* (London: s.n., 1770), 57–62.

43. Denis Diderot, "Epicuréisme," in Diderot and d'Alembert, *Encyclopédie* (1751–1777), vol. 5 (1755), 784.

44. Louis-Antoine-Léon Saint-Just, *Rapport sur le mode d'exécution du décret contre les ennemis de la révolution* ([Paris]: Imprimerie nationale, 1794).

45. Louis-Antoine-Léon Saint-Just, *Rapport sur les factions de l'étranger* (Laval, France: Dariot, 1794), 14.

46. Claude Adrien Helvétius, *De l'esprit* (Paris: Durand, 1758), 411. On Helvétius, see David Wootton, "Helvétius: From Radical Enlightenment to Revolution," *Political Theory* 28 (2000), 307–336.

47. The lazy censor was Jean Pierre Tercier; see D. W. Smith, "The Publication of Helvétius's *De l'esprit* (1758–59)," *French Studies* 18 (1964), 333–334; Raymond Birn, *Royal Censorship of Books in Eighteenth-Century France* (Stanford, Calif.: Stanford University Press, 2012), 28–32.

48. This was translated into English in 1774; an expanded version appeared in French in 1776, and was translated into English in 1792 under the title *Agriculture and Population: The Truest Proofs of The Welfare of The People.*

49. *Pace* Werner Stark, "A Forerunner of Marxism: François-Jean De Chastellux," *Economica* 8 (1941), 203–207.

50. François Jean Chastellux, *De la félicité publique* (Paris: Renouard, 1822), 27.

51. This is a view also presented in Pierre-Paul Le Mercier de La Rivière, *L'ordre naturel et essentiel des sociétés politiques,* 2 vols. (London: Nourse, 1767), 1:42–43: "La multiplication & le bonheur des hommes sont deux objets tellement enchaînés l'un à l'autre dans le systéme de la nature qu'il n'est sur la terre aucune puissance qui ait le pouvoir de les séparer. Humainement parlant, le plus grand bonheur possible consiste pour nous *dans la plus grande abondance possible d'objets propres à nos jouissances, & dans la plus grande liberté possible d'en profiter.*"

52. Saint-Lambert, introduction to Helvétius, *Le bonheur* (1772), iii–iv.

53. On du Châtelet's translation of Mandeville, see Felicia Gottmann, "Du Châtelet, Voltaire, and the Transformation of Mandeville's Fable," *History of European Ideas* 38 (2012), 218–232.

54. Emilie du Châtelet, *Selected Philosophical and Scientific Writings,* ed. Judith P. Zinsser (Chicago: University of Chicago Press, 2009), 349, 355.

55. Ibid., 358–359.

56. Nicholas Cronk, *Voltaire: A Very Short Introduction* (Oxford: Oxford University Press, 2017), 61.

57. Du Châtelet, *Selected Writings* (2009), 360, 362.

58. Keith Thomas, *The Ends of Life: Roads to Fulfilment in Early Modern England* (Oxford: Oxford University Press, 2009), 8–43.

59. Judith P. Zinsser, *La dame d'esprit: A Biography of the Marquise du Châtelet* (New York: Viking, 2006), 25.

6. THE STATE: CHECKS AND BALANCES

1. I use 2013 figures from "List of Countries by Public Sector," Wikipedia, https://en.wikipedia.org/wiki/List_of_countries_by_public_sector.

2. "UK National Debt," Wikipedia, https://commons.wikimedia.org/wiki/File:UK_GDP.png; "What Is the Total National Debt?," Usgovernmentspending.com, http://www.usgovernmentspending.com/us_national_debt_chart.html. The

key study of the growth of the state is John Brewer, *The Sinews of Power: War, Money, and the English State, 1688–1783* (New York: Knopf, 1989).

3. David Hume, "Of Public Credit," in *Essays and Treatises on Several Subjects*, 2 vols. (London: Millar, 1764), 1:394; David Hume, *The History of England: From the Invasion of Julius Cæsar to the Revolution in 1688*, 8 vols. (London: Cadell, 1778), 5:475. See also John Christian Laursen and Greg Coolidge, "David Hume and Public Debt: Crying Wolf?," *Hume Studies* 20 (1994), 143–149; and Istvan Hont, "The Rhapsody of Public Debt: David Hume and Voluntary State Bankruptcy," in *Jealousy of Trade: International Competition and the Nation State in Historical Perspective* (Cambridge, Mass.: Harvard University Press, 2005), 325–353.

4. Peer H. H. Vries, *State, Economy and the Great Divergence: Great Britain and China, 1680s–1850s* (London: Bloomsbury Academic, 2015), 72–73. Peer Vries, "Public Finance in China and Britain in the Long Eighteenth Century" (working paper, Department of Economic History, London School of Economics, 2012) is a helpful survey. For inflation in this period, see Elizabeth W. Gilboy, "The Cost of Living and Real Wages in Eighteenth Century England," *Review of Economic Statistics* 18 (1936), 134–143.

5. Vries, *State, Economy and the Great Divergence* (2015), 186.

6. Ibid., 100; Tom Clark and Andrew Dilnot, *Long-Term Trends in British Taxation and Spending*, Institute for Fiscal Studies Briefing Note 25, 2002, https://www.ifs.org.uk/bns/bn25.pdf; "OECD.Stat" (database), Organisation for Economic Co-operation and Development, http://stats.oecd.org/Index.aspx ?DataSetCode=REV; "Hauser's Law," Wikipedia, https://en.wikipedia.org /wiki/Hauser%27s_law.

7. Benedict Anderson, *Imagined Communities: Reflections on the Origin and Spread of Nationalism* (London: Verso, 1983); Linda Colley, *Britons: Forging the Nation, 1707–1837* (New Haven, Conn.: Yale University Press, 1992).

8. David Hume, "Of Public Credit," in *Political Discourses* (Edinburgh: Kincaid and Donaldson, 1752), 132.

9. Geoffrey S. Holmes, "Gregory King and the Social Structure of Pre-industrial England," *Transactions of the Royal Historical Society*, 5th ser., 27 (1977), 41–68.

10. See, for example, Isaac de Pinto, *Traité de la circulation et du crédit, contenant une analyse raisonnée des Fonds d'Angleterre* (Amsterdam: Rey, 1771), which was translated into English in 1774 (Smith owned a copy). On credit in this period, see Craig Muldrew, *The Economy of Obligation: The Culture of Credit and Social Relations in Early Modern England* (New York: St. Martin's, 1998); and Carl Wennerlind, *Casualties of Credit: The English Financial Revolution, 1620–1720* (Cambridge, Mass.: Harvard University Press, 2011).

11. David Hume, "That Politics May Be Reduc'd to a Science," in *Essays, Moral and Political,* 2 vols. (Edinburgh: Kincaid, 1741–1742), 1:27–48.

12. It is often said that Hobbes, in the opening paragraph of *Leviathan,* compares the state to an automaton such as a clock; this is not true. Hobbes argues the state is an artificial person, and, for all his materialism, he does not think that people (or states) are automata. The context of this passage is, of course, the Cartesian claim that animals (but not people) are automata. See Samantha Frost, *Lessons from a Materialist Thinker: Hobbesian Reflections on Ethics and Politics* (Stanford, Calif.: Stanford University Press, 2008), 21–23, 177n24; Bernard Gert, "Hobbes and Psychological Egoism," *Journal of the History of Ideas* 28 (1967), 504.

13. *The Founders' Constitution,* ed. Philip B. Kurland and Ralph Lerner, 5 vols. (Chicago: University of Chicago Press, 1987), 1:394.

14. Montesquieu, *The Spirit of Laws,* trans. T. Nugent, 2 vols. (London: Nourse and Vaillant, 1750), 1:36.

15. James Madison, *James Madison's Notes of Debates in the Federal Convention of 1787 and Their Relation to a More Perfect Society of Nations.,* ed. James Brown Scott (New York: Oxford University Press, 1918), 99, 106.

16. Adam Smith, "The History of Astronomy," in *Essays on Philosophical Subjects,* ed. Joseph Black, James Hutton, and Dugald Stewart (London: Cadell and Davies, 1795), 44–45.

17. David Hume, "Of the Balance of Trade," in *Political Discourses* (1752), 79–100; David Hume, "The Parties of Great-Britain," in *Essays* (1741–1742), 1:121.

18. Anne-Robert-Jacques Turgot to David Hume, 1767, in David Hume, *Writings on Economics,* ed. Eugene Rotwein (Madison: University of Wisconsin Press, 1970), 211–212. For Turgot's economic theory, see Anne-Robert-Jacques Turgot, "Reflections on the Formation and the Distribution of Wealth," in *Turgot on Progress, Sociology and Economics,* ed. Ronald L. Meek (Cambridge: Cambridge University Press, 2010), 119–182.

19. Benjamin Constant, "On Ancient and Modern Liberty," in *Modern Political Thought: Readings from Machiavelli to Nietzsche,* ed. David Wootton (Indianapolis: Hackett, 2008), 558–569 (my translation).

20. David Hume, "Of the Independency of Parliament," in *Essays* (1741–1742), 1:79–92.

21. John Adams, *A Defence of the Constitutions of Government of the United States of America,* 3 vols. (London: Dilly, 1787–1788), 3:291; *Federalist No. 55, Independent Journal,* 13 February 1788.

22. Garry Wills, *Explaining America: The Federalist* (Garden City, N.Y.: Doubleday, 1980). See also David Wootton, introduction to *The Essential Federalist and*

Anti-Federalist Papers, ed. David Wootton (Indianapolis: Hackett, 2003), ix–xxxix.

23. Walter Bagehot, *The English Constitution* (London: Chapman and Hall, 1867), 11–12.

24. Government of the United Kingdom, The Data Retention Regulations 2014, https://www.legislation.gov.uk/ukdsi/2014/9780111118894; Government of the United Kingdom, The Investigatory Powers Act 2016, http://www.legislation.gov.uk/ukpga/2016/25/contents/enacted/data.htm.

25. David Hume, "Of the Independency of Parliament," in *Essays* (1741–1742), 1:84–85.

26. David Hume, "Of Some Remarkable Customs," in *Political Discourses* (1752), 154.

27. The phrase "checks and balances" is already found in Joseph Galloway, *Historical and Political Reflections on the Rise and Progress of the American Rebellion* (London: Wilkie, 1780), 32, and (the text is identical) in Galloway, *Reflections on the Rise and Progress of the American Rebellion* (London: Paramore, 1780), 24. This is perhaps the source for Adams, *A Defence of the Constitutions* (1787–1788), 1:1 (where the phrase keeps recurring). For an earlier discussion of this topic, see David Wootton, "Liberty, Metaphor, and Mechanism: Checks and Balances and the Origins of Modern Constitutionalism," in *Liberty and American Experience in the Eighteenth Century,* ed. David Womersley (Indianapolis: Liberty Fund, 2006), 209–274.

28. *The Spectator,* ed. Joseph Addison and R. Steele, 8 vols. (London: Buckley and Tonson, 1712–1715), 7:235 ("check and bridle"); Marchamont Nedham, *Interest Will Not Lie: Or, a View of England's True Interest* (London: Newcomb, 1659), 24 ("check and curb"). Another common phrase is "clog the Wheels of Government"; see Charles Davenant, *Essays Upon Peace at Home and War Abroad* (London: Knapton, 1704), 113 (the wheels here being the wheels of a cart or coach, not a clock).

29. Jonathan Swift, *A Discourse of the Contests and Dissensions Between the Nobles and the Commons in Athens and Rome* (London: Nutt, 1701), 5–6.

30. James Harrington, *The Common-Wealth of Oceana* (London: Chapman, 1656), 20 ("libration"); 4 ("overballance"); Montesquieu, *Persian Letters,* trans. J. Ozell, 2 vols. (London: Tonson, 1722), 2:100.

31. Charles I, *His Majesties Answer to the XIX Propositions of Both Houses of Parliament* (London: Barker and the Assignes of John Bill, 1642), 18 (ed. of 30 pages); Thomas Fairfax, *A Declaration of His Excellency Sir Thomas Fairfax, and His Councell of Warre* (London: Whittington, 1647), 5.

32. John Trenchard, *An Argument Shewing That a Standing Army Is Inconsistent with a Free Government* (London: s.n., 1697), 4.

33. Thomas Hobbes, *Leviathan, Or, the Matter, Forme, and Power of a Common Wealth, Ecclesiasticall and Civil* (London: Crooke, 1651), 96.

34. See Niccolò Machiavelli, *Discourses on Livy*, bk. 1, ch. 3, in Niccolò Machiavelli, *The Chief Works and Others*, trans. and ed. Allan H. Gilbert, 3 vols. (Durham, N.C.: Duke University Press, 1989), 1:201–202; Niccolò Machiavelli, *History of Florence*, bk. 7, ch. 1, in Machiavelli, *Chief Works* (1989), 3:1336–1337.

35. John Trenchard, *A Short History of Standing Armies in England* (London: s.n., 1698), iii–iv; the same can be found, with slightly different wording, in Trenchard, *Free Thoughts Concerning Officers in the House of Commons* (London: s.n., 1698), 1–2.

36. See Clifford Siskin, *System: The Shaping of Modern Knowledge* (Cambridge Mass.: MIT Press, 2016).

37. David Wootton, *The Invention of Science: A New History of the Scientific Revolution* (New York: Harper, 2015), 431–448; Walter Charleton, *Physiologia Epicuro-Gassendo-Charletoniana, or A Fabrick of Science Natural Upon the Hypothesis of Atoms* (London: Heath, 1654), 30; Ralph Cudworth, *The True Intellectual System of the Universe: The First Part, Wherein, All the Reason and Philosophy of Atheism Is Confuted and Its Impossibility Demonstrated* (London: Royston, 1678).

38. Joseph Butler, *Fifteen Sermons Preached at the Rolls Chapel* (London: Knapton, 1729), ix (a passage which does not appear in the edition of 1726).

39. David Hume, *Dialogues Concerning Natural Religion* (s.l.: s.n., 1779), 17.

40. Henry St. John Bolingbroke, *A Dissertation Upon Parties* (London: Haines, 1735), 108, 137, 103.

41. *Federalist No. 51*, *Independent Journal*, 6 February 1788.

42. Edward Spelman, introduction to Polybius, *A Fragment Out of the Sixth Book of Polybius: Containing a Dissertation Upon Government in General, Particularly Applied to That of the Romans*, ed. Edward Spelman (London: Bettenham, 1743), v, vi, viii.

43. Jean-Louis de Lolme, *The Constitution of England: Or An Account of the English Government* (London: Kearsley, 1775), 240–41.

44. Jean-Louis de Lolme, *The Constitution of England, or An Account of the English Government* (London: Robinson and Murray, 1784), 444.

7. PROFIT: THE INVISIBLE HAND

1. Adam Smith, *The Theory of Moral Sentiments* (London: Millar, 1759), 348–351. For a discussion of this and the immediately preceding passage, and the difficulties they present for attempts to read Smith as a virtue ethicist (as in Ryan Patrick Hanley, *Adam Smith and the Character of Virtue* [New York: Cambridge

University Press, 2009]), see Lisa Hill, "'The Poor Man's Son' and the Corruption of Our Moral Sentiments: Commerce, Virtue and Happiness in Adam Smith," *Journal of Scottish Philosophy* 15 (2017), 9–25.

2. My first point rejects the argument of Emma Rothschild, "Adam Smith and the Invisible Hand," *American Economic Review* 84 (1994), 319–322. My second point adopts the arguments of Lisa Hill, "The Hidden Theology of Adam Smith," *European Journal of the History of Economic Thought* 8 (2001), 1–29; and Peter Harrison, "Adam Smith and the History of the Invisible Hand," *Journal of the History of Ideas* 72 (2011), 29–49. My third point approves the approach of Jonathan Sheehan and Dror Wahrman, *Invisible Hands: Self-Organization and the Eighteenth·Century* (Chicago: University of Chicago Press, 2015). On Smith's natural theology, see Paul Oslington, ed., *Adam Smith as Theologian* (London: Routledge, 2011). Nicholas Phillipson, *Adam Smith: An Enlightened Life* (New Haven, Conn.: Yale University Press, 2010), presents Smith as holding the same views on religion as Hume (244), but Smith happily lectured on natural theology (132–133). Smith was a lifelong admirer of Voltaire (58, 190), and Voltaire always presented himself as a deist, not an atheist. On Voltaire's religion, René Pomeau, *La religion de Voltaire* (Paris: Nizet, 1956). Smith's account of the happiness of mankind may be compared with that of Voltaire in *De l'égalité des conditions* (1738; translated into English in two separate editions the same year), which maintains that God has made the world such that everyone has an equal opportunity to attain happiness. (Voltaire changed his mind in light of the Lisbon earthquake of 1755; Smith evidently did not.) See also, on the happiness of the poor, Jacques Necker, *On the Legislation and the Commerce of Corn* (London: Longman, 1776), 32–33.

3. David Wootton, *The Invention of Science: A New History of the Scientific Revolution* (New York: Harper, 2015), 544–554. See also Francis Fallon, "One Damned Thing before Another," *International Journal of Philosophical Studies* 26 (2018), 90–105.

4. *Oxford English Dictionary (OED) Online*, http://www.oed.com, s.v. "economy," updated June 2008. "Our national economy": Jonas Hanway, *Proposal for County Naval Free-Schools* (n.l.: n.p., [1783]), appendix, 42. Cantillon (posthumous, 1755) uses "this economy," and at least on one or two occasions the term seems to be used in the modern sense; from Cantillon's French it is translated into English in Postlethwayt's *Universal Dictionary* (1752–1754); see Richard Cantillon, *Richard Cantillon's Essay on the Nature of Trade in General: A Variorum Edition*, ed. Richard van den Berg (Abingdon, England: Routledge, 2015), 99. For later developments, see Margaret Schabas, *The Natural Origins of Economics* (Chicago: University of Chicago Press, 2005), 1–4. *OED Online*, updated June 2008, gives "economics" unaccompanied by the adjective "rural" as

dating to 1839. But note Edmund Burke, *Thoughts and Details on Scarcity Originally Presented to the Right Hon. William Pitt in the Month of November 1795* (London: Rivington and Hatchard, 1800), vi (where "rural" may be implied).

5. David Hume, "Of Liberty and Despotism" (later revised and retitled "Of Civil Liberty"), in *Essays, Moral and Political*, 2 vols. (Edinburgh: Kincaid, 1741–1742), 1:175.

6. Ernest Campbell Mossner, "Hume's Early Memoranda, 1729–1740: The Complete Text," *Journal of the History of Ideas* 9 (1948), 508; Hume was echoing Nicholas Barbon, writing in 1690; see Istvan Hont, *Jealousy of Trade: International Competition and the Nation-State in Historical Perspective* (Cambridge, Mass.: Harvard University Press, 2005), 8–9. On the reading of Machiavelli's *Discourses on Livy*, 1.37, proposed in Chapter 1 of the present volume, Machiavelli does have something, at least implicitly, to say about trade. On the emergence of a link between commerce and political power, see Andrew Fitzmaurice, "The Commercial Ideology of Colonization in Jacobean England: Robert Johnson, Giovanni Botero, and the Pursuit of Greatness," *William and Mary Quarterly* 64 (2007), 791–820.

7. Moses I. Finley, "Aristotle and Economic Analysis," *Past and Present* 47 (1970), 3–25. I think Finley was basically right to claim that there was no ancient Greek economic theory, although I realize views differ on this matter. For example, Scott Meikle, *Aristotle's Economic Thought* (Oxford: Clarendon, 1995) argues that Aristotle had an economic theory, but one fundamentally unlike ours.

8. Niccolò Machiavelli to Francesco Vettori, 9 April 1513, in Niccolò Machiavelli, *The Portable Machiavelli,* ed. and trans. Peter Bondanella and Mark Musa (Harmondsworth, England: Penguin, 1979), 65.

9. On the 1620s, see Paul Slack, "The Politics of English Political Economy in the 1620s," in *Popular Culture and Political Agency in Early Modern England and Ireland: Essays in Honour of John Walter,* ed. Michael J. Braddick and Phil Withington (Woodbridge, England: Boydell, 2017), 55–72.

10. Wootton, *The Invention of Science* (2015), 200.

11. Ibid., 164.

12. Cantillon, *Essay on the Nature of Trade . . . Variorum Edition* (2015), 77, 227.

13. David Hume, "Of Public Credit," in *Political Discourses* (Edinburgh: Kincaid and Donaldson, 1752), 126–127. Hume doubted that the term had any meaning when used in the context of the national debt.

14. Adam Smith, *An Inquiry into the Nature and Causes of the Wealth of Nations,* 2 vols. (London: Strahan and Cadell, 1776), 2:209.

15. S. Todd Lowry, "The Archaeology of the Circulation Concept in Economic Theory," *Journal of the History of Ideas* 35 (1974), 429–444.

16. Thomas Hobbes, *Leviathan, Or, the Matter, Forme, and Power of a Common Wealth, Ecclesiasticall and Civil* (London: Crooke, 1651), 130; William Petty, *A Treatise of Taxes and Contributions* (London: Brooke, 1662), 11. The same (though here the word "circulation" appears) may be true of T. L., *Animadversions on Two Late Books* (London: Hensman, 1673), 6.

17. Joseph Hill, *The Interest of These United Provinces* (Middelburg, England: Berry, 1673), fol. F2r.

18. Richard Haines, *The Prevention of Poverty* (London: Brooke, 1674), 3–4.

19. Slingsby Bethel, *An Account of the French Usurpation Upon the Trade of England* (London: s.n., 1679), 13; Gilbert Burnet, *The History of the Reformation of the Church of England. The First Part* (London: Chiswell, 1679), 3; Anonymous, *Popery and Tyranny: Or the Present State of France in Relation to Its Government, Trade, Manners of the People, and Nature of the Countrey* (London: s.n., 1679), 11.

20. Nicholas Barbon, *An Apology for the Builder* (London: Cave Pullen, 1685), 30.

21. Bethel, *French Usurpation* (1679), 3.

22. For the original, see "Systême figuré des connoissances humaines," in *Encyclopédie, ou dictionnaire raisonné des sciences, des arts et des métiers,* ed. Denis Diderot and Jean le Rond d'Alembert, The ARTFL Encyclopédie, http://encyclopedie.uchicago.edu/content/systême-figuré-des-connaissances-humaines-0. For a 1780 elaboration, see Manuel Lima, *The Book of Trees: Visualizing Branches of Knowledge* (New York: Princeton Architectural Press, 2014), 65.

23. Clifford Siskin, *System: The Shaping of Modern Knowledge* (Cambridge Mass.: MIT Press, 2016).

24. James H. Burns, "Bolingbroke and the Concept of Constitutional Government," *Political Studies* 10 (1962), 264–276. *OED Online,* first published 1893, gives Bolingbroke in 1735 as the first clear usage of "constitution" to mean "the system or body of fundamental principles according to which a nation, state, or body politic is constituted and governed" (as opposed to earlier usages, to refer, for example, to monarchy or aristocracy). Graham Maddox, "Constitution," in *Political Innovation and Conceptual Change,* ed. Terence Ball, James Farr, and Russell L. Hanson (Cambridge: Cambridge University Press, 1989), 59, finds it in Locke in 1703. But it appears to be widely used at the time of the Putney Debates; see, for example, Andrew Sharp, *The English Levellers* (Cambridge: Cambridge University Press, 1998), 33, 102, 104, 105, 108, 109, 110, 114, 115, 117, 120, 121, 122, 123, 129. It is important to note the remark in John Greville Agard Pocock, *The Ancient Constitution and the Feudal Law* (Cambridge: Cambridge University Press, 1987), 261: "It may be conceded here [in the reissue of a book first published in 1957] that the term 'constitution,' as used throughout this book, has not been systematically cleared of anachronism." "Ancient constitu-

tion," I might add, is originally used in an ecclesiastical context; the phrase "the ancient constitution of the kingdom" does not predate the English Civil War. On the absence of a concept of "constitution" (in the modern sense) before the Civil War, see John Humphreys Whitfield, *Discourses on Machiavelli* (Cambridge: Heffer, 1969), 141–162; and Glenn Burgess, *Absolute Monarchy and the Stuart Constitution* (New Haven, Conn.: Yale University Press, 1996), 127–164.

25. Adam Smith, "The History of Astronomy," in *Essays on Philosophical Subjects,* ed. Joseph Black, James Hutton, and Dugald Stewart (London: Cadell and Davies, 1795), 3–93.

26. Smith, *The Wealth of Nations* (1776), 2:125.

27. David Wootton, "Liberty, Metaphor, and Mechanism: Checks and Balances and the Origins of Modern Constitutionalism," in *Liberty and American Experience in the Eighteenth Century,* ed. David Womersley (Indianapolis: Liberty Fund, 2006), 209–274.

28. Smith, *The Wealth of Nations* (1776), 2:257. On checks and controls, see, for example, David Hume, "Of the Independency of Parliament," in *Essays* (1741–1742), 1:84.

29. David Hume "Of the Balance of Trade," in *Political Discourses* (1752), 79–100.

30. Cantillon, *Essay on the Nature of Trade . . . Variorum Edition* (2015), 202–203. Bert Tieben, *The Concept of Equilibrium in Different Economic Traditions: An Historical Investigation* (Cheltenham, England: Elgar, 2012), 96–122, discusses the concept (but not the word) "equilibrium" in Dudley North, and both the word and the concept in Pierre de Boisguilbert.

31. Smith, *The Wealth of Nations* (1776), 1:17.

32. Jacob Viner, *Religious Thought and Economic Society: Four Chapters of an Unfinished Work,* ed. Jacques Melitz and Donald Winch (Durham, N.C.: Duke University Press, 1978), 131–140; David Wootton, introduction to *Divine Right and Democracy: An Anthology of Political Writing in Stuart England,* ed. David Wootton (Harmondsworth, England: Penguin, 1986), 74–75; Jacob Viner, *Essays in the Intellectual History of Economics,* ed. Douglas A. Irwin (Princeton, N.J.: Princeton University Press, 1991), 180–181, 185–188; Pierre Force, *Self-Interest before Adam Smith: A Genealogy of Economic Science* (Cambridge: Cambridge University Press, 2003), 76–78; Hont, *Jealousy of Trade* (2005), 46–51. For examples in North (1691) and Boisguilbert (1705), see Tieben, *The Concept of Equilibrium* (2012), 108–109, 114.

33. Smith, *The Wealth of Nations* (1776), 1:66–178 (bk. 1, chs. 7–10), lays out Smith's theory of competition—on which, see Tony Aspromourgos, *The Science of Wealth: Adam Smith and the Framing of Political Economy* (London: Routledge, 2009), 65–134. It is radically different from later theories; see, for example, F. A. Hayek, "Competition As a Discovery Procedure," in *The Market*

and Other Orders, ed. Bruce Cladwell (Chicago: University of Chicago Press, 2014), 304–313; and Richard Tuck, *Free Riding* (Cambridge, Mass.: Harvard University Press, 2008), 156–204.

34. *OED Online,* s.v. "oligopoly," updated March 2004.

35. Thomas More, *Utopia,* ed. David Wootton (Indianapolis; Hackett, 1999).

36. David Wootton, "The Fear of God in Early Modern Political Theory," *Historical Papers / Communications historiques* 18 (1983), 56–80; David Wootton, "Lucien Febvre and the Problem of Unbelief in the Early Modern Period," *Journal of Modern History* 60 (1988), 695–730; David Wootton, "New Histories of Atheism," in *Atheism from the Reformation to the Enlightenment,* ed. Michael Hunter and David Wootton (Oxford: Clarendon, 1992), 13–53.

37. Pierre Bayle, *Lettre à M.L.A.D.C., où il est prouvé par plusieurs raisons tirées de la philosophie [et] de la theologie que les comètes ne sont point le presage d' aucun malheur* (Cologne: s.n., 1682); reissued in expanded form as Pierre Bayle, *Pensees diverses: Ecrites à un docteur de Sorbonne a l'occasion de la cométe qui parut au mois de decembre 1680* (Rotterdam: Leers, 1683); for an English translation, see Pierre Bayle, *Miscellaneous Reflections, Occasion'd by the Comet Which Appear'd in December 1680: Chiefly Tending to Explode Popular Superstitions,* 2 vols. (London: Morphew, 1708).

38. On Renaissance theories of laughter as a means of social control, see Quentin Skinner, "Hobbes and the Social Control of Unsociability," in *The Oxford Handbook of Hobbes,* ed. A. P. Martinich and Kinch Hoekstra (Oxford: Oxford University Press, 2016), 432–450.

39. Bayle, *Miscellaneous Reflections* (1708), 1:269–296, 2:329–396.

40. Bernard Mandeville, *The Fable of the Bees: Or, Private Vices, Publick Benefits* (London: Roberts, 1714).

41. Smith, *The Wealth of Nations* (1776), 1:70.

42. Hume, "Of the Balance of Trade," in *Political Discourses* (1752), 83–84.

43. Ibid., 85.

44. Hume, "Of the Balance of Power," in *Political Discourses* (1752), 101–114.

45. See Jonathan Swift, *A Discourse of the Contests and Dissentions between the Nobles and the Commons in Athens and Rome,* ed. Frank H. Ellis (Oxford: Clarendon, 1967); Wootton, "Liberty, Metaphor, and Mechanism" (2006), 108–112; and Michael Sheehan, *The Balance of Power: History and Theory* (London: Routledge, 2007).

46. The classic discussion is Otto Mayr, *Authority, Liberty, and Automatic Machinery in Early Modern Europe* (Baltimore: Johns Hopkins University Press, 1986).

47. Smith, *The Wealth of Nations* (1776), 1:453, 2:1, 278.

48. Mill would appear to be an exception, since, if the *OED Online* is to be believed, he originated "scarcity value" (entry first published 1910), "balance of payments" (first published 1885), and "wages-fund" (first published 1921). But one must, as usual, doubt the reliability of the *OED*, particularly of its older entries: it gives 1690 as the first use of "balance of trade," a term which appears in the very title of Misselden's *The Circle of Commerce: Or The Ballance of Trade* (1623). And it gives 1793 as the first use of "competition" in a commercial context, although the concept had been carefully defined by Steuart in 1767. I find "balance of payments" being used by Sir James Steuart in 1772 and "wages fund" by Arthur O'Connor in 1794. Which leaves only "scarcity value."

49. That human beings ought to be entirely self-interested in their behavior was also a standard claim among the physiocrats. See, for example, Victor de Riqueti de Mirabeau, *Lettres sur le commerce des grains* (Amsterdam: Desaint, 1768), 109, 196–197, 338; and Pierre-Paul Le Mercier de La Rivière, *L'intérêt général de l'état; ou, La liberté du commerce des blés* (Amsterdam: Desaint, 1770), 13, 99.

50. Some key discussions, in chronological order: Richard Teichgraeber, "Rethinking Das Adam Smith Problem," *Journal of British Studies* 20 (1981), 106–123; Laurence Dickey, "Historicizing the 'Adam Smith Problem': Conceptual, Historiographical, and Textual Issues," *Journal of Modern History* 58 (1986), 580–609; Russell Nieli, "Spheres of Intimacy and the Adam Smith Problem," *Journal of the History of Ideas* 47 (1986), 611–624; Spencer J. Pack, "Adam Smith on the Virtues: A Partial Resolution of the Adam Smith Problem," *Journal of the History of Economic Thought* 19 (1997), 127–140; Robert Sugden, "Beyond Sympathy and Empathy: Adam Smith's Concept of Fellow-feeling," *Economics and Philosophy* 18 (2002), 63–87; Leonidas Montes, "Das Adam Smith Problem: Its Origins, the Stages of the Current Debate, and One Implication for Our Understanding of Sympathy," *Journal of the History of Economic Thought* 25 (2003), 63–90; Lauren K. Hall, "Two Invisible Hands: Family, Markets, and the Adam Smith Problem," in *Propriety and Prosperity: New Studies on the Philosophy of Adam Smith,* ed. David Hardwick and Leslie Marsh (London: Palgrave MacMillan, 2014), 240–253; Istvan Hont, *Politics in Commercial Society: Jean-Jacques Rousseau and Adam Smith,* ed. Belá Kapossy and Michael Sonenscher (Cambridge, Mass.: Harvard University Press, 2015), 25–47.

51. See Albert O. Hirschman, *The Passions and the Interests: Political Arguments for Capitalism before Its Triumph* (Princeton, N.J.: Princeton University Press, 1977), 108–110, and the epigraphs to the present volume.

52. Hume, "Of the Independency of Parliament," in *Essays* (1741–1742), 1:85.

53. Exactly the same issue is apparent in Daniel Defoe's writings a half century earlier; see Hans H. Andersen, "The Paradox of Trade and Morality in Defoe," *Modern Philology* 39 (1941), 23–46.

54. With obvious modifications, this argument also applies to the claim (e.g., Nieli, "Spheres of Intimacy" [1986], and Hall, "Two Invisible Hands" [2014]) that Smith intended sympathy to govern relations with family and friends, and self-interest to govern relations with strangers. Entrepreneurs who constantly offer special deals to relatives and friends must, unless they have few of either, soon go out of business. The market is thus a system, an iron cage, from which one cannot escape—Smith surely understood this, but, unlike Cantillon, he places little emphasis upon it.

55. For a bibliography of Toussaint, see Ulrike Müller, "François Vincent Toussaint: Les Mœurs—The Manners—Die Sitten, Bibliography," http://www.encore.at /mam/toussaint/lesmoeurs.html. There is more than one English translation. Toussaint published a partial retraction; see François-Vincent Toussaint, *Éclaircissement sur les moeurs: par l'auteur des Moeurs* (Amsterdam: Rey, 1762), in which he claimed (unconvincingly) that he had intended his book to be compatible with orthodox Catholicism. The demand for his book in English suggests there was a market for undogmatic theism which was not being met by either clerical or enlightened authors. My attention was originally caught by an AbeBooks bookseller's entry for a copy of *Manners* offered for sale by Chapel Books of Saxmundham, England: "Item Description: W. Johnston, London, 1749. Hardcover. Book Condition: VG+. First edition. xlvi, 211, [ix] index. Paper slightly yellowed, pages otherwise very good with a little faint foxing. Heraldic crest to pastedown, and the ownership name of Thos Davison, Ferry Hill, to the head of the title page. [In 1754, Davison founded 'Mr Davison's Hospital' '—for six unmarried women, to be daughters and widows of burgesses' in Newcastle: who knows but that this book may have stirred him to such an act?]". The bookseller evidently drew on John Baillie, *An Impartial History of the Town and County of Newcastle Upon Tyne* (Newcastle upon Tyne, England: Anderson, 1801), 315. Davison and his sisters provided £1,200 for the hospital; see William Hutchinson, *A View of Northumberland with An Excursion to the Abbey of Mailross in Scotland. By W. Hutchinson,* 2 vols. (Newcastle upon Tyne, England: Charnley, 1778), 2:403; Eneas Mackenzie, *A Descriptive and Historical Account of the Town and County of Newcastle Upon Tyne* (Newcastle upon Tyne, England: Mackenzie and Dent, 1827), 531. In 1755 Davison also gave £500 for a trust to set young men up in business; see Baillie, *Newcastle Upon Tyne* (1801), 388; and *The Proceedings and Reports of the Town Council of the Borough of Newcastle* (Newcastle upon Tyne, England: Charnley, 1839). He also subscribed five pounds, five shillings per annum to the infirmary; see *Stat-*

utes, Rules and Orders, Agreed to at the General Meeting of the Subscribers, on Thursday the 21st of March 1750–1: For the Government of the Infirmary for the Sick and Lame Poor &c. (Newcastle upon Tyne, England: s.n., 1751), 45. He had been in business at least since 1719; some of his financial dealings are recorded in the Shafto (Beamish) Papers (http://reed.dur.ac.uk/xtf/view ?docId=ark/32150_s1v979v309q.xml), the Clayton and Gibson Papers (http:// reed.dur.ac.uk/xtf/view?docId=ark/32150_s14q77fr330.xml), in Add. Ms. 805 (http://reed.dur.ac.uk/xtf/view?docId=ark/32150_s1th83kz336.xml) at Durham University, and in the Northumberland Archives (http://discovery.nationalarchives .gov.uk/details/r/2b9a9cd4-6733-437f-b012-705e44ab7adb). His sister Timothia left £20 to the poor in her will; see John Brand, *The History and Antiquities of the Town and Country of the Town of Newcastle Upon Tyne* (London: White, 1789), 274. Davison's genealogy can be found at "Davison 2," Stirnet, https://www .stirnet.com/genie/data/british/dd/davison2.php.

56. François-Vincent Toussaint, *Manners: Translated From the French of Les Moeurs: Wherein the Principles of Morality, or Social Duties . . . Are Described in All Their Branches* (London: Johnston, 1749), 200.

57. Robert Surtees, George Taylor, and James Raine, *The History and Antiquities of the County Palatine of Durham*, 4 vols. (London: Nichols, 1816–1840), 3:279–290. The first three of Davison's chosen sentences are from Micah 6:8; the last is his own. The tomb no longer exists; I thank Mary Kell, the churchwarden, for searching for it.

58. Hence Defoe's coinage, "reason of trade."

59. Lisa Hill, "Adam Smith on Thumos and Irrational Economic Man," *European Journal of the History of Economic Thought* 19 (2012), 1–22.

60. For the impartial spectator, someone else's future pleasures are just as important as present pleasures. As Smith, *The Theory of Moral Sentiments* (1759), 362–363, notes, "Hence arises that eminent esteem with which all men naturally regard a steady perseverance in the practice of frugality, industry and application, though directed to no other purpose than the acquisition of fortune. The resolute firmness of the person who acts in this manner, and in order to obtain a great though remote advantage, not only gives up all present pleasures, but endures the greatest labour both of mind and body, necessarily commands our approbation. That view of his interest and happiness which appears to regulate his conduct, exactly tallies with the idea which we [spectators] naturally form of it. There is the most perfect correspondence between his sentiments and our own, and at the same time, from our experience of the common weakness of human nature, it is a correspondence which we could not reasonably have expected. We not only approve, therefore, but in some measure admire his conduct, and think it worthy of a considerable degree of applause. It is the

consciousness of this merited approbation and esteem which is alone capable of supporting the agent in this tenor of conduct. The pleasure which we are to enjoy ten years hence interests us so little in comparison with that which we may enjoy to day, the passion which the first excites, is naturally so weak in comparison with that violent emotion which the second is apt to give occasion to, that the one could never be any balance to the other, unless it was supported by the sense of propriety, by the consciousness that we merited the esteem and approbation of every body, by acting in the one way, and that we became the proper objects of their contempt and derision by behaving in the other."

61. Smith, *The Theory of Moral Sentiments* (1759), 341, 343, 344, 349.

62. I confess that this passage contains an autobiographical element. I happen to own the fine watch listed in this will; see "Will of James Britnell Wingyett (1842)," UK and Ireland Geneaology, http://www.genuki.org.uk/big/eng/DEV/Plymouth/JamesWingyett1842. A gray parrot is among the many other luxuries listed there.

63. Emily C. Nacol, *Age of Risk: Politics and Economy in Early Modern Britain* (Princeton, N.J.: Princeton University Press, 2016), 102.

64. Thus "A Great part, perhaps the greatest part of human happiness and misery arises from the view of our past conduct, and from the degree of approbation or disapprobation which we feel from the consideration of it." And "The man who, not from frivolous fancy, but from proper motives, has performed a generous action, when he looks forward to those whom he has served, feels himself to be the natural object of their love and gratitude, and by sympathy with them, of the esteem and approbation of all mankind. And when he looks backward to the motive from which he acted, and surveys it in the light in which the indifferent spectator will survey it, he still continues to enter into it, and applauds himself by sympathy with the approbation of this supposed impartial judge. In both these points of view his own conduct appears to him every way agreeable. His mind, at the thought of it, is filled with chearfulness, serenity, and composure. He is in friendship and harmony with all mankind, and looks upon his fellow-creatures with confidence and benevolent satisfaction, secure that he has rendered himself worthy of their most favourable regards. In the combination of all these sentiments consists the consciousness of merit, or of deserved reward." Smith, *The Theory of Moral Sentiments* (1759), 253–254, 187–188. Smith's friends believed that he secretly gave substantial sums to charitable purposes, but that he was ingenious in concealing his benefactions. See William Playfair, "The Life of Dr. Smith," in Adam Smith, *An Inquiry Into the Nature and Causes of the Wealth of Nations*, ed. William Playfair, 2 vols. (Hartford, Conn.: Cooke, 1811), 1:xxiii; and John Rae, *Life of Adam Smith* (London: Macmillan, 1895), 437. But one must note that his will contained no

charitable bequests, and that the evidence of Smith's charitable activity is unreliable.

65. Smith, *The Wealth of Nations* (1776), 2:340–348.

66. Cantillon's original text survives in French; "undertaker" is a contemporary translation of the French word *entrepreneur*. Cantillon, *Essay on the Nature of Trade . . . Variorum Edition* (2015), 130–131.

67. Smith, *The Wealth of Nations* (1776), 1:487, 495.

68. Tuck, *Free Riding* (2008), argues that free riding is an invisible problem for Smith; and it is in that it does not occur to him that anyone other than a beggar might be a free rider.

69. See, in particular, Hill, "Hidden Theology" (2001); Sugden, "Beyond Sympathy and Empathy" (2002); and Harrison, "History of the Invisible Hand" (2011).

8. THE MARKET: POVERTY AND FAMINES

1. *Hansard*, H.C. Deb., 22 June 1831, IV cc247-48.

2. Louis Paul Abeille, *Faits qui ont influé sur la cherté des grains en France & en Angleterre* (s.l.: s.n., 1768), 46. See also Victor de Riqueti, Marquis de Mirabeau, *Lettres sur le commerce des grains* (Amsterdam: Desaint, 1768), 141–142, 235.

3. Jacques Necker, *On the Legislation and the Commerce of Corn* (London: Longman, 1776), 300. For another example, see Paul Slack, "The Politics of English Political Economy in the 1620s," in *Popular Culture and Political Agency in Early Modern England and Ireland: Essays in Honour of John Walter,* ed. M. J. Braddick and P. Withington (Woodbridge, England: Boydell Press, 2017), 69: "famine without dearth." An anonymous author writing in 1769 distinguishes between an absolute dearth / famine (when there is no food to eat) and a relative dearth / famine (when the poor cannot afford to eat): Anonymous, *Réflexions sur le commerce des bleds* (Amsterdam: La veuve Pierres, 1769), 30. On the moment of publication of Necker's book, see Jean-Antoine-Nicolas Caritat de Condorcet, *Réfléxions sur le commerce des bleds* (London: s.n., 1776), vii–viii; and Cynthia A. Bouton, *The Flour War: Gender, Class, and Community in Late Ancien Régime French Society* (University Park: Pennsylvania State University Press, 1993). Modern scholarship, when considering opposition to the physiocratic doctrine of free trade in grain, has focused on Galiani rather than Necker; but, as his critics acknowledged, Necker's book was a runaway success, with four French editions within two years and an English translation, despite refutations by Nicolas Baudeau, Jean-Pierre-Louis de Luchet, André Morellet, Augustin-Joseph-Louis-Philippe de Rossi, and no fewer than three by Condorcet. It is thus not surprising that Smith read Necker and not (as far as we can tell) Galiani. On Necker and the grain trade, see Denis Diderot's letter

to Necker of 12 June 1775, https://fr.wikisource.org/wiki/Correspondance
_(Diderot)/67; Glenn Hueckel, "Smith's Mutiny on the Bounty: The Perils of
Polemic" (working paper, Claremont Institute for Economic Policy Studies,
2002); and Gilbert Faccarello, "'Nil Repente!' Galiani and Necker on Economic
Reforms," *European Journal of the History of Economic Thought* 1 (1994),
519–550. Emma Rothschild, "Social Security and Laissez Faire in Eighteenth-
Century Political Economy," *Population and Development Review* 21 (1995),
711–744, takes the side of Condorcet against Necker; but note that Condorcet
did not write, in Jean-Antoine-Nicolas Caritat de Condorcet, *Lettre d'un laboureur de Picardie, à M. N**** (s.l.: s.n., 1775), "in the assumed voice of 'a laborer from Picardie'" (Rothschild, 722); Condorcet's fictional *laboureur* is a
tenant farmer who employs laborers, an educated younger son from a wealthy
family who is down on his luck; see Condorcet, *Lettre d'un laboureur*, 30–31,
and the elaborate biography given at 45–51. He socializes not with the agricultural laborers, but with the parish curate, and, in the local town, with the mayor,
the bishop's deputy, and the chief of police. Naturally he favors the policies
of the physiocrats.

4. James Woodforde, *The Diary of a Country Parson, 1758–1802*, ed. John Beresford (Norwich, England: Canterbury, 1999), 322.

5. John Bohstedt, *The Politics of Provisions: Food Riots, Moral Economy, and
   Market Transition in England, c. 1550–1850* (Abingdon, England: Ashgate,
   2010), 192, 189; Roger Wells, *Wretched Faces: Famine in Wartime England,
   1793–1801* (Gloucester, England: Sutton, 1988).

6. Edward P. Thompson, "The Moral Economy of the English Crowd in the Eighteenth Century," *Past and Present* 50 (1971), 126.

7. John Beresford, introduction to Woodforde, *Diary* (1999), xv.

8. Thompson, "Moral Economy" (1971), 136.

9. The classic formulation of the contrary view is Herbert Butterfield, *The Whig
   Interpretation of History* (London: Bell, 1931).

10. I first find *esprit de système* in the *Mercure galant* for April 1709; then in Jean
    LeClerc's *Bibliothèque ancienne et moderne* 10 (1718), after which it becomes
    commonplace. In English, "the spirit of system" first appears in one of the
    dissertations added by an anonymous author to Jean Philippe René de La Blé-
    terie, *The Life of Julian the Apostate* (Dublin, s.n., 1746). For Smith's man of
    system, see Adam Smith, *The Theory of Moral Sentiments*, 2 vols. (London:
    Strahan, 1790), 2:110.

11. Adam Smith, "The History of Astronomy," in *Essays on Philosophical Subjects*,
    ed. Joseph Black, James Hutton, and Dugald Stewart (London: Cadell and
    Davies, 1795), 44–45 (machines), 93 (Newton).

12. There is an extensive literature on Smith's Newtonianism; see, for example, Eric Schliesser, "Some Principles of Adam Smith's Newtonian Methods in the Wealth of Nations," *Research in the History of Economic Thought and Methodology* 23 (2005), 33–74; and Leonidas Montes, "Newton's Real Influence on Adam Smith and Its Context," *Cambridge Journal of Economics* 32 (2008), 555–576.

13. Quotations from *The Wealth of Nations* in this chapter are from Adam Smith, *The Wealth of Nations,* ed. R. H. Campbell, A. S. Skinner, and W. B. Todd, 2 vols. (Oxford: Clarendon, 1976). There are no important variations between the first edition and the copy text.

14. Dugald Stewart, "Account of the Life and Writings of Adam Smith," in Smith, *Essays on Philosophical Subjects* (1795), lxxxi–lxxxii.

15. Andrew S. Skinner, "Adam Smith (1723–1790): Theories of Political Economy," in *A Companion to the History of Economic Thought,* ed. Warren J. Samuels, J. E. Biddle and J. B. Davis (Oxford: Blackwell, 2008), 108.

16. I owe this point to Cormac Ó Gráda; see Richard Cantillon, *Richard Cantillon's Essay on the Nature of Trade in General: A Variorum Edition,* ed. Richard van den Berg (Abingdon, England: Routledge, 2015), 203.

17. Amartya Sen, *Poverty and Famines: An Essay on Entitlement and Deprivation* (Oxford: Clarendon, 1981), 160.

18. Thompson, "Moral Economy" (1971).

19. Thompson, "The Moral Economy Reviewed," in *Customs in Common* (London: Merlin, 1991), 259–351; William James Booth, "On the Idea of the Moral Economy," *American Political Science Review* 88 (1994), 653–667.

20. A similar view of Smith is presented by Michel Foucault; see Callum Williams, "Famine: Adam Smith and Foucauldian Political Economy," *Scottish Journal of Political Economy* 62 (2015), 171–190.

21. Royal Swedish Academy of Sciences, "The Sveriges Riksbank Prize in Economic Sciences in Memory of Alfred Nobel 1998," press release, 14 October 1998, Nobel Prize, http://www.nobelprize.org/nobel_prizes/economic -sciences/laureates/1998/press.html; Sen, *Poverty and Famines* (1981). See also Amartya Sen, "Starvation and Exchange Entitlements: A General Approach and Its Application to the Great Bengal Famine," *Cambridge Journal of Economics* 1 (1977), 33–59; Amartya Sen, "Ingredients of Famine Analysis: Availability and Entitlements," *Quarterly Journal of Economics* 96 (1981), 433–464. Sen is perhaps best known for his claim that there has never been a famine in a democracy—a claim made in *Development as Freedom* (1999), and before that in Amartya Sen and Jean Drèze, *Hunger and Public Action* (1989).

22. Amartya Sen, *The Argumentative Indian: Writings on Indian History, Culture, and Identity* (Harmondsworth, England: Allen Lane, 2005), 193; Sen uses the

abbreviation FAD but not FEE in *Poverty and Famines* (1981); however, he does use FEE in "Ingredients of Famine Analysis" (1981).

23. Emma Rothschild, "Adam Smith and Conservative Economics," *Economic History Review* 45 (February 1992), 74–96; Emma Rothschild, "Commerce and the State: Turgot, Condorcet and Smith," *Economic Journal* 102 (1992), 1197–1210; Emma Rothschild, "Social Security and Laissez Faire" (1995); Emma Rothschild, "The Debate on Economic and Social Security in the Late Eighteenth Century," *Development and Change* 27 (1996), 331–351; Emma Rothschild, *Economic Sentiments: Adam Smith, Condorcet, and the Enlightenment* (Cambridge, Mass.: Harvard University Press, 2001). Sen and Rothschild have published together, and are related by marriage; but it should be noted that in *Poverty and Famines,* 160–161, Sen had taken the standard, laissez-faire view of Smith. Rothschild's line is adopted in Williams, "Famine" (2015). For a vigorous defense of the traditional view, see Mike Hill and Warren Montag, *The Other Adam Smith* (Stanford, Calif.: Stanford University Press, 2014), 235–342. For a generally convincing critique of Sen on Bengal, see Cormac Ó Gráda, "'Sufficiency and Sufficiency and Sufficiency': Revisiting the Great Bengal Famine of 1943–44," in *Eating People Is Wrong, and Other Essays on Famine, Its Past, and Its Future* (Princeton, N.J.: Princeton University Press, 2015), 38–91; and Cormac Ó Gráda, *Famine: A Short History* (Princeton, N.J.: Princeton University Press, 2009), 159–194. For an application of Sen to early modern England, see Robert W. Fogel, *Second Thoughts on the European Escape from Hunger: Famines, Price Elasticities, Entitlements, Chronic Malnutrition, and Mortality Rates* (Cambridge, Mass: National Bureau of Economic Research, 1989).

24. One passage in Smith is always quoted in favor of a radical rather than conservative reading of *The Wealth of Nations:* Smith said that when wages are regulated it is to benefit employers so that when, quite exceptionally, one finds a regulation which benefits employees it is "always just and equitable" (I.x.c.61)—an example he gives is requiring wages to be paid in money not goods. Smith was not saying—obviously—that any possible regulation of wages to benefit employees is a good thing, merely that the very few regulations of that sort that do exist are a good thing, because in general Parliament responds to the wishes of employers, not employees. Despite the efforts of Rothschild, one can't find in Smith an argument for a legislated minimum wage.

25. Steven L. Kaplan, *Bread, Politics and Political Economy in the Reign of Louis XV* (The Hague: Martinus Nijhoff, 1976); Keith Michael Baker, "State, Society, and Subsistence in Eighteenth-Century France," *Journal of Modern History* 50 (1978), 701–711; Dena Goodman, *The Republic of Letters: A Cultural History of the French Enlightenment* (Ithaca, N.Y.: Cornell University Press, 1994), 183–232.

26. Jacques Necker, *Sur la législation et le commerce des grains,* 2 vols. (Paris: Pissot, 1775), cited in Smith, *The Wealth of Nations* (1976), V.ii.k.78; and André Morellet, *Réfutation de l'ouvrage qui a pour titre Dialogues sur le commerce des bleds* (London: s.n., 1770), sig. a4rv.

27. Hence the English translation of Necker, *Sur la législation et le commerce des grains* (1775) as Necker, *On the Legislation and the Commerce of Corn* (1776).

28. Bohstedt, *The Politics of Provisions* (2010), 106.

29. Arthur Young, *The Farmer's Letters to the People of England: Containing the Sentiments of a Practical Husbandman . . . The Second Edition, Corrected and Enlarged* (London: Nicoll, 1768), 31.

30. Andrew B. Appleby, "Grain Prices and Subsistence Crises in England and France, 1590–1740," *Journal of Economic History* 39 (1979), 865–887; John Walter and Roger Schofield, "Famine, Disease and Crisis Mortality in Early Modern Society," in *Famine, Disease and the Social Order in Early Modern Society,* ed. John Walter and Roger Schofield (Cambridge: Cambridge University Press, 1989), 1–74; David R. Weir, "Markets and Mortality in France, 1600–1789," in Walter and Schofield, *Famine, Disease and the Social Order in Early Modern Society,* 201–234; Karen J. Cullen, *Famine in Scotland: The "Ill Years" of the 1690s* (Edinburgh: Edinburgh University Press, 2010). Though Cantillon, who lived in France 1715–1720, said it was commonplace there to see laborers and their children starve to death; see Cantillon, *Essay on the Nature of Trade . . . Variorum Edition* (2015), 82–83.

31. Charles Smith, *A Short Essay of the Corn Trade, and the Corn Laws* (s.l.: s.n., 1758), 56.

32. Bruce M. S. Campbell and Cormac Ó Gráda, "Harvest Shortfalls, Grain Prices, and Famines in Preindustrial England," *Journal of Economic History* 71 (2011), 859–886.

33. Smith was echoing Arthur Young's *Political Arithmetic* of 1774 (a copy of which was in his library); Young had said that he did not think it easy "to declare what season, wet or dry, best suits the production of corn in *England;* the soil is so various, such tracts of sand, sandy loams, gravels, chalks, and other soils, to which a wet year is as suitable as a dry one to clays. So many tracts of clay and wet loams, to which a dry year is as suitable as a wet one to sand." Arthur Young, *Political Arithmetic. Containing Observations on the Present State of Great Britain; And the Principles of Her Policy in the Encouragement of Agriculture* (London: Nicoll, 1774), 45. The argument that in England the harvest never entirely fails goes back at least to Davenant in 1699; see Karl Gunnar Persson, *Grain Markets in Europe, 1500–1900: Integration and Deregulation* (Cambridge: Cambridge University Press, 1999), 8. Smith did not consider disease or frost, which are rarely a major problem with grain crops; both are capable of

destroying a potato crop—the freezing of seed potatoes was a significant factor in the Irish famine of 1740, and blight was the cause of the great Irish famine of 1845–1852. He was, though, aware that a rice harvest might be vulnerable to bad weather.

34. Rafael Dobado-González, Alfredo Garcia-Hiernaux, and David E. Guerrero, "The Integration of Grain Markets in the Eighteenth Century: Early Rise of Globalization in the West," *Journal of Economic History* 72 (2012), 671–707.

35. Dale Edward Williams, "Were 'Hunger' Rioters Really Hungry? Some Demographic Evidence," *Past and Present* 71 (1976), 70–75. For studies of bad years of increased mortality, see John Dexter Post, *Food Shortage, Climatic Variability and Epidemic Disease in Preindustrial Europe: The Mortality Peak in the Early 1740s* (Ithaca, N.Y.: Cornell University Press, 1985); and John Dexter Post, "The Mortality Crises of the Early 1770s and European Demographic Trends," *Journal of Interdisciplinary History* 21 (1990), 29–62.

36. See M. Messance, *Recherches sur la population des généralités d'Auvergne, de Lyon, de Rouen . . . avec des reflexions sur la valeur du bled, tant en France qu'en Angleterre, depuis 1674 jusqu'en 1764* (Paris: Durand, 1766), 291, a book owned and carefully read by Smith.

37. On the importance of poor relief in England, see Post, "The Mortality Crises" (1990), 60, 62.

38. Rothschild, "Commerce and the State" (1992).

39. For a similar argument, see Condorcet, *Réfléxions sur le commerce des bleds* (1776), 33–34.

40. Geoffrey Brennan and Philip Pettit, "Hands Invisible and Intangible," *Synthèse* 94 (1993), 191–225; Garrett Hardin, "The Tragedy of the Commons," *Science* 162 (1968), 1243–1248. See also Adam Smith, *Lectures on Jurisprudence*, ed. Ronald L. Meek, D. D. Raphael and P. G. Stein (Oxford: Clarendon, 1978), 497.

41. One of his sources is Messance, *Recherches sur la population* (1766), 287–288, and the accompanying tables.

42. For evidence that Smith's analysis was sound see, for example, Rothschild, "Commerce and the State" (1992), 1200; and Sen's study of famine in the Sahel in *Poverty and Famines,* 113–30.

43. In the nineteenth century there was much opposition to such interventions in the market, supposedly on Smithian principles; see Sen, *Poverty and Famines* (1981), 160–161; and Rothschild, "Adam Smith and Conservative Economics" (1992). Malthus sought to analyze the consequences of such intervention (and did not entirely oppose it). Sen, *Poverty and Famines* (1981), 174–84 provides a sophisticated reexamination of the issues, which I simplify greatly here.

44. Thompson, "Moral Economy" (1971), 122–126.

45. Condorcet, *Réfléxions sur le commerce des bleds* (1776), 25, i–iv, 34, 136, 189. Condorcet had earlier expressed his support for free trade in corn in Nicolas Caritat de Condorcet, *Lettres sur le commerce des grains* (Paris: Couturier père, 1774).

46. Condorcet, *Réfléxions sur le commerce des bleds* (1776), 88–89.

47. Ibid., 31–42. See also Jean-Antoine-Nicolas Caritat de Condorcet, "Monopole et monopoleur" (originally published as a pamphlet in 1775), in *Correspondance secrète, politique & littéraire, Ou, Mémoires pour servir à l'histoire des cours, des sociétés & de la litterature en France, depuis la mort de Louis XV,* 18 vols., London: Adamson, 1787–1790), 2:52–58, repr. in Jean-Antoine-Nicolas Caritat de Condorcet, *Oeuvres de Condorcet,* ed. F. Arago and A. O'Connor, 12 vols. (s.l.: s.n., 1847–1849), 11:37–58.

48. Smith, *The Theory of Moral Sentiments* (1759), 350.

49. On our greater concern for the welfare of the rich and powerful, see Smith, *The Theory of Moral Sentiments* (1790), 2:89–90 (VI.ii.1.20). For, on the other hand, Smith's critical views on inequality, see Dennis C. Rasmussen, "Adam Smith on What Is Wrong with Economic Inequality," *American Political Science Review* 110 (2016), 342–352.

50. Ferdinando Galiani, *Dialogues sur le commerce des bleds* (London: s.n., 1770), 183–185; but here I follow Ferdinando Galiani, *Dialogues entre M. Marquis de Roquemaure, et Ms. Le Chevalier Zanobi: The Autograph Manuscript of the* Dialogues sur le commerce des bleds, ed. Philip Koch (Frankfurt am Main: Klostermann, 1968), 180–181 (my translation). See also Anonymous, *Réflexions* (1769), 43–44, on the inadequacy of charity in times of famine.

51. In other words, Smith did not misjudge the scale of supply variation, but he failed to grasp the implication of the inelasticity of demand (see Campbell and Ó Gráda, "Harvest Shortfalls, Grain Prices, and Famines in Preindustrial England" [2011], 875–877). He had in his library the text in which Davenant formulated what is now called the King–Davenant Law (see G. Heberton Evans, "The Law of Demand: The Roles of Gregory King and Charles Davenant," *Quarterly Journal of Economics* 81 [1967], 483–492), but he may have been misled by Quesnay and Turgot into thinking the issue was less acute than Davenant had claimed (see Philippe Steiner, "Demand, Price and Net Product in the Early Writings of F. Quesnay," *European Journal of the History of Economic Thought* 1 [1994], 231–251; Karl Gunnar Persson, "The Seven Lean Years, Elasticity Traps, and Intervention in Grain Markets in Pre-industrial Europe," *Economic History Review* 49 [1996], 692–714; and Karl Gunnar Persson, *Grain Markets in Europe, 1500–1900: Integration and Deregulation* [Cambridge: Cambridge University Press, 1999], 47–64; see also Pierre-Paul Le Mercier de La Rivière, *L'intérêt général de l'état* [Amsterdam: Desaint, 1770],

NOTE TO PAGE 203

112–121, 165). Moreover, although the physiocrats had a theory of demand inelasticity, they rarely deployed it for the simple reason that it was constructed to
deal with unrealistically large variations in production. Instead, their standard
account of sharply rising prices argued that responsibility lay not with a
(modest) shortfall in production but with a lack of competition among grain
merchants, which they termed "monopoly." Thus dearth they insisted was
usually not "real" but "fake" (Mercier de La Rivière, *L'intérêt général de l'état*
[1770], 161, 246, 249, 257, 286; Bigot de Sainte-Croix, *Avis du Parlement de
Dauphiné, sur la libre circulation des grains & la réduction naturelle des prix
dans les années de cherté. Adressé au Roi le 26 avril 1769* [s.l.: s.n., 1769], 73, 97,
99, 125). Their argument depended on the (mistaken) claims that modest
shortfalls ought to have only minor consequences for prices, and that in the European grain market, centered on Amsterdam, there was little variation in price
from year to year (see Victor de Riqueti, Marquis de Mirabeau, *Lettres sur le
commerce des grains* [Amsterdam: Desaint, 1768], 125, 180–181, 282; and
Sainte-Croix, *Avis du Parlement de Dauphiné* [1769], 68–69). They exagger-
ated the extent to which there was (or could be, before the steam engine) a
unified European grain market, and their claim that prices moved only within
a narrow range was false (see the tables of Dutch grain prices, taken from Nico-
laas Wilhelmus Posthumus, *Inquiry into the History of Prices in Holland,* vol.
2, *Commodity Prices* [Leiden: Brill, 1964], which can be downloaded from
"List of Datafiles," International Institute of Social History, http://www.iisg.nl
/hpw/data.php). Smith was presumably misled by this literature into thinking
that competition alone could eliminate dearth and famine. But he was at fault
in failing to address the question of the inelasticity of demand, which was well
established in the literature. See, in addition to Davenant and the physiocrats,
James Steuart, *An Inquiry Into the Principles of Political Economy,* 2 vols.
(London: Millar and Cadell, 1767), 1:293 (grain prices double if supply falls by
one-sixth); Jacques Necker, *Sur la législation et le commerce des grains,* 2 vols.
(Paris: Pissot, 1775; a book consulted by Smith), translated as Jacques Necker,
On the Legislation and the Commerce of Corn (London: Longman, 1776),
66–76, 205–206, 257–258, 351–352, 367–368. Necker's argument was adopted
in Thomas Pownall, *A Letter From Governor Pownall to Adam Smith . . .
Being An Examination of Several Points of Doctrine, Laid Down in His
"Inquiry Into the Nature and Causes of the Wealth of Nations"* (London: Almon,
1776), 30; see also James Anderson, *Observations on the Means of Exciting
a Spirit of National Industry: Chiefly Intended to Promote the Agriculture,
Commerce, Manufactures, and Fisheries, of Scotland. In a Series of Letters to a
Friend . . .* (s.l.: Cadell, 1777), 526, 312. Though Smith's revisions of 1784 took

into account some criticisms of his discussion of the corn trade, this issue remained unaddressed.

52. Smith, *The Wealth of Nations* (1976), 274.

53. Smith's failure to mention charity brings him close to the laissez-faire arguments of the physiocrats. Thus Mirabeau held that in a true free market system, harvest failure and starvation would be unlikely to occur, but if they did, no one would be responsible and no one would be under an obligation to take remedial action. The fault would lie with nature, with the sun and the rain; see Mirabeau, *Lettres* (1768), 176. Necker, by contrast, held that that poor had a right to life, and that this imposed an obligation on society to come to the assistance of the starving; see Jacques Necker, *Eloge de Jean-Baptiste Colbert: Discours qui a remporté le prix de l'academie françoise, en 1773* (Paris: Brunet et Demonville, 1773), 33. Necker also maintained, in *Sur la législation et le commerce des grains* (1775), that a free market would not create an automatic harmony of interests between the different social classes, and so government intervention and regulation would always be necessary. It is not anachronistic to use the word "class" in this context, *pace* Peter Laslett, *The World We Have Lost: England before the Industrial Age* (London: Methuen, 1968), ch. 2. Although it is rarely used in the modern sense by Adam Smith, who generally writes about "a particular class" or "particular classes," it is used frequently in a new sense by the physiocrats and, following them, by Necker and his translator and by Smith when expounding the views of the physiocrats. See, for example, Pierre-Paul Le Mercier de La Rivière, *L'ordre naturel et essentiel des sociétés politiques,* 2 vols. (London: Nourse, 1767); Anne-Marie Piguet, *Classe: Histoire du mot et genèse du concept: Des physiocrates aux historiens de la Restauration* (Lyon: Presses universitaires de Lyon, 1996). The role of the physiocrats in shaping the modern language of class is missing, for example, from Raymond Williams, *Keywords: A Vocabulary of Culture and Society* (New York: Oxford University Press, 1976), and Dror Wahrman, *Imagining the Middle Class: The Political Representation of Class in Britain, c. 1780–1840* (Cambridge: Cambridge University Press, 2003). Thus, if the physiocrats developed the first theory of economic classes, it was Necker who was the first theorist of class conflict; see Necker, *On the Legislation and the Commerce of Corn* (1776), 5–6, 85–86, 93, 104, 176–177, 265–267, 363–365, 413–416, 438–439.

54. See Smith, *Lectures on Jurisprudence* (1978), 525.

55. The standard catalog of Smith's library is now Hiroshi Mizuta, *Adam Smith's Library: A Catalogue* (Oxford: Clarendon, 2000).

56. On dearths in France over the previous two hundred years, see Mercier de La Rivière, *L'intérêt général de l'état* (1770), chs. 29–33.

57. Anonymous, *The Groans of Ireland, in a Letter to a Member of Parliament* (Dublin: s.n., 1741), 3.

58. Jonathan Swift, *A Modest Proposal for Preventing the Children of Poor People from Being a Burthen to Their Parents, or the Country, and for Making Them Beneficial to the Publick* (Dublin: Harding, 1729), 6, 7. See also Ryan Patrick Hanley, "Style and Sentiment: Smith and Swift," *Adam Smith Review* 4 (2008), 88–105.

59. There was no centrally organized poor relief system in Ireland (or Scotland); see David Dickson, "In Search of the Old Irish Poor Law," in *Economy and Society in Scotland and Ireland, 1500–1939,* ed. Rosalind Mitchison and Peter Roebuck (Edinburgh: Donald, 1988), 149–159; and Larry Patriquin, "Why Was There No Old Poor Law in Scotland and Ireland?," *Journal of Peasant Studies* 33 (2006), 219–247.

60. James Kelly, "Jonathan Swift and the Irish Economy in the 1720s," *Eighteenth-Century Ireland/Iris an dá chultúr* 6 (1991), 7–36.

61. Samuel Fleischacker, *On Adam Smith's* Wealth of Nations: *A Philosophical Companion* (Princeton, N.J.: Princeton University Press, 2004), 218–220, replying to Istvan Hont and Michael Ignatieff, "Needs and Justice in the Wealth of Nations: An Introductory Essay," in *Wealth and Virtue: The Shaping of Political Economy in the Scottish Enlightenment,* ed. Istvan Hont and Michael Ignatieff (Cambridge: Cambridge University Press, 1983), 1–44.

62. Smith, *The Wealth of Nations* (1976), IV.v.b.3. Compare Mirabeau, *Lettres* (1768), 254.

63. Ferdinando Galiani, *Dialogues sur le commerce des bleds,* ed. Fausto Nicolini (Milan: Ricciardi, 1959), 373.

64. Ronald L. Meek, *The Economics of Physiocracy: Essays and Translations* (Cambridge, Mass.: Harvard University Press, 1963), 138–149.

65. Robert Sibbald, *Provision for the Poor in Time of Dearth and Scarcity: Where There Is an Account of Such Food as May Be Easily Gotten When Corns Are Scarce or Unfit for Use: And of Such Meats as May Be Used When the Ordinary Provisions Fail, or Are Very Dear* (Edinburgh: Watson, 1699), 3, 24.

66. Steuart, *An Inquiry into the Principles of Political Economy* (1767), 1:113.

67. Smith, *The Theory of Moral Sentiments* (1759), 364–70 (pt. 4, sec. 2).

68. Ibid., 110.

69. Rothschild, "Adam Smith and Conservative Economics" (1992), 86–88. On Burke's *Thoughts and Details on Scarcity,* see Donald Winch, "The Burke-Smith Problem and Late Eighteenth-Century Political and Economic Thought," *Historical Journal* 28 (1985), 231–247; and Richard Bourke, *Empire and Revolution: The Political Life of Edmund Burke* (Princeton, N.J.: Princeton University Press, 2015), 886–893.

70. Edmund Burke, *Thoughts and Details on Scarcity: Originally Presented to the Right Hon. William Pitt, in the Month of November, 1795* (London: Rivington and Hatchard, 1800), 4, 18, 44.

71. Lisa Hill and Peter McCarthy, "Hume, Smith and Ferguson: Friendship in Commercial Society," *Critical Review of International Social and Political Philosophy* 2 (1999), 43.

72. Burke, *Thoughts and Details on Scarcity* (1800), 18; for Pufendorf's views, see Samuel Pufendorf, *The Whole Duty of Man According to the Law of Nature*, ed. Ian Hunter and David Saunders (Indianapolis: Liberty Fund, 2003), 110. For Ferguson, see Hill and McCarthy, "Hume, Smith and Ferguson" (1999), 43. See also Smith, *The Theory of Moral Sentiments* (1759), 172, 365–368, 423–424.

73. Anonymous, *The Groans of Ireland* (1741), 3.

74. Galiani, *Dialogues sur le commerce des bleds* (1770), 183–184. Translation from Hill and Montag, *The Other Adam Smith* (2014), 277. (This passage does not appear in the manuscript edited by Philip Koch.) Galiani had seen famine; see John Robertson, *The Case for the Enlightenment: Scotland and Naples 1680–1760* (Cambridge: Cambridge University Press, 2005), 387.

9. SELF-EVIDENCE

1. Herbert Lawrence Ganter, "Jefferson's 'Pursuit of Happiness' and Some Forgotten Men: I," *William and Mary Quarterly* 16 (1936), 422–434; Herbert Lawrence Ganter, "Jefferson's 'Pursuit of Happiness' and Some Forgotten Men: II," *William and Mary Quarterly* 16 (1936), 558–585. See also Garry Wills, *Inventing America: Jefferson's Declaration of Independence* (New York: Doubleday, 1978), 240–255; Darrin M. McMahon, *The Pursuit of Happiness: A History from the Greeks to the Present* (London: Allen Lane, 2006), 314–333; and James E. Crimmins, "Happiness, Pursuit of," in *The Bloomsbury Encyclopedia of Utilitarianism*, ed. James E. Crimmins (New York: Bloomsbury).

2. George Anderson, *An Estimate of the Profit and Loss of Religion* (Edinburgh: n.p., 1753), 19.

3. Julian P. Boyd and Gerard W. Gawalt, *The Declaration of Independence: The Evolution of the Text* (Charlottesville, Va.: International Center for Jefferson Studies at Monticello / Library of Congress, 1999), 67.

4. No one, as far as I can tell, ever pursued felicity. The "pursuit of fame" is, however, a common phrase, which tells against the argument of Arthur M. Schlesinger, "The Lost Meaning of 'The Pursuit of Happiness,'" *William and Mary Quarterly* 21 (1964), 325–327.

5. Jean-Jacques Burlamaqui, *The Principles of Politic Law, Being a Sequel to the Principles of Natural Law* (London: Nourse, 1752), 222. The phrase "safety and happiness" occurs in the Declaration of Independence, in the context of the people's right to make war on their rulers.

6. Jean-Jacques Burlamaqui, *The Principles of Natural Law, in Which the True Systems of Morality and Civil Government Are Established* (London: Nourse, 1748), 51, 46–47.

7. Ibid., 15, 50.

8. Ibid., 46, 49.

9. John Locke, *Two Treatises of Government* (London: Churchill, 1690), 305.

10. *Spectator* 8, no. 624, 24 November 1714.

11. John Locke, *An Essay Concerning Humane Understanding* (London: Awnsham and Churchil, 1694), 139 (bk. 2, ch. 21, sec. 43; see also secs. 47, 51, 52, 56, 59): Locke seeks to reconcile this view with his doctrines of uneasiness and free will.

12. Peter Paxton, *Civil Polity: A Treatise Concerning the Nature of Government* (London: Wilkin, 1703), 35.

13. Thomas Morgan, *Physico-Theology, or a Philosophico-Moral Disquisition Concerning Human Nature* (London: Cox, 1741), 108.

14. David Hume, "The Stoic," in *Essays, Moral and Political*, 2 vols. (Edinburgh: Kincaid, 1741–1742), 2:119.

15. Morgan, *Physico-Theology* (1741), 97.

16. Thomas Rutherforth, *An Essay on the Nature and Obligations of Virtue* (Cambridge: Bentham, 1744), 153.

17. Robert Clayton, *The Religion of Labour: A Sermon Preach'd in Christ-Church, Dublin* (Dublin: Grierson, 1740), 7; William Warburton, *A Critical and Philosophical Commentary on Mr. Pope's Essay on Man* (London: Knapton, 1742), 86.

18. Julien Offray de La Mettrie, *L'homme machine* (Leiden: Luzac, 1748), 89; Julien Offray de La Mettrie, *Man a Machine* (London: Owen, 1749), 46.

19. Adam Smith, *The Theory of Moral Sentiments* (London: Millar, 1759), 490–520 (pt. 7, sec. 3).

20. Francis Hutcheson, *An Essay on the Nature and Conduct of the Passions and Affections* (London: Smith and Bruce, 1728), 216, 33; Francis Hutcheson, *An Inquiry into the Original of Our Ideas of Beauty and Virtue* (London: Darby, 1725), 252–253; David Hume, *A Treatise of Human Nature*, 3 vols. (London: Noon, 1739–1740), 2:248.

21. Smith, *The Theory of Moral Sentiments* (1759), 1–3 (passage in brackets added in 1790).

22. John P. Reeder, *On Moral Sentiments: Contemporary Reponses to Adam Smith* (Bristol, England: Thoemmes, 1998), 70, 66; see also 72, 74–75 (as discussed

in Istvan Hont, *Politics in Commercial Society: Jean-Jacques Rousseau and Adam Smith,* ed. Belá Kapossy and Michael Sonenscher [Cambridge, Mass.: Harvard University Press, 2015], 29–30).

23. Hume, *An Enquiry* (1751), 21–22.

24. William Wollaston, *The Religion of Nature Delineated* (s.l.: s.n., 1722), 27.

25. Thomas Reid, *Essays on the Active Powers of Man* (Edinburgh: Bell, 1788), 226.

26. Adam Ferguson, *An Essay on the History of Civil Society* (Edinburgh: Millar and Caddel, 1767), 79, 87.

27. Joseph Butler, *Fifteen Sermons Preached at the Rolls Chapel* (London: Knapton, 1729), 217, 228, xvii. The preface is new in this, the second edition, but the text of sermon 11 also differs considerably from that of the first (1726), and these passages are new in 1729. Variations between the first and second editions are recorded in Butler, *The Works of Bishop Butler,* ed. J. H. Bernard, 2 vols. (London: Macmillan, 1900). On Butler, see especially R. G. Frey, "Butler on Self-Love and Benevolence," in *Joseph Butler's Moral and Religious Thought,* ed. Christopher Cunliffe (Oxford: Clarendon, 1992), 243–267.

28. *Fifteen Sermons Preached at the Rolls Chapel* (London: Knapton, 1726), 223; in the second edition the passage ends: "till we are convinced that it will be for our Happiness, or at least not contrary to it"; Butler, *Fifteen Sermons* (1729), 229. On this passage, Terence Penelhum, *Butler* (London: Routledge, 1985), 73–76.

29. Butler, *Fifteen Sermons* (1726), 54; identical in Butler, *Fifteen Sermons* (1729), 54–55.

30. Anthony Ashley Cooper Shaftesbury, *Characteristicks of Men, Manners, Opinions, Times,* 3 vols. ([London]: [Darby], 1711), 1:115–116.

31. Adam Smith, *Essays on Philosophical Subjects,* ed. W. P. D. Wightman, J. C. Bryce, and I. S. Ross (Oxford: Oxford University Press, 1980), 242–254.

32. Louis-Jean Levesque de Pouilly, *Theory of Agreeable Sensations,* trans. Jacob Vernet (London: Owen, 1749), 219, 93.

33. Smith, *The Theory of Moral Sentiments* (1759), 284, 285.

34. Ibid., 167–168.

35. David Hume, *Essays and Treatises on Several Subjects. Containing An Enquiry Concerning the Principles of Morals,* 4 vols. (London: Millar, 1753), 3:189 (the first edition, *An Enquiry Concerning the Principles of Morals* [London: Millar, 1751], 187, differs), 21.

36. David Wootton, *The Invention of Science: A New History of the Scientific Revolution* (New York: Harper, 2015), 377; see also René Descartes to Elisabeth of Bohemia, 15 September 1645, in Elisabeth of Bohemia and René Descartes, *The Correspondence between Princess Elisabeth of Bohemia and René Descartes,* ed. Lisa Shapiro (Chicago: University of Chicago Press, 2007), 112.

37. Fernando Vidal, *The Sciences of the Soul: The Early Modern Origins of Psychology,* trans. Saskia Brown (Chicago: University of Chicago Press, 2011).

38. George Makari, *Soul Machine: The Invention of the Modern Mind* (New York: Norton, 2015), 216–218.

39. Locke was acutely aware of problems of translation; see, for example, his claim that what philosophers say in Greek about φύσις and in Latin about *natura* makes no sense when said in English about "nature." John Locke, *Mr. Lockes Reply to the Right Reverend the Lord Bishop of Worcester's Answer to His Second Letter* (London: Churchill, 1699), 254–255. Strangely, there is no discussion of the absence of the word "mind" in French in *Dictionary of Untranslatables: A Philosophical Lexicon,* ed. Barbara Cassin, Emily Apter, Jacques Lezra, and Michael Wood (Princeton, N.J.: Princeton University Press, 2014). The issue seems to have been invisible, both to the original compilers of the French edition, and the editors of the English adaptation. By the same token, there is no English word for *esprit;* Helvétius's *De l'esprit* was translated as: Claude Adrien Helvétius, *De L'esprit; Or, Essays on the Mind and Its Several Faculties* (London: Dodsley, 1759).

40. We happily say that Descartes invented the mind / body problem. But, though he has satisfactory words, in both Latin and French, for "body," there was no satisfactory word for "mind" available to him in Latin or French. So he wrote in the second of his *Meditations on First Philosophy* (1641), "Nihil nunc admitto nisi quod necessario sit verum; sum igitur praecise tantùm res cogitans, id est, mens, sive animus, sive intellectus, sive ratio, voces mihi priùs significationis ignotae. Sum autem res vera, & vere existens; sed qualis res? Dixi, cogitans." This became, in the contemporary translation of the Duc de Luynes, "Je n'admets maintenant rien qui ne soit nécessairement vrai: je ne suis donc, précisément parlant, qu'une chose qui pense, c'est-à-dire un esprit, un entendement ou une raison, qui sont des termes dont la signification m'était auparavant inconnue. Or je suis une chose vraie, et vraiment existante; mais quelle chose? Je l'ai dit: une chose qui pense." Both texts can be found at "Descartes' Meditations," Wright State University, http://www.wright.edu/~charles.taylor /descartes/intro.html. In the English translation of 1680 this is rendered as, "In short therefore I *am* only a *thinking thing,* that is to say, *a mind* or a *soul,* or *understanding,* or *Reason,* words which formerly *I* understood not; I am a *Real thing,* and *Really Existent.* But what sort of thing? I have just now said it, *A thinking thing*." René Descartes, *Six Metaphysical Meditations,* trans. William Molyneux (London: Tooke, 1680), 16. A review of the long entry for "mind" in the *Oxford English Dictionary* will establish that the meaning of the word "mind," before Locke, was not necessarily more obvious in English than in

Latin. That the concept of "the mind" is itself an invention, a construction, is established in Bruno Snell, *The Discovery of the Mind: The Greek Origins of European Thought* (Oxford: Blackwell, 1953).

41. La Mettrie, *L'homme machine* (1748), 103; Julien Offray de La Mettrie, *Man a Machine* (London: Smith, 1750), 55 (the relevant page is missing from the 1749 edition on Eighteenth Century Collections Online).

42. The subtitle of Hume's *Treatise of Human Nature* is *Being an Attempt to Introduce the Experimental Method of Reasoning into Moral Subjects.*

43. Smith, *The Theory of Moral Sentiments* (1759), 285.

44. John Maxwell, "The Promulgation of the Law of Nature," in Richard Cumberland, *A Treatise of the Laws of Nature,* trans. John Maxwell (London: Knapton, 1727), 122; John Maxwell, "Of the Imperfectness of the Heathen Morality," in Cumberland, *Treatise* (1727), clxvi. For Shaftesbury's use of "system" see, for example, Shaftesbury, *Characteristicks* (1711), 2:286-287.

45. Leo Catana, *The Historiographical Concept "System of Philosophy": Its Origin, Nature, Influence, and Legitimacy* (Leiden: Brill, 2008).

46. Joseph Glanvill, "Essay VII: The Summe of My Lord Bacon's New Atlantis," in *Essays on Several Important Subjects in Philosophy and Religion* (London: Baker and Mortlock, 1676), 50.

47. David Fordyce, *Dialogues Concerning Education,* 2 vols. (London: s.n., 1745), 2:201.

48. Cesare Beccaria, *An Essay on Crimes and Punishments* (London: Almon, 1767), 22.

49. Wootton, *The Invention of Science* (2015), 163-247.

50. Michael Sheehan, *The Balance of Power: History and Theory* (London: Routledge, 2007), 43.

51. They are the only sort discussed in Otto Mayr, *Authority, Liberty, and Automatic Machinery in Early Modern Europe* (Baltimore: Johns Hopkins University Press, 1986).

52. Shaftesbury, *Characteristicks* (1711), 2:63.

53. One can read Butler's cool hour passage in this way; see Penelhum, *Butler* (1985), 73-74.

54. John Locke, *An Essay Concerning Humane Understanding. Fourth Edition, with Large Additions* (London: Churchill and Manship, 1700), 222.

55. La Mettrie, *Man a Machine* (1749), 24. Compare Bernard Mandeville, *The Fable of the Bees: Or, Private Vices, Publick Benefits* (London: Roberts, 1714), 30; and Bernard Mandeville, *The Fable of the Bees; Part II* (London: Roberts, 1729), 331.

56. Frank H. Durgin, "The Tinkerbell Effect: Motion Perception and Illusion," *Journal of Consciousness Studies* 9 (2002), 88-101.

57. Nicholas Barbon, *A Discourse of Trade* (London: Milbourn, 1690), preface.

58. Voltaire wrote, around 1750, "Peu de commerçants ententend [*sic*] le commerce général. Une boutique veut décréditer sa voisine, Lyon veut écrazer Tours. L'homme public soutient tout." Voltaire, *Voltaire's Notebooks,* 2 vols., ed. Theodore Besterman (Geneva: Institut et Musée Voltaire, 1952), 2:311. See also J. Massie, *A Representation Concerning the Knowledge of Commerce as a National Concern* (London: Payne, 1760). John Millar, on the other hand, in a posthumous essay, regarded the organization of a trading interest as something which happened automatically: "By a constant attention to professional objects, the superior orders of mercantile people become quick-sighted in discerning their common interest, and, at all times, indefatigable in pursuing it . . . the merchant, though he never overlooks his private advantage, is accustomed to connect his own gain with that of his brethren, and, is therefore, always ready to join with those of the same profession, in soliciting the aid of government, and in promoting general measures for the benefit of their trade." John Millar, *An Historical View of the English Government,* 4 vols. (London: Mawman, 1803), 4:136. Thus an historical process comes to seem natural once it has been completed.

59. Margaret Thatcher, interview with Douglas Keay on 23 September 1987, *Women's Own,* 31 October 1987, 8–10.

60. John Bossy, "Some Elementary Forms of Durkheim," *Past and Present* 95 (1982), 3–18 (but see also Phil Withington, *Society in Early Modern England* [Cambridge: Polity, 2010], 130); Brent Nongbri, *Before Religion: A History of a Modern Concept* (New Haven, Conn.: Yale University Press, 2013); Noah Millstone, *Manuscript Circulation and the Invention of Politics in Early Stuart England* (Cambridge: Cambridge University Press, 2016); Edward P. Thompson, *The Making of the English Working Class* (London: Gollancz, 1963).

61. Padraic X. Scanlan, *Freedom's Debtors: British Antislavery in Sierra Leone in the Age of Revolution* (New Haven, Conn.: Yale University Press, 2017), 5.

62. The classic text is Peter Winch, *The Idea of a Social Science and Its Relation to Philosophy* (London: Routledge and Kegan Paul, 1958).

63. Rosemary H. Sweet, "Topographies of Politeness," *Transactions of the Royal Historical Society* 12 (2002), 355–374.

64. I take "entanglement" from Erwin Schrödinger's 1935 account of his thought experiment (now known as Schrödinger's cat) which illustrates a paradox in quantum physics. His word is *Verschränkung.* J. L. Austin, *How to Do Things with Words* (Cambridge, Mass.: Harvard University Press, 1962) studies one aspect of this entanglement, but there is an equally significant book to be written entitled How to Say Things with Deeds; both require an intersubjective un-

derstanding, a shared language, a set of social conventions regarding what can be done, what can be said, and how they entangle with each other. Another type of entanglement is encapsulated in Le Corbusier's statement "Une maison est une machine-à-habiter," in Le Corbusier, *Vers une architecture* (Paris: Crès, 1923), 73: the house both reflects a "form of life" (the phrase is Ludwig Wittgenstein's) and it makes possible a form of life. Le Corbusier wanted both to understand our form of life and to change it.

65. See, for a related example, Simon R. Charsley, *Wedding Cakes and Cultural History* (London: Routledge, 1992).

66. Arthur Herman, *How the Scots Invented the Modern World* (New York: Crown, 2001) is the popular version of this story.

67. On this issue there was a sustained debate, focusing on the question of "luxury"; see Christopher J. Berry, *The Idea of Luxury: A Conceptual and Historical Investigation* (Cambridge: Cambridge University Press, 1994).

68. The identification of an overarching system of this sort raises methodological issues. The system in question is not a Weberian ideal type, a Lovejoyian unit idea, a Kuhnian paradigm (though I use the term "paradigm" myself), or a Foucauldian episteme, although it owes something to each of these. I would prefer to describe it (in Wittgensteinian terms) as an interrelated set of language games, which relate to an interrelated set of forms of life. It is, I think, possible to specify the Enlightenment paradigm more precisely than, for example, "civic humanism," another broad category often employed by historians. And this, of course, makes it easier to confirm or falsify the argument presented here.

69. Thomas Hobbes, *Humane Nature, or The Fundamental Elements of Policie* (London: Bowman, 1650), 117.

70. Ferguson, *An Essay on the History of Civil Society* (1767), 79.

APPENDIX A. ON EMULATION, AND ON THE CANON

1. See, for example, Quentin Skinner, *Visions of Politics,* vol. 1, *Regarding Method* (Cambridge: Cambridge University Press, 2002).

2. Willy Maley, "A View of the Present State of Ireland (1596; 1633)," in *A Critical Companion to Spenser Studies,* ed. Bart Van Es (Basingstoke, England: Palgrave Macmillan, 2006), 210–229.

3. A classic example would be Quentin Skinner's 1972 reading of Hobbes's *Leviathan* alongside Anthony Ascham's *Of the Confusions and Revolutions of Governments* (1649); see Kinch Hoekstra, "The De Facto Turn in Hobbes's Political Philosophy," in *Leviathan after 350 Years,* ed. Tom Sorell and Luc Foisneau (Oxford: Oxford University Press, 2004), 33–75.

4. They are already linked together in Albert O. Hirschman, *The Passions and the Interests: Political Arguments for Capitalism before Its Triumph* (Princeton, N.J.: Princeton University Press, 1977), 107–108.

5. On which, see Sophus A. Reinert, *Translating Empire: Emulation and the Origins of Political Economy* (Cambridge, Mass.: Harvard University Press, 2011), 29–33.

6. Slack has produced a series of studies, culminating in Paul Slack, *The Invention of Improvement: Information and Material Progress in Seventeenth-Century England* (Oxford: Oxford University Press, 2015). Barbon's argument is echoed in Edward Chamberlayne and William Petty, *The Present State of England* (London: Whitwood, 1683), 61. Emulation is presented as a thoroughly bad thing in Richard Lawrence, *The Interest of Ireland in Its Trade and Wealth Stated* (Dublin: Howes, 1682); and William Petyt, *Britannia Languens, Or, a Discourse of Trade* (London: Baldwin, 1689).

7. For the probable influence of Barbon and North on Mandeville, see Bernard Mandeville, *The Fable of the Bees: Or, Private Vices, Publick Benefits*, ed. F. B. Kaye, 2 vols. (Oxford: Clarendon, 1924), 1.xcv–xcvi, c–ci, 108–109. On which authors on trade might be considered obscure, see Julian Hoppit, "The Contexts and Contours of British Economic Literature, 1660–1760," *Historical Journal* 49 (2006), 79–110.

8. Christopher J. Berry, *The Idea of Luxury: A Conceptual and Historical Investigation* (Cambridge: Cambridge University Press, 1994).

9. Smith held that often workers took days off not because they were lazy, or had satisfied their immediate needs, but because they had pushed themselves beyond their physical limits. Adam Smith, *An Inquiry into the Nature and Causes of the Wealth of Nations*, 2 vols. (London: Strahan and Cadell, 1776), 1:100–101. On Saint Monday, see Edward P Thompson, "Time, Work-Discipline, and Industrial Capitalism," *Past and Present* 38 (1967), 56–97. The laziness argument had, however, a long afterlife; it is advocated by the anonymous translator of Jacques Necker, *On the Legislation and the Commerce of Corn* (London: Longman, 1776), 177–181: "it is a melancholy truth, that nothing but the fear, nay the feeling of want, will make men in general labour with due assiduity. . . . Who has not heard of Saint Monday?"; and in James Anderson, *Observations on the Means of Exciting a Spirit of National Industry* (Edinburgh: Cadell and Elliot, 1777), 277: "necessity alone induces men to work." It is rebutted (indeed refuted) in M. Messance, *Recherches sur la population des généralités d'Auvergne, de Lyon, de Rouen . . . avec des reflexions sur la valeur du bled, tant en France qu'en Angleterre, depuis 1674 jusqu'en 1764* (Paris: Durand, 1766), 287–288, a book admired by Smith.

10. Nicholas Barbon, *A Discourse of Trade* (London: Milbourn, 1690), 15; see also Andrea Finkelstein, "Nicholas Barbon and the Quality of Infinity," *History of Political Economy* 32 (2000), 83–102.

11. [Nicholas Barbon], *A Discourse Shewing the Great Advantages that New-Buildings and the Enlarging of Towns and Cities Do Bring to a Nation* (London: s.n., 1678), 5. The attribution to Barbon originates in Paul Slack, "Perceptions of the Metropolis in Seventeenth-Century England," in *Civil Histories: Essays Presented to Sir Keith Thomas,* ed. Peter Burke, Brian Harrison and Paul Slack (Oxford: Oxford University Press, 2000), 175–177.

12. Dudley North, *Discourses upon Trade: Principally Directed to the Cases of the Interest, Coynage, Clipping, Increase of Money* (London, Basset, 1691), 14–15. This is an early example of an invisible hand argument—on which, see Chapter 7.

13. Adam Smith, *The Theory of Moral Sentiments* (London: Millar, 1759), 127.

14. Daniel Defoe, *A Tour Thro' the Whole Island of Great Britain,* 3 vols. (London: Strahan, 1724), 1:109. Thomas Nettleton found the contemporary obsession with making money "ridiculous and absurd. . . . Yet as preposterous as this may seem to be, 'tis the *reigning Passion* of the present Age: To get Riches by right Methods, or by wrong, is grown the prevailing Aim, and most fashionable Pursuit." Thomas Nettleton, *Some Thoughts Concerning Virtue and Happiness: In a Letter to a Clergyman* (London: Batley, 1729), 54–55. The passage disappears from later editions, perhaps because it no longer seemed quite so preposterous.

15. Timothy Brook, *Vermeer's Hat: The Seventeenth Century and the Dawn of the Global World* (London: Profile, 2008); Neil McKendrick, John Brewer, and J. H. Plumb, *The Birth of a Consumer Society: The Commercialization of Eighteenth-Century England* (London: Europa, 1982).

APPENDIX B. DOUBLE-ENTRY BOOKKEEPING

1. *Oxford English Dictionary,* s.v. "impute" (published 1899).

2. Jean [John] Calvin, *Sermons . . . Upon the Ten Commandemements of the Law,* trans. J. Harmer (London: Bishop, 1579), 127; Jean [John] Calvin, *The Sermons . . . Vpon the Fifth Booke of Moses Called Deuteronomie,* trans. A. Golding (London: Bishop, 1583), 577–578, 582, 585, 589, 610, 857–858, 914; Jean [John] Calvin, *Sermons . . . Upon the Booke of Job,* trans. A. Golding (London: Bishop, 1584), 433.

3. Peter Barker, *A Iudicious and Painefull Exposition Vpon the Ten Commandements* (London: Jackson, 1624), 75.

4. Richard Carpenter, *Three Profitable Sermons* (London: Constable, 1617), 54–55.

5. Zacharias Ursinus, Henry Parry, and David Pareus, *The Summe of Christian Religion, Delivered* (London: Bowtell, 1645), 647.

6. William Day, *A Paraphrase and Commentary Upon the Epistle of Saint Paul to the Romans* (London: Kirton, 1666), 92.

7. Walter Cross, *Two Sermons One on the Subject of Justification, the Other on the Imputed Righteousness . . . By Which We Are Justified* (London: Attwood, 1695), 31.

8. Thomas Watson, *The Beatitudes, Or, A Discourse Upon Part of Christs Famous Sermon on the Mount* (London: Smith, 1660), 647.

9. Major Algood, *A Sermon Preached at the Funeral of . . . Mr. Georg Ritschel, Late Minister of Hexham in Northumberland* (London: Hall, 1684), 12. Virtually the same wording is to be found in Robert Parsons and Edmund Bunny, *A Booke of Christian Exercise Appertaining to Resolution . . . Accompanied Now with a Treatise Tending to Pacification* (London: Wight, 1584), 10; Robert Parsons, *The Seconde Parte of the Booke of Christian Exercise, Appertayning to Resolution* (London: Waterson, 1590), 15; Lewis Thomas, *Seauen Sermons, Or, the Exercises of Seuen Sabbaoths* (London: Sims, 1599), 13; Mathew Stoneham, *A Treatise on the First Psalme* (London: Burre, 1610), 58; Robert Mossom, *The Preachers Tripartite in Three Books* (London: Newcomb, 1657), 72; and Christopher Jelinger, *Heaven Won by Violence, Or, A Treatise Upon Mat. 11, 12* (London: s.n., 1665), 93. Several of these appeared in more than one edition.

10. John Downame, *A Gvide to Godlynesse* (London: Weuer and Bladen, 1622), 90.

APPENDIX C. "EQUALITY" IN MACHIAVELLI

1. See, for example, Robert Sparling, "The Concept of Corruption in J. G. A. Pocock's *The Machiavellian Moment*," *History of European Ideas* 43 (2017), 156–170. But see, on equality, Giovanni G. Balestrieri, "'Equalità' e 'Inequalità' in Machiavelli," *Teoria politica* 33 (2007), 129–137.

2. For the frequent breakdown of "civil equality," see Stuart Carroll, "Revenge and Reconciliation in Early Modern Italy," *Past and Present* 233 (2016), 101–142. On the comparatively successful methods used to maintain it in Florence, see Andrea Zorzi, "Contrôle social, ordre public et répression judiciaire à Florence à l'époque communale: Éléments et problèmes," *Annales. Histoire, Sciences Sociales* 45 (1990), 1169–1188. I take it that when Machiavelli refers to inequality in *Discourses*, 1.17, it is primarily civil inequality he has in mind, not, as is assumed in Quentin Skinner, *Visions of Politics*, vol. 2, *Renaissance Virtues* (Cambridge: Cambridge University Press, 2002), 176, inequality of wealth; this seems to follow from the elaboration of Machiavelli's argument in 1.18, though here and in 3.16 he does also have in mind inequality of wealth, for, as he

makes clear in 1.2, he believes there is a connection between *avarizia* and the breakdown of the rule of law, or *civile inequalità.* In 3:3 Piero Soderini is described as refusing to seize power in a coup d'état because he would have had to use the laws to destroy *civile equalità:* in other words, he would have had to use the laws to deny his opponents equal treatment under the law by killing or banishing them. Machiavelli thinks that Soderini was wrong not to seize power (an example of Machiavelli advocating—*pace* Skinner, *Renaissance Virtues* [2002], 205—*modi straordinari;* see also *Discorsi* 1:4): proof, surely, that for Machiavelli *civile equalità* was not an end in itself, but at best a means to an end, and sometimes even an obstacle to the creation of the sort of republic of which Machiavelli approved. Just as noblemen were killed on sight in the republics of Germany, so Soderini should have seen the need to kill the *ottimati* who wanted to see the return of the Medici. But even this would not have been sufficient to create in Florence the sort of equality, both civil and economic, that existed in the German cities.

3. Niccolò Machiavelli, "A Discourse on Remodeling the Government of Florence," in *The Chief Works and Others,* 3 vols., trans. and ed. Allan H. Gilbert (Durham, N.C.: Duke University Press, 1989), 1:107.

4. Ibid., 1:101.

5. See Yves Winter, "Plebeian Politics: Machiavelli and the Ciompi Uprising," *Political Theory* 40 (2012), 736–766, esp. 744, 753; John P. McCormick, "Faulty Foundings and Failed Reformers in Machiavelli's Florentine Histories," *American Political Science Review* 111 (2017), 204–216; and John P. McCormick, *Machiavellian Democracy* (Cambridge: Cambridge University Press, 2011).

6. Niccolò Machiavelli, *The History of Florence,* 3:13, in *The Chief Works* (1989), 3:1160.

7. On this antithesis, see a series of publications by Quentin Skinner on the classical or neo-Roman conception of liberty, beginning with Quentin Skinner, *Liberty before Liberalism* (Cambridge: Cambridge University Press, 1988). Even the Levellers, over a century later, would find it difficult to defend the claim that servants should have a right to vote; see David Wootton, "Leveller Democracy and the Puritan Revolution," in *The Cambridge History of Political Thought,* ed. J. H. Burns and Mark Goldie (Cambridge: Cambridge University Press, 1991), 412–442.

APPENDIX D. THE GOOD SAMARITAN

1. For a parallel discussion of this theme, see Katherine Ibbett, *Compassion's Edge: Fellow-Feeling and Its Limits in Early Modern France* (Philadelphia: University of Pennsylvania Press, 2018), 98–133.

2. Nehemiah Rogers, *The Good Samaritan; Or An Exposition on That Parable Luke X. Ver. XXX–XXXVIII* (London: Saubridge, 1658), 91–92.

3. Henry Hammond, *A Paraphrase, and Annotations Upon All the Books of the New Testament* (London: Davis, 1659), 225

4. Archibald Symmer, *A Spirituall Posie for Zion* (London: Sheares, 1629), 5.

5. Thomas Pierce, *Philallelpa, Or, the Grand Characteristick Whereby a Man May Be Known to Be Christ's Disciple* (London: Royston, 1658), 13–14.

6. William Gould, *The Generosity of Christian Love* (London: Royston, 1676), 23.

7. John Boys, *The Autumne Part From the Twelfth Sundy* [sic] *After Trinitie, to the Last in the Whole Yeere* (London: Aspley, 1613), 41.

8. Rogers, *The Good Samaritan* (1658), 93.

9. John Gage, *The Christian Sodality, or Catholick Hive of Bees* (s.l.: s.n., 1652), sig. O1r, p. 193.

10. Martin Luther, *Special and Chosen Sermons* (London: Vautroullier, 1578), 399. Luther's interpretation follows Augustine, and so similar views are also presented by Catholics. See, for example, Henry More (1586–1661, a Jesuit and not the Cambridge Platonist), *The Life and Doctrine of Our Saviour Iesus Christ* (Ghent: Graet, 1656), 111.

11. I have come across one striking protest against such interpretations: "The authors of free will runne here into an Allegory, affirming that the condition of Adam after his fall is described vnder the Type of ye wounded man. Whereupon they inferre that ye power of well doing was not altogether extinct in him, bycause hee is only sayd to be halfe deade. . . . As vaine also is that other Allegory, the which notwithstandinge hath bene so well lyked of many that it hath bene receiued as an Oracle. They haue fayned this Samaritan to bee Christe, bycause hee is our keeper: They say that Wyne, and Oyle was powred into the Wound, bycause Christ doth heale vs with Repentance and the promise of grace. Thirdly, they say that Christe doth not by and by restore health, but doth commende such as are to bee cured to the Church for a while. In this and such lyke, the Scriptures are vnreuerently handled, the true sence beinge transfigured into shadowes." (Augustin Marlorat, *A Catholike and Ecclesiasticall Exposition of the Holy Gospell After S. Marke and Luke,* trans. T. Tymme [London: Marsh, 1583], 193.)

12. Richard Holland, *The Good Samaritane. A Sermon Preached at the Parish-Church of St. Magnus the Martyr* (London: Back, 1700), 11.

13. Henry Smith, *The Poore Mans Teares* (London: Wright, 1592), 107.

14. William Fleetwood, *A Sermon Preached at Christ-Church, Before the Governors of That Hospital, on St. Stephen's Day* (London: Brewster and Chiswell, 1691), 24.

15. William Johnson, *Deus Nobiscum. A Sermon Preached Upon a Great Deliverance at Sea* (London: Crook, 1664), 129, thanks a compassionate friend who has been a Good Samaritan to him, but the friend is not named.

16. James King, *The Good Samaritan Exemplify'd in the Charitable Christian* (London: Hills, 1708). Matthew Griffith, *The Samaritan Revived* (London: Johnson, 1660), sig. a2r, aims "to personate the good Samaritan," but he does so by binding up the wounds of the body politic.

APPENDIX E. PRUDENCE AND THE YOUNG MAN

1. Ryan Patrick Hanley, *Adam Smith and the Character of Virtue* (New York: Cambridge University Press, 2009), esp. 100–131.

2. Adam Smith, *The Theory of Moral Sentiments* (London: Millar, 1759), 341–343.

3. Adam Smith, *The Theory of Moral Sentiments,* 2 vols. (London: Strahan, 1790), 2:52–53, 58–59.

4. See Emily C. Nacol, *Age of Risk: Politics and Economy in Early Modern Britain* (Princeton, N.J.: Princeton University Press, 2016), 100–105.

5. Adam Smith, *An Inquiry into the Nature and Causes of the Wealth of Nations,* 2 vols. (London: Strahan and Cadell, 1776), 1:505.

6. Hanley, *Adam Smith and the Character of Virtue* (2009), 115.

7. Smith, *The Wealth of Nations* (1776), 1:129.

8. David Hume, *The Life of David Hume, Written by Himself* (London: Strahan and Cadell, 1777), 6.

9. See Pascal Bonenfant, "Wages," http://www.pascalbonenfant.com/18c/wages .html.

10. G. E. Mingay, *English Landed Society in the 18th Century* (London: Routledge and Kegan Paul, 1963), 26.

11. John Baillie, *An Impartial History of the Town and County of Newcastle upon Tyne* (Newcastle upon Tyne, England: Anderson, 1801), 279–280, 388.

12. These prices come from a search of booksellers' catalogs on Eighteenth Century Collections Online (https://www.gale.com/primary-sources/eighteenth-century -collections-online). Some 170 entries for new and secondhand copies of *The Wealth of Nations* can be located by adopting the following search procedure: In advanced search under Title, enter "catalogue," then in an Entire Document box, enter "Wealth of Nations." Sort the results by date. This produces 173 results, of which one appears to be a false positive as it bears the date "[1742]," but it does in fact include Smith's *Wealth of Nations*. A proportion of these results contain more than one entry, but a roughly equal proportion do not specify prices or are catalogs of libraries; adding "Adam Smith" as a further

search term only produces twenty-five results, a sample of around 14 percent of the whole. It would be tempting to use such figures to compare the total sales of different works, but they are inherently biased: the more expensive a book, the more likely it is to be sold by a bookseller who publishes a catalog. For comparison, Locke's *Essay* cost between eight shillings and twelve shillings ("neatly bound") new, and between two shillings and six pence and nine shillings secondhand; *The Theory of Moral Sentiments* sold for six shillings new, and three shillings and six pence or four shillings and four pence secondhand; Nettleton's *Treatise on Virtue* cost four shillings and Toussaint's *Manners* three shillings, both bound.

13. Elizabeth Boody Schumpeter, "English Prices and Public Finance, 1660–1822," *Review of Economics and Statistics* 20 (1938), 23; see also William D. Nordhaus, "Do Real-Output and Real-Wage Measures Capture Reality? The History of Lighting Suggests Not," in *Economics of New Goods*, ed. Timothy F. Bresnahan and Robert J. Gordon (Chicago: University of Chicago Press, 1996), 27–70.

14. J. Massie, *Calculations of the Present Taxes Yearly Paid by a Family of Each Rank, Degree, or Class* (London: Payne, Owen, and Henderson, 1761), nos. 25–27. Massie believed two hundred pounds to be the minimum income for a gentleman (no. 12). A detailed budget for a family on 390 pounds per annum is to be found in Mary Johnson, *Madam Johnson's Present: Or, Every Young Woman's Companion* (London: Fuller, 1759), 187–188, though a bachelor could live more cheaply. In this family the head of the household would have had to buy books out of the four shillings per week set aside for his "Pocket Expences." See also Anonymous, *The economist. Shewing, in a variety of estimates, from fourscore pounds a year to upwards of 800l. how comfortably and genteely a family may live with frugality for a little money*, 14th ed. (London: J. Bell, 1776). For an agricultural laborer's wage, see Jacques Necker, *On the Legislation and the Commerce of Corn* (London: Longman, 1776), 177. See also Robert D. Hume, "The Economics of Culture in London, 1660–1740," *Huntington Library Quarterly* 69 (2006), 487–533; and Abigail Williams, *The Social Life of Books: Reading Together in the Eighteenth-Century Home* (New Haven, Conn.: Yale University Press, 2017), 95–126.

15. Baillie, *An Impartial History* (1801), 388.

16. Daniel Defoe, *The Compleat English Tradesman: Volume II; In Two Parts; Part I: Directed Chiefly to the More Experienc'd Tradesmen* (London: Rivington, 1727), 177–178. The advice to a young man starting out is in Daniel Defoe, *The Complete English Tradesman: In Familiar Letters, . . . Especially for Young Beginners* (London: Rivington, 1726).

17. For a discussion of risk in Smith, see Nacol, *Age of Risk* (2016), 98–123. For the origins of the word "risk," see *Oxford English Dictionary Online,* 3rd ed., updated June 2010; although Nacol appears to cite this edition (2n5), she seems to be relying on the 2nd ed., 1989.

18. Smith, *Theory of Moral Sentiments* (1790), 2:55.

19. Destructive change is not peculiar to industrial capitalism; see, for example, the account of the decline of Ipswich in Daniel Defoe, *A Tour Thro' the Whole Island of Great Britain,* 3 vols. (London: Strahan, 1724), 1:62–66.

20. Richard Cantillon, *Richard Cantillon's Essay on the Nature of Trade in General: A Variorum Edition,* ed. Richard van den Berg (Abingdon, England: Routledge, 2015), 109.

21. Cantillon, *Richard Cantillon's Essay on the Nature of Trade . . . Variorum Edition* (2015), 125.

22. Smith, *The Wealth of Nations* (1776), 2:342.

23. Smith, *The Theory of Moral Sentiments* (1759), 285–286.

24. Defoe, *The Compleat English Tradesman: Volume II* (1727), 19.

APPENDIX F. "THE MARKET"

1. Emma Rothschild, "Commerce and the State: Turgot, Condorcet and Smith," *Economic Journal* 102 (1992), 1200. I would like to thank Iain Hampsher-Monk for drawing this issue to my attention.

2. David Hume, "Of Money," in *Political Discourses* (Edinburgh: Kincaid and Donaldson, 1752), 55.

3. The *Oxford English Dictionary,* s.v. "market," updated December 2000, gives numerous earlier usages that might be called "abstract" rather than "concrete"; the puzzle is when "market" used in a loose or metaphorical sense turns into a new, generalized concept of commercial exchange.

Illustration Credits

Page vi: "Ragione di Stato," from Cesare Ripa, *Iconologia* (1603). Zentralbibliothek Zürich.

Page x: Title page and frontispiece from William Percey, *The Compleat Swimmer* (London: Printed by J. C. for Henry Fletcher, 1658). Image provided courtesy of Forum Auctions.

Page 10: Frontispiece from Thomas Hobbes of Malmesbury, *Leviathan or the Matter, Forme and Power of a Common Wealth Ecclesiasticall and Civil* (1651). Private Collection / Bridgeman Images / XJF106673.

Page 36: Title page from Niccolò Machiavelli, *Discorsi* (London: John Wolfe, 1584). Reproduced by kind permission of the Syndics of Cambridge University Library, Syn.7.58.76.

Page 66: Title page from David Hume, *A Treatise of Human Nature* (London: John Noon, 1739). Photo © Granger / Bridgeman Images.

Page 88: Title page from John Locke, *An Essay Concerning Humane Understanding,* 2nd ed. (London, 1694). St. Catharine's College, Cambridge, H.3.24.

Page 114: Title page from Pierre Bayle, *Pensées diverses, écrites à un docteur de Sorbonne à l'occasion de la Comète qui parut au mois de Décembre 1680* (Rotterdam: R. Leers, 1683). Reproduced from the author's collection.

Page 134: Title page from John Adams, *A Defence of the Constitutions of Government of the United States of America* (Philadelphia: Hall and Sellers, 1787). John Rylands Library, the University of Manchester.

Page 154: Title page from Adam Smith, *The Theory of Moral Sentiments* (London: Andrew Millar, 1759). Collection of Stuart Warner.

Page 177: Title page from François-Vincent Toussaint, *Manners* (London: J. Rivington, 1749). Reproduced from the author's collection.

Page 186: Title page from Jonathan Swift, *A Modest Proposal* (Dublin: S. Harding, 1729). Private collection / Bridgeman Images.

Page 218: The Declaration of Independence, printed by John Dunlap (broadside) (1776). The National Archives, Image Library, CO 5 / 40.

Page 368: Frontispiece from *Index librorum prohibitorum,* SSmi D. N. Benedicti XIV (Rome, 1758). Reproduction courtesy of Linda Hall Library.

Acknowledgments

This book began as a series of six Carlyle Lectures given at the University of Oxford in February and March 2014 under the title "Power and Pleasure, 1513–1776." I would like to thank the Faculty of History and All Souls College for inviting me to give the lectures. The historians of Oxford (including the Regius Professor) and the fellows of All Souls gave me such a warm welcome that the whole experience—which I had expected to be rather intimidating—was a delight. I particularly want to thank those fellows of All Souls who kept coming, lecture after lecture, either because they found the subject interesting or because they have a particularly strong and collective sense of obligation. Parts of Chapters 4 and 6 were also exposed to criticism in Cambridge in 2017: Chapter 4, at the invitation of Chris Meckstroth, was discussed at a meeting of the Research Seminar in Political Thought and Intellectual History (with Tom Sorrell commenting), and Chapter 6 at a workship on artificial intelligence organized by David Runciman and funded by the Leverhulme Trust.

My original idea was that power and pleasure can be pursued without limit, and I soon wanted to add profit to these two, so I wrote in 2016 two further lectures on profit, the first of which I gave as a paper to the Department of History at the University of Sheffield, and the second of which I gave as a lecture, first at the University of Wisconsin–Madison, and then, much revised, as the 2017 Besterman Lecture at the University of Oxford. To all these audiences I am indebted for their criticisms and their encouragement.

A number of friends and colleagues have read parts of the book in draft: Robert Black, Susan Brigden, Bill Connell, Simon Ditchfield, Ryan Patrick Hanley, Christine Henderson, Lisa Hill, Cormac Ó Gráda, and Blair Worden. Francis Fallon, Paul Rahe, Ritchie Roberston, Alicia Steinmetz, and Stuart Warner generously read the whole thing and made a number of characteristically incisive comments. I am grateful to all of them for their advice. I owe a particular debt to my colleague David Clayton, who set up an undergraduate course in which I found myself teaching the Bengal Famine—proof, if proof were needed, that compulsory modules are not only good for students but are also good for professors. Mara van der Lugt has kindly corresponded with me about Pierre Bayle; David Norbrook, Catherine Wilson, and Samuel Zeitlin have helped with Thomas Hobbes and Lucretius; Richard Bourke has advised on "class"; and Niall O'Flaherty has helped with David Hume.

My colleagues in the History Department of the University of York have been wonderfully supportive over the years, and I thank Simon Ditchfield for organizing my teaching schedule in the spring of 2014 so that I never had to be in two places at once. I wrote this book while on a year's leave funded by the Leverhulme Trust. This is the second time the trust has supported me, and I cannot thank it enough.

It has been a pleasure to work with Ian Malcolm, my editor, who is based near Oxford and who demonstrated his commitment by attending the original lectures. Susannah Stone did picture research, and Ian Craine did the index; I have worked with them before and hope to work with them again. I would also like to thank all those who have worked to see this book through the press, particularly its designer, Dean Bornstein, and John Donohue of Westchester Publishing Services, who has been a marvel. My greatest debt is to Alison Mark; as always, she read the whole thing several times; more important, there would be no book without her. The many faults that remain are, of course, mine alone.

Frontispiece from *Index librorum prohibitorum* (8°) (1758).

The Catholic Church systematically opposed the views discussed in this book. Of the authors with which we have been concerned the following appear in the Index of Forbidden Books of 1758 (whose frontispiece is reproduced on the facing page): Niccolò Machiavelli, Francesco Guicciardini, Michel de Montaigne, Giovanni Botero, Giulio Cesare Vanini, Thomas Hobbes, Benedict de Spinoza, Samuel von Pufendorf, Abraham Nicolas Amelot de la Houssaye, Pierre Bayle, Pierre Nicole, John Locke, Lord Shaftesbury (in Denis Diderot's translation), Bernard Le Bovier de Fontenelle, Bernard Mandeville, Montesquieu, Jonathan Swift, Voltaire, Julien Offray de La Mettrie; a 1759 supplement added Helvétius and the *Encyclopédie ou dictionnaire raisonné des sciences, des arts et des métiers,* edited by Denis Diderot and Jean le Rond d'Alembert. David Hume and Claude Yvon were added in 1761, Jean-Jacques Rousseau in 1762, Cesare Beccaria in 1766, Paul Henri Thiry, Baron d'Holbach in 1770, Laurence Sterne in 1819, Pietro Verri in 1826, and Jeremy Bentham in 1835.

Index